# Philosophy and the Law of Torts

When accidents occur and people suffer injuries, who ought to bear the loss? Tort law offers a complex set of rules to answer this question, but until now philosophers have offered little by way of analysis of these rules.

In eight essays commissioned for this volume, leading legal theorists examine the philosophical foundations of tort law. Among the questions they address are the following: How are the notions at the core of tort practice (such as responsibility, fault, negligence, due care, and duty to repair) to be understood? Is an explanation based on a conception of justice feasible? How are concerns of distributive and corrective justice related? What amounts to an adequate explanation of tort law?

This collection will be of interest to professionals and advanced students working in philosophy of law, social theory, political theory, and law, as well as anyone seeking a better understanding of tort law.

Gerald J. Postema is Cary C. Boshamer Professor of Philosophy and Professor of Law at The University of North Carolina at Chapel Hill. He is the author of *Bentham and the Common Law Tradition* (1986) and the editor of *Jeremy Bentham: Moral and Legal Philosophy* (2001) and *Racism and the Law: The Legacy and Lessons of Plessy* (1997).

# Cambridge Studies in Philosophy and Law

*Some other books in the series:*

# Philosophy and the Law of Torts

*Edited by*

Gerald J. Postema

The University of North Carolina at Chapel Hill

CAMBRIDGE UNIVERSITY PRESS
Cambridge, New York, Melbourne, Madrid, Cape Town, Singapore, São Paulo

Cambridge University Press
The Edinburgh Building, Cambridge CB2 8RU, UK

Published in the United States of America by Cambridge University Press, New York

www.cambridge.org
Information on this title: www.cambridge.org/9780521622820

First published 2001
This digitally printed version 2007

*A catalogue record for this publication is available from the British Library*

*Library of Congress Cataloguing in Publication data*

Philosophy and the law of torts / edited by Gerald J. Postema.
p.   cm. – (Cambridge studies in philosophy and law)
Includes bibliographical references and index.
1. Torts – Philosophy.   I. Postema, Gerald J.   II. Series.
K923 P49     2001
346.03´01–dc21
00–065174

ISBN 978-0-521-62282-0 hardback
ISBN 978-0-521-04175-1 paperback

# Contents

# Contributors

BRUCE CHAPMAN, Professor of Law, University of Toronto

JULES COLEMAN, John A. Garver Professor of Jurisprudence and Philosophy, Yale University

MARK GEISTFELD, Professor of Law, New York University School of Law

GREGORY C. KEATING, Professor of Law, University of Southern California

STEPHEN R. PERRY, John J. O'Brien Professor of Law and Professor of Philosophy, University of Pennsylvania

GERALD J. POSTEMA, Cary C. Boshamer Professor of Philosophy and Professor of Law, University of North Carolina at Chapel Hill

ARTHUR RIPSTEIN, Professor of Law and Philosophy, University of Toronto

MARTIN STONE, Professor of Law, Duke University

BENJAMIN C. ZIPURSKY, Associate Professor of Law, Fordham University

# 1

# Introduction

## Search for an Explanatory Theory of Torts

### GERALD J. POSTEMA

To an old-fashioned English lawyer, Sir Thomas Holland once said, common law is "a chaos with a full index" (Holmes 1870, p. 114). Anglo-American tort law, having evolved case by particular case, retains the common law character of its origins more than any other department of law. It is likely to strike a reader of any standard casebook to be little more than indexed chaos. Yet, at least since Holmes in the early twentieth century jurists and legal scholars have sought to identify some unifying and rationalizing themes or aims. Only lately, in the last generation or so, have philosophers signed on to this project as well. Over the past decade especially the philosophical contribution to this project has become increasingly sophisticated. As one might expect, this increased attention and sophistication has led on the whole to greater refinement of theoretical options rather than to increasing consensus with regard to one of those options. The essays commissioned for this book take theoretical reflection on the foundations of tort law in new directions. Each voice is distinctive, and there is a considerable degree of disagreement among the contributors on some key issues, but there is also more than a little agreement about the object of theoretical reflection and, in broad strokes, the appropriate methodology directing this reflection.

The primary aim of these essays is not critical or justificatory; rather they seek to contribute to the articulation and defense of an explanatory account of tort law. They seek to deepen our understanding of this corner of the law and the practice to which it gives structure. As we shall see, the appropriate methodology for this kind of study is contested. For the most part, essays in this book follow, and some of them spend considerable time defending (see essays by Stone and Coleman), a broadly "interpretive" methodology, which takes seriously, at least as a point of departure, the categories and patterns of reasoning of participants in tort practice, predominantly judges and lawyers.

## I. First Attempts

With these patterns and categories in mind, it is useful to identify core elements of tort practice, even if we find later that we must refine our understanding of the boundaries of this core. Tort law, it appears, has certain distinctive *substantive* rules as well as a distinctive procedural and conceptual *structure*. (See Section II of Stone's essay for a detailed description of these core elements of tort law.) The substantive law of unintentional torts in Anglo-American jurisdictions is dominated by negligence liability, with pockets of strict liability. The conceptual structure of torts is reflected in the litigation process. The substantive rules of tort liability are announced and enforced in case-by-case adjudication between private parties. A private party initiates the proceedings against another private party claiming on its behalf a right to recover damages from the defendant for losses caused by the defendant's act in breach of a duty of care. The state vindicates or rejects plaintiff's claim, but is not a party to the litigation. The litigation process, and the framework of concepts and rules governing the court's assessment of claims made in litigation, reflect an essentially private, bilateral structure. Plaintiff claims that defendant's wrongful action violated a duty of care to her and caused her injury, and she claims compensation for her wrongful loss from the party who injured her.

## Naïve Moral Theory

Reflecting on these substantive and structural features of torts, a theoretically inclined observer might entertain the hypothesis that the primary objective of tort law is to vindicate the moral rights of individuals unjustly invaded by the culpable actions of others and to hold injurers to their moral duties to compensate the losses they wrongfully cause their victims. A moral theory of torts seems to be indicated by the dominant vocabulary of tort. For to act with careless disregard for the rights and interests of others seems not only legally wrong but also a moral failing, and people ought to bear the costs of their moral failings. Tort liability would seem to back up these moral judgments. It punishes these failings and grants redress to those who suffer the harm they cause.

This proposal needs refinement. First, we need to distinguish two different objectives this naïve moral theory might attribute to tort law, objectives issuing from distinct perspectives from which ordinary tort practice can be viewed. The *prescriptive* point of view regards social interaction wholesale, or *ex ante,* and considers how it might be influenced or guided with publicly articulated rules and standards. Viewed from the prescriptive vantage point, tort law defines ground rules for players on the field of risk-creating social interaction. The substantive rules of tort seek to guide the conduct of the players, prescribing certain modes of conduct and prohibiting other modes, and tort litigation seeks to enforce these rules. The *remedial* perspective, in contrast, deals in retail with concrete situations, specific parties, and the misfortunes they suffer. Our moral theory must decide which perspective to take and how to relate these objectives.

Second, naïve moral theory must explain the bilateral structure of tort law. To say, as it does, that tort law mirrors and serves background morality just raises further questions. For example, does the relationship between the parties to tort litigation have any antecedent moral significance? Aren't they typically strangers, not conspicuously related in any morally significant way? If there is a morally significant relationship between them as private parties, one that distinguishes them from all other citizens and justifies treating them in the special way tort practice does, why think the state through the law has any title to intervene in matters between them? Law, we might argue, has a mandate to do the public's business, but what mandate or title does it have to intervene in strictly private matters?

However, investing in attempts to refine the naïve moral theory looks like a bad idea. For, if we probe beneath the surface vocabulary of torts to actual doctrines that give legal life to this vocabulary, we discover a reality that is, to a naïve observer, a shocking departure from our considered moral judgments. A few examples will suffice to make the point. Tort law appears to be utterly indifferent to the culpability of the injurer. A momentary lapse of care by one agent can result in liability for massive losses (Waldron 1995), while other agents, equally guilty of such lapses, or guilty of much greater lapses, escape liability entirely. It's all a matter of luck. Tort law puts all its liability chips on luck-dependent causation. Similarly, one may be liable in tort for losses even if one has taken every reasonable precaution to avoid them; indeed, one may be liable even if one has a recognized legal right to act in the way that injured another. And these cases are not merely exceptions or marginal deviations from a core with a firm moral focus, for the legal notion of negligence itself departs sharply from the ordinary moral notion. We are prepared to hold morally blameworthy those who injure others intentionally or knowingly, and even those who do so inadvertently so long as the agent failed to pay sufficient attention to the risks involved in her action. We regard the failure as the *agent's,* in virtue of a failure of the agent's moral control center. Ordinary morality attaches culpability to a state of mind – indifference, carelessness, or the like (Sverdlik 1993). However, as judged by the law, negligence is strictly a property of conduct, not of the agent's state of mind. Law, it appears, redirects our critical aim and thereby misses the moral target of culpability entirely. Moreover, the standard of conduct defined by negligence law is especially resistant to morally obvious excuses. It holds everyone to what the average reasonable person would do, taking no account of the individual agent's available information or mental capabilities.

## *A Positivist Response*

Of course, this systematic departure of legal doctrine from considered moral judgments sharing the same vocabulary does not surprise any reader of Holmes's "Path of Law" (Holmes 1920). Long ago law may have sprung from moral judgments and concerns, but, Holmes reminded us, it has a logic and a life of its own, and only confusion results from taking its vocabulary at face value. Explanatory tort theory, then, must begin its theorizing from a resolutely non-moral quarter, or at least so it appeared to Holmes and the tradition of tort theorizing he sired (Goldberg and Zipursky 1998, esp. pp. 1752–69). Seen in cold analytical light, he argued, law is a device for achieving certain public goals. Tort law in particular announces and enforces public standards of conduct with the aim of deterring the most harmful and costly forms of social behavior and indemnifying its victims. For this purpose, notions of culpability are simply out of place and "objective" definitions of due care are the most effective. Moreover, for Holmes, public norms of tort prescribe "absolute duties," duties not owed to anyone in particular. Tort litigation is distinctive, of course, because it offers recourse to private parties to vindicate their legal rights, but, on the Holmesian view, this is merely an arrangement of convenience, which is justified, in the best case, in terms of effective prosecution of violations of the public norms, or at least as less costly than alternatives. In brief, tort law, on this view, is a matter of private enforcement of public norms. This militantly non-moral theory is not, of course, entirely devoid of moral, or quasi-moral, notions. In particular, it presupposes a vaguely utilitarian notion of social good in terms of which the aim of public norms and the institutions of private enforcement could be understood and assessed. That quasi-utilitarian framework privileges the prescriptive point of view on tort practice, rationalizes without (explicitly) moralizing the basic doctrines of tort, and offers a strictly instrumental explanation of the distinctive bilateral structure and process of tort litigation.

The theoretical foundations of Holmes's approach remained in a rudimentary state until a group of legal academics, lead by Calabresi (1970), and Landes and Posner (1987), deployed modern economic concepts and models of explanation to construct a comprehensive and systematic theory of tort law (see Shavell 1987). In the place of Holmes's vaguely utilitarian rationalizing standard, economic analysis proposed the notion of efficiency, defined in terms of wealth maximization (or sometimes, less precisely, social welfare maximization). With the precision tools of welfare economics, theorists were able to analyze and explain systematically the basic components of tort law, both its substance and its structure. Following Holmes, it adopted a predominantly prescriptive theoretical perspective. The mode of explanation was broadly "functionalist" (see the essays by Stone and Coleman). It identified a goal of the tort system as a whole (e.g., wealth maximization) and sought to explain all the component elements of the system, and their complex relationships, as means of achieving this independently defined goal.

The economic theory of torts has proved enormously influential in legal academic circles. The influence is not difficult to explain: its basic conceptual elements are relatively simple and intuitive, its analytical tools are very powerful, and it promises truly to rationalize without thereby also recommending. As a bonus, it provides resources for explaining not only the traditional core of accident law, but also some of its more radical departures from orthodoxy, for example, developments in product liability, especially market-share liability. Over the course of the last three decades, it has become the dominant theory of torts. It is the theory to meet and beat.

## II. Moral Theories Refocused and Refined

In recent years the economic theory has been challenged from a number of different quarters. The essays by Stone and Coleman in this book develop one influential line of attack that strikes at the foundations of the theory. They both charge that it fails adequately to explain the distinctive bilateral structure of tort law. They argue that, far from explaining why tort law grants standing only to plaintiffs who can claim to have been injured by a specific defendant and why that defendant alone must indemnify this plaintiff, economic analysis makes this essential link utterly mysterious. More fundamentally, they charge that the functionalist methodology of economic analysis in general is simply unsuited to provide an explanation of the system and practice of tort law. A very different methodological approach is needed, they argue. New conceptual and normative resources must also be developed in the place of the conceptual apparatus of economics. Challengers have looked again to the categories of personal or political morality, but, fully aware of the pitfalls of the naïve moral approach, they have undertaken to refine these categories and to articulate them for the rather different context of tort practice.

Keating, Perry, Ripstein, and Zipursky join Stone and Coleman in the search for a more satisfying alternative to familiar economic explanations of tort practice along these lines. These essays disagree about whether the appropriate frame of reference is political morality or personal morality and whether the organizing concept is one of distributive justice or of corrective justice, but there is broad agreement that an "interpretative" rather than functionalist methodology is to be preferred. Geistfeld and Chapman take a different tack. Unwilling to abandon the economic model entirely, they seek rapprochement in quite different ways between the economic model and emerging alternative justice models of explanation. Geistfeld explicitly defends the economic model against substantive criticisms like those of Stone and Coleman, but at the same time finds merit in the more sophisticated moral models that have been proposed. He argues that the two approaches are complementary. Like economic analysis, Chapman starts from the same headwaters in the theory of rational choice, but he finds resources there for a systematic integration of the very different values represented by economic analysis and competing moral theories.

### *From the Prescriptive Point of View: Distributive Justice*

Sophisticated "moral" theories fall into two groups depending on whether they accord theoretical priority to the prescriptive perspective or to the remedial perspective. One group largely accepts the theoretical template inherited from

Holmes and the economic theory, but rejects their fundamental organizing principles and goals. Public norms of care and conduct in social life, they argue, serve justice, rather than wealth- or welfare- maximization. Rather than focusing on personal moral responsibility as reflected in judgments of culpability, these theories take the basic normative questions posed by tort law to be questions of political fairness, specifically matters of distributive justice.

KEATING. George Fletcher's well-known fairness theory adopted this perspective (Fletcher 1972). Gregory Keating, in his contribution to this book, develops a theory from a similar perspective. Keating sets his inquiry in the political community. He maintains that standards of negligence and strict liability are best seen as the products of an attempt to balance the competing liberty and security interests of citizens. Adopting a Rawlsian-contractarian model of argument, he asks: What would potential injurers and victims, regarded as free and equal moral persons, seeking to establish social conditions for pursuit of their conceptions of the good, accept as fair rules for creating and imposing risk. Three broad principles for selecting and interpreting liability rules would emerge, he argues. First, risks are fairly imposed only when they promise to work to the long-run benefit of those most disadvantaged by it (namely, potential victims). Second, security interests take priority over liberty interests when the risks are grave (e.g., death, serious injury). These principles suggest the third: The benefits and burdens of a risky activity are balanced when the *harms* it causes are reciprocal in the risk community. Fletcher argued that impositions of risk on others are fair if those on whom the risk is imposed by the activity have equal opportunity and right to impose the same kind or amount of risk on the initial imposers. In contrast, Keating argues that actual harms, not just the risks of them, must be distributed reciprocally.

With these three general principles in hand, Keating sets out first to account for the division of labor between negligence and strict liability standards in tort law. Keating's "interpretative" account, however, appears to takes a decidedly critical or reforming tack at this point. Regarding activities involving grave risks, he argues (*pace* current tort law) for a presumption in favor of strict liability over negligence liability, on the ground it tends to encourage more effective and extensive reduction of the risks and distributes the costs of the materialization of those risks more fairly. This is especially true where there are adequate liability insurance markets for participants in the activities in question. Because insurance greatly eases the burden of compensating victims, it reduces the burden on liberty created by strict liability. This line of reasoning also supports enterprise or market-share liability, because it disperses the costs of non-negligent accidents across all parties benefiting from participation in large-scale, systematically organized risky activities.

Keating also argues that his contractarian principles help explicate the average reasonable person standard of due care for negligence liability. Keating argues that the familiar Hand Formula for determining reasonable precautions does not properly reflect the priority of security over liberty interests that free and equal citizens would insist on. Rather, at least where the injuries risked are severe, they would insist on a "disproportionality" test, which requires risk imposers to take all feasible precautions short of eliminating the risky activity.

Keating, it is interesting to note, assumes that the relevant parties to the contractarian deliberations are potential injurers and their potential victims, viewed as partners of sorts in patterns of risky social interaction. Given his starting point, this assumption may be surprising. Distributive justice takes the perspective of the political community as a whole. But, then, members of this community other than injurers and victims might also have stakes in the norms adopted for regulating risky conduct, since they or the community at large stand to benefit from and to bear some of the costs of conduct (or reductions in the level of certain activities) in accord with the rules of liability adopted. One wonders whether they should also be included in the deliberations. If so, might not third parties, or the community at large, also be considered a potential bearers of costs of risks that materialize? Nothing in the theoretical frame that Keating proposes requires that we pay special attention to specific injurers and victims. This, of course, leaves the apparent bilateral structure of tort practice unexplained. At least three responses are open to someone inclined to Keating's approach. First, one can argue in a reformist mode that there is no deep justification of the bilateral structure and, thus, that it should be phased out of tort practice. Second, one can try to fit his account of the substantive norms of tort liability to the Holmesian/economic theory template and offer an instrumental rationalization of the bilateral structure. Third, one can take seriously Keating's framing assumption that the class of relevant parties is restricted to potential injurers and victims and seek to identify a deep explanation for it, perhaps in some notion of corrective justice. Following this third tack, one might seek to integrate what looks like a manifestly political, distributive justice view of the substantive norms of tort law into a private, corrective justice frame.

## Remedial Theories

Some tort theorists will welcome the potential expansion of the normative framework implicit in Keating's approach, but others will argue that it seriously compromises the conceptual integrity of tort practice. If they remain sympathetic with Keating's work, they would insist on the third response mentioned above. For them, structure shapes substance in the domain of tort law, and, hence, the remedial perspective is theoretically prior. The primary aim of liability rules, on this view, is not to guide conduct, but to determine who should bear the costs of certain kinds of misfortunes, especially those occasioned by human actions. This shift of focus is reflected in the moral concepts on which many of these remedial moral theories rely. For example, *duties* to repair injuries or losses are said to fall to those *responsible* for those losses. But, as Perry makes very clear in his essay for this volume, the concern here is not responsibility for actions, but rather responsibility for outcomes, and *outcome responsibility* is not tied directly to blame or a right to punish, but rather with "ownership" of losses. Hence, the moral concern of responsibility from this remedial perspective shifts from conditions of culpability (the focus of naïve moral theory) to conditions of liability. Similarly, duties to repair are said to be *owed by* a responsible injurer *to* her victim. Perry and Coleman insist that this implies that the duty generates an "agent-specific" reason for the injurer to act. Moreover, her reason applies to her specifically precisely because of some special relationship between her and her victim. So, not only is the reason specifically addressed to the injurer, but also her action in fulfillment of the duty is specifically directed to her victim.

COMPENSATORY JUSTICE. The remedial perspective on tort practice does not by itself favor one particular moral theory of the practice. Although there is wide agreement among legal philosophers that justice is the relevant moral concept around which the theory should be constructed, it is possible to move from this plateau in quite different directions. One direction is marked by the notion of compensatory justice. On this view, justice requires that losses that are undeserved or arbitrary from a moral point of view be offset. However, this notion is not likely to illuminate tort practice, since it looks to an ideal distribution of benefits and burdens and not necessarily to any historical event, let alone human action, as an essential component of the case for compensation. Compensatory justice is simply distributive justice applied to particular social conditions.

The "annulment theory" once defended by Jules Coleman (Coleman 1992b) is a refined version of a compensatory justice principle. The annulment thesis calls for compensation of wrongful losses, that is, losses caused by wrongful actions. It focuses on the causal upshots of wrongdoing and so might seem to be an attractive starting point for a justice-based theory of torts. However, as Coleman came to see, the focus on annulling wrongful losses is one-sided. It cannot explain the allegedly fundamental bilateral structure of tort practice and it offered no special reason for imposing a duty to compensate on the doer of the wrong.

RESTORATIVE JUSTICE. Restitution, rather than mere compensation, might seem to be a more promising point of departure. On this view, the unjust losses are departures from or distortions of a just set of holdings caused by some rights-violating action. Justice requires that those who take goods without their owner's consent return them to their owner; by the same token, the losses one imposes on others against their will must be "returned" to their "owner." Something like this idea of restorative justice seems to underlie the libertarian theory of tort liability. It has resources for explaining the traditional bilateral structure of torts and it utilizes a recognizable and plausible moral concept, but it faces two major objections. First, both Perry and Coleman argue that the strictly empirical notion of causation at the heart of this theory cannot bear the weight of determining who "owns" the losses resulting from social interactions. Second, restitution theory subordinates justice in tort litigation entirely to distributive justice. The principle of restitution is arguably a relatively trivial implication of distributive justice, and this holds the justice pursued in torts litigation hostage to an assessment of the justice of the *status quo ante.* One distinctive feature of the duty to repair in torts is that it is imposed at least relatively independently of consideration of the background conditions of the parties.

CORRECTIVE JUSTICE. Some philosophers have concluded that the notion of justice that provides the conceptual structure of tort practice is conceptually distinct from distributive justice. It is a species of what has traditionally been called "commutative justice" – justice between particular persons arising from their commerce, exchange, and interaction. In the tort theory sweepstakes, such "corrective justice" theories appear to pose the most serious challenge to the hegemony of the economic theory, and versions of corrective justice theories have in recent years become increasingly sophisticated. The richness, variety, and sophistication of this theoretical approach are apparent in the essays by Stone, Perry, Coleman, and Ripstein and Zipursky.

PERRY. Stephen Perry does not set out to defend directly the explanatory thesis that tort practice seeks to do corrective justice between the parties in tort litigation; rather, he articulates the conception of corrective justice that, in his view, must figure in that explanation. Tort liability, he claims, rests on a notion of personal responsibility. To understand his point it would be useful to distinguish two notions of responsibility that seem to be at work in discussions of corrective justice in this book. We can distinguish between *ascribing* (or imputing, or attributing) responsibility to a person, on the one hand, and *assigning* (or allocating) responsibility, on the other. When we assign responsibility we give a certain person a task, make it his business. One mark of this task-oriented feature of assigned responsibility is that we speak in the plural of duties and responsibilities. Responsibilities may be assigned for many different kinds of reasons, among them reasons of expediency, efficiency, justice, or fairness. Also one can assume such responsibilities voluntarily, or find them assigned to one, for example, as part of a role in which one finds oneself. One may also have some task responsibility because one did something to bring about the situation calling for the task. In this case, one *has* that *responsibility* because one is *responsible* for the situation. The latter is a different notion of responsibility. At its core is not the notion of a job, or task, or business, but rather the notion of accountability typically tied to features of a person's character, actions, or the outcomes of those actions. This kind of responsibility is ascribed or attributed.

Although Perry does not use the terms I have introduced, we can use them to state his thesis. If tort law serves corrective justice, he argues, then tort law assigns responsibility – that is, liability and hence duties to repair – on the basis of judgments of ascribed responsibility. His essay seeks to articulate the notion of ascribed outcome-responsibility relevant to corrective justice and the link between outcome-responsibility and the duties corrective justice imposes on injurers to compensate their victims. He maintains that judgments of corrective justice are formulated in a two-stage process. First, we identify the parties who are outcome-responsible for the losses; then, we determine whether any of the outcome-responsible parties were at fault or imposed the risk of the harm suffered on the party suffering it, and if so we assign obligations to them to compensate the victims. Most of Perry's essay is devoted to articulating and defending his notion of outcome-responsibility, but he also suggests, although in less detail, the bases for judgments of fault and risk imposition.

On Perry's account, an agent A is outcome responsible for some state of affairs if and only if (1) A causally contributed to bringing about that state of affairs; (2) A had the capacities necessary to foresee that the state of affairs might be produced by her action; and (3) A had the ability and opportunity, on the basis of what A could have foreseen, to avoid the state of affairs. Perry distinguishes his view from two rivals that also make personal responsibility the ground of assignments of corrective justice responsibilities. The libertarian requires only causal contribution, whereas more robust moral theories call for some degree of actual advertence on the part of the agent (either actual intention or at least awareness of the likelihood of the harmful outcome). Perry's account adds to the causal contribution condition the requirement that the outcome responsible agent have the capacity to foresee and avoid the outcome, but *only* this capacity, not any actual advertence. His account of outcome-responsibility, then, is "objective" in the sense that no state of mind (even indifference) is requisite, but it is still "subjective" in the sense that the requisite capacities are assessed individually. On his view, we must ask with respect to each party whether he or she actually possessed the capacities to foresee and avoid the outcomes in question. The capacities of an average reasonable person are not the relevant test. This links outcome-responsibility closer to our ordinary moral notion of responsibility, but it also raises the question whether Perry can square it with the more strongly "objectivist" tendencies in modern Anglo-American tort law.

Outcome-responsibility, Perry argues, is not sufficient to ground a corrective justice obligation to compensate losses, for in many cases both parties in an accident meet the conditions of outcome-responsibility and so it does not provide in itself the basis for assigning exclusive "ownership" of the losses to one of the parties. Typically, losses result from the interaction of activities, not from actions of a single agent. Whether the risks of the harm resulting from this interaction are unilaterally imposed or jointly created is a matter that cannot be settled by strictly empirical criteria, Perry argues, but only with the aid of normative standards. These normative standards enable us to identify which of the two parties, if either, was at fault, and only the fault, or fault-like unilateral imposition of risk, of an outcom-responsible party can ground a duty of that party to compensate the accident victim. This is not, as he was once inclined to say (Perry 1992b, p. 497), a question of "localized distributive justice," but rather consideration of fault (or something akin to it) is a natural extension of the perspective on responsibility and interaction that determined the conditions of outcome-responsibility as he defined them. The relevant question at this point is not: Who in fairness ought to bear this loss? but rather: Is it true of either party that he or she *should have* foreseen and avoided what they could have foreseen and avoided? This inquiry remains in the mode *ascribing* responsibility, rather than *assigning* responsibility.

To answer this question, Perry says, we need to look again at the nature of the interaction between the activities of the outcome-responsible parties. He observes that conventional norms structure a large part of meaningful social interaction into recognized and accepted patterns. These norms and patterns enable us to distinguish between joint risk creation and unilateral impositions of risk. Risks normally resulting from the interaction of activities falling within conventionally structured and accepted patterns of interaction are jointly created and so not a sufficient basis for assigning an obligation to compensate losses to one of the parties. Within accepted patterns of social interaction, one acts with due care if any additional precautions (or any reduction in the level of the activity) would cost one more than the probability-discounted value of the precaution to potential victims of the risks. However, if one acts outside of a recognized pattern of interaction, or if others have much less control over the potential risks than one has, or if the risks one's activity creates are greater than normal within the range, or one can reduce the risks at a cost less than the probability-discounted value of the precaution, one can be said to impose the risks on others. In those cases, the risks are properly said to be one's own, and, should those risks materialize, the resulting losses are properly said to be one's fault, and on that basis one can be held to a duty to the victim to repair the victim's losses. On the other hand, if the losses are the materialization of risks jointly created and neither enhanced by one party's action nor reducible by not unreasonably costly precautions, then the loss remains the responsibility of the initial victim.

STONE. Martin Stone agrees with Perry that we must seek an explanation of tort practice in its relationship to corrective justice, but he disagrees with Perry about how this relationship should be understood. Corrective justice, as Stone understands it, cannot be defined entirely apart from the patterns of analysis and reasoning characteristic of participants in tort practice. Rather, corrective justice, given expression in tort practice, just is the concrete realization of a certain distinct albeit abstract moral concern. While the abstract concept gives shape and direction to characteristic legal reasoning in this domain, that reasoning, in turn, gives content to the abstract idea because it deals with concrete situations and parties. Thus, to grasp this moral concern, we must look at the practice more intensely and ask what kind of moral ideal is expressed in characteristic reasoning in this practice.

The relevant moral concern, Stone submits, is moral equality, understood as a norm for a part of the domain of commutative justice consisting of non-voluntary interpersonal relations. Corrective justice, in his view, is focused not on relations between the parties mediated by their common membership in a community, but rather on moral equality between parties immediately related, that is, related as private individuals. This is not to deny the moral importance of the former concern, the proper concern of distributive justice; it is merely to assert the moral significance of a different concern.

This abstract notion of moral equality shapes the remedial question raised by tort litigation, Stone maintains, by putting formal constraints on reasons that support legal judgments in this domain. Equality of this kind, he says, requires "correlativity of reasons" – that is, it requires that the reasons grounding defendant's liability for the losses must be of the same kind and force as the reasons grounding plaintiff's entitlement to damages for those losses. More specifically, considerations that count in favor of plaintiff's recovery must to the same extent count in favor of liability of the defendant. For example, suppose a plaintiff makes a claim in tort against a particular defendant. This claim must pick out some feature of the loss plaintiff suffers such that it justifies not only entitling the plaintiff to damages, but also imposing liability for those damages on this defendant. Plaintiff's suffering the loss is not enough because it does not pick out this defendant as the uniquely appropriate bearer of the losses. But it cannot be something simply about the defendant that makes him liable (like, for example, that he did wrong or intended to harm the plaintiff). For either it does not pick out this particular plaintiff (defendant may have wronged no one, or wronged someone else), or it protects the defendant from liability without duly considering features of the plaintiff, allowing, as it were, the defendant to determine unilaterally what he can be held liable for. The loss suffered must be wrongful loss and the wrong must be wrong done by the defendant to the sufferer. The ground for entitlement and liability must arise from features of the situation that pertain to both parties equally. It must be such that it accords equal status to the interests of both parties in liberty and security. This provides the framework for judicial deliberation. To determine more precisely what the appropriate rules would be, Stone argues, requires not that we construct some ideal or hypothetical perspective, but rather that we engage in reasoning typical of tort judges. In this way, Stone's corrective justice approach rejects Keating's apparatus.

COLEMAN. Jules Coleman opens his defense of a corrective justice account of tort practice in the same methodological key as Stone's essay. Like Stone, he argues that we can best deepen our understanding of tort practice, not in functionalist fashion by showing how it promotes some value defined entirely apart from the practice. He proposes to explain tort via the notion of corrective justice, but he insists, like Stone, that tort practice and corrective justice are conceptually interdependent.

On the one hand, he argues that corrective justice illuminates tort practice in two ways. First, the abstract principle of corrective justice relates to each other certain other normative concepts that figure prominently in legal reasoning in torts. This principle – that individual persons who are responsible for wrongful losses have a duty to repair those losses – puts in intelligible order and relations of dependency the concepts of wrong, loss, responsibility, duty, and repair. This template rationally organizes the core elements of tort practice and provides an intelligible structure for the practical inferences made by participants in it. Second, the core concept of corrective justice, fairness, links this principle and the institution to which it gives shape to other fundamental political principles and their corresponding institutions and practices. In turn, all the political institutions that fairness structures and rationalizes give shape to the concept of fairness, with the result that shifts in our understanding of fairness in other political contexts may be felt in the shape it gives to the concerns of corrective justice. In these two ways, corrective justice rationalizes tort practice, giving it a coherent and intelligible structure, relating it to other similar political aims, and making it answerable to broader political concerns and values.

On the other hand, Coleman argues, the concept of corrective justice depends for its content on tort practice. Tort practice turns the ideal of corrective justice into a set of regulative principles and concrete duties; it determines which losses are compensable, what counts as repair of them, which actions are wrong, and under what conditions losses are the responsibility of an individual. Against Perry, Coleman maintains that no notion of personal responsibility with roots outside the context of tort practice has any relevance to questions of corrective justice. The notion of responsibility on which determinations of tort liability – the duty to repair wrongful losses – depend is strictly a political notion in his view. (In his conclusion, Coleman argues that there is a more fundamental notion of responsibility lying behind the responsibility defined by tort practice, but it is not the ascriptive notion of personal morality, but rather a fundamental concept of liberal political theory.)

This part of Coleman's view seems to rest on an observation and an assumption. First, he observes that tort law, as a specific form of legal practice, is fundamentally a coercive arm of the state. Hence, conditions of its legitimacy must reflect conditions of the legitimacy of the state's exercise of coercive authority in general. This, he concludes, makes corrective justice a concept of political morality. He assumes that questions of political morality must be answered entirely apart from any reliance on personal morality, that the two domains are theoretically independent. This assumption has two important implications. First, it settles the question we asked earlier about how to reconcile the apparently private focus of tort litigation with its nature as a public institution. Coleman's straightforward answer is: tort practice is *public* practice, an integral part of the state's apparatus of coercive authority. So its organizing moral concept must reflect the public nature of the practice. Second, it blocks any attempt to understand and articulate corrective justice as a principle of *interpersonal,* i.e., non-political, relations.

Coleman's theory of tort law, then, is intended to be expressive, pragmatic, and practice-dependent, and its organizing concept, corrective justice, is understood as fundamentally a concept of political morality. Thus, corrective justice, for Coleman, is a kind of *political fairness* – reciprocity between free and equal individual citizens – concerned with the state's allocation of life's misfortunes due to human agency to individuals. Distributive justice is another kind of political fairness, also concerned with the allocation of misfortunes, but distinct from corrective justice in that it is concerned only with misfortunes due to nature as it were. In the domain of human agency, the governing notions are action, duty, wrong, and repair of the relevant misfortunes; and the misfortunes falling into this domain are those that can properly be said to be someone's responsibility. This notion of responsibility, as we have already seen, is defined politically. Some costs consequent upon people's actions and interactions belong to some agents, some belong to other agents, and some may belong to no agents at all. Which costs belong to which agents – who is responsible for which costs – cannot be determined by any normatively neutral notion of causation or agency, Coleman argues. This can be determined only by determining what individual citizens owe to each other with respect to potential costs associated with, or consequent upon, their actions. To use terminology I introduced earlier, the notion of responsibility in play here appears to be assigned responsibility, not ascribed responsibility. This explains why determination of who bears a duty to repair losses, which Perry thinks is a significant *further* moral conclusion from a determination of responsibility for losses requiring further substantial argument, Coleman regards as a direct implication of a determination of responsibility. The responsibility assigned just is the duty to compensate.

This fairness framework both illuminates tort practice and it depends on it, in Coleman's view. For fairness requires that individuals clean up their own messes, and prohibits them from displacing the costs of their activities onto others, where the costs of their activities is determined by the duties of care they bear. An institution which requires those who breach those duties of care to repair the losses that subsequently occur when the risks of their wrongful actions materialize, would seem to serve this ideal of political fairness nicely. Moreover, the practice would impose duties of repair not on just anyone who might be able to bear the losses (or who might even be best able to bear them), but only on those who brought them about by their wrongful actions. This duty, then, would have precisely the effect on practical deliberation that this branch of political fairness, corrective justice, calls for, namely it would impose on wrongdoers "agent-specific" reasons to repair the victims' losses. At the same time, we can determine specifically for which costs of an agent's activities he or she is responsible only by looking for guidance to the specific rules and doctrines of tort practice. The content of corrective justice fairness is dependent on the practice of corrective justice, that is, on concrete tort practices.

## III. Theoretical Responses to Recalcitrant Phenomena

Critics, including Stone and Coleman in this book, have argued that the economic theory of torts fails adequately to explain core features of tort practice. Yet moral theories, whether rooted in notions of retributive, distributive, or corrective notions of justice, also seem to face serious problems of "fit." For example, corrective justice theories that make the causal link between parties central to their critique of economic theory and to their accounts of the tort system have difficulty with modern developments of products liability. More generally, tort practice appears to be too heterogeneous to submit easily to the strictures of any single-valued explanatory theory. Some part of the tort balloon seems to pop out, regardless of the shape of the explanatory box we construct.

### *Monist Strategies*

Two broad responses to recalcitrant phenomena are open to these theories: monism or pluralism. The monist insists that there is only one fundamental explanatory principle or value, so apparently recalcitrant phenomena must be explained in its terms or explained away. The *robust* monist response simply denies the recalcitrant phenomena status as tort law. This denial can take one of two forms. The *purist* holds that whatever does not fit the conceptual or normative pattern of the core of the tort system falls outside that system and so is not properly the concern of a theory of torts. The *reformist* argues that we should regard the outliers as *mistakes* and undertake to reform the tort law according to the image projected by the favored theory.

In contrast, a *modest* monist response claims to be able to explain the core elements of tort practice, and makes no pretense of offering a unified explanation of the entire practice. (Perry seems to adopt this modest view.) Modesty always seems sensible, of course, and there is something to be said for the modesty in this context. (Early sections of Geistfeld's essay offer some useful support for this line of thought.) After all, tort law has a long and very complex history. Over that history society's view of the aims of the practice could have changed while leaving in place more or less remarkable vestiges of earlier practice. New aims could arise and old ones pass away, or make way partially for new ones. Opportunistic reforms might reshape part of the system without achieving a wholesale revision according to a single coherent plan. Moreover, institutional inertia enables practices to go on for a very long time even when their point is uncertain, highly contested, or even lost to view. These observations are so obvious that any pure monist explanatory theory is likely to strike one as decidedly otherworldly.

Yet, sensible as it may seem, modest monism faces problems of its own. It needs to defend its claims regarding the constituency of the core of the practice, but it is very difficult to do so without begging some of the most important questions in play. Moreover, if modest theory leaves a substantial part of the system entirely without explanation, or explains it only historically and pragmatically, the practice is likely to appear incoherent. At the very least, modest theory must give us some reason to think that the chaos does not infect the privileged core. This suggests, perhaps, that modest theory is sensible, but only insofar as it is regarded as a resting place on the road to a full explanation, rather than a place to call home.

RIPSTEIN AND ZIPURSKY. Not satisfied with this modest approach, Ripstein and Zipursky take a different tack. They seek to defend corrective justice against the claim that it cannot account for recalcitrant tort phenomena. They focus on what may be the toughest cases for corrective justice theories to account for: market-share liability doctrines and mass torts. It is widely believed that leading cases in this area, notably *Sindell* and *Hymowitz,*[1] abandon the core requirement of causation for tort liability, replacing it with the rule that a defendant company is liable for that share of the plaintiff's injury proportional to its share of the market for the injurious product. However, Ripstein and Zipursky argue that some (but not all) forms of market-share liability are entirely consistent with the traditional tort law and corrective justice.

This is true of cases that follow *Sindell,* they argue. The *Sindell* court did not challenge the fundamental doctrine of causation, in their view, but rather shifted the traditional evidential burden from plaintiff to defendant in a way that is consistent with concerns of corrective justice. It did so on the ground that the defendant was not entitled to the benefit of the traditional presumption that its activities did not injure the plaintiff in cases in which plaintiff had presented persuasive evidence that defendant's products had injured a substantial number of persons, but was merely unable to line up injured plaintiff with injury-causing defendant. Fairness between the parties ordinarily supports imposing the burden of proof on the complaining party, since the complaining party is accorded in the name of corrective justice the right to initiate litigation. But in this kind of case, the court argued, fairness supported shifting that burden (with the understanding that the presumption thus shifted was rebuttable). Commitment to the causation requirement was essential to the argument for shifting the burden, not irrelevant to it, our authors argue. Moreover, the same key corrective justice notions of causation and duties of non-injury explain the court's market share solution. Defendants could correctly argue that they could not fairly be held liable for more harm than they actually did, so the court held them liable only for that share of the harm which was proportional to their market share.

Still, the analysis Ripstein and Zipursky propose has a critical, reformist edge. For on their reading, the *Hymowitz* court and those that have followed it misunderstood *Sindell*. *Hymowitz* simply held defendants liable in proportion to their national market share and did not permit any defendant to avoid liability by showing it had not injured the plaintiff, thereby summarily dispensing with the individualized causation requirement. *Hymowitz,* they argue, was a mistake. While *Sindell,* on its reading, extends traditional tort doctrine consistent with the core commitments of corrective justice, *Hymowitz* undermines those foundations, and thereby opens tort litigation to serious objections. They argue that serious problems of structural fairness arise precisely because tort practice no longer can defend its relegation of choice of defendant, and rights to demonstrate negligence, to a private party. When considered as a matter primarily of doing corrective justice between the parties, tort law's private bilateral structure makes normative sense. When tort law is turned to public aims it invites assessment in terms of standards of procedural fairness appropriate to public enforcement of public norms, standards which tort practice conspicuously fails to satisfy.

### Pluralist Strategies

Two essays in this book represent a pluralist response to recalcitrant phenomena. Pluralists accept that the tort system may be driven by a number of different aims or values. They undertake to identify a manageable set of such aims or values and explain the tort system in terms of them, but it is incumbent on the pluralist to show how tort practice maintains its coherence in light of its multiple aims or values. The theorist can try to do so in a number of ways. The limiting case of this project is to find some way in which the apparently different values can be seen nevertheless to be reducible to a single common value. This is, of course, merely disguised monism. A quite different strategy is to *compartmentalize* – that is, assign different aims or values to different parts of the tort system. Coherence of the system is maintained, on this view, by institutional separation of the differently motivated parts. This seems to be the strategy of Coleman's "mixed theory" (Coleman 1992a), which sought to reconcile recalcitrant products liability doctrines with his corrective justice explanation of the system's core. The essays in this book by Chapman and by Ripstein and Zipursky point out difficulties with this strategy. Grafting a limited at-fault pool onto a general system of corrective justice, as Coleman seems to propose for mass tort cases, represents an unstable compromise between two very different ways of managing injuries and regulating behavior, Ripstein and Zipursky argue. Allowing the plaintiff to select her defendant and prove fault level makes sense in a corrective justice context, and raises no general questions of procedural fairness, but those concerns loom large once the objective is state-imposed penalty for wrongful behavior. Moreover, persons injured by negligent parties who are not in a recognized group are restricted to recovery from their injurers, with the result that a wrongfully injured party's ability to recover will depend on structural features of an industry, which are arguably irrelevant from a fairness point of view. This suggests that we should seek to seal off the compensation institutions even more tightly. Chapman argues, however, that this will be very difficult to do while maintaining the integrity of each of the institutional spheres. It will be difficult to exclude competing concerns (for example, excluding deterrence considerations from the sphere of corrective justice), and increasing demands for coordination of the spheres will be felt.

GEISTFELD. Two other approaches to reconciling the admittedly plural aims of the tort system are represented in this volume. Mark Geistfeld seeks to show that some compelling different aims are in fact *interdependent*. He begins by arguing that, while corrective justice (or more generally "moral theory") does a good job explaining a substantial part of the tort system, economic theory does an equally good job of explaining a substantial part and that these parts overlap, although not perfectly. Thus, viewed from the perspective of "positive analysis" – that is, description or explanation of the system – the two theoretical approaches are better seen as complementary rather than as competitors, he suggests.

But he does not leave his irenic proposal there; he argues further that in certain important respects the theories are mutually dependent. Economic theory, he argues, is "conceptually incomplete." It presupposes that the practice has a purpose, or more specifically that there is an appropriate social welfare function in terms of which to assess outcomes, but cannot supply such a purpose out of its own resources. The purpose, or social welfare function, must come from moral theory. By the same token, he argues, moral theory is "pragmatically incomplete." It needs economic theory to guide implementation of its ends or enforcement of its deontological rules.

CHAPMAN. Geistfeld's irenic proposal, however, seems to assume that moral theories will inevitably take a broadly consequentialist shape, or at least have a substantial consequentialist component. So, his pluralist strategy does not seem to be available to corrective justice theories, like Stone's or Perry's, which resolutely insist on a non-consequentialist understanding of the aims they propose for the tort system. Bruce Chapman offers a more ambitious pluralist strategy that might hope to do so.

Reflecting on alternative responses to Arrow's famous impossibility theorem in decision theory, Chapman offers a systematic proposal for a pluralist account of the tort system by showing how rational decision-making with multiple values is possible. He begins his application of these reflections to tort theory with the observation that problems due to the irreducible plurality of values arise most forcibly when we must weigh one competing value against another. In the context of accident law, problems arise if we think that corrective justice, deterrence, compensation, and social welfare apply equally *and simultaneously* to all alternatives. Chapman calls this the "neutrality" assumption. He argues, however, that if we allow these considerations to bear on issues or the choice of alternatives in an ordered sequence, we can often manage the problem. The outcome or decision we ultimately arrive at will, of course, depend on the sequence in which the alternatives come up – it will be "path dependent." That sequence may be arbitrary, but Chapman suggests that it can also be rationally ordered. Not all path dependence is vicious or arbitrary; some orderings of the sequence of issues and questions to be considered, and so of the values to be consulted, can be rationally structured. The trick, of course, is to justify the partition and sequencing of issues.

Tort law, he maintains, provides a conceptual structure for taking up different normative questions in a rationally ordered sequence that plausibly accommodates each of them. This structure is evident, for example, in the way in which the process of tort litigation puts issues in sequence. It is also evident in the way courts determine whether defendant took all reasonable precautions to avoid plaintiff's injury. Consider the second example. Famously, the Hand Formula requires only that defendant take that precaution the cost of which to him is at least marginally less than the cost of the injury that might thereby be prevented, discounted by its likelihood of occurring if the precaution is not taken. This, it is often argued, serves a deterrent function contributing to an efficient level of accident prevention. From a corrective justice point of view, the Formula fails to recognize that risk is a relational concept; it considers exclusively the cost of the precaution to the defendant. However, a more complex standard set by Lord Reid in *Bolton v. Stone*,[2] arguably takes this corrective justice perspective into account and yet has a place for welfare or efficiency directed deterrence considerations, Chapman argues. First it distinguishes "real" or foreseeable risks from "far-fetched" risks and imposes no liability for the latter when they materialize. Plaintiff cannot reasonably claim the defendant had a duty to protect her against that kind of risk, Reid argued. Second, Reid partitioned "real" risks into "substantial" ones and "small" ones. Regarding substantial risks he held that defendant's burden of providing the precaution is irrelevant; plaintiff's right to security prevails. But plaintiff does not prevail absolutely for real risks, for defendant is liable for the materialization of small real risks only if the cost of precautions to prevent these risks is not considerable. This invites a Hand-like calculation of the burden of precaution at this later stage of consideration, Chapman contends.

This example is complex both regarding the proper interpretation of the court's rule in *Bolton*, and regarding the values at issue in it (compare Keating's rather different understanding of the values at stake in this case), but it nicely illustrates Chapman's approach. For the *Bolton* rule partitions the issue of determining what counts as reasonable precaution in negligence litigation into a sequence of issues arguably bringing to bear considerations of corrective justice at early stages and deterrence-welfare or efficiency at later stages. The sequence greatly affects the outcome of the determination and yet no one of the relevant values is given absolute weight.

Of course, to show that a set of issues is sequenced is not yet to show that the sequence is rational or reasonable. To show that the sequence is "conceptually" structured is sufficient to dispel the sense that the path dependence is strictly arbitrary, but that too is not enough to make us comfortable with its rationality. To respond to this reasonable demand for justification of the sequence by bringing to bear some more comprehensive normative principle that can show us why it is appropriate to locate one value at point A in the process and another at point B is doomed. For it is just another version of the demand for ultimate commensurability of the relevant values that, by hypothesis, cannot be met. Chapman's approach is promising only if the rationality or reasonableness of the sequence can be demonstrated *in situ,* that is, only if we can manifest the reasonableness of a sequence with regard to the specific concerns and issues in question at each point. If we accept that there is no single principle or value to which all others can be reduced or made to serve – that is, if we accept the irreducible plurality of values – then this is our only option short of skepticism. However, if we remain uncomfortable with this option, we might wonder whether the discomfort is the product of a disappointed monism and the hope that all rational choice can be structured systematically by means of a small set of abstract principles. If we are willing to consider the possibility of rational decision making that is structured more concretely and pragmatically, then Chapman's approach will appear to be a promising beginning. Moreover, it might be partnered with the methodological proposals of Stone and Coleman to give even greater content and structure to their suggestions.

However, while Chapman's proposal is intriguing, he would no doubt concede that at this point in its development it offers a framework for explanation, but not yet a full-fledged explanatory theory. Even in partnership with the Stone-Coleman methodological suggestions, the task remains to show that the tort law does structure decision-making in such a way as to give important competing values of corrective justice, deterrence, compensation, cost spreading and the like due consideration, not only in this or that corner of the practice but in all its corners. And it must be shown – not in the abstract once and for all, of course, but context by context – that the way it partitions issues and structures decision making is reasonable. It's a difficult, but worthy, task.

Clearly, the work of making a coherent whole out of the indexed chaos of modern tort practice remains unfinished. Perhaps, though, the essays in this volume will help readers better grasp the shape of key conceptual and normative issues involved and more easily to identify and avoid some theoretical dead ends. They have sharpened some useful analytical tools and made ready some important conceptual materials from which to build an adequate explanatory theory. However, compared to philosophical work on other areas of law, criminal law for example, philosophical reflection on the law of tort is still in its infancy. It is hoped that the loose ends, uncompleted models, sketched new ideas, as well as the well-honed arguments and sharpened analytical tools, stand as an invitation to further work in this fertile field.

I conclude with a note of gratitude to Jeremy Ofseyer and Tom Holden, who helped me in the early stages of preparation of this book. I am greatly in debt to Sean McKeever, who spent many long hours helping me prepare it in its later stages. Gratitude is due also to the Law School and the Philosophy Department of the University of North Carolina at Chapel Hill, and to the National Humanities Center, which supported the UNC Law and Philosophy Workshop at which the papers published in this book were first presented.

### Notes

1. *Sindell v. Abbott Laboratories,* 607 P. 2d 294 (Cal. 1980); *Hymowitz v. Eli Lilly Co.,* 539 N.E. 2d 1069 (N.Y. 1989).
2. *Bolton v. Stone* [1951] A.C. 850 H.L.

# 2

# A Social Contract Conception of the Tort Law of Accidents

GREGORY C. KEATING[1]

Competing conceptions of the law of accidents take fundamentally different views of its task. Economic conceptions of the subject suppose that accident law should promote the general welfare, conceived as the satisfaction of people's preferences for their own well-being, and counted as wealth. Wealth – willingness to pay – measures welfare. The price that prospective victims will pay for risk-reducing precautions reveals the intensity of their preferences for safety, just as the price that prospective injurers will pay for the right to forego such precautions reveals the intensity of their preferences for imposing risk. By reducing risks until a dollar more spent on prevention yields less than a dollar's worth of increased safety, cost-minimizing liability rules maximize both the wealth and the welfare generated by accident producing activities (Cooter and Ulen 1988). Indeed, even when wealth and intensity of preference are imperfectly aligned, the maximization of wealth figures in the maximization of well-being; imperfections in the congruence between wealth and welfare are best cured by maximizing wealth in accident law and redistributing it through tax law (Kaplow and Shavell 1994).

Libertarian conceptions of the subject start from an apparently opposite premise – from the conviction that the law of accidents should protect individual rights, not promote the general welfare. They suppose that we each have a natural right to the integrity and inviolability of our persons, and that this right entitles us to be free of injuries inflicted by others. The task of accident law is to protect the inviolability of our persons, by requiring either *ex ante* consent to risk as the precondition for, or *ex post* compensation for harm as the price of, accidental injury (Nozick 1974, p. 54).

My aim in this paper is to sketch the outlines of a third view,[2] one that is liberal in general and Kantian in particular. It is liberal – as opposed to libertarian – in that it is driven by the value of fairness as much as by the value of freedom. Like libertarianism, this third view conceives of the central problem of accident law as a problem of human freedom. When the law of accidents licenses the imposition of a risk, it enhances the freedom of some and imperils the security of others. Those who impose the risk are set free to pursue valuable ends and activities, and their pursuit endangers the security of others' lives, limbs, and property. When the law of accidents forbids the imposition of some risk, it does the reverse – it curbs the freedom of prospective injurers and enhances the security of potential victims. Risk impositions thus pit the liberty of injurers against the security of victims and the law of accidents sets the terms on which these competing freedoms are reconciled. Its task is to find and fix terms that are fair.

The view is Kantian because of the way that it articulates these ideas of freedom and fairness. It brings the idea of fair terms of cooperation among free and equal persons to bear on the law of accidents, supposing that the task of accident law is to reconcile liberty and security on terms that both injurers and victims might freely and reasonably accept. What terms might those be? Terms that reconcile freedom from accidental injury and death at the hands of others, and freedom to impose risks of injury and death on others, in a way which gives free and equal persons reasonably favorable circumstances for pursuing the aims and aspirations that give meaning to their lives. The next three sections of this paper respectively explain the basic elements of this conception, sketch its approach to the choice between negligence and strict liability, and bring it to bear on the concept of reasonable care.

## I. The Conception

Just how to understand Kant's legacy in moral, political, and legal theory is, of course, a matter of dispute. My own use of Kant brings to bear the general understanding of his moral conception found in John Rawls' work and in the work of moral and political philosophers sympathetic to Rawls – Thomas Scanlon, Thomas Nagel, Barbara Herman, and Joshua Cohen, among others. More particularly, I appropriate the understanding of Kant's contribution to social contract theory found among these scholars. Before I explain the fundamentals of this conception as I understand and use it, however, let me say a bit about how I am going to use the conception.

In *A Theory of Justice,* Rawls draws a distinction between ideal and non-ideal ethical theory. Ideal theory seeks to determine principles of justice for a nearly just society; non-ideal theory seeks to determine how best to proceed under circumstances of less than ideal justice.[3] It is natural to think that the use of Rawls' kind of Kantian theory will proceed in one of these two ways. The kind of tort theorizing that I am engaged in, however, puts the conception of society as a system of fair cooperation among free and equal persons to a different – a third – kind of use. It puts this conception to *interpretive* use.[4] It asks how this conception might help us to understand, justify and (in part) criticize the law of accidents.

Putting the conception to interpretive use means that we are not "applying it" by asking questions about the articulation of ideal theory such as: "What set of principles and institutions would the parties behind the veil of ignorance adopt for addressing the problem of accidental injury and death?" "At what stage – constitutional or legislative – would they adopt those principles?" "Would they reach the problem of accidental harm at all? Or is that not part of the 'basic structure' of society to which Rawls' principles of justice are meant to apply?"[5] Nor are we "applying" Rawls' conception by asking, in light of its concepts and principles, questions of non-ideal theory such as "What, all things considered, is the best way to handle the problem of accidental harm in our less than just society?" "What ought we do about the existing injustices of the law of torts?"

Rather, by putting the Kantian moral conception found in Rawls' work to *interpretive use* we are asking questions such as "How far can we use this moral conception to understand, justify and criticize *from within* the law of accidents as we presently find it?" "How far can we understand that law to be concerned with the fair reconciliation of liberty and security?" "Does a Rawlsian conception of reasonableness illuminate the concept of reasonableness in the law of negligence?" "In the law of nuisance?" My aim, in short, is to use this moral conception to get both explanatory and critical purchase on the law of accidents. We are hoping to offer an account that explains what, if anything, in our accident law is valuable; why it is valuable; and how we might take what is of value in it and extend its influence.

Clarifying the interpretive character of the use being made of Kantian moral and political theory may dispel misunderstandings that have their roots in the distinction between ideal and non-ideal theory, but it invites another kind of misunderstanding. It is tempting to suppose that any use of a systematic moral conception (libertarianism, utilitarianism, liberalism) to "interpret" a field of law must be a "top down" (Posner 1992) endeavor – theory's effort to grasp and remake practice in its own image. Interpretation, as I conceive it, is not top down in this sense; it proceeds both from the top down and from the "bottom up." An interpretive theory seeks to illuminate, justify and partially criticize the practice that it theorizes, but it is also shaped by its encounter with that practice. In the case at hand, the animating thought is that the values of freedom and fairness are, in fact, among the values embraced by the law of accidents as we know it.[6] Bringing theory to bear on our law of accidents enables us to put the best face on those values, and so on the practice that they animate.

For example, the concept of reasonableness is central both to the law of negligence and to Kantian moral and political theory. The law of negligence insists that we owe each other reasonable care. Rawls distinguishes reasonableness from rationality, and attaches great weight to the distinction. We act rationally when we pursue our own interests, aims and aspirations in an instrumentally intelligent and informed way. We act reasonably when we show due regard for the interests of others – when we pursue our own aims and aspirations on terms that provide both ourselves and others fair opportunity to pursue our respective aims and aspirations. The canons of rationality govern the choices of individuals and associations with shared final ends; the canons of reasonableness govern the choices we make as members of a community of equal persons with diverse and incommensurable ends. Bringing Kantian theory to bear on tort practice thus illuminates the significance of negligence law's attachment to reasonableness rather than rationality – a significance obscured by the prevailing economic account of the matter – and helps to justify that attachment (Keating 1996, pp. 311–13, 341–82).

Conversely, the categories of liberty and security used by this theory to describe the stakes in accidental risk imposition show how that theory is reshaped by its encounter with tort practice. These categories are not taken from some preexisting list of liberties set out in some canonical Kantian text. In part, they are extracted from the practice by generalizing the stakes at issue in accidental risk impositions. And in part our sense of the stakes is shaped by viewing them through the lenses of the theory. We ask "How do risk impositions affect the pursuit of a conception of the good over the course of a complete life?" In answering this question, we come to see that substantial measures of liberty – understood as the freedom to impose risks of physical injury and death on others – and security – understood as freedom from accidental injury at death at the hands of others – are specialized kinds of primary goods. Each is important to the pursuit of a conception of the good over the course of a complete life.

This articulation of the theory through its encounter with tort practice is only to be expected. The subject matter of the tort law of accidents[7] is quite different both from the subject matter of justice for the basic structure of society, and from the individual actions that are the subject of ethics. Even if the same general moral conception can be applied to all three domains, it must be tailored to the domain at hand.

So much for how I propose to use Kantian social contract theory. What, exactly, are the substantive ideas that I propose to put to this interpretive use? The core idea of the conception is one of political society as a system of cooperation among persons who are free and equal, rational and reasonable. *Free* in the democratic sense of being politically independent. Democratic citizens yield their independence only to a political authority capable of commanding their unforced consent – because that authority is constituted in accordance with principles of justice suitable for ordering the fundamental terms of their life in common.[8] *Equal* in the sense of being free and independent, but also in the sense that they each possess the capacities for self-governance and fair treatment of others sufficiently to be fully participating members of society. *Rational* in the sense that they are each able to form, revise and act from a conception of the good – a set of aims and aspirations for their lives (Rawls 1993, pp. 48–54, 302). The capacity for "critically reflective self-governance" shared by all free and equal persons gives each such person both the ability to, and a fundamental interest in, shaping his or her life in accordance with some conception of its point (Scanlon 1988, pp. 151, 174–5). Democratic citizens are thought to be *reasonable* because they have a sense of justice – they are prepared to abide by fair terms of cooperation so long as others abide by those terms as well.

This framework addresses the problem of political justice, conceived in a certain way. So conceived, the problem arises both from the fact of scarcity and from the fact of reasonable disagreement over the good. On the one hand, co-operation enables the production of material wealth, but not so much that all wants can be satisfied. Moderate scarcity is thus the order of the day. On the other hand, a plurality of incommensurable conceptions of the good – a plurality of convictions about what is valuable and worth doing – is a natural outgrowth of conditions of political freedom (Rawls 1993, p. 36). Unchecked by constraints of law and justice these diverse conceptions are fertile sources of bitter and divisive conflict. The task of principles of justice is to order competing claims to scarce resources, and to fix the terms on which people may pursue their diverse conceptions of the good. The challenge is to find or fashion terms of cooperation that free and equal persons, who hold diverse and incommensurable conceptions of the good, might reasonably accept so long as others do so as well.

It follows from this specification of the problem that the terms of social co-operation among free and equal citizens will have to be justified independent of any *specific* conception of the good. There is no shared final end – such as the pursuit of maximal preference satisfaction, or the maximization of wealth – that can be used to commensurate costs and benefits to different people. Comparisons among citizens must therefore be made through the use of criteria of interpersonal comparison that are "objective," not "subjective." Subjective criteria of interpersonal comparison evaluate "the level of well-being enjoyed by a person in given material circumstances or the importance for that person of a given benefit or sacrifice . . . solely from the point of view of that person's tastes or interests" (Scanlon 1975, p. 72). Objective criteria appraise burdens and benefits in terms that are "the best available standard of justification that is mutually acceptable to people whose [aims, aspirations and] preferences diverge" (Scanlon 1975; see also Scanlon, 1991). When persons' conceptions of the good are diverse and incommensurable, justification must proceed by appealing to objective criteria of well-being, because only objective criteria can prove mutually acceptable. Here, too, Kantian theory converges with, underpins, and illuminates tort law's firm commitment to objective criteria of interpersonal comparison (Keating 1996, pp. 367–73).

The comparison of burdens and benefits requires not only criteria of comparison, but also some benchmark of comparison. One kind of benchmark, found in the Lockean tradition of social contract theory, compares the distribution of burdens and benefits under some proposed principle of justice against a fixed historical baseline.[9] The Kantian tradition in social contract theory takes a different tack: It compares the allocations of burdens and benefits under one proposed principle against the alternatives – against the allocations proposed by other principles. There is a strong structural resemblance between this procedure and tort practice.[10] In choosing between negligence and strict liability, and in assessing whether a duty of reasonable care was breached because a particular precaution should have been taken, we compare the allocation of burdens and benefits effected by different alternatives.

If the fundamental idea of Kantian social contract theory is the idea of society as a system of cooperation among free and equal persons, a fundamental task of principles of justice on this account is to find terms of cooperation that express the freedom and equality of democratic citizens, recognizing that these citizens hold diverse and incommensurable conceptions of the good. Kantian political theory approaches that task by asking, "What terms would free and equal persons themselves agree to, if they were to reach agreement under ideal conditions?" Ideal conditions, in brief, are conditions untainted by any bargaining advantages; informed by a correct understanding of the consequences of alternative principles and arrangements; and based on the fundamental interests of democratic citizens in realizing their own conceptions of the good, consistent with a like freedom for others to do so as well. The underlying intuition that the device of uncoerced agreement models is the intuition that just arrangements must treat the fundamental interests of those they affect equally and adequately, so that the terms of social cooperation are to the advantage of each and every participant.

To bring this general conception to bear on the law of accidents, we must first characterize the interests at stake in risk impositions, bearing in mind that our general aim is to establish favorable conditions for persons to pursue their conceptions of the good over the course of complete lives. The tort law of accidents governs risks that are the by-product of beneficial activities. The benefits vary widely: some risky activities increase income and wealth, others offer amusement and challenge, and still others pursue ends of great urgency (saving life, for example). Yet however varied the interests benefited by risk impositions, the interests threatened are essentially the same. The tort law of accidents is preoccupied with activities that impose risks of serious bodily harm and even death, both upon those who undertake them and upon those who are exposed to them. Here, then, we have the heart of the problem. On the one hand, the freedom to impose risk is valuable, because it enables people to engage in activities that bring material benefits, psychic well-being, and meaning to their lives. On the other hand, at least some risks of accidental injury and death pose grave threats to our well-being. The security of our persons and property is at least as urgent a good as liberty. "Security," John Stuart Mill remarked, "no human being can possibly do without; on it we depend for all our immunity from evil and the whole value of all and every good, beyond the passing moment, since nothing but the gratification of the instant could be of any worth to us if we could be deprived of everything the next instant . . ." (Mill 1861, p. 53). Yet when risks of the sort that occupy accident law are at stake, enhancing the security of some impairs the liberty of others.

Folding this back into a Kantian framework, we can say that both liberty and security are preconditions of effective rational agency. For Kantian social contract theory, person's interest in pursuing a conception of the good – a conception of what is worthwhile and valuable in life – is a one of their deepest and most settled interests. Whatever a person's conception of the good is, a substantial measure of security is a precondition of its pursuit. So, too, is a substantial measure of liberty. Liberty and security as we have specified them are, in short, "primary goods" – goods that free and equal persons need in adequate measure if they are to pursue their conceptions of the good, whatever those may be. The challenge is to reconcile the two on terms that provide favorable – ideally the most favorable – circumstances for persons who wish to pursue their conceptions of the good over the course of their lives.[11]

The question of how best to reconcile the pursuit of activities we value with the physical and psychological integrity that those activities can jeopardize is, of course, an issue that each of us must face individually. What ends are worth the risks they entail? Are the risks of death and disfigurement that are the price of scaling Mount Everest worth the glory of reaching its summit? Are increased risks of cancer worth bearing as the price of performing path-breaking medical research? Are they worth bearing as the price of earning a living? This kind of individual choice is not, however, the chief concern of the law of accidents. The problem of accidental harm is a problem of social choice, a matter of reconciling the competing claims of liberty and security for a plurality of persons.

Because the final aims and aspirations of free and equal persons are diverse and incommensurable, the principles of social choice differ markedly from those of individual choice. Individually, it may be rational to expose ourselves to risks that it would be unreasonable to impose on others. The *rationality* of exposing oneself to a risk depends on the end furthered by the exposure, the importance that one attaches to furthering that end, and the efficacy with which the exposure will further those values. The canons of rationality thus give wide rein to individual subjectivity, and are naturally expressed in the language of cost–benefit efficiency. Individuals are free to value the burdens and benefits of risks by any metric they choose, and it is surely natural for them to value burdens and benefits by their own subjective criteria of well-being. It is also perfectly rational for individuals to run risks, measured by their own subjective criteria of well-being, whenever the expected benefits of so doing exceed the expected costs, and to decline risks whenever the reverse is true.

It is not, however, *reasonable* for us to settle questions of interpersonal risk imposition by recourse to the canons of rationality. The circumstance where we voluntarily expose ourselves to risks in the pursuit of our own ends is very different from the circumstance where others involuntarily expose us to risks in the pursuit of their ends. In a world where persons affirm diverse and incommensurable conceptions of the good, those who are put at risk generally do not value the ends pursued through the relevant risk impositions in the way that those imposing the risks do. This difference between individual and social choice strips the argument that a risk should be borne because it pursues a worthy end at an acceptable cost of its force. Given the reasonable diversity of persons' final aims and aspirations, the justification for accepting risk impositions by others is not common acknowledgment of some shared final end, but mutuality of benefit. It is reasonable to expose other people to risks of serious injury and even death when it is fair to do so; and it is fair to do so, when they, too, stand to gain from the imposition of those risks.

Prospective victims stand to benefit from the imposition of risks upon them in either of two ways. First, they might benefit because, *ex ante,* the imposition of those risks works to their long-run benefit, even though they do not impose them, or benefit from being free to impose them. For example, given the importance of driving to our daily lives (this, from someone who lives in Los Angeles), we may all stand to benefit from the transport of large quantities of gasoline over the roads, even though it creates risks of massive explosion, and even though most of us never expect to make use of the legal right to transport gasoline in this manner.[12]

Second, victims may stand to benefit from the imposition of risks upon them because they do – again *ex ante* and over the long run – stand to benefit from receiving the reciprocal right to expose others to equal risks. The right to impose risks *on* others can justify the imposition of equal risks on us *by* others, because the right to impose risks secures the liberty essential to the pursuit of a conception of the good. For example, we may each gain more from the mundane freedom to take our cars on the road than we lose through the hazards so created. When – within a community of risk – the right to impose risks of a certain kind *ex ante* benefits each affected person's liberty more than it burdens each affected person's security, it is fair to ask each member of the community to bear the imposition of the same kind of risk by others.

The underlying criterion that justifies the imposition of risks in both cases is one of *ex ante* long-run benefit to those disadvantaged by particular risk impositions.[13] Those disadvantaged by particular risk impositions are prospective victims – those who stand to gain nothing from the impositions in question, but whose lives, limbs and personal property is put in peril by them. And their long-run benefit is no longer than the course of a normal life. Were it longer, they could not expect to reap the benefits of the risk impositions at issue. Precisely because this criterion licenses only those risks that are to everyone's benefit, free and equal persons, uncoerced by any differences in bargaining power, and concerned to reach agreement on principles that would secure for each of them favorable and mutually beneficial terms of accidental risk imposition would agree to its adoption. When mutuality of benefit is realized in this way, no one's life or limb is sacrificed to the greater good of others, and we each gain more from the right to impose certain risks than we lose from having to bear exposure to equivalent ones.

Kantian social contract theory thus confirms and articulates an intuition voiced by the rhetoric of fairness that recurs throughout the American law of torts. Issues of interpersonal risk imposition are fundamentally matters of fairness, not matters of efficiency. The question is not "Do the expected benefits of this risk exceed its expected accident costs?" but "Is it fair for one person to put another's life, limbs, and personal property in peril in this way?" The answer the theory gives is that it is fair when so doing is to the long run expected advantage of the person imperiled.

With these basic ideas in hand, we are in a position to sketch how Kantian social contract theory views two of the central issues in accident law, namely, the choice of an appropriate liability rule, and the evaluation of the reasonableness of particular risk impositions (the problem of duty and breach in negligence law). These are both fundamental issues in tort law and theory, and issues that illuminate the fundamentals of a social contract conception. Social contract theory asks the same question of the choice between negligence and strict liability that it asks of the decision to take or forego a particular precaution: Which principle (in the case of the choice between negligence and strict liability) or ruling (in the case of due care) reconciles the competing claims of liberty and security in the most reasonable way?

## II. Choosing Between Negligence and Strict Liability

The law of accidents is now, and long has been, divided between two basic principles of liability: negligence and strict liability. Just how we should understand the difference between these competing principles of responsibility is, it so happens, a contested matter in its own right. Because some account of the essential difference between negligence and strict liability is necessary to frame the substantive question of how we should (and do) go about choosing between them, I propose, for the purposes of this paper, simply to note that I take the contrast between negligence and strict liability to be a distinction between "fault" and "conditional fault." So conceived, the fundamental difference between strict and negligence liability is this: Under strict liability, the payment of damages to those injured by the characteristic risks of an activity is a condition for the legitimate conduct of an activity.[14] Under negligence liability, the payment of damages is a matter of redress for the wrongful infringement of the property and physical integrity of others (Keating 1997, p. 1308–12). When strict liability is conceived in this way, it leads neither to "absolute" liability (as George Priest has argued), nor to a kind of surrogate negligence liability (as others including Gary Schwartz and Richard Posner seem to think), but to liability for the "characteristic" or "distinctive" risks of an activity. So-called characteristic or distinctive risks are those risks that the long-run careful conduct of a particular activity increases over and above their background level (Keating 1997, pp. 1287–92). The use of field burning as an agricultural technique, for example, increases the background risk of harm from fire.[15]

This specification of the difference sets the stage for us to address the difficult substantive question: Why is it that the fair allocation of responsibility for accidental harm among free and equal persons requires negligence liability in some circumstances and enterprise liability in others? Why is the payment of money damages to the victims of a risk (or an activity) sometimes rightly conceived as redress for wrongful infringement of the victim's security (and paid only when the infringement is wrongful) and other times rightly conceived as a condition for the legitimate conduct of an activity (and paid whenever the activity issues in a characteristic harm)?

This question is one that has a long-standing answer in the social contract tradition, albeit one that I think in need of some revision. More than twenty-five years ago, George Fletcher argued that the doctrinal division of labor between negligence and strict liability tracks reciprocity of risk imposition, and rightly so (Fletcher 1972). When risks are reciprocal once due care is exercised, both tort law and social contract theory favor negligence liability; when they are not, both tort law and social contract theory favor strict liability. We need to reconstruct Fletcher's argument to appraise its strength.

### A. Fairness as Reciprocity of Risk

Fletcher's central idea is that social contract theory favors negligence liability within a community of reasonable risk imposition, and strict liability when one community imposes risks on another (Fletcher 1972). A community of risk is one whose members impose reciprocal risks of harm on one another, thereby imposing and being exposed to identical risks. A community of *reasonable* risk imposition is one whose members impose only risks that confer more in the way of benefits on those who impose them than they inflict in the way of detriment on those who are exposed to them. When risks are reciprocal, then, each person relinquishes an equal amount of security and gains an equal amount of freedom. When *reasonable risks are reciprocal,* each member of the community that imposes and is exposed to them: (1) relinquishes an equal amount of freedom; (2) gains an equal amount of security; and (3) gains more in the way of freedom than they lose in the way of security.

Reciprocity of risk once due care has been exercised thus defines a community of equal freedom, benefits each of its members, and fairly apportions the burdens and benefits of the risks that it licenses. Subjecting reasonable reciprocal risks to strict liability increases neither freedom nor fairness. Strict liability does not increase either freedom or security because it bears only on the distribution of non-negligent accident costs.[16] It does not improve the fairness of the distribution of the burdens and benefits of risk imposition because its adoption simply "substitute[s] one form of risk for another – the risk of liability for the risk of personal loss" (Fletcher 1972, p. 547).

Matters are different when risks are non-reciprocal even if injurers exercise due care. Strict liability does and should apply to risks that are reasonable but nonreciprocal. Some risks are reasonable because they are to the long-run advantage of those imperiled by them, but they are not mutually beneficial in the full sense that reciprocal risks are. For example, given the importance of driving to our daily lives, each of us may benefit from the transport of large quantities of gasoline over the roads, even though this method of transporting gasoline creates risks of massive explosion, and even though most of us never expect to make use of the legal right to transport vast quantities of gasoline in this manner.[17] It follows that the prospective victims of non-reciprocal risk impositions are not fully compensated for bearing these risks by the right to impose equal risks in turn.[18] The imposition of non-reciprocal risks is not part of a normal life, and the value of the right to impose such risks does not offset the disvalue of having to bear exposure to them.

Subjecting non-reciprocal risks to strict liability offsets this unfairness, insofar as *ex post* compensation can redress the harm victims suffer. By ensuring that those injured by non-reciprocal risk impositions are – so far as possible – fully compensated for their injuries, strict liability effects a more robust mutuality of benefit. Risk is unfairly distributed *ex ante,* but the costs of accidents issuing from those risks are fairly distributed *ex post.* The damages paid under strict liability are, then, not redress for wrongful infringement of another's security, but a condition for the legitimate conduct of activities whose reasonable risks are not mutually beneficial in the strong sense that reasonable reciprocal risks are. Fletcher's account thus captures the fact that negligence is a matter of fault and strict liability a matter of conditional fault, and explains why this should be so.

The connection between Fletcher's account and Kantian social contract theory should be evident. Social contract theory seeks to secure favorable and fair conditions for equal persons to pursue their conceptions of the good over the course of complete lives. For the particular package of risk impositions licensed by the law of accidents to realize these aspirations, several conditions must be met. First, the gain conferred on our liberty by the right to impose certain risks must exceed the loss to our security from having to bear exposure to such risks. The requirement that reciprocal risks be reasonable entails the satisfaction of this condition. Second, the terms of reasonable risk imposition must be terms of equal freedom. Reciprocity of risk defines a regime of equal freedom because reciprocity exists when risks are equal in probability and gravity. When risks are equal in these respects, persons relinquish equal amounts of security and gain equal amounts of liberty.

Third, social contract theory asks that the burdens and benefits of risk be fairly distributed. When reciprocal risks are imposed for reasons that are both good (that is, sufficient to justify the diminutions of security that they involve) and equally good, reciprocity of risk also defines a regime of mutual benefit. When these conditions are met, each person is *benefited* because, for each person, the loss of security occasioned by granting to others the right to expose her to risks of a certain probability and magnitude is more than offset by the freedom of action that a regime of reciprocal risk imposition grants to her, namely, the right to impose risks of equal probability and magnitude on others. When reasonable risks are reciprocal, each person's freedom of action is *equally* benefited and each person's security is equally burdened. Reciprocity of reasonable risk imposition thus defines a circumstance where risk is fairly distributed.

Thus, under a regime where risks equal in probability and magnitude are imposed for reasons that are both sufficient and equally good, we acknowledge both the importance of leading our lives in accordance with our aims and aspirations, and the equal value of the aims, aspirations, and lives of others. We acknowledge the former by being willing to expose ourselves to reasonable risks in pursuit of our aims and aspirations. We acknowledge the latter by accepting equal risk impositions by others. The former is central to our status as free persons; the latter is central to our status as equal persons. The Kantian logic behind making reciprocity of risk imposition (once due care has been exercised) the master criterion for choosing between negligence and strict liability becomes evident when reciprocity is understood in this way. Taking reciprocity to require that risks be equal in probability and magnitude, and be imposed for reasons that are both equally good and sufficient, makes reciprocity of risk a test for the fair reconciliation of liberty and security so far as *risk – not harm –* is concerned.

This account of the reciprocity of risk criterion is open to a number of objections. For one thing, there is reason to doubt that the law of accidents really does exhibit the logic of reciprocity as Fletcher conceived it. Much (perhaps most) of modern enterprise liability imposes strict liability on circumstances where the underlying risks seem at least arguably reciprocal (Keating 1997, p. 1295, esp. note 91). For another thing, there is reason to doubt that the ideal of reciprocity can be made into an operational criterion for the choice of liability rules in as straightforward a way as Fletcher supposes (see Keating 1997, pp. 1317–27). I want to put these problems to the side, however, because I believe that the central problem with the argument lies elsewhere. The central problem is that Fletcher's account underrates the attractiveness of strict liability to social contract theory. Strict liability may often strike a fairer balance between liberty and security than negligence does, even when reasonable risks are reciprocal. Harm need not be reciprocal even when risk is, and it is reciprocity of harm that is essential to the fair apportionment of the burdens and benefits of risky activities.

To understand why Fletcher underrates the general attractiveness of strict liability, we must first bear in mind that social contract theory evaluates the case for a particular liability regime by asking if it is to the long-run advantage of those it disadvantages.[19] To apply this criterion to the choice between negligence and strict liability, however, we need to refine Fletcher's approach, because it focuses disproportionately on the *ex ante* distribution of risk as distinguished from the *ex post* distribution of harm. Negligence and strict liability distribute the benefits and burdens of reasonable risk impositions in markedly different ways. Negligence singles out the victims of non-negligent accidents for comparatively great burdens, whereas strict liability targets the injurers who harm those victims. We must, therefore, compare the disadvantages that negligence liability imposes on the victims of non-negligent accidents with the disadvantages that strict liability imposes on those who inflict non-negligent injuries.

The burdens of these *most* disadvantaged classes of persons come to the fore, because those most disadvantaged are those with the most to complain about. For a liability rule to be fully justified, the rule must be shown to be to long-run advantage of those it most disadvantages, even though they suffer more under it than anyone else does.[20] For Fletcher's argument to succeed, then, it must be the case that, when risks are reciprocal, the victims of non-negligent accidents are better off over the long run bearing the costs of the accidents that befall them – as they do under negligence liability – than they would be under a regime of strict liability – which would secure them compensation for those costs.

Strict liability is more attractive to social contract theory than Fletcher thinks, for three reasons. First, when risks are grave, persons' interests in security are, on the whole, more in need of protection than their interests in liberty. Strict liability protects persons' security more than negligence does; it induces greater risk reduction and it provides compensation to the victims of non-negligent accidents. Second, Fletcher's argument overrates the importance of risk, and underrates the importance of harm. Once we assign appropriate importance to harm, strict liability becomes more attractive. Third, Fletcher's claim that it is unfair to impose strict liability on reciprocal risks assumes that strict liability simply shifts a concentrated harm from the victim who has suffered the harm to the injurer who inflicted. When non-negligent accidents are insurable, however, strict liability disperses an activity's non-negligent accident costs across all those who participate in the activity. This distribution of the burdens and benefits of reasonable risk is fairer than the distribution effected by negligence liability.

Starting with the first of these arguments: Our interest in security is entitled to more protection than our interest in liberty if and when risk impositions threaten a significant chance of death or debilitating injury. To the extent that they do so, they threaten the premature end, or the severe crippling, of our agency. In general, the burdens to our liberty that follow from our need to take risk-reducing precautions do not pose similar threats to our capacities to pursue our ends over the course of complete lives. For the burden to liberty to be comparable to the burden to security effected by death or severe debilitation, risk-reducing precautions would have to effect the cessation or the crippling, of the risky activity. This will rarely be the case. To the extent, then, that accident law concerns itself with activities that can and do impose grave risks, we have reason to favor security over liberty in designing our accident law. Strict liability tends to do this.

Strict liability tends to protect security more effectively than negligence does because it awards damages for all of the injuries occasioned by an activity's characteristic risks, not just for those that might have been prevented by the exercise of due care. Because damages can undo much of the harm that injuries inflict – the costs of treatment and rehabilitation, for instance – awarding damages to all the victims of an activity's characteristic risks, not just those whose injuries issue out of unreasonable risk impositions, undoes a substantial measure of the harm done by those injuries.[21] Making injurers pay for all of the accidents characteristic of their activities also tends to induce more extensive and effective risk reduction, for two reasons. First, it places the responsibility for selecting precautions in the hands of the party likely to be most expert in the matter – the injurer itself.[22] Second, it induces that party to comb through its activity in search of effective risk-reducing measures – it induces injurers to adjust the levels at which they engage in their activities as well as the care with which they conduct them, for example.[23] When security is seriously jeopardized by substantial risks of death and grievous injury, then, social contract theory has reason to be favorably disposed toward strict liability.

### B. Fairness as Reciprocity of Harm

Fletcher's second mistake is to place too much weight on reciprocity of *risk*, and it, too, leads him underrate the attractiveness of strict liability. The claim is that *ex post* compensation is unnecessary when reasonable risks are reciprocal. The presence of in-kind compensation eliminates the need for explicit monetary compensation by tort liability. When risks are reciprocal, those who are exposed to risk are compensated for bearing that exposure by their right to impose similar risks in return. This is compensation in-kind and it justifies dispensing with the payment of damages when reasonable and reciprocal risks issue in harm.

The argument is flawed, but not because it makes use of the idea of in-kind compensation. The flaw lies in its emphasis on risk. What counts is not reciprocity of *risk* but reciprocity of *harm*. Risk rarely impairs the ability to pursue a conception of the good over the course of a complete life; it is harm – physical injury and death – that wreaks havoc with people's lives.[24] Reciprocity of risk does provide compensation in-kind for bearing a risk, but it does not provide compensation in kind for bearing the harm that issues from the risk. Risk can be fairly distributed while harm is unfairly concentrated, and it is harm that matters. Reciprocity of risk therefore cannot justify a regime of negligence liability. Only reciprocity of harm can provide in-kind compensation for bearing harm.[25]

When might reciprocity of harm justify negligence liability? Reciprocity of harm might justify negligence liability when (1) the risks at issue precipitate harms of relatively modest magnitude; and (2) those who suffer such harm inflict similar harms on others within the community of risk in fairly short order. The relative modesty of a risk favors departing from a regime of strict liability because the urgency of reducing a risk diminishes with its magnitude. Furthermore, putting the special case of death to one side, the urgency of the victim's need for contemporaneous compensation increases with the seriousness of the injury. A short time span between the suffering and the infliction of an injury by a given member of a community of risk favors dispensing with monetary compensation because it keeps accounts in balance. When the time lag between injuring and being injured is long, a regime that relieves injurers of the duty to compensate their victims is likely to leave accounts out of balance.[26] Some injurers will reap benefits that they will not be required to repay; some victims will bear losses that they will never have occasion to recoup. Insisting on contemporaneous compensation is the only way to keep accounts in balance.

By contrast, the circumstances described in Justice Bramwell's famous statement of the "live-and-let-live" rule of nuisance law justify dispensing with the requirement of compensation (and indeed with certain duties of precaution) because both relative modesty of risk and reciprocity of *harm* are present:

The instances put during the argument, of burning weeds, emptying cesspools, making noises during repairs, and other instances which be nuisances if done wantonly or maliciously, nevertheless may be lawfully done. It cannot be said that such acts are not nuisances, because, by hypothesis they are; and it cannot be doubted that, if a person maliciously and without cause made close to a dwelling-house the same offensive smells as may be made in emptying a cesspool, an action would lie. Nor can these cases be got rid of as extreme cases, because such cases properly test a principle. Nor can it be said that the jury settle such questions by finding that there is no nuisance, though there is. . . .

There must be, then, some principle on which such cases must be excepted. It seems to me that that principle may be deduced from the character of these cases, and is this, viz., that those acts necessary for the common and ordinary use and occupation of land and houses may be done, if conveniently done, without submitting those who do them to an action. . . . There is obvious necessity for such a principle as I have mentioned. It is as much for the advantage of one owner as of another for the very nuisance the one complains of, as the result of the ordinary use of his neighbour's land, he himself will create in the ordinary use of his own, and the reciprocal nuisances are of a comparatively trifling character. The convenience of such a rule may be indicated by calling it a rule of give and take, live and let live.[27]

Bramwell's observations, however, are tailored to the special circumstances of nuisance law. Nuisance law and negligence law address different kinds of harm. Nuisance law addresses harmful fallout from an activity – fallout that interferes with another's use and enjoyment of their land. The fallout is typically either continuous or – if continual – very frequent. The interference – while substantial enough to disrupt the reasonable use and enjoyment of land – is not devastating. Negligence law – being part of law of accidents proper – addresses sudden explosions of standing risks into substantial injuries. *Rylands v. Fletcher*, for example, is an instance of accidental harm, not nuisance, because the collapse of Rylands' reservoir flooded Fletcher's mine. (It took him four months to pump the water out.) Had the water seeped out of Rylands' reservoir on a regular basis and substantially increased the existing percolation of water through Fletcher's mine, Fletcher's claim would have been one for nuisance.

It is clear how reciprocity of harm can be desirable in the nuisance context. There are certain everyday annoyances – ordinary interferences with the use and enjoyment of property – that each of us is better off bearing than curtailing. We each gain more from the right to impose similar interferences on others than we lose from having to bear such impositions by others. The reciprocity of the interference makes the payment of compensation superfluous. We are each compensated in-kind. Accidental injury to life, limb and property is, however, substantially more serious in magnitude than continuous low-level interference with the use and enjoyment of property. Non-negligent risk impositions can and do explode into death and disfigurement.[28] Given the substantial gravity of the harms with which negligence is concerned, it is natural to ask "What is the appeal of reciprocity of harm in this context?" "Why would it ever be better to bear such risks without compensation than with compensation?"

In the negligence context, reciprocity of harm exists when the non-negligent level of risk imposition is the background level of risk imposition, the level of "inevitable risk." Inevitable risk is risk whose reduction is not consistent with the flourishing of valuable activities; it is the price of freedom to act. Inevitable risk is mutually imposed and reciprocal in a broad sense. In the course of our normal lives, each of us imposes non-negligent risks of injury on each other. While we do so in the course of different activities, we do so in roughly reciprocal ways, at least in the long run.[29] Even though the magnitude of the harms that can issue from background risk impositions is great, the probability of such harms is low enough to justify treating background risk impositions as less grave than those "reasonably foreseeable" risks that the law of accidents seeks to reduce to more reasonable levels.[30] The risk that a six-year-old child will be inspired by a toy lighter to set himself on fire is too low to be reasonably foreseeable. We are each better off bearing background risks than we are trying to regulate them through tort liability. Negligence liability is thus appropriate not when reasonable risks are reciprocal, but when the residual level of reasonable risk imposition – the level remaining once due care has been taken – is low enough to merge into the background level of mutually imposed risk that is the price of the freedom to act.[31]

Without reciprocity of harm, the case for subjecting a set of risks to a regime of negligence liability is only convincing if strict liability would disrupt the liberty of injurers so greatly that its disruptive effects equal those that negligence inflicts on victims. Consider the risks of the road (Fletcher's principal example of reciprocal risk imposition) in this regard. The residual risks of reasonably careful driving are substantial; they probably exceed the normal level of non-negligent risk imposition. The time lag between one's turns as non-negligent injurer and victim of a non-negligent accident is likewise quite long.[32] Although rough reciprocity of risk may be present, rough reciprocity of harm is not. The case for imposing strict liability is therefore presumptively quite strong.

What might be said against imposing strict liability? Perhaps that doing so would impair the liberty of motorists as injurers as much or more than negligence would impair the security of motorists as victims. During the latter half of the nineteenth century, if not now, negligence liability for automobile accidents may have been justified because the institution of liability insurance was in its infancy. Without the institution of liability insurance, a regime of strict liability might have brought financial ruin upon injurers by imposing upon them the financial costs of accidents that they should not have prevented. When this is so, strict liability may disrupt the liberty of injurers so greatly that its disruptions threaten to cripple the activity and equal those that negligence inflicts on victims. Under these circumstances, motorists may be better off under negligence liability. Bearing the costs of non-negligent accidents may be to their long-run advantage, especially if they can insure themselves against non-negligent injury through loss insurance.

In short, reciprocity of harm, not reciprocity of risk, is the touchstone of fairness. The burdens and benefits of an activity are in balance only when the harms that it causes are fairly distributed. The ideal of fairness thus creates a strong presumption that – when the residual harms issuing from a regime of reciprocal risk imposition exceed the background level of inevitable risk imposition – strict liability ought to be imposed, even though the burdens and benefits of the underlying risks are, *ex ante,* fairly distributed. To rebut that presumption, we must show that the burden to injurers' liberty effected by the imposition of strict liability equals or exceeds the burden to victims' security of leaving non-negligent accident costs on the shoulders of victims.

## C. Fairness as Proportionality of Burden and Benefit

When we place the case for negligence liability on this relatively narrow ground, however, we pave the way for it to be undermined by the rise of adequate liability insurance markets. Liability insurance eases the burden of compensating the victims of non-negligent accidents, thereby diminishing the burdens that strict liability (in the special form of no-fault automobile insurance) places on the liberty of those who inflict non-negligent accidents. Because automobile accidents wreak havoc with lives, limbs and property, victims have good reason to demand compensation for them. Because no-fault insurance supplies such compensation, we have strong reason to favor it over negligence liability, other things equal.[33] The risks of driving remain roughly reciprocal as the institution of insurance advances, but the case for strict liability – here in the special guise of no-fault automobile insurance – grows in tandem with the rise of adequate liability insurance.

Insufficient attention to the importance of insurance is the third and perhaps the most important weakness in reciprocity of risk theory. The argument that it is unfair to impose strict liability on reciprocal risks because doing so merely shifts the financial costs of non-negligent accidents from victims to injurers assumes a particular social world – one in which risks are concentrated on the single injurer that inflicted the harm, rather than being dispersed across the class of persons who impose risks of the same kind. In part because the institution of insurance has improved, and in part because the world has grown more insurable, we live in a markedly different social world from the one this argument assumes. In our world, enterprise liability is often able to achieve fairness in its fullest sense by making burden and benefit symmetrical. In our world, the imposition of strict liability upon an activity can disperse the costs of its non-negligent accidents across all those who benefit from the risk impositions that issue in those accidents (Keating 1997, 1331–36, 1351–56). This is just what a fully realized scheme of no-fault insurance would do – and no-fault insurance is enterprise liability in the special form of compulsory first-party loss insurance.

When strict liability spreads the costs of the non-negligent accidents across those who benefit from the creation of the relevant risks, its comparative advantage over negligence liability is greater than ever. It is plainly fairer to spread the costs of accidents arising out of the characteristic risks of an activity across those who profit from the activity, than it is to leave those who have the misfortune to get in the activity's way to bear those costs as best they can.

The distinction that counts here is one between two *idealized* social worlds. The social world presupposed by the argument that strict liability merely shifts concentrated harms is the *world of acts;* our social world is, in large part, a *world of activities.* The differences between the two worlds are in part a matter of the transformation of the characteristic features of many risk-imposing activities, and in part an artifact of the improvement of the institution of insurance. The world of acts is a world of "isolated, ungeneralized wrongs"; the world of activities is a world in which certain risks are the regular and routine "incidents of certain well-known businesses" (Holmes 1920). In the world of acts, risk impositions are *discrete* one-shot events. The actors who impose risks are independent of one another, and actuarially small. In this world, non-negligent harms are as haphazard and unpredictable as natural disasters. Just as one might have the bad luck to be struck by lightning, so, too, one might have the bad luck to be struck by a man raising a stick high behind him as he struggles to break up a dogfight.[34] In the world of acts, the typical actor is an individual or a small firm who creates risk so infrequently that harm is not likely to materialize from its actions alone, and the typical accident arises out of the independent actions of natural persons or small firms engaging in similar activities on an occasional basis. Viewed as a whole, the actions of these actors are diffused and disorganized, and even their combined activity may be actuarially small.

The random dogfight that precipitated *Brown v. Kendall* nicely typifies torts in the world of acts. Dog owners were then – and pretty much are now – a diffuse and disorganized group. The risks of physical injury and death that each dog owner imposed were too actuarially small to make the infliction of serious personal injury on someone else an ordinary and predictable part of individual dog ownership. Each dog owner is an actuarially small actor, and the risks imposed by her are independent of, and uncorrelated with, the risks imposed by each other owner. Under these circumstances, liability rules shift, but do not spread, the financial costs of accidental injury.[35] In the world of acts, the imposition of strict liability "substitute[s] one form of risk for another – the risk of liability for the risk of personal loss" (Fletcher 1972, p. 547).[36] It may well be fair to make this substitution,[37] but it will not be fair *because* strict liability spreads the costs of non-negligent harms across the class of those who impose like risks.

At the opposite pole from the world of acts is the world of activities. In the world of activities risks are *systemic*. Systemic risks arise out of a continuously repeated activity (the manufacture of Coke bottles, the supplying of water by a utility, the transport of gasoline) that is actuarially large. "Accidental" harm is statistically certain to result from such risks: If you make enough Coke bottles, some are sure to rupture;[38] if you transport enough gasoline, some tankers are sure to explode;[39] if you never inspect water mains and leave them in the ground long enough, some are sure to break.[40]

In the world of activities, the typical injury arises not out of the diffuse and disorganized acts of unrelated individuals or small firms, but out of the organized activities of firms that are either large themselves, or small parts of relatively well-organized enterprises. The defendant in *Lubin v. Iowa City* is large in the first sense: A single entity is responsible for the piping of water through underground pipes, for laying and maintaining those pipes, for charging consumers for the water so transported, and so on. The transportation of large quantities of gasoline in tractor trailers on highways is large in the second sense: The firms that do the transporting may (or may not) be small and specialized, but they are enmeshed in contractual relationships with those who manufacture and refine the gasoline, those who operate gasoline stations, those who manufacture tractor trailers, and so on.

In the world of activities, the financial costs of accidental injuries characteristic of certain activities *can* be spread fairly across those activities. In this world, accidents arise out of circumstances that satisfy the basic criteria of in-surability. Foremost among these criteria is the law of large numbers.[41] The more the law of large numbers is met, the more risks are certain not only to issue in harms, but also to issue in harms with predictable regularity. When an activity is large enough, the accidental harm associated with its conduct is predictable, and the cost of that harm can be foreseen and priced into the activity. In the purest version of the world of activities, actors (enterprises) themselves satisfy the requirements of the law of large numbers. When enterprises themselves are actuarially large, they tend to engender non-negligent accidents in a regular and calculable way, and the costs of those accidents can be factored into the costs of conducting the enterprise. The costs of manufacturing and distributing Coke can include the costs of injuries from exploding Coke bottles; the costs of supplying water to households and businesses can include the costs of the damage caused by broken water mains.[42]

The respective spheres of these two worlds, and the location of the boundary between them, are partly artifacts of the cost and effectiveness of insurance mechanisms. Domesticated dogs may not be systemically related but they are abundant; they were quite plentiful in the late nineteenth century; and many of them must create roughly similar risks of serious physical injury or property damage. Whether domesticated dogs can be pooled into an insurable "activity" depends in large part on how well and how cheaply the mechanisms of insurance pooling can be made to operate. If those mechanisms can be made to operate well enough and cheaply enough, then this apparently canonical corner of the world of acts can be brought into the world of activities.

The movement from the world of acts to the world of activities thus provides another reason to favor strict liability (in its enterprise form) over negligence liability. Enterprise liability distributes the financial costs of non-negligent harms more fairly than negligence does, dispersing them across those who benefit from the imposition of the underlying risks. But it also strengthens the preexisting case for strict liability. That case is rooted in the greater relative urgency of persons' interests in security when risks are grave, and in the benefits that compensation confers both on those put at risk, and on those actually injured. Even in the world of activities, each natural person has only one life to lead. Serious accidents wreak havoc with that life just as much as they do in the world of acts; their incidence and their impact still need to be minimized so far as reasonably practicable. For enterprises, by contrast, accidental injury and death are far more predictable and far less disruptive. Enterprises live in – indeed they constitute – the world of activities. Enterprises are therefore able to anticipate those accidents that issue from their characteristic risks, minimizing their incidence in advance, and dispersing their costs after the fact.

Whatever the merits of Fletcher's argument that, in the world of acts, strict liability is as disruptive of liberty as negligence is of security, in the world of activities, the choice between strict liability and negligence is no longer a choice between equally grave disruptions of security and liberty. In the world of activities, strict liability does not shatter the freedom of injurers by forcing them to bear the concentrated costs of accidents whose incidence they cannot anticipate any more accurately than victims. In the world of activities, strict liability forces enterprises to bear the eminently foreseeable costs of their characteristic risks – costs whose incidence they are in an excellent position to estimate and minimize *ex ante,* and to disperse *ex post.*

Negligence liability places much greater burdens on the security of victims. It asks them to bear the characteristic risks of others' activities – risks that they either cannot control or cannot reasonably be asked to control[43]; risks whose materialization may well prove devastating; risks whose incidence is, from their perspective, largely beyond meaningful prediction. As compensation for these threats to their security, a regime of negligence liability offers victims a boon to liberty, namely the right to impose equivalent characteristic risks on others without the duty to repair any ensuing harm to natural persons or their property. The benefit to freedom here is less than the burden to security: Few, if any, of us stand to benefit much from the right to expose others to the level of drunkenness characteristic of the Coast Guard's activity, the risk of pipe breakage characteristic of a waterworks' activity, or the risks of fire and explosion characteristic of transporting huge quantities of gasoline by tractor trailer. For victims to benefit in this way, they would have to be engaged in either the same, or an equivalent, (level of) activity.

In the world of activities, then, the choice between strict liability and negligence is a choice between a grave disruption of security, and a more modest disruption of liberty. Enterprise liability strikes a more favorable balance between the competing claims of liberty and security than negligence liability does, because enterprise liability disrupts the liberty of injurers less than negligence impairs the security of victims. Enterprise liability thus secures more favorable conditions than negligence for persons to pursue their conceptions of the good over the course of their lives.

### III. Duty and Breach: "Due Care as Reasonableness"

The question of due care – of which risks impositions are permissible and which risk-reducing precautions necessary – raises the same question in a more particularized form. The question is the same, because the issue, once again, is how to strike a reasonable balance between liberty and security. The question is more particular because it applies to risk impositions and precautions in particular cases, rather than to the choice between competing principles of responsibility for large classes of cases. This greater particularity has an important consequence. Each and every risk imposition cannot be to everyone's advantage. Every time we cross the street on a mundane errand, for example, we are exposed to risks from which we have more to lose than to gain. What we can hope is that the particular risks impositions licensed by the law of duty and breach are to the long-run advantage of those most disfavored by the risks licensed – those who stand to lose their lives and limbs.

Reasonable care, then, is the level of care that fairly reconciles the conflicting liberties of injurers and victims. The liberty that injurers gain from imposing risks must be balanced against the security that victims lose through bearing those risks. Conversely, the liberty that injurers give up when they are forced to take precautions must be balanced against the benefits those precautions afford to the property and physical integrity of victims. The "fair" level of care is determined by the principle of proportionality: Injurers must take precautions commensurate with the gravity and probability of the risks that they create. And victims can only insist on precautions whose benefits to their security exceed the burdens that they impose on the liberty of injurers.

In one common circumstance, the fair reconciliation of liberty and security calls for pushing the level of precaution beyond the cost-minimizing point. When the risk at issue puts life and limb in substantial danger of severe injury, and when the cost of increased precaution is modest, fairness calls for taking those risk-reducing precautions – up to the point where further precaution either reduces the risk to an unreasonable level, or threatens the continuation of the activity itself.

When are injuries severe? When they fundamentally disrupt the normal course of a life, or the pursuit of a conception of the good, in a way that the payment of compensation cannot rectify or dissipate. Death is the paradigmatic severe injury. It brings the course of a life to a premature close, forever cutting short the pursuit of a conception of the good; it cannot be rectified by the payment of compensation; and it cannot be dispersed into innumerable smaller harms and distributed across a class of prospective injurers. Serious and incurable disease and severe and permanent physical injury are next in order of severity. Ordinary property damage, by contrast, is on the other end of the continuum. Its occurrence disrupts but does not destroy the course of a life; it can be undone by the payment of compensation; and it can be dispersed into innumerable smaller harms and distributed across a class of prospective injurers. When are increased precaution costs modest? When they are merely monetary and their monetary cost is dispersed across a class of potential injurers in small increments. And when is a risk substantial? When it is great enough to threaten a significant chance of premature death or severe and irreversible injury over the course of a normal life span. What is significant? One death in a million lives? One in a hundred thousand? One in ten thousand? That is not so easy to say, and must be left to another day.

This approach to the calculus of risk under the Hand Formula is the natural extension of tort law's singling out of physical integrity and personal property for heightened, equal, and inalienable protection.[44] That singling out is, in turn, an acknowledgment of the importance of bodily integrity to our capacity to pursue our conceptions of the good.

To be sure, there is a paradox here: Kantian social contract theory adheres to the principle that precautions ought to be proportionate to risks imposed, but concludes that security is entitled to special weight in the calculus of risk. The appearance of contradiction disappears, however, once we connect the principle of proportionality with the social contract conception of the interests at stake in accidental risk imposition, and the proper terms of interpersonal comparison. When the question of what level of precaution is reasonable is framed as a matter of comparative burdens and benefits to freedom of action and security, the evaluation of the costs and benefits of various risks and precautions becomes a *qualitative* one. We must ask how various risks and precautions burden persons in their pursuit of the aims and aspirations that give meaning to their lives. Qualitative evaluation, in its turn, leads to placing special weight on the security of victims because serious physical injury and death characteristically burden persons in the pursuit of their conceptions of the good far more than the financial costs of increased precaution do. Conceptions of the good are developed and pursued over the course of complete lives. Thus, substantial risks of serious injury threaten grave disruption to our pursuits of happiness, and accidental death brings those pursuits to a premature close.

In fact, if the probability is great enough, the mere threat of injury or death can itself be debilitating. If that threat is great enough, it discourages persons from participating in activities that have important roles to play in their conceptions of the good, or may drain those activities of all their joy simply by producing enormous anxiety and fear. Modest increases in money spent on precaution, by contrast, burden persons' capacity to realize their conceptions of the good in more minor and incremental ways. The disparity is especially great when the incremental costs of increased precaution are dispersed across all those who benefit from an activity, while the harms it causes are concentrated on a few unlucky victims. When a risk is severe in magnitude and substantial in probability, and when the cost of increased precaution is decreased income and wealth, dispersed across a class of potential injurers, fixing the point of reasonable precaution beyond the point of cost-justified precaution is the fair response to the qualitative difference between the burden of bearing the risk and the burden of reducing it.

Third and last, Kantian social contract theory holds that the canons of reasonableness frequently run out before the choice between a particular risk and a particular precaution can be made. Negligence adjudication often grapples with close cases – in the domain where relatively few risks or precautions are either reasonable or unreasonable as a matter of law. The specification of reasonable precautions therefore requires us to draw (as the law of negligence itself does) on subordinate doctrines and institutional arrangements, on custom or convention, statutes and the deliberative sense of juries. Custom, legislative judgment, and jury verdicts close the gap left by applying the general canons of reasonableness to particular risks and precautions, and they do so by identifying those precautions that serve as natural focal points for reasonable persons seeking to sustain a mutually beneficial form of social cooperation on fair terms. (Or so social contract theory argues.) Each of these devices also draws on its own distinctive principle of legitimacy – custom on reasonable reliance, statutes on legislative supremacy, and jury verdicts on their deliberative democratic character. Taken together, these doctrines and institutions fill the zone where precautions are neither reasonable nor unreasonable *as a matter of law.*

Throughout its articulation of these substantive claims, Kantian social contract theory elaborates its commitment to "objective" criteria of interpersonal comparison, and argues that tort law's reliance on such criteria is a bulwark of our mutual freedom. The importance of objective valuation is a theme that runs throughout the social contract interpretation of the doctrine of due care. In developing that theme, social contract theory displays and specifies its distinctive account of what objective valuation is, and how it proceeds.

These ideas need to be unpacked, and the claims that they make articulated and defended. We can begin this task by returning to the principle of proportionality, and its paradoxical embrace of disproportion and discontinuity.

## A. Precaution and Proportionality

The idea of proportionality is a straightforward one. Indeed, it is nothing more than the natural (and, at least in the case law, dominant) noneconomic interpretation of the Hand Formula: The extent of precaution should be proportional to the magnitude and probability of the harm threatened by a particular risk imposition. In cases where the probability of the risk is very, very low – so that the risk might be described as a "mere possibility," not "reasonably foreseeable" [45] – the principle of proportionality calls for no precaution at all. Some level of risk is simply the price of freedom to act, and that level of risk is the background level. With certain inescapable variations, ordinary activities, carefully conducted, produce mutually imposed and mutually beneficial risks.[46] Because these risks are the price of ordinary activity, we are all better off bearing them than attempting to reduce them.

Typical negligence cases, however, involve risks whose probability is low, but not very, very low, and whose magnitude is significant. The risks created by having inspectors crawl underneath temporarily parked trains to inspect their undercarriages for cracks[47] are typical of such risks, as are the costs (slower operation of the trains, more disruptive inspections, reduced income) of the precautions that would reduce or eliminate those risks (blowing a whistle or visually inspecting trains before moving them, discontinuing the practice of crawling beneath temporarily parked trains). What does the principle of proportionality call for in these kinds of cases?

One influential answer holds that tradeoffs between precaution and accident costs should be made along a razor's edge, where a penny's saving in precaution costs is equated with a penny's saving in losses of life and limb.[48] Does this test of efficient precaution also fairly reconcile liberty and security? Not on the facts of *Davis;* the test ignores qualitative differences between the costs of the risk and the costs of reducing it. In cases like *Davis* risk impositions burden the security of victims by threatening (and inflicting) death and dismemberment, whereas increased precaution burdens the liberty of injurers by increasing the monetary cost of their activities. When the injury producing activity is an enterprise like Consolidated Rail, that cost of precaution is dispersed across a large number of natural persons, none of whom bears a heavy burden. Commensurating these conflicting interests in dollar terms and adding the dollars up obscures the qualitative distinctions that are at the heart of the case. Irreversible injuries to life and limb are on one side of the equation; injuries that are irreparable, total and beyond dispersion or redistribution. Monetary costs of precaution are on the other side; those costs are not just qualitatively less grave, they are also distributed across a broad class of persons and in modest increments. Cost–benefit analysis fails to register these qualitative distinctions.

Negligence law, by contrast, generally *is* sensitive to the fact that life itself is at stake in its calculations. The circumscribed domain and inalienable character of accident law reflect in part the value of life itself (Keating 1996, p. 345). So, too, the law distinguishes gross negligence, recklessness, and conduct egregious enough to justify the award of punitive damages, both from ordinary negligence and from each other at least partly by the degree of indifference to the value of human life that they exhibit.[49] The calculus of risk ought to be similarly sensitive. The fundamental interest that underlies both the forms of liberty at stake in accidental risk imposition is an interest in having favorable circumstances to form and pursue one's conception of a worthwhile human life. Substantial risks of serious physical injury and death threaten this interest more than reductions in wealth or income effected by increased precaution costs do, especially when those reductions are widely dispersed.

The question, then, is how to register the greater relative importance of security when risks are significant, and when life and limb lie on one side of the equation and monetary costs of precaution on the other. What general test does Kantian social contract theory – does fairness – lead to in these circumstances? Not, I think, to the balancing of marginal costs and benefits, but to the taking of those precautions that are reasonably feasible – those precautions that can be taken without threatening the survival of the risky but beneficial activity itself. Only the cessation of an activity threatens to impair anyone's pursuit of a conception of the good as gravely as premature death and permanent disability do, and then only if the activity is an important and hard to replace one. When risks are significant, and when life and limb are pitted against wealth and income, then, we should reduce risks to the point where they are either no longer unreasonable, or where further reduction would jeopardize the continuation of the activity itself.[50]

Part of the reason for rejecting the balancing of marginal costs and benefits is that Kantian social contract theory rejects the idea that total costs, monetized and added up, are what count. For, just as total utility is experienced by no one, so, too, total wealth is enjoyed by no one.[51] We ought, rather, attend to the burdens and benefits borne and enjoyed by the affected classes of persons, namely, injurers and victims. And, in assessing the significance of these, we should attend both to their incremental and their absolute levels. We should attend to incremental levels because "[c]ontractualist morality relies on notions of what it would be reasonable to accept, or reasonable to reject, which are essentially comparative." We should attend to absolute levels because the reasonableness of accepting or rejecting a particular burden depends in part on how much it "hurt[s] me in absolute terms" (Scanlon 1982, p. 113). Indeed, the *absolute* seriousness of the threat to the victim's well-being is the fundamental reason Kantian social contract theory embraces the reasonable feasibility test in the first place.

Recall that Kantian social contract theory directs our attention to those who fare worst under a particular regime. In the case of accidental risks impositions, those who fare worst are those who stand to lose, through premature death, the very capacity to pursue their conceptions of the good of the course of a complete life. How might risk impositions nonetheless be to their long-run advantage? In part, because the right to engage in the same or similar activities is to the long-run advantage of those whose deaths are threatened by the particular risk impositions in question. But this leaves open just what risks are to the advantage of those imperiled by those activities – and that is our present concern. The reasonable feasibility criterion identifies those risks that work to the long-run advantage of those put in peril by particular risks. That criterion gives the greatest possible protection to their security, consistent with the continuation of the valuable activity itself.

Because the harm wrought to the pursuit of a conception of the good by premature death is very great, and because the harm wrought by permanent disability and disfigurement can be almost as great, securing substantial protection against such harms is important indeed. This, the reasonable feasibility test does. If (and only if) the benefits of a mutually beneficial activity are important enough, the right to engage in the activity is to the long-run advantage of those imperiled by its risks – either directly or by reciprocity – and the cessation of the activity works to their disadvantage. So long as the benefit is significant enough, fixing the point of precaution at the point of reasonable feasibility is therefore to the long-run disadvantage of those whose lives and limbs are put in peril by risky, but mutually beneficial, activities. Pressing the point of precaution beyond the point of reasonable feasibility is not.

Does this reasonable feasibility criterion give injurers ground for complaint? I think not. So long as the activity itself can be made reasonably safe without endangering its long-term viability, the burden that the reasonable feasibility criterion imposes on their liberty is less than the burden that significant risks impose on the security of victims. Only the cessation of the activity (and ones like it) threatens to cripple injurers' pursuits of the aims and aspirations that give meaning to their lives, in the way that disfigurement and premature death threatens to cripple victims in their pursuit of their respective ends and aspirations.

Framed as I have framed it here, the reasonable feasibility test applies to only one kind of circumstance – the circumstance where life and limb are pitted against wealth and income – and even then difficult questions of application will arise. Circumstances where life and limb are pitted against life and limb are an entirely different matter.[52] When the cost of the precaution is a reduction in the probability that life or limb will be saved, the interests at stake are identical – the security of the victim is being traded off against the security of the person for whose benefit the risk is being imposed. When the interests at stake are identical in this way, there is no reason to adopt a criterion that tilts in favor of risk reduction in the way that the reasonable feasibility test does. Such a test simply puts into place an arbitrary bias against saving the life for whose benefit others are put at risk. In yet other circumstances, the reasonable foreseeability test would tilt in the wrong direction. For example, when an injurer risks injury to property to save life and limb, we have reason to tilt in favor of the risk imposition and against its reduction.[53]

Circumstances where prospective victims benefit from the use of the risky instrumentality also present special problems. We know that it is reasonably feasible to make knives safer by dulling their blades to the point that they do not cut. But we also know that this is absurd, because it deprives users of the principal benefit that they secure from knives.[54] But not all cases are so easy. How should we evaluate the level of precaution appropriate for a subcompact car, for instance? Is a precaution reasonably feasible if it would increase the size of the car to the point where its classification would change? If its cost would price a substantial number of subcompact car consumers out of the market? How do the concerns that animate the reasonable foreseeability test interact with those that animate the consumer expectation test?[55]

We cannot explore, let alone answer, all of these questions here, but we can illustrate this conception of reasonable care by bringing it to bear on the famous American negligence case, *Helling v. Carey*.[56] *Helling* both illustrates the circumstance where the monetary burdens of a precaution may exceed its monetary benefits by a hair's breadth (or more) without making the precaution not reasonably feasible, and sheds light on how Kantian social contract theory conceives of the choice between mandatory precautions and warnings. The plaintiff in *Helling* brought a malpractice suit against her ophthalmologists, alleging that her permanent visual damage resulted from their failure to diagnose and treat her glaucoma (*id.* at 982). Consistent with the custom of the profession, the defendants had not routinely tested the plaintiff for glaucoma because she was under forty, and the incidence of glaucoma for persons under forty was believed to be 1 in 25,000 (*id.* at 982–3). Setting aside the normal rule that, in medicine, customary care is due care,[57] the court ruled "*as a matter of law,* that the reasonable standard that should have been followed under the undisputed facts of this case was the timely giving of this simple, harmless pressure test to this plaintiff and that, in failing to do so, the defendants were negligent."[58]

In support of its ruling, the court stated:

> The incidence of glaucoma . . . may appear quite minimal. However, that one person, the plaintiff in this instance, is entitled to the same protection, as afforded persons over 40, essential for timely detection of the evidence of glaucoma where it can be arrested to avoid the grave and devastating result of this disease. The test is a simple pressure test, relatively inexpensive. There is no judgment factor involved, and there is no doubt that by giving the test the evidence of glaucoma can be detected. The giving of the test is harmless if the physical condition of the eye permits. (*id.*)

Put in Hand Formula terms, the high magnitude of the harm, the low cost of the precaution, and the high efficacy of the precaution offset the low probability of the harm, and require the precaution to be taken.

In finding ophthalmologic custom wanting as a matter of law, the *Helling* court stressed two features of the case. First, the issue did not involve special medical expertise.[59] The question, rather, was what due care required, given the probability and magnitude of the harm, and the costs of the precaution necessary to avert that harm. This, the opinion insists, is a matter for the court (*id.* at 983). Second, the cost of the precaution was simply not commensurate with the magnitude of the harm it would prevent. The cost of the precaution is the increased time and expense borne by the 24,999 patients who do not have glaucoma but who must nonetheless submit to a harmless test for it, and the harm that precaution prevents is "the grave and devastating result of this disease" (*id.*).

The first argument is sound from a social contract perspective because questions of reasonable risk imposition are questions about the reconciliation of the competing liberties of different persons. They are thus public in both their subject matter – the rights of persons against one another – and in their institutional form – as aspects of public, legal institutions. The court's second justification is likewise sound, but the reasons why are more complex. *Helling,* like *Marshall v. Gotham,* is not an accident among strangers – that is, an accident arising out of the involuntary exposure of victims to risks by injurers. It is an accident among participants in a joint enterprise. Indeed, in a deep sense, the victims and injurers are the same people. Patients expose themselves – not others – to burdens and risks by taking and foregoing precautions. They suffer the permanent blindness of glaucoma when it occurs, and they bear the financial costs and the inconvenience of the pressure test.[60] These circumstances make contract a live alternative to tort: Instead of deciding what is best for patients, we might educate them about glaucoma and its prevention and let them decide whether to have the test administered.

Nevertheless, for social contract theory, these facts do not call for supplanting tort with contract. Unlike *Marshall v. Gotham,* in which the precaution of timbering the entire mine both enhanced the security and burdened the freedom of the miners who bore the risk of "slickenside," the precaution at stake in *Helling* places a very modest burden on liberty, while enhancing security considerably. Persons concerned with advancing conceptions of the good over complete lives would have strong reason to insist that the precaution be taken. Permanent blindness at an early age has a devastating impact on a person's life, and on a person's pursuit of her aims and aspirations. Because exposure to the risk of glaucoma does not further a plausible conception of the good, the fact that injurers expose themselves, not others, to injury by foregoing the pressure test does not distinguish *Helling* from cases where injurers expose others to risks.[61] The test should be administered because the cost of foregoing it is exposure to a devastating and wholly preventable disease, whereas the cost of administering it is minor inconvenience and modest expense. Given the strength of the case for taking the precaution, a contract regime should be rejected. The burden of education and decision that such a regime imposes is substantial, and that burden yields little, if any, benefit.

Invoking the reasonable feasibility test, the point is that the magnitude of the harm that the precaution in *Helling* averts is great, and the costs of the precaution – the minor inconvenience and modest expense of a simple pressure test for 24,999 people – do not threaten the long-run viability of the activity. Those costs are dispersed across all those at risk from the disease and the impact on any single person's liberty is minimal. Whatever the *total* dollar cost of the pressure test, the costs borne *by each patient* are quite modest.

Put this way, however, the argument might appear paternalistic. Because we believe that no reasonable forty year old would gamble with her eyes by foregoing a pressure test, we shall not offer her the opportunity to do so. While I think that this charge is overstated – the market is not a paternalistic social institution because it fails to satisfy every idiosyncratic whim, or eccentric taste, of every consumer – the case for insisting that pressure tests be given instead of leaving the choice of whether or not to take them in the hands of patients is not, I think, paternalistic in any meaningful sense of the word. It rests on the conclusion that a warning regime reconciles the liberty and security of diverse persons less reasonably than a regime of mandatory precaution (mandatory pressure tests) does.

Kantian social contract theory holds that a warning regime reconciles freedom and security less reasonably than a negligence regime of mandatory pressure tests does, because it burdens the interests of many reasonable people while furthering the freedom of few idiosyncratic or irrational ones. The point of the argument that a regime of mandatory pressure tests is paternalistic is that there are some patients who – perhaps because they are irrational, or perhaps because they are desperately poor, or perhaps because they a psychologically peculiar –

would prefer to forego the test and pocket the money saved. The fact that their conduct might be objectively foolish, is not sufficient reason to override their own decisions about how best to lead their lives.

Social contract theory need not decide if this argument is correct. Its endorsement of a negligence regime of mandatory pressure tests does not rest on the claim that those who would forego the test and pocket the money saved are so irrational that their preferences for their own welfare should be paternalistically overridden. Its point, rather, is that both a warning regime and a negligence regime place burdens on those subject to them, and the burdens of a negligence regime are less than those of a warning regime. A negligence regime burdens those who would prefer to forego the test (while visiting an ophthalmologist) by denying them the opportunity to do so. A warning regime burdens those who see no advantage in being given the choice of whether or not to take the test, and are burdened by being required to make that decision. If the correct decision is clear to anyone who is neither irrational nor idiosyncratic, the burden of education and decision imposed by the warning regime is not worth the benefits of the choice it enables.

A negligence regime reconciles the competing claims of liberty and security (for a plurality of persons who hold diverse conceptions of the good) better than a warning regime does, because the burdens that it imposes on the freedom of the idiosyncratic few are less than the benefits that it confers on the freedom of the rational and reasonable many. So too, the burdens that a warning regime imposes on the security of the rational and reasonable many, are greater than the benefits such a regime confers on the freedom of the idiosyncratic few. Social contract theory's endorsement of a negligence regime over a warning one therefore rests not on a "paternalistic" judgment that irrational preferences for one's own welfare should be overridden, but on a qualitative and comparative evaluation of how these two possible regimes reconcile the competing claims of a plurality of persons.

This interpretation of *Marshall* shows, I believe, that the social contract approach to matters of reasonable care, with its focus on questions on reasonable foreseeability can supply answers in actual cases. That test is, however, indeterminate in a wide range of cases. Any of a number of precautions within some broad zone may be reasonable and it may be difficult to select the most reasonable; it may be difficult to appraise the relative burdens that possible precautions impose on liberty and security; it may be more important to agree on one precaution than to identify the single best one, and so on. In an enormous number of cases, then, we must consider other negligence doctrines and institutions, such as custom, statutes, and jury adjudication in order to settle on an appropriate level of precaution. Before we touch upon these other doctrines, however, we need to examine the concept of the "average reasonable person" (ARP). So doing will enable us to flesh out the concept of reasonable care, both as it is found in the law and as Kantian social contract theory reconstructs it.

## B. The Conduct of Reasonable Persons

One of the curious facts about the law of duty and breach is that its principal concepts are formulated in two distinct doctrines. One is the Hand Formula's "calculus of risk." The other is "average reasonable person doctrine." Just how to situate and connect these doctrines is a standing issue in tort scholarship. Scholarship in the "scientific policy-making" tradition,[62] preeminently law and economics, has tended to assign pride of place to the Hand Formula. Conceiving of social choice as individual choice writ large, law and economics has tended to reduce the average reasonable person to an economically rational one, and has read the Hand Formula as a straightforward invitation to cost-benefit analysis (Keating 1996, pp. 332–7). Social contract theory, by contrast, belongs in the "ordinary observer" tradition, and it emphasizes the significance of ARP doctrine.

There are three principal reasons why Kantian social contract theory thinks ARP doctrine significant. First, the concept of reasonableness (especially as distinguished from the concept of rationality) is central to social contract theory. The prominence of the concept of reasonableness in tort law is, consequently, important to social contract theory. Social contract theory is concerned both to resist the reduction of reasonableness to rationality, and to articulate the special character of reasonable conduct. Second, when ARP doctrine specifies particular standards of care, it assigns the kind of high value to security that social contract theory argues for. Third, ARP doctrine asserts that risks and precautions must be appraised by "objective" criteria, and fleshes out a set of such criteria. The template of reasonableness fashioned by the doctrine, is therefore both a confirmation of, and crucible in which to test, several of the main claims of social contract theory.

ARP doctrine performs at least three distinct tasks: (1) It holds that some precautions are required as a matter of law;[63] (2) It articulates substantive duties of care for certain classes of persons (the awkward, the insane, experts, children) and the activities that parallel them; and (3) It specifies the qualities of the reasonable person. The first way that the doctrine supports the social contract conception of due care is by placing great relative weight on victim security in its articulation of duties.[64] Where injurers claim that they should owe a reduced standard of care because of their diminished capacities to exercise due care, the victim's security starkly conflicts with the injurer's freedom of action. In these cases, affording adequate protection to the security of prospective victims conflicts with the precept that it is unfair to hold actors liable for conduct they could not have helped. ARP doctrine comes down overwhelmingly on the side of security at the expense of freedom of action (and fairness to the diminished capacities of injurers),[65] and so assigns high relative value to security.

Persons with poor judgment are held to the same standard of care as those with good judgment, regardless of their ability to conform to that standard.[66]

Children engaged in adult activities, and those with permanent mental disabilities, are held to the same standard as adults with normal capacities.[67] Finally, novices engaged in dangerous activities are held to the same standard as persons of normal competence.[68] These rules place a tremendous burden on the pertinent classes of injurers: They must measure up to a standard of care that exceeds their abilities, or forego the relevant activities.

Justifying these rules is a difficult matter. The assumption that most actors, with sufficient effort, are capable of exercising the same level of care as the average reasonable person may justify the general rule. But that assumption seems unrealistic in the case of children and the permanently disabled. A better explanation is that society is lodging its judgments of negligence deeper than it usually does, by finding children and disabled persons who engage in activities beyond their competence negligent in their choice of activity. This seems partly correct. The cases seem to be pinning implicit responsibility on parents for the conduct of their children and implicit responsibility on guardians for the conduct of insane persons.[69]

The question remains, however, why responsibility should be driven so deep. Here the answer seems to lie in the great relative value of security and the threat to security posed by making duty commensurate with capacity. Precisely because of their diminished capacities, children and the disabled impose great and non-reciprocal risks: Children driving cars and powerboats are far more dangerous than adults engaging in the same activities. Moreover, the shortage of effective victim precautions compounds the threat to security created by diminished capacity. Our ability to identify those cars on the road that are driven by children (or uncontrolled epileptics), and to steer clear of them, is poor. Relaxing the standard of care for such persons would debilitate security even further by undermining our capacity to estimate the risks of undertaking various activities, and by preventing us from regulating our exposure to risk on the basis of such estimates.

Exceptions to the general rule that all actors will be held to the standard of the average reasonable person further illustrate the priority that American accident law assigns to security. For example, children engaged in childlike activities are held to a lower standard of care – a standard appropriate to their age and maturity (Keeton, Sargentich, and Keating 1998, pp. 186–8). As a class, childlike activities, such as riding bicycles and peddling paddleboats, are inherently less risky than adult activities, such as driving cars and operating powerboats.[70] Moreover, because children engaged in childlike activities are often readily identifiable or exposed to view (in fact, the activities themselves often identify their participants as children), prospective victims can often take additional precautions to guard against any increased risks associated with the children's diminished capacities.[71] Lowering the standard of care for children engaged in childlike activities is thus compatible with the assignment of a high priority to security: Responsibility is lowered as risk to others is lowered.

Conversely, ARP doctrine holds experts to a *higher* standard of care.[72] Experts tend to impose greater risk because they tend to engage in more dangerous activities. Moreover, by virtue of their greater knowledge and skill, experts are able to exercise greater care for the protection of prospective victims.[73] Responsibility is increased as risk and capacity for care are increased. Beginners, by contrast, do not impose less risk by virtue of their lower skill; if anything, they impose more. Thus, by holding experts to a higher standard of care, and beginners to the same standard of care as persons of normal competence, tort law favors security over freedom of action.

In setting the standards of care for experts, children, and beginners, ARP doctrine treats the level of risk created by an activity as a two-way ratchet, and the capacity for care as a one-way ratchet. When both the level of risk and the capacity for care increase, duty increases; when both the level of risk and the capacity for care diminish, duty decreases. But when capacity diminishes without a corresponding decrease in risk creation, duty remains constant. This pattern is even more telling evidence of the great value that ARP doctrine assigns to security. Because experts have the ability to take greater care, our demand that they do so is less onerous, and thus more reasonable. Yet, although those with lesser capacities may be unable to meet a standard of ordinary competence, we are justified in demanding more of them because those lesser capacities put others at greater, not lesser, risk.

Finally, the exculpation of actors in "those exceptional cases of loss of consciousness resulting from injury inflicted by an outside force, or fainting, or heart attack, or epileptic seizure, or other illness which suddenly incapacitates the driver of an automobile when the occurrence of such disability is not attended with sufficient warning or should not have been reasonably foreseen"[74] is also consistent with the substantial value of security. No effective precautions can be taken against sudden, unforeseeable disabilities. Holding actors liable for them would debilitate freedom of action without securing any corresponding gain to security. In sum, ARP doctrine tilts strongly towards the protection of security.

## C. The Template of Reasonableness

So far I have stressed the *substantive* content of average reasonable person law – namely, its assignment of greater relative weight to security than to freedom of action. But social contract theory sees *methodological* significance in ARP doctrine as well: It shows how the concept of reasonableness might be used as a template for determining permissible risk impositions and proper precautions. ARP doctrine shows how the concept of reasonableness can be used to identify precautions that enable social cooperation on fair terms among free and equal persons. By drawing upon a sufficiently definite and rich account of the particular aims and dispositions that characterize reasonableness; taking advantage of the fact that questions of permissible risk imposition and appropriate precaution are *embedded in ongoing mutually beneficial practices;* and making use of "normalizing assumptions," ARP doctrine fashions a template for identification of reasonable precautions.[75]

Taking up this larger task will, however, prove easier if we first address the subordinate issue of how burdens and benefits to injurers and victims are to be measured and compared. ARP doctrine is famous for its objective character, and Kantian social contract theory is insistent in its embrace of objective criteria of interpersonal comparison. Unsurprisingly, social contract theory's constructive account of ARP doctrine deploys an objective approach to interpersonal comparison, and endeavors to show that body of law's commitment to objective standards in its best light. To pave the way for this constructive account, however, we must first explain why the use of subjective criteria of interpersonal comparison is unreasonable.

1. THE UNREASONABLENESS OF SUBJECTIVE VALUATION. Objective criteria identify goods whose importance can be acknowledged by persons who hold diverse and incommensurable conceptions of the good, whereas subjective ones employ people's tastes or preferences for their own well-being (Scanlon 1975). Because persons who affirm diverse conceptions of the good can agree upon the importance of being able to lead one's life in accordance with one's aspirations, and because basic liberties are the necessary "background conditions" for this enterprise, basic liberties are objective criteria of interpersonal comparison (Rawls 1993, pp. 178–90). The categories of "liberty" and "security" employed in this paper are likewise objective.

ARP doctrine is firmly committed to objective valuation: It makes its calculations of reasonableness not by investigating the values that the persons involved in risk impositions place on the liberty interests at stake, but by insisting that the value which the law attaches to those liberty interests be accepted by the persons whose interests they are.[76] Indeed, ARP doctrine rejects subjective valuation as utterly *irrelevant in principle.* Settled negligence doctrine holds that extraordinary risks can be imposed only in the name of objectively important ends (Keating 1996, p. 369). For example, leaping in front of an onrushing train to rescue children in imminent danger of death is not negligent, despite the high magnitude and probability of the risk involved.[77] So, too, it is not negligent for policemen and firemen to speed when they are saving life and limb from grave and imminent danger (Keating 1996, p. 357, note 150), but it surely would be negligent for me to speed simply to get a good spot at the beach on a hot summer's day.[78] Speeding wildly in pursuit of a good place at the beach is a canonical instance of unreasonableness, because the end being pursued is trivial and the risk being imposed is great – no matter how intensely I might care about it and no matter how indifferent my prospective victims might be about the risk I imposed. The intensity of my preference for getting to the beach early has no weight at all within the framework of negligence analysis. What counts is the *objective* importance of my end. Life and limb are fundamental interests – they are central to the security and integrity of persons. Getting to the beach early is an ordinary interest, akin to countless other interests whose urgency is very modest. Individually, these interests do not support especially grave risk impositions, although, taken collectively, they support the ordinary background level of non-negligent risk imposition.

Taking subjective valuation seriously would require the law to take the intensity of my preference for getting to the beach early as a critical variable affecting the amount of risk that I might impose. So doing would, however, countenance results wildly at odds with our sense of justice. For instance, teenagers who linger on railroad bridges in the path of onrushing trains, and then leap into the water below at the last possible moment, almost certainly place enormous value on the thrill of "cheating death."[79] Subjective valuation requires us to accept the paramount value that these teenagers place on cheating death by trestle jumping as the correct value for purposes of our calculations of permissible risk imposition. It therefore implies that the speed at which trains run, and the risks to which they expose their crews and passengers, should be acutely sensitive to the tastes of trestle-jumpers for cheating death. Subjective valuation might require that trains speed to put trestle-jumpers in peril, and then slam on their brakes at the last minute to avert that peril, thereby exposing crewmembers, passengers, and any bystanders unlucky enough to be nearby, to substantial risks of physical injury and death.

Yet the law of negligence would reject outright the idea that train engineers should behave recklessly toward their passengers – and toward bystanders – in order to satisfy the preferences of trestle-jumping teenagers for death-defying thrills. It seems just as plain that negligence law would condemn as *reckless* anyone who dawdled on a railroad bridge to experience the thrill of being nearly killed by onrushing trains. That sort of conduct evidences a deep disregard for the value of one's own life. Any duty that train engineers might have to take precautions for the benefit of such teenagers would not flow from the *subjectively* high value that they place on putting their lives at risk. That duty would flow from the *objectively* high value of human life, and would exist despite the failure of those whose lives were in danger to respect that value.

Taking lingering on railroad bridges as our concrete example, the critical objection to subjective valuation is not that it is *irrational* to risk one's neck for the thrill of cheating death, but that it is *unreasonable* to ask others to bear substantial risks so that you may do so. These are markedly different objections. The rationality of playing chicken with trains is essentially irrelevant to tort law, whereas the reasonableness of playing such games is the very essence of that law: Tort law is only tangentially about the risks that we *should impose on ourselves,* but centrally about the risks that we *should be permitted to impose on others.*

Put concretely and contextually, the unreasonableness of exposing others to substantial risks for the thrill of cheating death turns on two factors. First, as we have often emphasized, security is essential to the capacity to pursue a conception of the good over the course of a complete life. Thus, activities that substantially jeopardize the security of others place a tremendous burden on an important interest. Second, the burden of forgoing activities that expose others to significant risks in order to cheat death is not great. However important the thrill of cheating death may be to one's conception of the good, there are ways of experiencing it – rock or mountain climbing without ropes, opening one's parachute at the last possible moment during a skydive, diving into perilously shipwrecks – that do not require exposing others to substantial risk.

Turning back toward legal authority, it is hard not to be struck by the extent to which the contours of ARP doctrine respects the fundamental difference between imposing a risk on others and taking risks upon oneself. (This distinction is fundamental to the idea that risk imposition must be reasonable and is ignored by the idea that risk imposition must be rational.) Whatever our capacities, we are expected to exercise reasonable care when we impose risks on others, but we are allowed our weaknesses and idiosyncrasies when we are protecting ourselves from the carelessness of others. For example, children below a certain age are often held to be incapable of contributory negligence,[80] whereas children engaged in adult activities are held to an adult standard of care;[81] those with subpar mental capacities are held to the standards of those with normal capacities when primary negligence is at issue, but their limitations are generally considered when secondary (contributory or comparative) negligence is at stake.[82] Finally, we excuse victims from the duty to mitigate damages when mitigation would require them to act inconsistently with their moral or religious convictions, even if most of us would regard the convictions as odd at best, and evidently wrong at worst.[83] What counts is neither the objective validity nor the commonality of the beliefs involved, but the central role of conscience in the lives of free people, and the circumstances under which we ask others to bear the costs of our convictions. We may not ask innocent strangers to bear the costs of our idiosyncratic convictions; nor may those who have wronged us ask us to ease their burden by acting against our beliefs.

To summarize and generalize, ARP doctrine and social contract theory utilize objective valuation because of three serious problems with subjective valuation. The first problem with subjective valuation is that it licenses deeply nonreciprocal risk impositions and puts the reasonable at the mercy of the unreasonable. The reasonable – those who have less intense preferences for getting to beaches or soccer games, or who cultivate a modest sense of the importance of their own ends – will be denied by their reasonableness the right to impose grave risks on others. By contrast, the unreasonable – persons with intense preferences, or an immodest sense of the importance of their own ends – will, by virtue of their unreasonableness be entitled to impose great risks on others.

This asymmetry licenses unfairness: Persons engaged in identical activities (driving, for example) for identical reasons (to get to the beach) may impose very different risks on each other. Still more unfairly, those who temper their demands confer the benefits of their restraint *on* others, and are repaid for their restraint by being made to bear the extravagant demands *of* others. The reasonable throw lesser risks and bear greater ones, while the unreasonable throw greater risks and bear lesser ones. Subjective valuation upsets reciprocity of risk and undermines a regime of mutual benefit and equal freedom.

The second problem with subjective valuation is that it debilitates security by legitimating haphazard and unpredictable risk impositions. If actors were permitted to impose risks that were justified solely by their own subjective valuations of the ends that the risk impositions serve, we could not reliably predict the risks to which we might legitimately be exposed in pursuing any particular course of action. Drivers, for example, could no longer estimate the legitimate risks of freeway driving by assuming reasonable compliance with the rules of the road. The risks of freeway driving will vary with the subjective valuations that different drivers attached to their activities. If those subjective benefits vary greatly the legitimate risks of highway driving will vary wildly.[84]

Third, the uncertainty created by subjective valuation tends to erode the bases of fair social cooperation. Willing adherence to a scheme of social cooperation depends heavily (or so social contract theory supposes) on the scheme's being both fair and perceived to be fair. Subjective valuation tends to frustrate social cooperation by making the legitimacy of particular risk impositions turn on information which is rarely, if ever, publicly accessible – namely, the subjective valuations that actors actually do place on the ends that they are pursuing. Under a regime of subjective valuation, those who are prepared to honor the terms of social cooperation so long as others do so as well will have difficulty telling if their good faith is being reciprocated. For this reason, their confidence in the fairness of the scheme will diminish, as will their willingness to do their part.

Worse still, the principle of subjectively rational risk imposition creates powerful incentives to misrepresent, *ex post,* one's subjective valuation of the ends that justify risk impositions. In the absence of some credible way of distinguishing the sincere from the insincere, this is no small defect. When cheating is easy, profitable, and difficult to detect, the incentives both to cheat and to defect are great. Those who abide by the terms of social cooperation only so long as others do so will have reason to suspect that their good faith is not being reciprocated. They will thus have reason to defect.

Objective valuation succeeds where subjective valuation fails: It facilitates social cooperation on terms of equal freedom and mutual benefit. The pieces of ARP doctrine are not the ad hoc exercise in practical ingenuity that they are often taken to be, but the incarnation of an alternative general approach to interpersonal comparison.

**2. IDENTIFYING REASONABLE PRECAUTIONS.** As Mark Grady has shown, negligence adjudication operates as kind of filter (Grady 1989). Injured plaintiffs propose precautions that would have prevented the accidents that injured them, and these precautions are compared to the actual conduct of the defendant, with an eye to determining if the defendant acted reasonably in failing to take one or more of the plaintiff's proposed precautions. The task of due care doctrine is to provide the tools to make that judgment. By (1) drawing on the concept reasonableness itself, (2) exploiting the possibility that certain precautions are "natural focal points" of cooperation, and (3) making use of "normalizing assumptions," ARP doctrine performs this task.

The concept of reasonableness itself supplies important guidance because reasonable people approach the identification of appropriate precautions with certain dispositions and convictions. They assign substantial weight to security; they cooperate on fair terms with others who are prepared to reciprocate their cooperation; they do not prefer their interests to those of others;[85] and they restrain the intensity of their preferences so that they do not make demands upon others that they would not be prepared to honor themselves. When these convictions and dispositions are linked to the circumstances within which questions of reasonable precaution arise, and joined to normalizing assumptions about the importance of various kinds of interests, ARP doctrine fashions a filter that identifies some risk impositions as reasonable as a matter of law; condemns the failure to take certain precautions as *un*reasonable as a matter of law; and narrows the range of reasonable disagreement in the broad spectrum of cases that lie between these poles.

The residual problem of identifying reasonable precautions, moreover, does not arise in a vacuum. It arises among free and equal persons engaged in mutually beneficial activities. Accidents – even accidents among strangers – typically arise as by-products of mutually beneficial cooperative activities. Consider driving. Even though automobile accidents are a paradigmatic instance of accidents among strangers, persons engaged in driving are nonetheless participants in a complex and mutually beneficial form of social cooperation. The activity enables participants to pursue their own ends and requires each of them to take precautions for each other's benefit (observing the rules of the road, maintaining the brakes on their vehicles, moderating their intake of alcohol, and so on). The precise questions of reasonableness contested in automobile accident cases are highly contextualized. Particular risks are compared to the precautions that would eliminate them.

When reasonable people are engaged in an ongoing course of cooperation with each other they may be able to single out certain precautions as "natural focal points" (Schelling 1980; Johnson 1976) for their mutually beneficial cooperation. Given the background facts of the activity (the particular kinds of risks it imposes and the particular possibilities it presents for reducing those risks), the disposition to reasonableness, and the fundamental interests of reasonable persons, certain precautions will often prove salient. As Thomas Schelling points out, "[m]ost situations . . . provide some clue for coordinating behavior, some focal point for each person's expectation of what the other expects him to expect to be expected to do."[86]

Take the situation presented by *Delair v. McAdoo*.[87] *Delair* holds that all drivers must be held – as a matter of law – to be aware of the hazards of tires which are "worn through to the fabric" (and so must be found negligent for accidents caused by using tires in such condition) (*id.* at 184). The choice confronting the court is a restricted one – a choice between an objective rule requiring persons to know the dangers of worn-out tires, and a subjective rule exculpating people who make sincere but unsuccessful efforts to acquire the relevant knowledge. Once the choice is framed by the context of driving and by the alternative rulings available to the court, it is an easy choice for reasonable persons concerned to sustain a mutually beneficial form of social cooperation on fair terms to make. The subjective rule suffers from all of the vices that we have reviewed: It puts the security of other drivers at considerable risk; it increases the uncertainty surrounding the risks of the road; and it undermines the bases of social cooperation on fair terms. The objective rule offers all of the converse virtues: It protects the security of other drivers; it makes the risks of the road more predictable; and it underwrites social cooperation on fair terms. Moreover, it makes comparatively modest demands – the burden of examining *one's own* tires to determine if they are worn through to the fabric, and of recognizing the hazards posed by such tires – on prospective injurers. Holding drivers responsible for accidents caused by tires that are worn through to the fabric is therefore the salient solution to the problem presented by *Delair.* Similar justifications can be given for most of the rules of ARP doctrine, and the correct rule is, for the most part, similarly clear.

Exceptions to the general rule that all actors are held to the standard of the average reasonable person lend themselves to interpretation and defense as salient agreement points among reasonable persons engaged in mutually beneficial cooperation. It is reasonable, for example, to permit police and fire personnel to impose greater than average risks when responding to emergencies (Keating 1996, p. 369). Even persons who disagree about conceptions of the good can agree upon the urgency of preserving life and limb from grave and imminent harm. Moreover, police and fire personnel can alert potential victims of the added danger from their hazardous activities (by driving specially marked vehicles, by using flashing lights, and by sounding sirens), thereby permitting potential victims to take additional precautions for their own safety. Finally, because police and fire departments closely supervise and train their members, and because the conditions that permit greater risk imposition are objectively defined and publicly known,[88] courts can easily determine whether the power to impose increased risk is being properly exercised.

The relaxation of the duty of care for police and fire personnel also clearly demonstrates how appropriate solutions "depend on time and place and who the people are" (Schelling 1980, p. 58). The last three reasons that I have given for relaxing the duty of care exploit facts peculiar to police and fire personnel and so illustrate how ARP doctrine can incorporate the distinctive attributes of particular injurers, institutions, and victims.[89]

The third piece of the puzzle is ARP doctrine's use of normalizing assumptions. ARP doctrine draws tacitly, and social contract draws expressly, on normalizing assumptions. Such assumptions abound in our ordinary moral discourse.

Thus, for example, we take it as given for purposes of moral argument that it is very important that what one wears and whom one lives with be dependent on one's choices and much less important that one be able to choose what other people wear, what they eat, and how they live. And we do this despite the fact that there may be some who would not agree with this assignment of values.[90]

Normalizing assumptions are necessary if we are to carve out sufficient space for persons to pursue their diverse conceptions of the good on fair terms.

*Delair,* for example, relies implicitly on such assumptions. Like ARP doctrine generally, *Delair* rejects outright the economic argument that we should, if possible, examine the costs of care that individuals face in taking a particular precaution. Implicitly, the court draws on the normalizing assumption that the injurer's benefits from continuing to use worn tires are not important to the pursuit of a plausible conception of the good. They are, on the contrary, the benefits of laziness, inexcusable ignorance, or insufficient regard for the well-being of others. Because these are character flaws, not elements of a conception of the good, they are entitled to no weight at all in the calculus of risk.

The doctrines delineating the duties of children demonstrate the role of normalizing assumptions even more clearly. From a subjective viewpoint, the cost of holding children engaged in adult activities to an adult standard of care seems very high. If, however, we subscribe to the normalizing assumption that engaging in adult activities has no place in the normal development and maturation of children, the objective cost of care is very low. By contrast, the normalized benefits of holding children to an age-appropriate standard when they participate in age-appropriate activities is very high, because, unlike participation in adult activities, participation in age-appropriate acts is an important part of healthy development.[91] In short, the doctrines delineating the duties of children are anomalous if conceived in terms of individualized (and subjective) cost, but sound if conceived in terms of normalized (and objective) cost.

These examples are anything but anomalous. ARP doctrine is normalizing through and through. In order to fix the boundaries of our freedoms and responsibilities, the doctrine rejects the use of individualized values for the simple but powerful reason given in *Vaughan:* A rule measuring the adequacy of care by individual capacities to take care "would leave so vague a line as to afford no rule at all."[92] The doctrine, therefore, requires "in all cases a regard to caution such as a man of ordinary prudence would observe" (*id.*). In this way, the terms of reasonable cooperation and the grounds of normalization are intimately related.

These two ideas – normalizing assumptions and reasonable precautions as those that form natural focal points for fair cooperation between free and equal persons – complete the social contract interpretation of due care. With these concepts, the social contract interpretation achieves its vision of equal freedom in three ways. First, by assigning high relative value to security, the interpretation provides the most favorable conditions for the pursuit of conceptions of the good over the course of complete lives. Second, the interpretation brings *comparative* clarity to the practice of determining duties of care by its insistence on, and conception of, objective valuation. This comparative clarity itself strengthens our freedom. Third, ARP doctrine as social contract theory conceives it adjudicates – rather than legislates – the terms of reasonable risk imposition, and this protects both liberty and security. It protects the liberty of injurers by holding them liable only for imposing risks that they should have been able to recognize, *ex ante,* as unreasonable. It protects the security of victims by ensuring that they will not be at the mercy of unreasonable risk impositions. This third aspect of ARP doctrine's protection of our freedom is both an illustration of the second aspect, and a matter that requires more explanation.

In establishing norms of reasonableness, ARP doctrine can be either legislative or adjudicative: The doctrine is legislative if it prescribes canonical norms of reasonableness and requires persons to honor those norms; it is adjudicative if it acknowledges and honors preexisting norms recognized by reasonable persons. Thus, in applying ARP doctrine, courts may either formulate new norms, and so *prescribe* the terms of reasonable behavior, or they may acknowledge existing norms, and so *describe* the norms that reasonable persons engaged in the practices should arrive at by themselves (Johnson 1976, pp. 172–7).

This is a distinction that matters. Freedom from retroactively imposed legal penalties and liabilities is an important aspect of our freedom, one protected by the rule of law itself. If ARP doctrine merely articulates the judgments that reasonable persons would reach when confronted with the matter at hand, the doctrine respects preexisting rights instead of creating rights retroactively. It therefore realizes the rule of law and secures freedom from retroactive penalties.[93] When reasonable precautions are salient and courts competent, persons who act reasonably will find that the reach of their responsibilities is (reasonably) clear even in the absence of judicial precedent, customary practice, or statutory prescription. People who behave reasonably will not have their freedom violated by the judicial creation of retroactive duties and liabilities.

Two statutory negligence cases – *Martin v. Herzog*[94] and *Tedla v. Ellman*[95] – illustrate the difference between the legislative and adjudicative roles of reasonableness, and show how ARP doctrine can be fundamentally adjudicative. *Martin* lays down the rule that the unexcused violation of a statutory prohibition is negligence *per se.*[96] *Tedla* carves out an exception to that rule. The plaintiffs in *Tedla* were wheeling a baby carriage full of junk along the right side of the road one Sunday evening after dark. "[V]ery heavy Sunday night traffic" was headed in the opposite direction, so the plaintiffs chose to walk with the lighter traffic on the other side of the road.[97] Plaintiff's decision to walk with – not into – traffic appeared to be contributory negligence *per se* because, although it was consistent with customary practice, it was contrary to a recently enacted statute. Yet the court came down on the side of customary practice, creating an exception to the statute for the circumstances of this case (see *id.* at 991). The driving force behind the court's opinion was not some conclusion about the intention of the legislature, but the evidently greater reasonableness of the customary practice in comparison with the legislative prohibition. Under the circumstances, walking with the traffic was clearly safer than walking against it.

*Tedla* thus supports the argument that judicial determinations of reasonableness under ARP doctrine are meant to announce the norms of reasonable behavior, not to legislate them. When actors hit upon reasonable precautions and legislatures do not, legislation, as well as judicial precedent enshrining statutes as authoritative specifications of reasonable behavior, must yield. This is as it should be. While the determination of duties of care is a matter of and for public moral reasoning, it is a matter of reasoning about the natural duties that persons owe to one another (Keating 1996, pp. 320–1). Legislation ratifies and specifies those duties; it does not create them. To be sure, ARP doctrine is not purely adjudicative; at the very least it requires people to behave reasonably. This requirement may seem legislative even if the norm of reasonableness itself derives from beliefs to which our practices and moral judgments, properly reconstructed, commit us.[98] This fact, however, does not undermine the adjudicative character of judgments of reasonableness: Such judgments follow the template of reasonable behavior; they do not form that template. Insofar as they do, the canons of reasonableness ensure that liability is not imposed retroactively, thereby realizing one of the liberties associated with the rule of law.

The flip side of this coin is the protection that an adjudicative approach to the determination of duty affords to the security of protective victims. When ARP doctrine and practice are adjudicative, reasonable victims will be in a better position to estimate the risks to which they will be exposed than they otherwise would be.

If the social contract articulation of due care doctrine realizes its vision of accident law as a realm of mutual freedom in three ways, it likewise achieves its conception of accident law as a realm of fair risk imposition in three ways. First, it spells out what it means for risks to be reciprocal: Reciprocal risks are risks that are equal in magnitude, equal in probability, and imposed for reasons that are both good enough to justify the perils they risk and equally good. Risk impositions that meet these criteria are fair because they are, *ex ante,* to the long-run advantage even of those they imperil. Second, this interpretation underwrites mutually beneficial social cooperation by seeking out precautions that are "natural focal points" for such cooperation. Third, it places social cooperation on a firm footing by making the terms of cooperation comparatively clear, and by making compliance with them publicly verifiable.

### D.  Subordinate Doctrines of Due Care

For all its importance, the template of reasonableness fashioned by ARP doctrine will not prescribe a specific level of precaution in a wide range of cases. Taken together, the Hand Formula and ARP doctrine provide general substantive and methodological criteria of reasonableness, but these criteria often fail to identify uniquely reasonable precautions. This is not so surprising: Social contract theory insists that the canons of reasonableness often leave substantial room for "reasonable" disagreement (Rawls 1993, pp. 54–8).

Negligence law responds to the indeterminacy of the general canons of reasonableness through subordinate doctrines that specify the concrete duties of care. To determine concrete standards of reasonableness, we must look to custom, jury adjudication, and statutes. Each of these doctrines draws support not only from its capacity to specify the precise terms of reasonable precaution, but also from its own distinctive principle(s) of political morality. When the canons of reasonableness fail to single out a particular precaution as the most reasonable one, the general norms of reasonableness cannot do all the work of legitimating particular precautions.

Custom, for example, draws its support from two sources – due care doctrine's quest for salient precautions, and the principle that reasonable reliance should not be disappointed. Customary precautions are salient; customary conduct *is* normal conduct; and what is normal is plainly relevant to, though not dispositive of, the question of what should be normal. Jury adjudication also serves to establish precautions in circumstances where the general canons of due care are indeterminate. This subordinate doctrine gathers its support partly from its identification of salient precautions and partly from independent moral principles. Salience is contextual. It "depends on time and place and who the people are" (Schelling 1980, p. 58). Insofar as juries presumably embody the culture and conventions of their communities, they are well suited to selecting contextually salient precautions. Salience is not the end of the matter, however. The practice of jury adjudication also has independent moral support because it brings the moral sense of the community to bear on controversial disputes. By virtue of its claim to articulate the sense of justice shared by a particular community (Wells 1990, pp. 208–10), jury adjudication legitimizes controversial outcomes even in the face of persistent disagreement. Finally, negligence law determines concrete standards of due care by deference to statutes. Legislative specification of precautions as mandatory surely makes those precautions salient. Equally sure, the principle of legislative supremacy and the duty to comply with just institutions[99] provide further – and independent – grounds for deferring to statutes.

These remarks, of course, only situate these aspects of due care law in relation to the general social contract conception of due care. Even this brief discussion, however, enables us to understand the basic role of, and justification for, these aspects of negligence law. It also clarifies a fundamental structural affinity between social contract theory and due care doctrine. Just as social contract theory "work[s] from a general framework for the whole to sharper and sharper determination of its parts" (Rawls 1971, p. 566), so, too, due care doctrine works from general canons of reasonableness to the specification of substantive duties through a sequence of doctrines. The Hand Formula and ARP doctrine specify general substantive and methodological criteria of reasonableness; jury adjudication, custom, and statutes specify concrete duties of care. Each stage in the sequence frames and limits the subsequent stages, and draws authority both from general notions of reasonableness and from its own distinctive principles (Rawls 1993, p. 262). Juries, customs, and statutes may set duties of care only insofar as they respect the boundaries set by the general canons (both methodological and substantive) of reasonableness. Within those boundaries, their own distinctive institutional principles (such as legislative supremacy) reinforce their authority. When they transgress against those boundaries, they forfeit their authority.

### Notes

[1] Professor of Law, USC Law School. I am grateful to participants in the UNC Law and Philosophy Workshop on Tort Law and Philosophy, and to the members of the Los Angeles Law and Philosophy Discussion group, for valuable comments and suggestions. Comments from Jules Coleman, Arthur Ripstein, Ben Zipursky, Scott Altman, and Lew Sargentich have been especially helpful.

[2] These three views do not exhaust the possibilities. A wide range of contemporary theories gather under the banner of "corrective justice." See, e.g., Wells (1990); Coleman (1992a); Weinrib (1995, pp. 56–83); Fletcher (1972, pp. 537–8).

[3] Rawls draws the distinction in Rawls (1971, pp. 8ff, 245ff).

[4] I have in mind the particular sense of "interpretive" found in the work of Ronald Dworkin. Dworkin (1986, pp. 45–86).

[5] On the "basic structure" see Rawls (1993, p. 257). I have been misleading on this score in the past. In Keating (1997, pp. 1302–4), I suggest that tort is part of the basic structure of society in Rawls' sense. It would have been better simply to say that tort is a coercive order of public norms, which protects urgent interests.

[6] See, e.g., *Fletcher v. Rylands*, L.R. 1 Exch. 265 (1866); *Rylands v Fletcher* L.R. 3 H.L. 330 (H.L. 1868); *Losee v. Buchanan*, 51 N.Y. 476 (1873); Bohlen (1926, pp. 344–50); Fried (1970, pp. 183–206); Fletcher (1972).

[7] This paper is overwhelmingly concerned with one branch of the law of accidents, namely,

the tort law of accidents. The distinctive feature of the tort law of accidents, in my view, is that it is a system that effects both reparation and risk regulation.

[8] For example, democratic citizens do not hold the status of children in a patriarchically conceived family. They are not inferior and dependent but equal and independent. See Locke (1980, ch. 2).

[9] *Losee v. Buchanan* appeals to this kind of fixed historical baseline in rejecting the reasoning and conclusion of *Rylands v. Fletcher.* See Keating (1996, pp. 314–17).

[10] The conception of reciprocity articulated by Lord Cairns' opinion in *Rylands v. Fletcher,* and developed by George Fletcher, adopts this approach. See Keating (1996, pp. 314–17). Social contract rhetoric in the case law of torts has thus taken both Kantian and Lockean forms.

[11] Thus "liberty" and "security" in the sense used here are not lexically superior to our interests in income and wealth in the manner of the liberties covered by Rawls' first principle of justice. "Liberty" and "security," as I use them, are general cover terms designed to characterize, at a fairly high level of generality, the stakes in accidental risk imposition. The burdens and benefits of risk include increases and losses in wealth and income, so there is no question of these freedoms being lexically prior to the primary goods of wealth and income. Thus, in judging the reasonableness of various risk impositions or liability rules, we should assess the significance of gains and losses in wealth and income in terms of their impacts on liberty and security.

In the past, I have expressed myself inadequately and inconsistently on this score. For example, the discussion on page 322 of Keating (1996) implies that our interests in security and freedom of action are lexically superior to our interests in wealth and income. The discussion on page 355 implies the opposite.

Why characterize the interests at stake in risk impositions as interests in freedom at all? Because risks and their reduction affect the space that we have to form, evaluate and act upon our aims and aspirations.

[12] The transport of gasoline in this manner precipitated the death of the plaintiff in *Siegler v. Kuhlman,* 502 P.2d 1181, 1187 (Wash. 1972).

[13] In an early use of Rawlsian ideas in legal theory, Frank Michelman proposes a similar criterion for determining when compensation should be granted for a "taking" under the just compensation clause. "A decision not to compensate is not unfair as long as the disappointed claimant ought to be able to appreciate how such decisions might fit into a consistent practice which holds forth a lesser long-run risk to people like him than would any consistent practice which is naturally suggested by the opposite decision" Michelman (1967, p. 1223).

[14] Legal doctrine and rhetoric often come very close to putting the matter this way. For example, *Koos v. Roth,* 652 P.2d 1255, 1262 (Or. 1982), a leading case on abnormally dangerous activity liability, explains that, under strict liability "the question is not whether the activity threatens such harm that it should not be continued. The question is who shall pay for harm that has been done." *Loe v. Lenhardt,* 362 P.2d 312, 317 (Or. 1961) explains the basis of abnormally dangerous activity liability in language that comes even closer to the language of conditional fault embraced in this paper: "The element of fault, if it can be called that, lies in the deliberate choice by the defendant to inflict a high degree of risk upon his neighbor, even though the utmost care is observed in so doing." The Comment on Clause (c) to §520 Abnormally Dangerous Activities of the *Restatement of Torts, Sec-*

*ond* (1977) observes that "the utility of [the injurer's] conduct may be such that he is socially justified in proceeding with his activity, but the unavoidable risk of harm that is inherent in it requires that it be carried on at his peril, rather than at the expense of the person who suffers harm as a result of it."

[15] *Koos v. Roth,* 652 P.2d 1255 (Or. 1982).

[16] Or so Fletcher's paper implies. In fact, there is reason to think that strict liability reduces the incidence of non-negligent risk impositions.

[17] Recall *Siegler v. Kuhlman.*

[18] See note 13, and accompanying text. The conduct of abnormally dangerous activities might be thought to be generally advantageous in this way.

[19] See text accompanying note 13.

[20] See Scanlon (1982). Bear in mind that to determine who is worst off we must compare those most disadvantaged by one regime with those most disadvantaged by the other.

[21] The fundamental principle of the tort law of damages is to make the plaintiff whole again. See, e.g., *Sherlock v. Stillwater Clinic,* 260 N.W.2d 169 (Minn.1977) ("The elementary principle of compensatory damages . . . seeks to place injured plaintiffs in the position that they would have been in had no wrong occurred").

[22] This is the fundamental lesson of Calabresi and Hirschoff (1972).

[23] Shavell (1987, pp. 21–6). Deterrence is a secondary aim, or by-product of the practice of awarding money damages. See e.g., *People Express Airlines, Inc. v. Consolidated Rail Corp.,* 100 N.J. 246, 268, 495 A.2d 107, 117 (1985) ("the imposition of liability should deter negligent conduct by creating incentives to minimize the risks and costs of accidents.").

[24] To be sure, there are special cases in which exposure to risk is itself a kind of harm. Exposure to carcinogenic toxins and radiation can result in risks of harm that persist long after the exposure ends, and this may count as a harm in itself. See, e.g., In re TMI, 67 F.3d 1103 (1995) (holding that exposure to radiation beyond a certain threshold fixed by regulation constitutes a harm regardless of subsequent personal injury). But these are exceptional, and distinctively modern, cases. Fletcher clearly has more typical (and traditional) cases in mind.

[25] Because our system of tort compensation is harm based, an argument establishing that it is fair not to compensate persons for their exposure to risk may strike many torts scholars as academic. Step back from the particularities of our tort law and survey the range of possible approaches to risk, and the significance of the argument becomes evident. For example, the argument from "in kind" compensation is important to social contract theory because it shows that reasonable reciprocal risk impositions are fair. While that may not justify subjecting them to negligence liability, it does justify letting the risks be imposed in the first place.

[26] In *Koos v. Roth,* 293 Or. 670, 652 P.2d 1255 (1982) Justice Hans Linde invokes the remark – attributed to Keynes – that "in the long run, we're all dead" to explain why the reciprocity of risk among neighboring farms created by field burning as an agricultural technique does not justify negligence liability. The time lag between injuring and being injured by field burning is great, as is the magnitude of the harm inflicted.

[27] *Bamford v. Turnley,* 122 Eng. Rep. 27, 32–33 (Ex. 1862) (Bramwell, B.).

[28] See e.g., *Kuhlman v. Seigler,* note 24 (sixteen-year-old driver killed by non-negligent explosion of gasoline tanker).

29   See note 45, and accompanying text.

30   *Van Skike v. Zussman,* 318 N.E.2d 244 (Illinois, 1974).

31   There is an affinity between this interpretation of the *domain* of negligence liability and the position taken by Lord Reid in *Bolton v. Stone* [1951] A.C. 850 H.L. (stating that people have a duty not to impose "substantial" risks on others – risks in excess of those ordinarily imposed during "the crowded conditions of modern life"). The idea that due care requires reducing risks to the background level is sometimes embraced by tort theorists, e.g., by Brudner (1995, pp. 191–2); Perry (1988, pp. 169–71). This idea is similar to the idea that I am suggesting here, the idea that negligence liability is fair only when the residual (reasonable) risks of an activity are low enough to merge into the background level of risk imposition.

32   The Owner's Manual for my 1992 Honda Accord wagon reports that an average driver can expect to be in one serious automobile accident during her lifetime.

33   Other things may not always be equal. If no-fault automobile insurance increases the incidence of serious accidents, its advantages over negligence liability diminish and disappear fairly quickly. We must either return to negligence liability or make offsetting adjustments elsewhere, such as increasing our direct regulation of driving safety.

34   These are the facts of *Brown v. Kendall* 60 Mass. (6 Cush.) 292 (1850).

35   The perfection of the institution of insurance can shift an activity out of the world of acts and into the world of activities. Contemporary homeowner's insurance usually covers policyholders for liability arising out of damage their domestic pets inflict on the persons and property of others.

36   Although the activity of dog owning itself might have been actuarially large, the independence of dog owners from each other effectively prevented nineteenth-century insurance mechanisms from stitching these independent and unrelated actors together into a unified enterprise.

37   See pp. 37–38.

38   *Escola v. Coca-Cola,* 150 P.2d 436 (1944).

39   See *Siegler v. Kuhlman,* note 12.

40   *Lubin v. Iowa City,* 131 N.W.2d 765 (1965) (waterworks chose not to inspect underground water mains, and to replace them only after they broke).

41   Mehr, Cammack, and Rose (1985) (the system of insurance is predicated on the law of large numbers, a theory under which the ability to predict collective losses supplants the impossibility of predicting individual losses).

42   *Escola v. Bottling Coca Cola Bottling Co. of Fresno,* 150 P.2d 436, 441 (1944) (Traynor, J., concurring); *Lubin v. Iowa City,* 131 N.W.2d 765, 770 (1964).

43   For discussion of the connection between the capacity to control a risk and strict liability, see Keating (1997, pp. 1356–9).

44   On this, see Keating (1996, pp. 342–6); Keating (1997, pp. 1296–1308).

45   In *Van Skike v. Zussman,* 318 N.E.2d 244 (Ill. App. Ct. 1974) a child set himself on fire after he won a toy lighter as a prize in a gumball machine, and tried to fill it with lighter fluid that he purchased from the store on whose premises the machine was located. He and his mother brought suit against Zussman, the operator of the gumball machine, among others, claiming that "[Zussman] knew of or should have known that he had placed his cigarette lighter dispensing machines in a store that sold flammable fluids" and, by implication, that placing the machines in the store created a risk of harm against which precautions

should be taken. The court concluded that these allegations failed to state a claim against Zussman on the ground that the "creation of a legal duty requires more than a mere possibility of occurrence" (*id.* at 247).

46  Compare Fried (1970, p. 193). Some variation in the risks "ordinarily" created by different activities seems inevitable. Driving endangers bystanders more than skateboarding, if only because cars are larger, heavier and faster than people on skateboards.

47  The train inspector in *Davis v. Consolidated Rail Corp.,* 788 F.2d 1260, 1262 (7th Cir. 1986) lost one leg below the knee and most of the foot on his other leg when the train he was inspecting started without warning.

48  *Duckworth v. Franzen,* 780 F.2d 645, 652 (7th Cir. 1985), cert. denied, 479 U.S. 816 (1986) (Posner, J.).

49  E.g., Hart and Honore (1985, p. 214, note 46) (describing recklessness as "flying in the face of an apparent and apprehended risk" and gross negligence as merely failing to adhere to a low standard of care); Keeton 1984 at 9–10, 211–14.

50  The test that I am proposing is similar to the "feasibility" standard favored by OSHA, and, more loosely, to one of the standards found in the law of nuisance. See *American Textile Manufacturers Institute v. Donovan* ("The Cotton Dust Case"), 452 U.S. 490, 101 S. Ct. 2478 (1981) (discussing "feasibility analysis" standard that requires the elimination or reduction of "significant risk[s] of material health impairment . . . 'to the extent such protection is technologically and economically feasible.'"), and §826(b) of the *Restatement of Torts, Second* (1979) (requiring compensation despite cost justification when "the financial burden of compensating for this and similar harm to others would not make the continuation of the conduct not feasible").

51  Total utility is widely rejected as a measure of human welfare for just this reason. See, e.g., Rawls (1971, pp. 161–6).

52  See, e.g., *Eckert v. Long Island Railroad,* 43 N.Y. 502, 506 (1871).

53  Cf. *Ploof v. Putnam,* 71 A. 188, 189 (Vt. 1908) ("One may sacrifice the personal property of another to save his life or the lives of his fellows.").

54  The contrast is not between life and limb and purely monetary costs of precaution, but between life and limb and the activities that the product enables.

55  On this test, see the materials in Keeton, Sargentich, and Keating (1998, pp. 705–49).

56  519 P.2d 981 (Wash. 1974).

57  *Id.* at 983. Cf. *Gates v. Jensen,* 92 Wn.2d 246, 595 P.2d 919 (1979).

58  *Helling,* at 983 (emphasis added).

59  *Helling,* at 982. Questions of special medical expertise dropped out because the court supposed (rightly or not) that the choice of the pertinent precaution and its efficacy were beyond dispute.

60  Or so I shall assume. It is virtually impossible to know whether all of the *financial* costs of the pressure test were passed through to the patients, though the patients necessarily bore the *time and inconvenience* of those tests. See generally Craswell (1991). And even if the costs were passed through, they may have been covered by insurance, in at least some cases. Because the tests benefited the patients, it would be normatively appropriate to make them bear their costs, and I shall therefore analyze the case on that assumption.

61  When exposure to a risk does further a plausible conception of the good, accidents involving participants in a shared enterprise differ greatly from accidents among strangers. Social contract theory supposes that persons are generally free to impose upon themselves

any risks that they think appropriate when such imposition is integral to the pursuit of a permissible conception of the good.

[62] The distinction between "scientific policy-maker" and "ordinary observer" perspectives is Bruce Ackerman's. See Ackerman (1977).

[63] See e.g., *Delair v. McAdoo*, 188 A. 181, 184 (Pa. 1936) (holding defendant negligent as a matter of law for driving a car whose tires were worn through to the fabric).

[64] In the case of the Hand Formula, formal doctrine does not do this, jury practice does.

[65] In one familiar formulation, two basic principles of tort law conflict – "No Liability Without [Subjective] Fault" and "As Between Two Innocents, Let the Person Who Caused the Damage Pay." Balkin (1986), – and ARP doctrine sides with the latter principle.

[66] Keeton 1984, at 176–7 ("The fact that the individual is a congenital fool, cursed with in-built bad judgment . . . obviously cannot be allowed to protect him from liability.").

[67] *Jolley v. Powell*, 299 So.2d 647, 649 (Fla. Dist. Ct. App. 1974); *Miller v. State*, 306 N.W.2d 554 (Minn. 1981); *Dellwo v. Pearson*, 107 N.W.2d 859, 863 (Minn. 1961); Keeton 1984, at 177.

[68] E.g., *Hughey v. Lennox*, 219 S.W. 323, 325 (Ark. 1920) (holding that an inexperienced driver is liable for injuries caused by his inexperience).

[69] See *Jolley*, 299 So. 2d at 649; *McGuire v. Almy*, 8 N.E.2d 760, 762 (Mass. 1937); *Breunig v. American Family Ins. Co.*, 173 N.W.2d 619, 624 (Wis. 1970).

[70] See, e.g., *Daniels v. Evans*, 224 A.2d 63, 64 (N.H. 1966); *Dellwo*, 107 N.W.2d at 863.

[71] As the court in Dellwo remarked: "A person observing children at play . . . may anticipate conduct that does not reach an adult standard of care or prudence. However, one cannot know whether the operator of an approaching automobile . . . is a minor or an adult, and usually cannot protect himself against youthful imprudence even if warned." *Dellwo*, 107 N.W.2d at 863 [citations omitted].

[72] See *Brillhart v. Edison Light & Power Co.*, 82 A.2d 44, 47 (Pa. 1951); *Public Serv. Co. v. Elliot*, 123 F.2d 2, 6 (1st Cir. 1941).

[73] See Keeton 1984, at 185 & nn.14–20.

[74] *Breunig v. American Family Ins. Co.*, 173 N.W.2d 619, 623 (Wis. 1970).

[75] One prominent task of ARP doctrine is to determine when and how the capacities of natural persons should be taken into account in appraising the reasonableness of their conduct. I shall be interested in this facet of the doctrine only insofar as it sheds light on the matter of valuation.

[76] *Restatement (Second) of Torts* § 283 cmt. e (1964).

[77] *Eckert v. Long Island Railroad*, 43 N.Y. 502, 506 (1871).

[78] A person who knowingly and willingly puts others in danger when "engaged in his ordinary affairs, or in the mere protection of property" is negligent. *Eckert*, at 506.

[79] John M. Glionna, "Trestle-Jumping Fad Puts Youths in Path of Danger," *L.A. Times*, Aug. 10, 1992, at A1 (quoting one trestle-jumping youth as saying, "at the peak of danger, you bail out. You cheat death. It's a feeling nothing else can beat."). In explicating the flaws in subjective valuation, I shall focus on the problems presented by injurers who have unusually intense preferences of a sort that lead them to want to impose great risks *on* others or themselves. But, with appropriate modifications, these difficulties might also be illustrated by focusing on victims who have unusually intense preferences for avoiding risk impositions *by* others.

[80] See, e.g., *Cusick v. Clark*, 360 N.E.2d 160, 163 (Ill. App. Ct. 1977).

[81] See, e.g., *Dellwo v. Pearson* at 863.

82  See, e.g., *De Martini v. Alexander Sanitarium, Inc.,* 13 Cal. Rptr. 564, 567 (Cal. Dist. Ct. App. 1961). For a general discussion of tort law's treatment of victims and injurers who are not "average," see Calabresi (1985, pp. 20–6).

83  *Lange v. Hoyt,* 159 A. 575, 577–8 (Conn. 1932); *Troppi v. Scarf,* 187 N.W.2d 511, 520 (Mich. Ct. App. 1971); *Friedman v. State,* 282 N.Y.S. 2d 858, 865–6 (N.Y. Ct. Cl. 1967).

84  The flip side of this coin is the problem of the emotionally hypersensitive plaintiff. If prospective victims could set up a duty of care whenever injurers disturbed their emotional tranquility, uncertainty would debilitate freedom of action. Social contract theory therefore supports tort law's general exclusion of purely emotional harm from its purview. See Keating (1996, pp. 346–7).

85  The reasonable person gives "an impartial consideration to the harm likely to be done the interests of the other as compared with the advantages likely to accrue to his own interests, free from the natural tendency of the actor, as a party concerned, to prefer his own interests to those of others." *Restatement (Second) of Torts* § 283 cmt. e (1964).

86  Schelling (1980, p. 57). The salience of certain solutions is a highly contextual matter. See Gibbard (1991) (reviewing Barry (1989)).

87  188 A. 181 (Pa. 1936).

88  There are usually statutory or administrative specifications of the circumstances under which police and fire personnel are permitted to impose greater risks.

89  It will, I hope, be plain that similar interpretations and justifications can be offered for other rules of ARP doctrine, including the doctrines (duties of care owed by children) and cases (*Martin v. Herzog* and *Tedla v. Ellman*) that I discuss for other purposes later in this section.

90  Scanlon (1988, p. 183). See generally Scanlon (1991), cf. Nozick (1974, p. 78–86); Coleman and Ripstein (1995).

91  See *Charbonneau v. MacRury,* 53 A. 457, 462 (N.H. 1931) (quoting Harry Shulman, (1928, p. 618), overruled on other grounds, *Daniels v. Evans,* 224 A.2d 63 (N.H. 1966). The relaxation of duty for children engaged in age-appropriate activities relies on normalizing assumptions in another, more descriptive, way. The doctrine supposes that age-appropriate activities impose less risk than adult ones and enable more victim precautions. See notes 69–71 and accompanying text. Precisely because the rules governing the duties of children respect the disproportionate value of security, and provide children with ample room to pursue their conceptions of the good, these rules represent salient solutions to the problems that they address, and natural focal points for reasonable cooperation.

92  *Vaughan v. Menlove,* 132 Eng. Rep. 490, 493 (C.P. 1837).

93  This involves two aspects of the rule of law – prospectivity and publicity. See Keating (1993, pp. 16–21, 27–9, 35–6); see also Dworkin (1978, pp. 165–6).

94  126 N.E. 814 (N.Y. 1920).

95  19 N.E.2d 987 (N.Y. 1939).

96  See *Martin,* 126 N.E. at 815.

97  See *Tedla,* 19 N.E.2d at 989.

98  But why should we think this idea of cooperation on reasonable terms legislative if it bubbles up from our experience of life under conditions of pluralism? See Rawls (1993, pp. 158–68).

99  For a discussion of this duty, see Rawls (1971, pp. 350–5).

# 3

# Responsibility for Outcomes, Risk, and the Law of Torts

STEPHEN R. PERRY*

## I. Introduction

Can there be a non-consequentialist moral theory of negligence law, or, more generally, can there be a non-consequentialist moral theory capable of justifying the imposition of tortious liability for unintentional harm? Most corrective justice theorists say yes, but the basis of that answer is hardly obvious on its face. After all, the predominant scholarly view is that the negligence standard of reasonable care is to be understood in utilitarian or economic terms, and this view is shared even by some who call themselves deontologists (Hurd 1996). Furthermore, the actions that bring about unintentional harm are not typically culpable or blameworthy, and sometimes they are not in any sense wrongful either. But the notions of culpability, blameworthiness, and wrongfulness lie at the heart of non-consequentialist theories of the criminal law, and it would not be implausible to think that they are central to non-consequentialist thought generally. It is true that negligence is characterized by the law as a species of "fault," but this clearly does not refer to fault in the core sense of wrongful action motivated or accompanied by a culpable state of mind. Moreover there are a number of circumstances in which tort law imposes strict liability for unintentional harm, and in these cases the law does not even purport to claim that the action giving rise to the harm is to be regarded as faulty. Is it possible to account in non-consequentialist terms for the full range of tortious liability for unintentional injury?

To answer the questions posed in the preceding paragraph, it will be helpful to draw the following distinction. Sometimes we say of a person, generally in a context in which blame or punishment is at stake, that he is responsible for some specific *action,* where the action in question consists, in the usual case, of reprehensible conduct of some kind. At other times we say rather that someone is responsible for a certain *state of affairs,* meaning that he is responsible for that state of affairs having come into being. If we focus on positive acts, as I intend for the most part to do in this article, and leave aside omissions, the states of affairs for which persons are typically regarded as responsible constitute the *outcomes* of actions that they have performed. The outcomes in question need not necessarily be bad or undesirable; we also speak of people as being responsible for bringing about good states of affairs. Adopting a term of Tony Honoré's,[1] I label this form of responsibility *outcome-responsibility*. Responsibility for reprehensible actions can by analogy be called *action-responsibility*.

It might be thought that outcome-responsibility is really no different from, or just a special case of, action-responsibility, since many actions include certain effects – outcomes – in their descriptions (e.g., an act of killing). But to equate outcome-responsibility with responsibility for (certain of) one's actions would, without more, beg some important questions. For example, perhaps we should only hold someone responsible for the *action* of killing another person if the action was in some appropriate sense culpable. We might, however, still think it right to hold someone who has killed another responsible for the *outcome* – the death itself – even if he or she had not behaved culpably in bringing that outcome about. We should also leave open the possibility that the two types of responsibility have different normative upshots (for example, one might call for punishment where the other calls for compensation). Finally, an outcome for which it seems appropriate to hold an agent responsible might simply be too remote from the originating action to count, under any plausible description, as part of that action. For present purposes I shall treat the term "outcome" as subsuming both the results and the consequences of actions, where a *result* is an effect entailed by a given description of an action and a *consequence* is a further effect distinct from, but still caused by, the action as described (Duff 1990, p. 42). Thus a death is the result of an act of killing, but in the case of an act of shooting it is a consequence only.

In this chapter, I shall argue that the general concept of outcome-responsibility underwrites the possibility of a non-consequentialist theory of tortious liability for unintentional harm. I shall also defend a particular conception of outcome-responsibility and show how that conception plays a fundamental role in explicating not just the theoretical foundations of tort law, but also its content. Central to the account of outcome-responsibility I develop, which I call the avoidability-based conception, is a certain understanding of the way in which the outcomes of one's actions can be said to be within one's control. More particularly, outcome-responsibility involves control in the form of a general capacity on the part of an agent to foresee an outcome and to take steps to avoid its occurrence. Outcome-responsibility thus conceived does not ordinarily give rise by itself to a moral obligation to compensate, although by normatively linking an agent to a harmful outcome it serves as the basis for such an obligation. Outcome-responsibility is, we might say, best envisaged as a plateau of responsibility that singles out the outcome-responsible agent as a *potential* cost-bearer. Further criteria must be met, however, before a moral obligation to compensate should be recognized and a corresponding legal obligation imposed.

Unintentional harm can be defined, for purposes of tort law, as harm to which an agent causally contributed but that he did not intend to bring about and that he was not substantially certain would occur.[2] Unintentional harm thus flows from action that poses not a certainty of harm, but only a risk. I shall argue that a certain understanding of the notion of risk is conceptually associated with outcome-responsibility in the avoidability-based sense, and that that understanding, which characterizes risk in epistemic terms, is required to explain the normative significance of risk in tort law (cf. Perry 1995, p. 321). The upshot is that the concept of outcome-responsibility helps to elucidate not just the moral foundations of a legal obligation to compensate, but also its substance or content. More particularly, it helps to elucidate the proper formulation of the standard of care in negligence law, as well as to explain why the law sometimes relies on a negligence standard and sometimes on a standard of strict liability.

The majority of theorists who have discussed the proper formulation of the negligence standard, or at least the majority who have discussed that issue from the perspective of corrective justice or individual responsibility, have implicitly assumed that there is some relatively straightforward, purely factual sense in which one person can be said to "impose" risks on another. They thus suppose that the relevant question for both tort law and tort theory is the following: which risks can acceptably be imposed on other persons, and which cannot be? But the initial assumption giving rise to that question is, I shall argue, mistaken. "Imposing a risk" on a person is not a simple factual state of affairs, like pointing a gun at him. So far as we can deal with the matter in purely factual terms, risk must be conceived in an objective rather than in an epistemic sense (Perry 1995, pp. 322–9), and it must generally be regarded as the joint creation of two interacting actors or activities rather than as something that one person has unilaterally imposed upon another. There is, to be sure, a sense in which one person can unilaterally impose a risk on someone else, and a distinction can accordingly be drawn between cases of joint risk creation and cases of unilateral risk imposition. But that distinction is based on an epistemic rather than on an objective conception of risk; more importantly, the distinction is normative rather than empirical.

To draw the distinction between joint risk creation and unilateral risk imposition, and to make explicit the norms that regulate instances of joint risk creation, we must have recourse, I shall argue, to the notion of an accepted, "normal" pattern of social interaction. The pattern of interaction between drivers and pedestrians is a good example, and one that illustrates the important point that our concern is not simply with risks that arise *within* a single activity, like driving. We are also concerned with risks that arise out of the interaction of two or more activities, like driving and walking. Jointly created risks are, very roughly, those that fall within the range of risks that is normally or customarily associated with a given pattern of social interaction. Such risks are properly regulated by a negligence rule, which is itself best understood by reference to a constrained form of cost–benefit analysis. Unilaterally imposed risks are of two kinds: first, those that arise within an established pattern of interaction but whose magnitude exceeds the normal range of risks within that pattern; and second, those that do not originate within an established pattern of interaction at all. Risks of the latter kind are typically associated with unusual activities that are dangerous in themselves, such as blasting; generally speaking, only the persons who engage in these activities, as opposed to those who might be injured by them, have any significant degree of control over the risks involved. Such risks are properly subject to a standard of strict liability.

## II. Non-Consequentialism and Liability for Unintentional Harm

Let me begin with the question of whether a non-consequentialist theory of tortious liability for unintentional harm is even possible. Heidi Hurd has argued, in an interesting recent article, that negligence law in particular cannot be understood in deontological terms, and must therefore be given a consequentialist interpretation (Hurd 1996). For present purposes, her most important set of arguments concerns the claim that risk-based theories of negligence cannot be deontological in character. She begins by noting that all deontological theories reject the consequentialist claim that wrongdoing consists in failing to maximize good consequences. Rather, deontologists define right and wrong in terms of compliance with, or violation of, agent-relative maxims which function as categorical prohibitions and whose violation cannot, therefore, be justified on consequentialist grounds (Hurd 1996, pp. 253, 267). Deontological maxims trump any contrary consequentialist calculations, but a deontologically permitted act may nonetheless be consequentially wrongful if it causes more bad consequences than good ones. After noting that defendants must generally be found to have both committed a wrongful act and to have done it culpably before they can be punished or found liable, Hurd goes on to suggest that the law "embraces a concept of wrongdoing within which is embedded the causation of harm" (Hurd 1996, p. 262). Thus the law and, according to Hurd, deontology, define wrongs as causally complex acts that subsume certain harmful results, such as killing, rape, and arson (Hurd 1994). (I use the term "result" here in the technical sense that was defined earlier.) Culpability is then understood by the law to consist either of certain mental states (e.g., an intention to bring about a prohibited harm) "or of the fact that the defendant had available to him evidence from which he should have formed a mental state concerning a prohibited harm (i.e., negligence)" (Hurd 1996, p. 262).

Hurd discusses four non-consequentialist theories of negligence law that purport to make liability turn on the creation of different kinds of risks, namely, non-reciprocal risks, unjustly enriching risks, substantial risks, and risks to particularly important interests. She argues that because the law premises liability on the causation of harm rather than on the creation of risk, all of these theories must, despite any appearance to the contrary, be understood as doing the same. From this Hurd concludes that each theory is offering an account of culpability, not an account of wrongdoing. This is just as well, she suggests, since risks cannot be wrongs in any event; to risk someone is not to harm them. There is, moreover, a conceptual problem in construing risks as wrongs: "It cannot be wrong to risk, because to risk is to act in the presence of available evidence that one will do wrong. Upon pain of vicious circularity, one cannot, as a conceptual matter, construe risks as wrongs. For to risk is to risk a wrong; and what is wrong cannot therefore be to risk" (Hurd 1996, p. 264).

Finally, Hurd suggests that, in addition to this conceptual difficulty, it is also morally unacceptable to say that risking is deontologically wrongful or culpable. This is because the violation of a deontological maxim is a categorically forbidden act that cannot be consequentially justified. But the modern world depends on activities that trade deadly risks against desirable consequences, such as building skyscrapers, setting high speed limits, and transporting toxic substances: "Unless deontologists are prepared to say that the myriad of risky activities that support our contemporary lifestyle are categorically wrong, or that the people who engage in them are necessarily culpable, deontologists must admit that even life is not so sacred that it cannot be risked asymmetrically, or substantially, or in an unjustly enriching manner, for good ends" (Hurd 1996, p. 265). After criticizing possible non-risk-based deontological theories of negligence, Hurd concludes that negligence law can only be explained in consequentialist terms. Having earlier noted that Learned Hand's formulation of the negligence standard "is patently and unapologetically consequentialist,"[3] she concludes that tort law "appears to preoccupy itself primarily with the concept of culpability that attaches to consequential wrongdoing, that is, negligence." (Hurd 1996, p. 272).

There are a number of problems with this critique of risk-based deontological theories of negligence.[4] The most fundamental of these, which grows out of the distinction between action-responsibility and outcome-responsibility, will be discussed later. Let me begin instead by considering a number of more specific difficulties that the critique encounters. The first of these concerns Hurd's claim that risks cannot be wrongs. She is right to maintain that risking harm is not itself harm (Perry 1995), from which it follows that a risk is not a wrong in the limited sense of a harmful act. It does not follow, however, that a risk cannot be a wrong in any sense. Hurd argues that it is viciously circular to construe risks as wrongs, but that is clearly a mistake. There is no circularity in defining a wrong as either an act that results in harm or an act that, in certain specified ways, risks causing harm.[5] It might be suggested that the second branch of this definition should be formulated as "risking causing a wrong" instead of "risking causing a harm," in which case the definition would formally be an inductive one; either way, however, there is no circularity. Leaving aside technical details of that kind, the main point for present purposes is that even if one accepts the claim that the central cases of wrongs are causally complex harmful acts – a claim whose justification I will not address in this article – there is no inherent conceptual difficulty in extending the notion of a wrong to include acts that merely risk harms.

Hurd has argued elsewhere that because risks are epistemic constructs, judgments of risk can only be deontologically relevant insofar as they give reasons for belief about the rightness or wrongness of conduct; they thus belong, she concludes, to the realm of culpability, not to the realm of wrongdoing (Hurd 1994, pp. 200–1). Without more, however, this argument provides no clear objection to the kind of extended definition of a wrong that was considered in the preceding paragraph. Rather the argument simply begs the question, by assuming from the outset that wrongs can only be harm-causing acts.[6] Why should it be thought to follow from the epistemic nature of risk that conduct that risks a wrong cannot itself be wrongful, at least under certain circumstances? Consider, for example, a possible action that the agent knows or should know carries a very high probability of death or serious physical injury to some other, particular, individual. Is it so implausible to think that performing that action is categorically forbidden (subject to deontologically acceptable excuses and justifications like self-defence), because to perform it would fail to show the proper respect that is inherently owed to another human being? Once this possibility is granted in *any* type of case involving risk, the conceptual point has been conceded; the argument then shifts to a debate about where to draw the appropriate line between wrongful and non-wrongful risks. The four specific theories of negligence that Hurd criticizes (that negligence consists of nonreciprocal risk creation, substantial risk creation, and so on) can be construed as differing attempts to draw just this line. Hurd does not offer specific criticisms of any of these theories; rather she dismisses them as viable theories of wrongdoing en masse, on the basis of the general claim that risks cannot be wrongs. But, as we have just seen, she offers no sustainable independent argument for that general claim.

However, let me suppose for the moment that Hurd is correct that risks cannot be wrongs. What about her second objection to the risk-based theories of negligence she is considering? This is, it will be recalled, that it is morally unacceptable to treat risky conduct as either deontologically wrongful or deontologically culpable, because the modern world depends on risky activities that are consequentially justified. At this point in her article Hurd is particularly concerned to undermine the view that these theories can plausibly be understood as deontological theories of culpability, since she has already concluded, on the basis of the conceptual argument just discussed, that they cannot be theories of wrongdoing. Hurd's own view is clearly that negligence is indeed best understood in terms of culpability, so that the only remaining question is whether this culpability is deontological or consequentialist in character. I should note that I have serious reservations about Hurd's stipulative definition of culpability as *either* negligence *or* a mental state like intention or knowledge, for the reason that culpability seems properly characterizable in terms of mental states only; negligence does not involve a "guilty mind" in the way that the other, core instances of culpability do. However, let me set those reservations aside. What are we to say about Hurd's argument that negligence cannot be given a deontological content, whether as a matter of wrongdoing or culpability, because we regard so many of our risky activities as justified by their good consequences?

The four risk-based theories Hurd is considering need not deny that risks can sometimes be consequentially justified. What they should be construed as saying, rather, is that certain risks cannot be run, so that consequentialist justification must take place within permissible deontological bounds. It is thus not enough to defeat this type of theory to point to the fact that risks are sometimes justified by their good consequences. What is required, rather, is either an argument that risks can *only* be justified consequentially, or else an argument that no deontologically satisfactory distinction can be drawn between acceptable and unacceptable risks. But Hurd offers neither kind of argument. She seems simply to suggest, without offering specific criticisms, that it is just obvious that none of the four theories she considers draws the appropriate distinction. As it happens I think that this conclusion is true,[7] although in the case of several of the theories the issue is hardly obvious. The important point, however, is that even a detailed refutation of each of the four theories would not show that a moral treatment of risk can only be consequentialist in character, or that a deontological theory of risk-taking is impossible.

The failure to show that a deontological theory of risk-taking is impossible does not, of course, entail that such a theory exists. I will argue in Section VII below that an appropriate deontological account of risk-taking – or, as I would prefer to say, an appropriate non-consequentialist account – can in fact be given. That account tells us, among other things, that the proper understanding of negligence involves a comparison of costs and benefits which closely resembles a constrained version of the Learned Hand Test. Although Hurd does not discuss them, somewhat similar nonconsequentialist interpretations of the negligence standard have been offered before.[8] It is obvious enough that the Hand Test can be given a consequentialist gloss, but it does not follow from this that the test is incapable of being understood in non-consequentialist terms and that it must be regarded, in Hurd's words, as "patently and unapologetically consequentialist." This is because the proper understanding of the negligence standard concerns not just its substantive content, but also its manner of justification.[9] I should note in passing that, although I lean to the view that negligence is best understood as wrongdoing rather than as culpability, I will not be further addressing that issue in the present essay. This is in part because it is not clear to me what turns on the distinction, even from the perspective of Hurd's own theoretical concerns.[10] The main reason, however, that I will not further address this question lies elsewhere. As I suggested earlier, the moral foundations of a non-consequentialist account of liability for unintentional harm must ultimately rest on the concept of outcome-responsibility. The precise normative status of the negligence standard within non-consequentialist moral theory is not, in the end, a central issue.

The considerations just adduced lead directly to a discussion of the more general problem with Hurd's critique of risk-based deontological theories of negligence. Recall her assertion that deontological theories all define right and wrong in terms of compliance with, or violation of, agent-relative maxims that function as categorical prohibitions. Given this starting-point, Hurd is naturally led to focus her inquiry on the question of whether the negligence norm is an agent-relative maxim of the appropriate kind. Built into this approach, however, is the implicit assumption that responsibility for one's actions as such, rather than responsibility for the outcomes of one's actions, must be the theoretical locus of a non-consequentialist theory of negligence law.[11] Hurd also makes the related assumption that if negligence law is to be understood in deontological terms, it must rest on essentially the same theoretical foundations as the criminal law. Both these assumptions can be discerned, for example, when Hurd writes that the distinction between culpability and wrongdoing "is deeply embedded in both tort and criminal law. Generally speaking, defendants must be found *both* to have done a bad act and to have done it culpably before they can properly be held liable or punished" (Hurd 1996, p. 262).

Perhaps Hurd is correct that the notion of deontology is limited to categorical prohibitions on actions. If so, I wish to suggest, the point is ultimately just a semantic one; so far as substantive moral theory is concerned, Hurd embraces too narrow a conception of non-consequentialism. Non-consequentialism in the most general sense concerns what Thomas Nagel calls "the action-centered aspects of morality," which he contrasts with the "outcome-centered aspects" that are the province of consequentialism:

The action-centered aspects of morality include bars against treating others in certain ways which violate their rights, as well as the space allotted to each person for a life of his own, without the perpetual need to contribute to the general good in everything he does. Such provisions are described as action-centered because, while they apply to everyone, what they require of each person depends on his particular standpoint rather than on the impersonal consequentialist standpoint that surveys the best overall state of affairs and prescribes for each person whatever he can do to contribute to it. (Nagel 1979, p. 85)

The "bars against treating others in certain ways" are, of course, Hurd's categorical deontological prohibitions. But, as this passage makes clear, morality's action-centered aspects also include the sphere of personal autonomy within which each person can pursue his or her own life unimpeded by the needs of others. One might be tempted to argue that this sphere exists only by virtue of the categorical prohibitions against treating others in certain ways, but that would be a mistake. The sphere of personal autonomy is an important substantive aspect of the non-consequentialist understanding of human flourishing, and not just a by-product of the idea that human beings cannot be treated in certain ways. It is an action-centered moral concept because many of the reasons that we have to pursue one object or goal in life rather than another are agent-relative in character; they are not agent-general reasons, applicable to others, to bring about generally desirable states of the world.

I wish to suggest that outcome-responsibility is a third aspect of non-consequentialist moral thought, in addition to the categorical prohibitions on certain forms of conduct and the existence of a sphere of personal autonomy. The basic idea is that, as a moral agent, I must take responsibility for certain of the outcomes of my actions, simply because they are the outcomes of *my* actions. This form of responsibility is conceptually distinct from action-responsibility, even though one possible conception of outcome-responsibility would limit the outcomes for which we are responsible to those that are the results of blameworthy actions. It is important not to be misled by the fact that outcome-responsibility focuses on "outcomes" into thinking that it is really one of the "outcome-centered aspects of morality" that Nagel says are the concern of consequentialism. Outcome-responsibility does not depend on any notion of maximizing good consequences. It is, moreover, concerned with outcomes considered not simply as states of the world, but rather as upshots of actions performed by moral agents. It is thus an action-centered moral notion in the specific sense described by Nagel, meaning that the reasons for action to which it gives rise – an obligation to compensate, for example, or perhaps a reason to apologize – are agent-relative rather than agent-neutral in character. Such reasons pertain to a particular person rather than to the world at large because at some point in the past he chose to perform an action that brought about the result or consequence for which he is now outcome-responsible. While different conceptions of outcome-responsibility will have different things to say about the character and content of these reasons for action, all will view them in agent-relative terms.

If corrective justice and, ultimately, tort law, are conceived in terms of outcome-responsibility rather than action-responsibility, then the core concern of a viable non-consequentialist theory of torts will not be with categorical prohibitions on conduct, Hurd's view to the contrary notwithstanding. Rather, the core concern will be, just as one would expect, with the outcomes of actions. For the reasons given in the preceding paragraph, a theory of corrective justice and tort law is not, merely by virtue of focusing on outcomes rather than on actions as such, necessarily consequentialist in nature. Furthermore, as was noted earlier, a non-consequentialist theory that focuses on outcomes can treat the precise non-consequentialist status of the negligence standard as a peripheral issue. Although I will not defend such a view in this article, it is even possible to envisage mixed consequentialist and non-consequentialist theories of tort. For example, a non-consequentialist conception of outcome-responsibility might underwrite the general possibility of liability for unintentional harm, leaving the content of the negligence standard to be justified in consequentialist terms. Hurd, however, would force the non-consequentialist to place action-responsibility at the heart of tort theory, thereby requiring him to show exactly how the negligence standard can be construed as a categorical deontological prohibition. If, however, the non-consequentialist character of tort law is defined by outcome-responsibility rather than by action-responsibility, then Hurd's challenge regarding the status of negligence creates a false dilemma.

Perhaps more importantly, Hurd's restricted understanding of non-consequentialism would seem from the outset to rule out the possibility of a non-consequentialist theory of strict liability. This is significant because many people have a strong pretheoretical intuition that strict liability can be understood in non-consequentialist terms, an intuition that Hurd in effect acknowledges when she writes that "strict liability, if purely applied, might be readily explained on deontological grounds" (Hurd 1996, p. 272). But because strict liability does not categorically prohibit anyone from doing anything and only requires them to pay compensation after the fact, its explanation plainly lies beyond the limited scope of Hurd's conception of non-consequentialism. Given that limited scope, it is, in fact, somewhat puzzling why she would think that strict liability could be given a deontological explanation.[12] A theory rooted in outcome-responsibility, on the other hand, does not necessarily have to point to any action-guiding norm that the defendant's harm-causing behavior violated before it can treat her as outcome-responsible for the harm and therefore as potentially liable for it in tort.[13]

### III. The General Concept of Outcome-Responsibility

In subsequent sections of this essay, I argue for the independence of outcome-responsibility from action-responsibility in non-consequentialist moral thought by defending in some detail a particular conception of the general concept, namely, the avoidability-based conception. According to the avoidability-based account, an agent is outcome-responsible for a harmful outcome if and only if he causally contributed to it, possessed the capacity to foresee it, and had the ability and opportunity to take steps, on the basis of what could have been foreseen, to avoid it. Before discussing the specifics of this conception of outcome-responsibility, however, it will be helpful to try to make clear some of the contours of the general concept. I will do this by discussing a number of other conceptions of outcome-responsibility besides the avoidability conception. Along the way, I will also consider how outcome-responsibility is related to action-responsibility.

Outcome-responsibility is, evidently, a species of responsibility, and, like most other responsibility concepts, it involves a notion of control.[14] In the case of action-responsibility, control is generally taken to mean that, in some appropriate sense, one could have acted otherwise. (There are, of course, differing philosophical understandings of what it means to say that one could have acted otherwise.) Outcome-responsibility assumes that the agent had control over his action of the kind posited by action-responsibility, but it also assumes that he had control over the outcome itself. Different conceptions of the general concept are grounded in differing views of what it means to have control over an outcome. There is a range of possibilities here. At one extreme, a person is regarded as having had the morally appropriate kind of control only if she acted with the intention of bringing that outcome about, either as an end or as a means to an end, and succeeded in doing so. Let me call this the achievement sense of outcome-responsibility. At the other extreme, a person is regarded as having had the morally appropriate kind of control over an outcome only if she acted and, in acting, caused the outcome. Because this account of outcome-responsibility tends to be associated with libertarian moral and legal philosophy, let me call it the libertarian conception.

The achievement conception of outcome-responsibility, which is applicable to both good and bad outcomes, is an important moral notion that is relevant not just to our practices of blaming and demanding compensation, but also to our practices of praising and giving credit. Suppose that I perform an action with the intention of bringing about some outcome. This means that I act under a certain description, with the intention of bringing about a type of outcome that is itself characterized by reference to a description I have in mind. Suppose further that I succeed in my aim, and that I do so more or less in the manner I intended. Clearly, the outcome can appropriately be said to have been under my control, at least so long as the epistemic probability of success was within a certain range.[15] To say that the outcome was under my control obviously does not mean that it was completely under my control; it does not mean, in other words, that I was destined to succeed. We always act with the knowledge that other factors in the world are at work, and the rough epistemic probability of success that we almost always have in mind takes account of the existence of such factors. But so long as the probability of success is not too low, and so long as the manner in which the outcome came about was not too far removed from what I either intended or should have expected as normal,[16] then I had control over the outcome. I am *responsible* for the outcome, in the sense that it can be attributed to my agency. I am properly regarded as its author.

Suppose once again that I act with the intention of bringing about a certain outcome and that, as before, my action causes the outcome to come about. But the manner of the outcome's occurrence is very far removed either from what I intended or should have expected as normal. For example, I am playing snooker, and announce that I am going to sink the black ball in the far corner pocket. It is a fairly straightforward shot, and I have enough skill (just) to make the epistemic probability of success not too unrespectable. However, the shot goes badly awry. The black ball caroms around the table a number of times, bouncing off the cushion and other balls along the way. Amazingly, however, it eventually rolls into the far corner pocket. Now in one sense I am responsible for this outcome, since I did cause it. Sometimes the word "responsible" is used simply to mean that an agent causally contributed to an outcome either in the but-for sense or, possibly, in some more restricted sense. This sense of responsibility is not without its uses, since I will still receive *credit* for the shot, within the rules of the game. But the outcome cannot be attributed to my agency in the achievement sense, and I am not properly regarded as its author. It was just a fluke. Thus praise for the shot, as opposed to credit within the rules of the game, would be odd or inappropriate. (Of course, it would be another story altogether if I had intended to make the shot in the manner in which it occurred.)[17]

I want to suggest that outcome-responsibility in the achievement sense comprises a fundamental element in our understanding of our own agency. I act in the world, intending to achieve some object. If the epistemic probability of success is not too low, then I have the capacity to achieve the outcome I have in mind. If my actions bring it about in a more or less normal manner, then I am responsible for its occurrence; it is properly attributable to the exercise of my agency. This is of course a retrospective judgment, but one that looks to the fact that I possessed the capacity to bring the outcome off, intended to do so, and succeeded. Under those circumstances, I can properly be said to have had control over it. Again, it is important to emphasize that this is partial control only. The knowledge that we only ever have partial or imperfect control over our interactions with the external world is itself a fundamental aspect of our sense of our own agency. Just as there is an epistemic probability that I will succeed in what I am attempting to do, so there is always a counter-probability I will fail. Moreover the manner of the outcome's occurrence must be either not too dissimilar to what I intended or else within the range of what I should expect as normal. Determining the appropriate ranges of epistemic probability and normality are, in part, normative questions, and it may be that the answers we give are partially dependent on the context. There is nonetheless a more or less determinate core conception of outcome-responsibility in the achievement sense that is central to our general understanding of ourselves as agents.

The achievement conception of outcome-responsibility supposes that control over an outcome turns in part on the actor's having possessed a certain state of mind. More particularly, it supposes that the actor acted with an intention to change the world in a certain way, and that he succeeded in that endeavor. This is a paradigmatic instance of one type of control over an outcome. But the actor's mental state is also regarded as important in certain theories of outcome-responsibility that focus, unlike the achievement conception but like the avoidability theory, on bad or harmful outcomes only. For such theories, what seems to matter in a judgment of outcome-responsibility is not intention as such, but rather *awareness* that one's action might bring about a certain type of outcome. Awareness is relevant to control in the following way: if an agent knew of the possibility that his action would or might cause a certain outcome, and if he had the capacity to act otherwise in the appropriate action-responsibility sense, then he could have avoided bringing the outcome about. In other words, control in this context means avoidability. I assume it is uncontroversial that awareness is *relevant* to avoidability. The stronger and more interesting claim is that awareness is not just relevant to, but necessary for, control in this sense. If that claim is correct, then an agent cannot be said to have been capable of avoiding an outcome unless he was aware at the time of acting that his action would or might cause it.

We can call theories that make the strong claim just discussed, and that accordingly make awareness a condition of outcome-responsibility for bad or harmful outcomes, advertence-based theories. The most important such theory maintains that an agent is responsible, in the robust sense of coming under a prima facie obligation to pay compensation, for and only for all the sufficiently proximate harmful outcomes that she intended, or that she was aware were likely to occur, and that she acted in blameworthy fashion in bringing about. Since action-responsibility is concerned with the determination of blameworthiness for reprehensible actions, this theory would bring outcome-responsibility very close to action-responsibility. Further variations on the advertence theme are also possible. For example, one might maintain that an agent is responsible, again in the robust sense of coming under a prima facie obligation to pay compensation, for and only for all the sufficiently proximate harmful outcomes that she intended or was aware were likely to occur, whether or not she was blameworthy in acting as she did. In this variation of an advertence theory, responsibility would extend to harmful outcomes that are the result or consequence of justified actions, including in particular those that are justified by natural necessity.[18]

No advertence-based theory seems capable, at least by itself, of accounting for the full scope of responsibility that we think people can come under for harmful outcomes. This is because we have a strong intuition that an individual can sometimes be responsible for harm even if she did not actually anticipate it (Coleman and Ripstein 1995, pp. 126–7). The law of torts reflects this intuition by imposing liability, on the basis of both strict and negligence-based standards, for a wide range of unintentional harms. The strongest argument for an exclusively advertence-based theory of responsibility for harmful outcomes must therefore be that no other conception of outcome-responsibility yields an acceptable understanding of what it means to have control over a bad or harmful outcome. This is the strong claim mentioned earlier that awareness is necessary for such control, and not simply a factor that would lead us to say that an agent had a particularly notable degree of control over an outcome. I argue in Section VI below that this claim is mistaken, and that in the case of harmful outcomes in particular the avoidability conception offers a morally more defensible account of control. Thus one can meaningfully be said to have had the power to avoid an outcome even when one was not aware at the time of acting that the outcome might eventuate. This is not to say that awareness is not a factor in our assessments of control, or that there is no room for a theory of outcome-responsibility that makes the agent's state of mind critical to control. Thus I am not claiming that we could do without the achievement conception; the type of control that is involved in bringing about an outcome at which one deliberately aims is, clearly, a crucial aspect of our understanding of agency. (Note that in the case of an intended harmful outcome, the achievement and avoidability conceptions will generally overlap.)

The libertarian conception of outcome-responsibility adopts quite a different understanding of control from the advertence-based theories. The basic idea is that I have a choice about whether or not to become active in the world. If I chose to act on a particular occasion, then I am properly regarded as having had control over whatever harmful outcomes my action caused. I could, after all, have avoided those outcomes simply by not acting, and that is so whether I foresaw the outcomes or not, or even whether they were foreseeable or not. The libertarian account equates outcome-responsibility for a harm that I cause someone else (as opposed to a harm that I bring upon myself) with a prima facie moral obligation to compensate the victim for her loss. As I have argued elsewhere, this is because libertarianism regards both the good and the bad outcomes that a person uniquely causes by her actions as an extension of her self-ownership, meaning her ownership of her physical person and her powers of agency (Perry 1997, pp. 363–73). In the case of a good outcome involving the production of a valuable asset, the upshot is a full liberal property right in the asset. This is the familiar libertarian thesis that individuals are entitled to the fruits of their labor; the wealth I produce through my own actions should not be subjected to redistribution by the state. In the case of a bad outcome involving harm to someone else, the upshot is an obligation to compensate the person who suffered the harm. Just as I have a moral right of property to the fruits of my labor, so also do I own, in a strong moral sense, the harms that I cause others. So far as tort law is concerned, the result is a regime of absolute liability.

The libertarian account of outcome-responsibility gives rise to a number of problems. I have discussed these at length elsewhere (Perry 1988, 1997; see also Coleman and Ripstein 1995, pp. 101–8), but let me briefly go over the two main difficulties. The first is that, in general, a harmful outcome to one person cannot plausibly be said to have been caused *uniquely* by the actions of someone else. Unintentional harm of a kind potentially subject to liability in tort is typically caused, on any plausible conception of causation, by actions of both parties; such cases involve a harmful interaction between persons rather than one person unilaterally acting upon, and thereby causing harm to, another. Ronald

Coase made this point some time ago in connection with the economic analysis of externalities (Coase 1960), but it is relevant to non-consequentialist theories of tort law as well. This fact about causation threatens any theory of absolute liability with serious indeterminacy. The libertarian defence of absolute liability that Richard Epstein offered in his early articles (Epstein 1973) for the most part avoids indeterminacy in the legal allocation of losses, but only at the cost of smuggling various notions of moral responsibility into the analysis of causation. The result, apart from a number of internal inconsistencies in the theory, was that he could not plausibly be regarded as presenting an account of causation at all. This is a dilemma that any ostensibly causation-based approach to tort liability will face. If the theory relies on a standard account of causation, it will give rise to significant indeterminacy. If it relies on a non-standard account that is specific to tort law, that account will inevitably extend beyond causation proper to include normative elements of some kind. In the case of Epstein's theory, the dominant normative element is a notion of epistemic risk that brings the theory closer to the avoidability conception of outcome-responsibility than to a true causation-based account (Perry 1988, pp. 161–6).

The second difficulty that the libertarian conception of outcome-responsibility encounters is related to the first. The focus now, however, is on the appropriate understanding of control rather than on the appropriate understanding of causation. Libertarianism claims that a person has control over the harmful outcomes she causes, even if she could not foresee those outcomes, because she could have chosen not to act in the first place. She had, so to speak, a second-order choice about whether or not to become an active being in the world. This assumes there is a morally non-arbitrary distinction between activity and passivity that is marked by the concept of causation: one, active party unilaterally acts upon and causes harm to another, passive party. The problem is that this picture of human interaction is mistaken not only from a conceptual point of view – because it involves an erroneous understanding of causation – but also from a moral point of view. There is no morally meaningful choice about choice. Even a choice to do absolutely nothing, which no one can sustain for very long anyway, has potential consequences for others that render a purely temporal distinction between activity and passivity quite arbitrary. Harm that arises from an interaction between persons is typically caused, as I have already noted, by actions of both parties, and responsibility for the harm is not determined by the fact that one of those actions was later in time than the other. In a moral sense, all autonomous persons must be regarded as active beings at all times.

While I have argued that both the libertarian and advertence-based theories of responsibility for harmful outcomes are problematic, both have nonetheless figured prominently in the philosophical tradition of theorizing about responsibility for harmful outcomes.[19] Such theorizing has not, for the most part, explicitly recognized an independent general concept of outcome-responsibility, but I would like to suggest that implicit in the tradition is precisely such a concept. At the core of that concept is the idea that responsibility for an outcome depends on control over the outcome, where control, in turn, depends on having had the power to act so as to avoid the outcome. A strong advertence theory insists that one can only be said to have had the power to avoid an outcome if one was aware at the time of acting that the outcome might occur.[20] Libertarianism, by contrast, argues that one can be said to have had that power simply by virtue of having caused the outcome, since one could have avoided it by choosing not to act.

The avoidability-based conception offers yet another understanding of both control and avoidability. It suggests, contrary to what libertarianism maintains, that both these notions have an epistemic dimension. There is, to be sure, a sense in which a young child who turns off a faucet avoids the outcome of the bathtub overflowing, even though he does not possess the cognitive capacity to appreciate the connection between what he has done and its consequence.[21] If he avoided the outcome, then he must in some sense have possessed the power to avoid it. This is not, however, the sense of avoidability with which outcome-responsibility should be concerned. At the same time, the avoidability conception does not goes so far as the advertence-based theories and insist that the epistemic aspect of avoidability involves actual awareness of the possibility that the outcome might come about. The power of avoidance depends, rather, on a general capacity to avoid. That general capacity is characterized, in turn, as a capacity to foresee an outcome and a related ability to take steps, on the basis of what could have been foreseen, to avoid it. The epistemic aspect of avoidability resides in the fact that the ability to take preventive steps depends in this way on the capacity to foresee. It depends, in other words, on the capacity to understand that in turning off the faucet one is preventing the bathtub from overflowing. One does not possess the requisite ability to avoid an outcome merely because one has the power to act in a way that would physically stop the outcome from happening.

Outcome-responsibility and action-responsibility are, while distinct concepts, clearly conceptually related in that both necessarily flow from an exercise of agency. But any further connection, and, in particular, the extent to which the two concepts are normatively related, depends on the particular conception of outcome-responsibility one has in mind. Action-responsibility is concerned with the determination of blameworthiness for having engaged in a reprehensible action. Ordinarily this requires both a wrongful act and a culpable state of mind. The advertence-based theory which requires that the agent's precipitating action have been blameworthy – let me call it the blame-based theory – obviously bears a very close moral relationship to action-responsibility. This is especially true given that the outcomes for which one would, according to that theory, be outcome-responsible will often be included in the relevant actions as results, in the technical sense of result that was defined earlier. The libertarian conception of outcome-responsibility, on the other hand, bears little moral relationship to action-responsibility. This is because libertarianism claims that a person can be responsible for outcomes that he not only was not blameworthy in causing, but that he might not have even foreseen.

So far as the moral relationship to action-responsibility is concerned, the avoidability conception of outcome-responsibility falls somewhere between libertarianism and the blame-oriented advertence theory. Like libertarianism, it permits responsibility for outcomes to extend beyond those caused by blameworthy actions. But, like the blame-based theory, it also involves a normative connection to blameworthiness, albeit a more complicated one. One way to characterize that connection is by means of H. L. A. Hart's capacity/opportunity principle, which says that "[w]hat is crucial is that those whom we punish should have had, when they acted, the normal capacities, physical and mental, for doing what the law requires and abstaining from what it forbids, and a fair opportunity to exercise those capacities" (Hart 1968, p. 152). This principle is nowadays generally regarded as a side constraint on judgments of action-responsibility.[22] It tells us that, in a case in which the question of action-responsibility for a harm-causing action is at issue, the actor must have had both the capacity to foresee the harm and the ability and opportunity to avoid it before he may be blamed or punished for his action. The criteria of foreseeability and avoidability thus qualify and constrain the fundamental judgments that an action was wrongful and performed with a culpable state of mind. The avoidability-based conception of outcome-responsibility takes these same two criteria – the capacity to foresee the harm and the ability, on the basis of such foresight, to avoid it – and treats them as necessary and sufficient conditions for responsibility for harmful outcomes as such. Thus what is a *constraint* on judgments of action-responsibility becomes the *core* of a judgment of outcome-responsibility. The blame-oriented theory, by contrast, sees the two types of judgment as almost identical. Libertarianism sees them as having almost nothing to do with one another.

So far as the relationship between outcome-responsibility and action-responsibility is concerned, then, the avoidability conception can be understood as falling between the opposed poles of libertarianism and the blame-based theory. Yet in another respect these latter two approaches resemble one another and contrast with the avoidability conception. Both libertarianism and the blame theory effectively equate outcome-responsibility with a prima facie moral obligation to compensate.[23] The avoidability conception, however, treats outcome-responsibility as a necessary but not a sufficient condition for the existence of such an obligation. As was noted earlier, outcome-responsibility is, on this view, a plateau of responsibility that is compatible with both strict and negligence-based regimes of liability in tort. I will argue in subsequent sections that outcome-responsibility is best conceived in this way, i.e., as a potential basis for, rather than as equivalent to, a moral obligation to compensate. For now I will simply observe that in *The Common Law* Oliver Wendell Holmes in effect defended the avoidability conception of outcome-responsibility in just this mediating form (Holmes 1963). Holmes criticized versions of both the blame-based theory and libertarianism, arguing that harm must be both reasonably foreseeable and avoidable before liability in tort can be imposed. But he did not, as some commentators have thought, treat foreseeability and avoidability as defining the content of negligence. Rather he treated them as the moral preconditions of tortious liability in general, where the standard of liability could be either strict liability or negligence (Rosenberg 1995, pp. 69–97). The choice between these two liability regimes was to be made on other grounds.

Finally, before turning to a more detailed discussion of the avoidability conception, it will be helpful to consider an argument advanced by Arthur Ripstein to the effect that responsibility of the kind underlying tort law – in my terms, outcome-responsibility – does not and cannot depend on any notion of control. Ripstein argues that "[i]f we relieve [the defendant] of responsibility for something he cannot control, we impose the same responsibility on [the plaintiff] for something that *he* could not control. There is no way to retreat to equating responsibility with control" (Ripstein 1994, p. 13). The argument, in other words, is that responsibility cannot depend upon control because responsibility cannot be avoided: if one party is not held responsible, the other will be. Ripstein makes clear an implicit presupposition upon which this conclusion rests when he writes that "'responsible for' means something like 'must bear the costs of'" (Ripstein 1994, p. 19 note 31). As Ripstein also puts the point, responsibility is a matter of answering the question, "Whose bad luck is this?" (Ripstein 1994, pp. 7, 10). This is said to be the fundamental question of *political* philosophy. Bad luck – and hence costs – are to be assigned on normative grounds, according to some appropriate conception of equality; in tort law this conception is determined, according to Ripstein, by the standard of care.

This is, however, a very problematic understanding of responsibility. We do not ordinarily think that one or the other of the parties to a harmful interaction must be regarded as responsible for the harm, any more than the law insists that one or the other of the parties must be held liable for it. If the defendant is not held liable, we do not impute liability to the plaintiff; it is just that the plaintiff must bear the loss because, as a matter of contingent fact, that is where it fell. Under those circumstances, no one is liable. The logic of responsibility is not precisely parallel to that of liability, since it is certainly possible for the person who suffers a loss to be responsible for its occurrence. But the two notions do have this in common: we do not insist that someone *must* be held either responsible or liable for a given harm.

There is a deeper point at issue here than the proper usage of the term "responsible for."[24] Ripstein maintains that responsibility for harmful outcomes is a political notion that rests on a conception of equality. This suggests in turn that the issue in tort law is one of allocating a loss between a plaintiff and a defendant on the basis of a criterion that in some appropriate sense treats the parties as equals. This makes the issue sound like one of distributive rather than corrective justice, and it comes as no surprise to learn that Ripstein believes the same conception of responsibility is at work in both areas. The difficulty is that distributive justice seems to take over the field entirely, leaving no room for any conception of corrective justice as traditionally conceived. It is thus not clear why we should be concerned, in allocating the costs of accidents, with a requirement that has always been regarded as fundamental to both corrective justice and tort law, namely, the requirement of causation. Why not, for example, share some costs, and perhaps all, across society as a whole?

Ripstein acknowledges that his political conception of responsibility allows for the general sharing of costs. The trouble is that a conception of responsibility that underwrites this possibility seems unable to account for our intuitions about personal responsibility for causing harm. Our concern in the latter context is not with the allocation of loss on the basis of norms of equality, but rather with the fact that one person has *done something* to another for which he is potentially morally accountable. The blame-based, libertarian, and avoidability-based conceptions of outcome-responsibility all provide different answers to the question of when one person has, in the appropriate moral sense, done something to someone else. It is true that, in tort law, if the defendant is not found liable, the loss remains with the plaintiff; as an empirical matter, someone must indeed bear the costs. But this does not mean that the plaintiff is necessarily *responsible* for the costs, nor do any of the theories just mentioned so regard him. He might be outcome-responsible for the harm he has suffered, but then again he might not be. Ripstein seemingly tries to finesse this issue by talking, in the tort context in particular, not just of bearing costs but of *bearing the costs of one's activities.* While this formulation does sound more like a conception of individual responsibility, the following point should be borne in mind. If the content of the notion of bearing the costs of one's activities is provided not by a conception of outcome-responsibility and an associated conception of control, but rather by the idea of distributing costs according to a norm of equality, then the notion is doing no work. Ripstein would do better if he were to drop the misleading talk of requiring people to bear the costs of their activities and were instead simply to speak of allocating costs in accordance with a conception of distributive justice.

He would do better still, however, to stop talking about responsibility altogether. Our intuitions about responsibility for harmful outcomes all consistently suggest that this is a moral rather than a political notion. An argument attempting to uproot these intuitions must do more than stipulatively define "responsibility" as "bearing costs" and then point out that responsibility cannot involve control because costs must always be borne by somebody, whether he had control over those costs or not.

## IV. Avoidability as the Basis of Outcome-Responsibility

In this and subsequent sections I wish to defend and further develop the avoidability-based conception of outcome-responsibility. In Sections V and VI, I will discuss the crucial elements of foreseeability and capacity respectively. First, however, I would like to say something further about the general character and justification of this conception. The basic idea, to repeat, is that an agent is outcome-responsible for a harmful outcome if and only if he causally contributed to it, possessed the capacity to foresee it, and had the ability and opportunity to take steps, on the basis of what could have been foreseen, to avoid it.[25] To say that someone had the capacity to foresee harm is, of course, perfectly compatible both with his having actually foreseen the harm and with his not having foreseen it; it is compatible, in other words, with both awareness of risk and lack of awareness. It should also be noted that to say that someone *could* have taken steps to avoid a harm does not mean that he *should* have done so. To say that he should have taken steps is to say that he was at fault in some way. Fault, in the form of negligence, is one possible standard for recognizing an obligation to compensate, but, as we shall see, strict liability is a possible standard as well. Strict liability may properly be imposed even when we cannot say that the defendant should have taken steps to avoid the relevant harm.

An important preliminary argument for the claims that, first, outcome-responsibility is an important non-consequentialist moral notion in its own right, and second, that responsibility for harmful outcomes is best understood in terms of the avoidability conception, is that both claims help to make comprehensive sense of our considered convictions about agency and responsibility generally. Thus we have a strong intuition that responsibility for outcomes is distinct from, and extends beyond, responsibility for actions. At the same time, however, we have a deep sense that our practices concerning responsibility are significantly interconnected. The most important point to note with respect to this latter point is that the notions of foreseeability and avoidability underlie not just outcome-responsibility in the avoidability sense, but also Hart's capacity/opportunity principle. This means, as we have seen, that the same moral elements that constrain a judgment of blameworthiness lie at the core of a judgment of outcome-responsibility for harm. This fact helps both to support and to articulate more precisely our strong sense that the concepts of action-responsibility and outcome-responsibility are fundamentally linked.

The avoidability conception similarly helps to make clear what it is that we find appealing about advertence-based theories of outcome-responsibility, and, more generally, why we think that awareness of a possible harmful outcome is relevant to a judgment of outcome-responsibility. Awareness is relevant because it suggests that the agent had the power to avoid causing the outcome and, in that sense, had control over it. A power to avoid an outcome based on awareness is, however, just a special case of the capacity to foresee and avoid outcomes that inheres in the avoidability conception. If an agent was aware of the likelihood of a given outcome and was capable of acting on that awareness to prevent its occurrence, then *a fortiori* he had the capacity to foresee the outcome and the ability to act, on the basis of what could have been foreseen, so as to avoid it. Here too, we find the linked notions of foreseeability and avoidability contributing to our overall sense of what it means to be a responsible moral agent.

Consider next the thesis that outcome-responsibility is a necessary but not a sufficient condition for the existence of a moral obligation to compensate for harm caused. The main argument for this thesis is that it offers the most coherent non-consequentialist account of our intuition that both negligence and strict liability can be appropriate standards for recognizing and enforcing an obligation to compensate. Outcome-responsibility in the avoidability sense is the moral element that these two standards have in common, as well as the philosophical foundation upon which each of the standards necessarily builds. Of course, the force of this argument depends in large part upon a more precise delineation of the role that the avoidability conception plays in characterizing and justifying the two standards within a single theory of corrective justice. These are matters that are taken up in Section VII.

Outcome-responsibility is a normative notion in the specific sense that it affects our reasons for action. According to the avoidability conception, it does so in a more diffuse way than either libertarianism or the blame-based theory. The blame-based theory equates outcome-responsibility with a prima facie obligation to compensate for intentional or knowing instances of harmful wrongdoing, while libertarianism equates outcome-responsibility with a prima facie obligation to compensate simply for causing harm. The avoidability conception, because it is a plateau of responsibility in the sense earlier described, sometimes grounds a negligence-based obligation to compensate, and sometimes an obligation of foresight-based strict liability. Sometimes, however, it grounds no obligation of compensation at all. Depending on the circumstances, it may do no more than give an agent a reason to apologize, obtain assistance, retract a statement, refrain from a certain course of action in the future, and so on.

The normative power of this conception of outcome-responsibility resides in the idea that the exercise of a person's positive agency, under circumstances in which a harmful outcome could have been foreseen and avoided, leads us to regard her as the author of the outcome. Others can appropriately say of her, and she can say of herself, that she did it, and this is true even if other factors (some of which might be the acts of other persons) also causally contributed to the harm.[26] The agent acted and caused harm under circumstances in which she had a sufficient degree of control to avoid its occurrence, and for that reason she has a special responsibility for the outcome that other persons do not have.

That we view outcome-responsibility as reason-affecting in this way is part of our deepest self-understanding of what it means to be a moral agent capable of both acting in the world and acknowledging responsibility for what one has done.

It is true that the mere fact of causal involvement in a harm can properly affect one's reasons for action in various weak ways.[27] For that matter, non-voluntary causal involvement (e.g., hitting someone while in the throes of an unpredictable epileptic fit), or involvement that is not causal at all (witnessing or coming upon the scene of an accident) may similarly affect one's reasons for action.[28] But, unlike outcome-responsibility, these circumstances affect reasons for action in ways that are not deeply rooted in the concept of moral agency itself. Rather they reflect the idea that we should, when directly confronted with occasions of human suffering, do what we can to alleviate that suffering. Such cases involve an overridable reason, not an obligation. In the absence of the key element of having caused an outcome over which one had control, these circumstances do not give rise to the possibility of a true non-consequentialist obligation, legitimately enforceable by the state, to compensate for loss. Only the moral proximity that comes from having caused harm that one could have foreseen and avoided can make the plaintiff and defendant "neighbors" in a sufficiently strong moral sense to ground an obligation of compensation.[29]

In the nature of things, the victim of a harmful interaction will have to bear the loss if no one else has an enforceable obligation to compensate her. If the other party to the interaction was outcome-responsible for the harm, then he potentially has such an obligation. He is properly singled out as a possible bearer of the loss, in a way that it would be unfair to single out anyone else who did not have a similar degree of control over the occurrence of the outcome.[30] But then we must ask, what else is required, in a case of unintentional harm, to justify an obligation to compensate? I shall deal with this question at some length in Section VII, but the short answer is as follows. There are two main circumstances in which an obligation to compensate is justified. The first arises when the actor was in an appropriate sense at fault; not only could he have avoided the harm, but he should have done so. The second is concerned with situations where the actor's outcome-responsibility can properly be said to involve, on normative grounds that we will presently explore, the imposition of a risk on the other person. The fact that there was an *imposition* of risk does not entail that the risk should not have been imposed, however, so a form of strict liability is involved.

A crucial aspect of outcome-responsibility in the avoidability sense is its understanding of what it means to have control over an outcome. As in the case of the achievement conception that was discussed in the preceding section, only partial or imperfect control is involved. A judgment of outcome-responsibility states after the fact that the actor could have foreseen the outcome of his action and taken steps to avoid it. This means, among other things, that taking those steps would in fact have avoided the outcome; otherwise, the actor's action was not a cause of what happened.[31] But the requisite understanding of control does not require that the actor could have known to a certainty that taking those steps would have avoided the harm. All that is required is that there have been, looking at the matter from the agent's perspective at the time that he acted, an epistemic probability exceeding a certain threshold that the outcome would have been avoided. The determination of that threshold is, as we shall see in Section VII, a normative matter.

Similarly, the requisite understanding of control does not require that the outcome have appeared to have been, again looking at the matter from the agent's perspective at the time that he acted, an inevitable consequence of *not* taking the relevant preventive steps. All that is required is that the harm be reasonably foreseeable. Foreseeability involves a notion of epistemic probability. The determination of what constitutes *reasonable* foreseeability is, as we shall see in Section VI, a normative matter. In general, the epistemic probability that will support a judgment of reasonable foreseeability need not be particularly high. In a case of unintentional harm, it is typically much more likely that the harmful outcome will not materialize than that it will. Nonetheless, given the facts that the actor caused the harm, could have foreseen it, and was in a position to avoid its occurrence, we rightly regard him as having had control over what eventuated.

The fact that both the achievement and avoidability conceptions of outcome-responsibility involve notions of control that are only partial or incomplete is relevant to the problem of moral luck. This is not an issue that I can deal with at length here, but at least a brief discussion is in order. Suppose that I unjustifiably shoot at someone with the intention of killing him. This is obviously a blameworthy thing to do, whether I succeed in killing my would-be victim or not. Now compare the situation where I succeed in killing the person with the situation where I do not. One of the puzzles of moral luck is why I should be regarded as *more* blameworthy, or at least as morally more responsible in some sense, in the situation where I succeed in killing than in the situation where I do not. By hypothesis, I did all I could at the time of the shooting to bring about the death; after I pulled the trigger, I had no further control over the situation.

However, the description of the puzzle just given is probably not the best way to look at the matter. We may assume, to begin, that I had appropriate control over my action (under the description of shooting with intent to kill), which is to say that the applicable criteria of action-responsibility, whatever they are, have been met.[32] If the shot misses, that action is all that I can be blamed for; there is no outcome, in the form of a death, for which I can be held responsible as well. If, however, the shot hits and kills my would-be victim – now no longer would-be – I am, in addition to being subject to blame for the act of shooting, outcome-responsible for the death; it is a consequence that I could have foreseen and taken steps to avoid. So I can appropriately be said to have had control over the outcome, even though the matter was out of my hands once I had taken my shot. This is because the ordinary concepts of control and responsibility that are at work here take into consideration the fact that other factors besides my efforts are in play, and that I therefore cannot guarantee my own success.[33] Moral luck is thus involved, but there is nothing puzzling or paradoxical about it. Given the way things turned out, I have an extra increment of responsibility that I would not have had in the alternative scenario. This is, to be sure, a different form of responsibility from blameworthiness. However, since I not only *could* have taken steps to avoid the outcome but, given the nature of my action, *should* have done so, it seems reasonable to think that in such cases outcome-responsibility has the effect of increasing blameworthiness. To put the point in the language of action, an act of deliberately killing another is inherently more blameworthy than an act of shooting at another with intent to kill.

Before we move on, two general points about the relationship between tort law and the avoidability conception of outcome-responsibility deserve mention here. The first concerns the requirement in tort of proximate causation (known in England as remoteness). Outcome-responsibility has a forward-looking aspect – foreseeability – and a backward-looking aspect – causation. In the context of negligence law in particular, the foreseeability aspect means, first, that the plaintiff must fall into a class of persons who were foreseeably put at risk of suffering harm of a foreseeable type, and second, that at least the initial harm the plaintiff suffered must have been of that foreseeable type. The first requirement is a matter of the duty of care,[34] while the second has come to be accepted as the basic principle of proximate cause.[35] In defending the avoidability conception, I am not, however, defending the thesis that "a defendant is responsible [in negligence law] for and only for such harm as he could reasonably have foreseen and prevented" (Hart and Honoré 1985, p. 255). There are many facets to the law of proximate cause in addition to the basic foreseeability principle. Some of these, moreover, seem to be built into the concept of outcome-responsibility itself. Consider, for example, our earlier discussion of the meaning of control under the achievement conception of outcome-responsibility. The outcomes for which a person is responsible under that conception must not only be intended but also "sufficiently proximate"; thus I am not outcome-responsible in the achievement sense for winning the lottery, or for sinking a snooker ball in the corner pocket if that outcome was just a fluke. Both the achievement and avoidability conceptions of outcome-responsibility are subject to a similar, normatively determined limitation along these lines. If a foreseeable type of harm occurs in too freakish or improbable a manner, there is insufficient control over the outcome to support a judgment of outcome-responsibility; if the harm was unintentional, there is also no liability in tort.

In law, some doctrines of proximate cause limit liability, even for foreseeable harm, while others extend liability, at times going beyond the foreseeable.

The doctrine discussed in the preceding paragraph is a limiting doctrine. Another is the rule that sufficiently culpable causal contribution by an intervening actor will relieve a negligent tortfeasor (but not an intentional wrongdoer) of liability. An example of an extending doctrine is the rule that a defendant is liable for both the tortious and non-tortious medical exacerbation of personal injury, so long as the exacerbation does not take too freakish or unusual a form. Another is the thin-skull rule, which holds that, so long as an initial injury to the person was foreseeable, the defendant is liable for all further personal injury, whether it is foreseeable or not, that flows directly from the initial harm. Yet another extending doctrine is embodied in the old legal saying that no intended result is too remote.

The examples just enumerated suggest, and many commentators on the subject have come to accept, that the legal concept of proximate causation is not a single moral principle but rather a grab bag of differing normative considerations. I suggested earlier that the limitation on liability in cases involving a freakish or highly improbable chain of events inheres in the concept of outcome-responsibility itself. Given the heterogeneous nature of proximate cause doctrines as a whole, however, there is no reason to think that they will all turn out to be aspects of outcome-responsibility. Some may have their source in principles or policies that are considered to be of independent normative significance in tort law. In the case of intervening culpable actors, for example, the independent principle might be something like this: blameworthiness generally trumps non-blameworthiness in the legal allocation of loss. It will not be possible to sort out all the complexities of the relationship between outcome-responsibility and proximate causation here, but the following point should be noted. It is quite conceivable that some of the extending doctrines of proximate cause lead to liability being imposed for harms for which the defendant was not truly outcome-responsible.[36] That does not seem to be a problematic conclusion, however, because tort law is a morally complex practice that weaves together many different normative strands. Sometimes the law imposes liability in tort for outcomes for which the defendant not only was not outcome-responsible, but which he did not – or at least probably did not – cause in fact. The doctrine of respondeat superior offers one such example, market-share liability another.[37] Thus my claim is not that outcome-responsibility must be present in every instance of liability in tort. It is, rather, that outcome-responsibility must be present in the central cases of tort liability, and that it must play a significant role in any theory which hopes to explain at least the fundamental principles of tort law in non-consequentialist terms.

The second general point I wish to mention here about the relationship between tort law and outcome-responsibility concerns omissions. For the most part, tort law imposes liability for unintentional harm only in situations where the defendant acted and, in acting, caused harm. It generally does not impose liability simply for failing to prevent harm. In the language of the common law, liability is ordinarily imposed for misfeasance but not for nonfeasance. This is fully in accord with the conception of outcome-responsibility that I have been developing, which supposes that outcome-responsibility for a harmful outcome requires not only that an agent have been able to prevent foreseeable harm, but that she actually have caused it by an action.[38] The reasons for this requirement cannot be fully explored here, but they have to do with the fact that outcome-responsibility is an aspect of our self-understanding as agents and is consequently only triggered by an exercise of agency. A related consideration is that non-consequentialism in the broadest sense involves a sphere of liberty or autonomy within which we are permitted to act unimpeded by the demands of others. We can, of course, incur affirmative obligations to others through special relationships and voluntary undertakings, and tort law properly imposes liability for harm that flows from the breach of these obligations.[39] But such liability is exceptional and, in my view, it is not even causal in character; omissions should not be regarded as causes (Moore 1999, pp. 31–4). None of this means, of course, that we do not owe positive duties that are rooted in considerations of, e.g., distributive justice. But these duties are unlikely to be owed to specific individuals, and hence are unlikely to ground obligations to compensate others for particular losses the latter have suffered.

From now on, unless otherwise indicated, I shall use the term "outcome-responsibility" to refer exclusively to the avoidability conception. In Section VII I will take up in greater detail the question of when, in the standard misfeasance cases, outcome-responsibility is translated into an enforceable obligation to compensate. First, however, we must deal with two possible objections to the account of outcome-responsibility that I have been developing. The first concerns the notion of foreseeability, and the second concerns the notion of capacity.

## V. The Coherence of Foreseeability

A key component of outcome-responsibility is provided by the concept of foreseeability. Foreseeability builds upon a notion of epistemic probability. To explain epistemic probability, we must first understand objective probability.[40] The most satisfactory account of objective probability (and hence of objective risk) looks to the relative frequency of an attribute (for example, the attribute of being involved in a car crash) within a reference class of events or objects that are in some appropriate way similar (for example, the class of instances of driving at 30 m.p.h. above the speed limit). Foreseeability is a function of epistemic probability, which looks not to relative frequency *tout court* but rather to the state of our knowledge of and beliefs about relative frequency. The most satisfactory account of epistemic probability maintains that such probabilities involve estimations of relative frequency that have been made, relative to a given body of evidence, in accordance with accepted standards of inductive reasoning and rational belief.[41] If such standards can properly be regarded as inter-subjectively valid, then there is a sense in which epistemic probability judgments can be said to be objective. This accords with the understanding of foreseeability that figures in tort law, which is usually labelled *reasonable* foreseeability. An event of a given type is said to be reasonably foreseeable if it would have been foreseen by a reasonable or ordinary person. What a reasonable or ordinary person would foresee must presumably be characterized by reference to, *inter alia,* appropriately informal, commonly employed, and, one hopes, intersubjectively valid standards for assessing relative frequencies.

However, an account of epistemic probability and foreseeability that is developed along the above lines runs up against the following objection. Suppose I am walking on the sidewalk near a building under construction, and one of the workers accidentally drops a brick on my head. Was this a foreseeable event? This depends on the epistemic probability of the event, which depends in turn on the objective probability. The difficulty is, there is no such thing as *the* objective probability of any given event. There are indefinitely many such probabilities, depending on which reference class of event-types, together with which attribute, we initially decide to focus on. Should we look to the class of events described as being present on a tall structure? Working on a construction site? Working on a construction site with bricks in an urban setting? Working on a construction site with bricks in an urban setting at a height of approximately 30 feet while wearing a checked jacket? The particular event that concerns us falls, we may assume, within all of these reference classes, and many more besides. Similar problems arise in specifying the attribute within the reference class, the relative frequency of which will give us an objective probability. Is the attribute the dropping of an object on a human head? The dropping of a brick on the head of a law professor? The dropping of a brick that produces an imprint of a minutely specified pattern on a law professor's skull? The event in question, we may assume, possessed all of these attributes, and many others as well. The objective probability, and hence the epistemic probability, and hence the judgment as to whether the event was foreseeable, are all relative to which reference class and attribute we decide to employ. But there is no correct or canonical answer to the question of which reference class and attribute we should choose. Thus the concept of foreseeability seems to be completely indeterminate.[42]

Notice that we have so far been talking about objective probabilities. Our concern is thus with the actual relative frequency of an attribute within a reference class, whatever that relative frequency might be. Presumably this is a determinate matter, whether or not we know what the relative frequency is, and whether or not we are even in a position to describe the relevant reference class or the attribute whose frequency yields the probability. It is sometimes said that probability is basically an epistemic phenomenon, and that the "real" probability of any event is one or zero. But this is wrong. Clearly there is a sense in which the probability of any event that has happened is one, since we can define a reference class containing that event alone. Perhaps there is also a sense in which we can say, in a deterministic universe, that the probability of an event that *will* happen is one, and that the probability of an event that did not happen or that will not happen is zero. The categories of cases mentioned in the preceding sentence are complicated, however, by the fact that the events in question do not (yet) exist, and so presumably cannot be referred to by a rigid designator. While it is perhaps possible to pick out such events by appropriately formulated and sufficiently precise definite descriptions, this is very far from our usual practice. Our usual practice, at least in the case of future possible events, is to speak of *types* of events, using general descriptions that in turn define different reference classes. As has already been noted, there is no correct or canonical answer to the question of which description we should use in trying to anticipate the future. Associated with different reference classes are different relative frequencies, and these will often lie between zero and one. Because these relative frequencies exist whether we know about them or not, they are objective and not just epistemic probabilities.

Two points emerge from the discussion in the preceding paragraph. First, objective probabilities besides one and zero exist. Second, there are many such objective probabilities that exist in connection with any given particular event (past, present, or future). Perhaps the best way to appreciate both points is to note that an objective probability is just a relative frequency, and a relative frequency is a property not of particular entities but rather of classes of (possible) entities.[43] In the case of events, a probability judgment thus necessarily applies, logically speaking, to event-types rather than to particular events. Since any given event is a token of many different event-types, there are many different objective probabilities that exist in connection with it. The resulting indeterminacy is built into the universe, and is not just a function of our epistemic limitations.[44] But since epistemic probability is a function of objective probability, the indeterminacy carries over to the concept of foreseeability.

On the basis of considerations similar to those that have just been canvassed, Michael Moore argues that foreseeability, understood as a criterion of proximate causation and, I assume, of duty of care, is not only an indeterminate but also an incoherent notion (Moore 1993). Moore characterizes the problem in terms of descriptions instead of reference classes, but the basic point is the same. As Moore points out, harm is only foreseeable under a description, and there is no uniquely correct description of any given harm. The more general the description, the likelier we are to say that the harm was foreseeable; the more restrictive the description, the less likely we are to say this. In making these points Moore recognizes that foreseeability is best understood as referring to *types* of harm rather than to particular instances of harm. This is because foreseeability is concerned with future rather than with existing or past events, and it is very implausible to suppose that it depends upon a relation between a mental state and a particular future event (Moore 1993, pp. 142, 147). The event in question does not, after all, yet exist. It therefore makes most sense to think that, in foreseeing possible future harm, we are not referring to particular harmful events but rather using a general description to pick out a certain type or category of harmful event.

Moore argues that to salvage the concept of foreseeability from indeterminacy and incoherence we need a shared typology of events that we do not, in fact, possess. But it is by no means evident that we do not possess such a typology, or, if not a full-blown typology, then at least a shared capacity to generate similar descriptions that can serve as the basis of foreseeability on particular occasions. Hart and Honoré suggest that in order to tame the problem of foreseeability and multiple descriptions "the first question to ask is not 'Was this harm foreseeable?' but 'Under what specific description which fits this harm has experience taught us to anticipate harm?'"[45] Dealing with the same problem in another context, they similarly maintain that the criteria of appropriate description, as well as the likelihood of the event in question (i.e., the relative frequency of the designated event-type within a larger class of event-types) will be supplied by considering the common knowledge available to ordinary persons.[46] While acknowledging that a certain degree of indeterminacy is unavoidable, they argue that the common knowledge and shared categories of ordinary persons are sufficient to make the foreseeability criterion workable across a wide range of cases.[47] This was also the conclusion of Clarence Morris (1952).

Hart and Honoré's approach to the problem of multiple descriptions thus suggests that the test for reasonable foreseeability in tort law should be the capacity of the *ordinary* person to foresee harm.[48] In the process of applying this test, the trier of fact will take account of (1) the level of generalization that ordinary persons typically bring to bear in describing and categorizing relevant event-types, and (2) the common knowledge that can be expected to be available to ordinary persons regarding the probability of those event-types. This approach is entirely in accord with modern tort doctrine. It is, moreover, a very plausible view of the matter. It is evident that typical human beings, or at least typical persons within a given society, share a roughly similar way of conceptualizing the world in which they live. As J. L. Austin expressed the point, we tend to perceive the world in terms of medium-sized dry goods, rather than break it down into larger, smaller, less stable, less contiguous, or more abstract entities. It seems reasonable to think that the similarities among our individual conceptual schemes are vastly greater than the differences, and that this fact is bound to be reflected in the categories we use to anticipate events in the future.

That we should agree to the extent that we apparently do about how to describe the world, and about which categories to use in describing it, is scarcely surprising, since a shared conceptual scheme is a very useful instrument from both the individual and the social perspectives.[49] Such a scheme facilitates cooperation, makes it easier to coordinate conduct, and helps to fix the reciprocal expectations we hold regarding one another's behavior. These points also serve to answer Moore's secondary argument that even if we do possess a common typology of harms, it could only have come about because of normatively irrelevant factors, such as the response-time it takes to recognize a particular thing as belonging to this category rather than to that one (Moore 1993, p.151). Such factors are indeed normatively irrelevant, but that does not entail that the same is true of the typology itself. A shared conceptual scheme, however it might have come about, is morally significant just by virtue of its existence. And because such a scheme strongly influences our expectations vis-à-vis one another and facilitates the coordination of our activities, that significance clearly extends to the characterization of foreseeable harm-types.

The considerations adduced by Hart and Honoré should not be taken to mean that people will always converge on the same categorization of events to such a degree that indeterminacy will be virtually eliminated from judgments of foreseeability. That is clearly far from the case, and Hart and Honoré do not claim otherwise. But the indeterminacy becomes manageable; there is enough agreement, enough of the time, to make foreseeability a normatively useful concept. It should also be noted that the manageability of the concept does not depend on our being able to say, with respect to a given situation of prospective action, that there must be just one way of categorizing the possible harm that might result. Generally there will be a number of perspectives from which the question of foreseeability can be raised, at which point the "typology of the ordinary" will help to channel how we think about what might happen in the future. There are two perspectives in particular that are of interest in the context of corrective justice and tort law. One is the perspective of the activity or action as such. If I engage in this activity at all, is harm to someone else foreseeable? The other perspective involves the particular manner of carrying on the activity. If I proceed in such and such a manner, is harm foreseeable? And if I take such and such precautions, will the risk be reduced or eliminated? The "untaken precautions" (Grady 1989) upon which we can expect attention to converge will be, again, suggested by the typology of the ordinary. We can call these two perspectives the activity perspective and the specific precaution perspective.[50] As we shall see in Section VII, they turn out to be useful in the explication of when outcome-responsibility gives rise to an obligation to compensate.

## VI. The Meaning of Capacity to Foresee

As I have characterized outcome-responsibility, a person is outcome-responsible for a particular result or consequence of her action if and only if she had the capacity to foresee the outcome and the ability to take steps to avoid it. But now we encounter another potential difficulty, which concerns what it means to say that a person has a capacity, and, in particular, a capacity to foresee. Two initial observations are in order here. First, if outcome-responsibility is to figure in a

theoretical interpretation of tort law, then it will have to be understood as in-
corporating an objective account of *reasonable* foreseeability along the lines
sketched at the beginning of Section V. But, second, it is natural to say that
avoidability, as a moral concept, must look to a subjective capacity to avoid
harm, and hence to a subjective capacity to foresee it. It was, after all, the presence of a measure of control that seemed to Holmes to confer moral force on
the notion of avoidability, and if we do not adopt a subjective view of the capacity to foresee and avoid harm, then there will presumably be cases of outcome-responsibility in which the actor had no meaningful control over the outcome. How, if at all, can these two points be reconciled?

The first point to be made in response to the question just posed is that we
are dealing here not with a single distinction between objectivity and subjectivity, but rather with a number of related such distinctions. The notion of reasonable foreseeability, as it figures in both tort law and in an acceptable account
of outcome-responsibility, is objective in its *content*. The law's determination
of which risks must be foreseen by an agent is based upon, among other things,
an appropriate understanding of the intersubjective criteria that underpin judgments of epistemic probability (more particularly, an understanding expressed
in terms of the judgments of an ordinary or reasonable person). The standard of
due care in negligence law is similarly objective in its content: the precautions
the law requires in a given situation of risk are determined by what a reasonable person, rather than the individual defendant, thinks should be done. But
norms are almost always objective so far as their content is concerned; it is not
up to the individual agent to decide what constitutes, say, murder. The notions
of reasonable foreseeability and due care are also objective in another sense,
which is that neither requires *advertence*. The individual agent need not be
aware, on the particular occasion, either that she is creating risks or taking inadequate precautions to prevent those risks from materializing. This is an important form of the objective/subjective distinction in criminal law. Strong
forms of the advertence-based theories of outcome-responsibility make the
claim, as we saw in Section III, that awareness of the risk of an outcome is a
necessary condition of having had control over that outcome. The basic idea is
that an agent does not have the power to avoid an outcome unless she was actually aware, at the time of acting, that her action might bring it about.

I will respond to the direct challenge of the advertence-based theories in a
moment. First, however, we need to observe that there is a third form of the ob-
jective-subjective distinction, in addition to those focusing on content and advertence, that is relevant to outcome-responsibility. This third distinction concerns the notion of capacity itself. An objective interpretation of the capacities
to foresee and avoid a harm would look exclusively to whether a reasonable or
ordinary person is capable of foreseeing that type of outcome and then acting
so as to avoid it. A competing subjective interpretation of capacity need not suppose, however, that an individual is actually aware of the possibility that he

might cause an outcome of the relevant type. Nor need such an interpretation assume that an individual who caused harm was capable of acting otherwise on that very occasion. Another possible subjective interpretation is that the capacities to foresee and avoid harmful outcomes are appropriately understood as *general* abilities that the individual who caused a given harm ordinarily succeeds in exercising in other, similar situations.[51] Whether the person was capable of foreseeing and avoiding the harm on the particular occasion may or may not be a meaningful question, but either way it is possession of the general capacity that matters, so far as moral responsibility is concerned. It is in this sense that the avoidability-based conception of outcome-responsibility treats the capacities to foresee and avoid harm as subjective.

Notice that, so far, we have done no more than establish a conceptual possibility concerning how one might understand the capacities to foresee and avoid a harm. This does not constitute a response to the substantive challenge of the strong advertence theories. The claim is simply that, in making judgments of outcome-responsibility for harmful outcomes, objectivity regarding content and advertence is perfectly compatible with subjectivity regarding the capacities to foresee and avoid, so long as we understand these capacities in the way described in the preceding paragraph. Even before we get to the challenge of the advertence theories, however, this understanding of the notion of capacity seems open to the following objection. What does it mean, exactly, to say that an individual possesses a general capacity? It seems implausible to say that this is a purely statistical notion that is based solely on the particular individual's rate of success in avoiding harm in other, similar, situations. For one thing, there does not seem to be any determinate baseline for judging what success rate would be sufficient for possession of the general capacity. If the notion of a general capacity cannot be understood purely statistically, however, it seems inevitable that it must be understood at least partly in normative terms. But if the notion of general capacity is normative in nature, then the worry arises that we must have recourse, in determining responsibility for outcomes, to judgments about what an actor should or should not have done. There is a concern, in other words, that we must look to action-guiding norms of the kind that figure in the negligence standard of reasonable care. But if that is true, outcome-responsibility seems to collapse into a conception of fault. There does not seem to be room for a separate, prior judgment of outcome-responsibility, of the kind the avoidability conception claims to involve.[52]

The answer to this objection is that, while the general capacities to foresee and avoid harm are to be characterized partly in normative terms, their characterization does not require reference to action-guiding norms. We are concerned with natural capacities that people really do have, but which they possess in differing degrees. Some people can foresee possible future outcomes more often than others, and some are sufficiently out of touch with reality that they possess only the most minimal capacity to predict the consequences of their actions. A line has to be drawn to determine what degree of the capacity a person must possess before he or she is capable of being outcome-responsible at all. We draw the line normatively, with an eye to what constitutes meaningful agency in the world. That, in turn, seems inevitably to require looking, not to action-guiding norms, but rather to the degree of capacity regularly exercised by ordinary or average people who strike us as possessing meaningful agency. That is a partly statistical exercise, but one guided by a normative ideal that emerges from our inquiry into what it means for beings like us to be agents; the ideal is not externally imposed. The issue resembles John Rawls' characterization of equal moral personality, which Rawls says is grounded in natural capacities for possessing a sense of justice and having a conception of the good (Rawls 1971, pp. 504–12). Like those capacities, the capacity to foresee outcomes is what Rawls calls a range property. In the case of Rawls' conception of moral personality, so long as you meet the minimum standard, you are entitled to equal justice. Similarly here, all those who meet the minimum standard are treated as having an equal capacity to foresee and avoid outcomes, and hence are subject in an equal degree to being held responsible for the consequences of their actions.

The determination that someone possesses the general capacities to foresee and avoid harm thus appeals to an idealized conception of the ordinary person (relativized, no doubt, to a certain context of action). This does not, however, make that determination objective rather than subjective in character. An objective understanding of capacity would say that an individual who caused harm should be regarded as outcome-responsible for it if an ordinary person would have foreseen the harm and would have been able to take steps to avoid it. The particular individual would then, in effect, be *deemed* to have the general capacity of the ordinary person. On the understanding of general capacity being defended here, however, the idealized ordinary person is simply a standard against which the abilities of the particular individual are measured. If the individual meets the minimum threshold that that standard sets, then he is not being deemed to possess the general capacity; he really does have it. No one succeeds in exercising such a capacity all the time, and it may well be a meaningless question to ask whether a person who failed to exercise it on a particular occasion could have done so on that very occasion. The capacity consists in being able to foresee and avoid outcomes in various sorts of circumstances on a sufficiently regular basis, where what counts as a sufficient degree of regular success is determined by the idealized conception of the ordinary person. Differences in degree are determined by different rates of success above the threshold. So it can be both meaningful and true of an individual to say that she had the capacity to foresee and avoid an outcome of a type that, as it happens, she did not foresee on the particular occasion. And this remains true even if there are other persons who have a higher general rate of success in anticipating outcomes.

The account just given of what it means to possess a general capacity clearly places a normative gloss on certain natural attributes. Normative considerations enter, first, in the idealization of the capacities of the ordinary person, and second, in the equal treatment of all those who meet the threshold that this idealization sets. At no stage do action-guiding norms have to be invoked.[53] Perhaps, however, it might be argued that this latter claim is, for the following reason, mistaken. Consider a manufacturing company that is contemplating whether or not to release a newly developed product onto the market. The company has to decide whether or not to do further safety testing. It will – and, according to the Learned Hand formulation of the negligence standard,[54] should – make that decision on the basis of a cost–benefit analysis. It must decide whether the benefits of further research, in the form of more information about the product's risks, are offset by the costs of undertaking that research. In fact, the argument continues, it is only by referring to such a cost–benefit analysis that we can say whether or not a given type of harm is reasonably foreseeable, i.e., whether or not it *should* be foreseen. Thus the notion of reasonable foreseeability inevitably involves more than the general capacity to foresee that I have been describing. It also involves reference to action-guiding norms of the kind that figure in the Learned Hand Test.[55]

It is true that action-guiding norms of the kind described in the preceding paragraph can affect what an actor should foresee. At the same time, action-guiding norms can only apply to us if we have the capacity to conform to norms, and the general capacity to foresee outcomes is plausibly thought to be implicated in the general capacity to conform to norms.[56] This would seem to require that at least some possible outcomes of actions that fall within the scope of an action-guiding norm be foreseeable independently of the application of that norm. Thus at least some harms must be independently foreseeable before a norm requiring a cost–benefit analysis can be brought to bear, and it is to those harms that the analysis of outcome-responsibility is directed. To put the point in terms of tort doctrine, there is a distinction between reasonable foreseeability, which is an issue of the duty of care, and reasonable conduct, which is an issue of the standard of care. To say that reasonable foreseeability necessarily involves action-guiding norms is to conflate these two notions. One must be able to foresee certain harms as an independent matter before one can say that, as a matter of reasonable conduct, further research is required into the risks of, say, a proposed new product. It is true that to say that further research is required is to say that the actor *should* foresee whatever further potential harms that that research would turn up. It is also true that the results of such research can affect what is properly taken to be reasonably foreseeable in the future. But neither point calls into question the distinction between reasonable foreseeability and reasonable conduct, nor does either point call into question the claim that the determination of what constitutes reasonable conduct depends in part on an independent ability to foresee certain outcomes.

In the example just discussed, is the company that negligently fails to carry out appropriate further research outcome-responsible for the harms that result from releasing its product onto the market? Yes. As we have just seen, the company could only be said to have been negligent if those harms were, under some perhaps fairly general description, foreseeable. Appropriate further research would no doubt have made the harm foreseeable under some more specific description which, if the results of such research were to become generally known, the ordinary person (or ordinary company) would henceforth be expected to employ. However, as things stand at the time the company makes its decision not to do further research, it is the more general description with which the ordinary person (or company) can be expected to be familiar. It is, therefore, that description that is most appropriate for the determination of outcome-responsibility.

The account I have been developing of what it means to possess a general capacity is offered as part of a general conception of outcome-responsibility. The treatment of these issues by tort law is, of course, a somewhat different matter. However, a natural doctrinal approach would be to set up a defeasible presumption, so that a defendant would be presumed to possess the general capacities of an ordinary person to foresee and avoid harm unless he could show that he did not possess those capacities. If the presumption were rebutted, then the defendant would have shown that he is not outcome-responsible for the harm, and he should be relieved of liability in tort. Holmes, for one, regarded the law as working in just this way: "[I]t will now be assumed that . . . the law presumes or requires a man to possess ordinary capacity to avoid harming his neighbors, unless a clear and manifest incapacity be shown" (Holmes 1963, p. 88). The pivotal cases are those involving serious mental disorders, and on this question the modern law is divided.[57] For present purposes, I will simply note that a plausible non-consequentialist theory of tort law must suppose that mental disorders serious enough to undermine the capacity to foresee and avoid harm should excuse the defendant from liability.

This brings us, finally, to the challenge of the advertence-based theories of outcome-responsibility. This challenge has been posed in its strongest form by Larry Alexander. Alexander focuses on negligence and, in particular, on the role of negligence in criminal law, but the question he raises is a matter of concern in tort law as well. Alexander argues, in effect, that the distinction I have drawn between subjectivity regarding capacity and subjectivity regarding advertence cannot be drawn. To have been capable of foreseeing an outcome a person must, according to Alexander, have actually been adverting to it at the appropriate moment of action:

If we take the defendant at the time of the "negligent" choice, with what he is conscious of and adverting to, his background beliefs, etc., then it is simply false that the defendant 'could have' chosen differently in any sense that has normative bite. For while it may be true that the defendant could have chosen differently in a sense relevant to the free will/determinism issue, it is false that in that situation, defendant had any internal reason to choose differently from the way he chose. . . . To have such a reason, a defendant will have to advert to that to which he is not adverting. But one has no control at such moments over what one is adverting to or is conscious of; try thinking of what you aren't thinking of, but should be. (Alexander 1990, pp. 99–101)

There are a number of points that can be made in response to this argument. First, there is neither a logical nor a practical difficulty involved in deciding to think about what you are not at present thinking about but should be. For example, suppose that I find myself day-dreaming while driving and make a conscious decision to pay attention to my speed, the state of the road, the proximity of other cars, and whatever other sources of risk the situation might hold. Choosing to initiate (or to maintain) mental states of this kind is a matter over which we exercise a great deal of control; in this respect "thinking about" ("paying attention to," "adverting to") differs from, say, "believing," because one cannot quite so simply choose to believe something. It is of course true that one cannot exercise *complete* control over the objects of one's thoughts, but that is beside the point; we do not have complete control over *any* aspect of our mental lives, our processes of practical reasoning, or the outcomes of our actions in the external world.[58] Hart maintains, quite plausibly, that most of us generally have sufficient control over our thought processes so as to make the attribution of responsibility for inadvertent negligence quite appropriate (Hart 1970, p. 151). And certainly this seems to be the attitude of most ordinary persons, who tend to hold themselves responsible for instances of inadvertent carelessness or negligence rather than simply saying "there was nothing I could do about it; it was completely beyond my control." Of course, holding someone responsible for an outcome, or taking responsibility oneself, does not amount to saying that the actor's mental state was culpable or his action blameworthy. So far as these latter judgments are concerned, advertence or the lack thereof is extremely relevant. That may mean, among other things, that inadvertent negligence should not be criminalized. But this simply serves to underscore the point that blameworthiness and outcome-responsibility, although they overlap, are distinct notions.

The second point I would make about Alexander's argument is that it is not clear what the sense is of "could have chosen differently" that he sets up in opposition to the sense he says is relevant to the free will/determinism issue. Only the former sense, he says, and not the latter, could have any normative bite in this context. Suppose, first, that one is an incompatibilist on the question of free will. Then one will presumably hold that the sense of "could have chosen differently" that is relevant to the free will/determinism problem entails that the agent could have acted differently even on the specific occasion. But that is a conclusion that surely has normative bite, so far as instances of inadvertent negligence are concerned. Suppose, on the other hand, that one is a compatibilist. Then the only sense of "could have chosen differently" that one can employ in assessing an agent's choices is surely some general capacity to act otherwise in similar circumstances, since by hypothesis determinism is true: on the specific occasion, the agent could not have chosen differently (assuming all antecedent conditions, including the precise state of the agent, are held constant). As Hart recognized, the situation in which there are, to use Alexander's phrase, no "internal reasons" before the actor's mind is in no relevant respect different from, say, a case of intentional killing, so far as the question of whether the actor could have done otherwise on the particular occasion is concerned: "For just as [an inadvertently careless person] might say, 'My mind was a blank' or 'I just forgot' or 'I just didn't think, I could not help not thinking' so the cold-blooded murderer might say 'I just decided to kill; I couldn't help deciding'" (Hart 1968, p. 156). As Hart further notes, evidence relating to the *general* capacities of the agent will be required in the case of both the inadvertently careless actor and the cold-blooded killer in order to establish their responsibility for the actions (and outcomes) in question. In each case that evidence will examine, among other things, the general history of the agent and of others like him.

Thus outcome-responsibility in the avoidability sense does not assume a conception of strong freedom of the kind associated with incompatibilism. It does not assume, in other words, that there were alternate possibilities open to an actor at the time that he acted, so that he could have done otherwise on that very occasion. By the same token, outcome-responsibility in the avoidability sense does not insist that there is no strong freedom. Reliance on the notion of a general capacity is a time-honored compatibilist technique, but my concern is not to defend compatibilism as such. It is, rather, to use that same technique to show that a person can properly be said to have had control over an outcome even if she was not aware when acting that that outcome might eventuate.

### VII. Action, Interaction, and the Meaning of Due Care

In this section I inquire further into, and focus more directly on, the relationship between outcome-responsibility and tort law. On the account of outcome-responsibility that I am advancing, the central question to be asked is this: did the actor have the capacity to foresee the harm, and if so did he have the ability to act on that foresight so as to avoid the harm? If the answer to this question is yes, then the actor is outcome-responsible for its occurrence. Outcome-responsibility does not by itself give rise to a moral obligation to compensate, but, I have suggested, it is the basis of such an obligation. If that is true, then it is a central strand in the moral foundation of both corrective justice and tort law (assuming, of course, that a corrective justice-type account of tort law can be made plausible, which is an issue that I do not directly address in this essay).

As was noted earlier, there are two main perspectives from which foreseeability can be judged. From the first, which I called the activity-perspective, we ask whether engaging in the activity at all, or at least engaging in it at a certain level, would lead an ordinary person to foresee one or more types of harm. To ask whether the actor could have taken steps to avoid the harm is, in the first instance, to ask whether the harm *would* have been avoided if he had ceased engaging in the activity altogether, or had engaged in it to a lesser extent. We must ask the question in this way, since if the harm would not have been avoided, the activity did not cause the harm and the question of the actor's outcome-responsibility does not even arise. In this sense, a judgment of outcome-responsibility is necessarily retrospective. However, this does not mean, from the actor's perspective at the time of acting, that ceasing to engage in the activity, or engaging in it to a lesser extent, would inevitably avoid the harm. Viewed from the *ex ante* perspective, we never have complete control over the outcomes of our actions. What the actor should have realized (whether or not he in fact did so) was that ceasing to engage in the activity, or engaging in it to a more limited extent, would have reduced the epistemic probability of harm. As for how much the epistemic risk must be reducible before the actor is properly regarded as outcome-responsible, this question is answered by reference to the idealized conception of the ordinary person that was discussed in the preceding section. Note that we have not yet reached the question of whether the risk was one that the actor *should* have taken steps to reduce or eliminate (or, alternatively, whether the risk was of such a nature that strict liability should be imposed).

The second perspective I called that of the specific precaution. The analysis is parallel, except that here we are focusing on the manner in which the activity is carried out. More particularly, we ask what specific precautions would it occur to an idealized ordinary person that he should consider employing in the course of his activity? If the type of harm that he should have foreseen does materialize, and if taking one or more of the specific precautions would have reduced the risk *ex ante* and, viewed *ex post*, would definitely have avoided the harm (i.e., failing to take the precautions was a cause of the harm), then he is outcome-responsible for its occurrence. Again, this does not mean that he *should* have taken the precautions in question. That question arises at a later stage of analysis.

In a strict liability case, foreseeability will generally be judged from the activity-perspective. In a negligence case, both the activity perspective and the perspective of the specific precaution will typically be in play. Both of these *ex ante* perspectives are doctrinally captured in negligence law by the notion of the duty of care. In the famous words of Lord Atkin, my "neighbors" in law are "persons who are so closely and directly affected by my act that I ought reasonably to have them in contemplation as being so affected when I am directing my mind to the acts or omissions which are called into question."[59]

It was noted in Section V that foreseeability is a function of epistemic probability. In the tort context, since a bad or harmful outcome is always in the offing, this means that foreseeability is a function of epistemic risk. This naturally leads us to question why outcome-responsibility should be viewed, as I have claimed, as a plateau of responsibility rather than as a prima facie obligation to pay compensation. Consider the following argument. If A is or ought to be aware that associated with her action is a risk of harm to B, then we are in effect saying that A, in acting, is *imposing* a risk on B. If that is true, it seems to be true whether the harm is foreseeable from the activity-perspective, the perspective of the specific precaution, or both. If, however, A has really imposed a risk on B, and if that risk materializes into harm, then the appropriate conclusion seems to be that A has imposed a cost on B. Why, then, should A not compensate B for the latter's loss? Why, in other words, is outcome-responsibility not equivalent to a prima facie obligation to compensate, where the associated regime in tort law would be one of general foresight-based strict liability?

The argument just sketched is an analogue of the libertarian argument for tort liability, except that risk-imposition takes the place of causation as the basis for determining when one person has imposed costs on another. The answer to the argument is, similarly, an analogue of the answer to the libertarian argument. Thus one of the problems with the argument just sketched is that we cannot proceed as readily as it supposes from the premise that A could foresee harm to B to the conclusion that A imposed a risk on B.[60] For one thing, many risks are properly regarded as a joint creation rather than as having been imposed by one person on another. This is particularly true within what we might call accepted patterns of interaction, such as driving. Drivers, at least when they are driving within the rules, do not so much impose risks on one another as jointly create risks to which they all are vulnerable. Individual outcome-responsibility still exists within such a pattern of interaction because the risks of driving are evident to most drivers; each can foresee, from the perspective of the activity itself, that he might be involved in an accident that could cause harm to himself or others. But no one person creates the risk, just as no one person causes the harm if an accident occurs. (On the causation point, recall our discussion of libertarianism in Section III.) And just as the mere fact of causal involvement is a poor basis for reallocating costs when both parties cause the harm, so the mere fact of being outcome-responsible is a poor basis for reallocating costs when both parties jointly created the risk that led to the harm. In such situations, both parties are outcome-responsible for what happened. Something more seems to be needed to ground an obligation to compensate, and we will explore what that something more is in a moment.

First, however, we need to ask, what does it mean to say that a risk is jointly created? Is it meaningful to say that objective risk is jointly created? We are, by hypothesis, talking about cases in which harm, if it occurs, will have been caused by the activities of two parties who interacted with one another. (This is the basic Coasean point.) The problem is complicated by the fact that it is impossible to specify a unique reference class that would allow us to say there is some relative frequency (whether we are aware of it or not) that comprises "the" objective risk. There are indefinitely many such reference classes, most of which we are unaware of, or at least are unable to describe. Still, we can at least say this. Consider a possible harmful interaction between Paul and George. Whatever the precise specification of the reference class of events and of the attribute denoting harm, there is almost always some action that George could take that would reduce the objective risk to zero. Similarly for Paul. They might not *know* this, but that is irrelevant so far as objective risk is concerned. Suppose an actual harmful interaction occurs: George loses control of his plane and lands on Paul at spot S. George could have decided not to go flying, or to fly in a direction away from S. Paul could have decided to have his picnic not at S but at T instead. Thus, except in very unusual circumstances, we can say that both parties to a (possible) harmful interaction create the objective risk. This is just a corollary of the basic Coasean point that actions of both parties cause the harm if it occurs.[61]

So objective risks of harmful interactions are almost always jointly created. Morally speaking, however, that is not a very interesting point. What matters from a moral perspective, of course, is epistemic risk. The question of when an epistemic risk should be regarded as jointly created or unilaterally imposed is an inherently normative one; the imposition of risk is thus not a simple factual state of affairs, like pointing a gun at someone. In sorting out joint from unilateral risk creation, it will be helpful to return to the notion of an accepted pattern of interaction that was introduced earlier. In the context of such a pattern of interaction risks do seem best regarded, intuitively speaking, as a joint rather than an individual creation. The example I gave was driving, but accepted patterns of interaction need not be limited to a single activity. Thus the interaction of drivers and pedestrians in modern society offers another example of an accepted pattern, even though the risks in question are for the most part risks for pedestrians and not for drivers. These risks arise not because they are "imposed" by drivers on pedestrians, but because of certain very general features of this mode of interaction that are so pervasive and fundamental that they can easily escape notice. Thus the risks would not exist (although perhaps different ones would), if pedestrians walked on walkways suspended above the streets, or on protected paths that were connected by tunnels beneath them. The risks would also be quite different if drivers were permitted to drive their cars on any public property (parks, sidewalks, etc.), and not just in certain designated areas (roads or highways). Accepted patterns of interaction involve very broad and well-entrenched social customs. The customs in question are, in effect, constitutive of much social behavior, and are so pervasive that they do not often rise to the level of explicit consideration in tort law. In this they differ from the specific customs, involving common precautionary practices to be found *within* more general patterns of interaction, that are quite often taken into account when courts determine the standard of care.[62]

How a particular pattern of interaction comes to be socially accepted is an exceedingly complex question, and not one that I can take up here. No doubt it involves, first, a sense of reciprocity, based on a general understanding that many people can and do engage in either of the interacting activities, and second, a sense that people who might engage in either of the activities will be aware of the risks and capable, within limits, of affecting the degree of risk to which they or others are exposed. Often, as in the driving examples, but not always, a public regime of regulation will confer explicit legislative approval on a set of constitutive or partially constitutive rules. Clearly the idea of coordinating the activities of a number of different persons is involved. Perhaps implicit social judgments of expediency and efficiency enter as well. But however acceptability is ultimately to be determined, I hope it will be agreed that the idea of an accepted pattern of interaction points to an existing, significant, and utterly pervasive normative phenomenon.

Let me turn, then, to the relation between patterns of interaction and the determination of when an obligation to compensate is owed. It will be helpful to begin with the standard of care in negligence law. It is sometimes suggested that fault in negligence law is a matter of one person imposing a substantial level of foreseeable risk on another; in support of this view Lord Reid's judgment in the case of *Bolton v. Stone*[63] is often cited. This suggests that what is involved is (1) the whole-cloth creation of a risk by one person who unilaterally imposes that risk on another person; and (2) the idea that the reasonableness or unreasonableness of the risk depends on whether it exceeds a certain undefined but constant ("substantial") level of seriousness. This is problematic, for at least three reasons. First, there does not seem in law to be any constant level of substantial risk that is taken to constitute negligence in all circumstances; the unreasonableness of risk seems to vary with the context. Second, it is not clear why, from the perspective of a theory of tort law rooted in notions of justice and individual responsibility, the unilateral imposition of *any* level of risk should be acceptable; the claim that there is a cut-off point between acceptable and unacceptable risks seems to suggest a consequentialist trade-off of some kind. Third, the determination of reasonable care at least sometimes seems to involve a form of cost–benefit reasoning, and this appears not to be permitted by the level-of-substantial-risk idea. The suggestion I wish to make is that these difficulties disappear, or at least become less pressing, if we understand the baseline for substantial risk to be, in a wide range of cases, the risks that are normally incident to a given pattern of interaction.

The basic idea is that while risks are, in a wide variety of circumstances, the product of joint action, individual actors will very often exercise some degree of control, and often a great deal, over the level of risk in particular circumstances. Thus I can increase the risk involved in driver-pedestrian interactions by driving recklessly, say, if I am a driver, or by habitually walking in the road, if I am a pedestrian. The baseline for determining what constitutes a "substantial" risk is the normal range of risks associated with the type of interaction in question. This baseline will vary from context to context, and in the case of some patterns of interaction, such as driving, it could be quite high. (This is the answer to the first of the three problems enumerated in the preceding paragraph.) Because the risk is jointly created and arises within the context of an accepted pattern of interaction, it is as though the baseline were, for these parties, zero; neither is unilaterally imposing a risk on the other. (Here we have at least the beginnings of an answer to the second problem.) Finally, it will often be the case that even *within* the normal range of risks, a person can, at perhaps very little cost to him or herself, significantly reduce the risk for others. This is a form of constrained cost–benefit analysis, and offers at least a starting-point for responding to the third of our three problems.

Let me try to push the cost–benefit idea a little further. Perhaps the negligence standard of fault should be understood, *within the confines of an accepted pattern of interaction,* as involving straightforward cost–benefit analysis along the lines of the Learned Hand Test. According to that test, a person is negligent if she fails to take precautions when B < PL, that is, when the cost or burden of precautions is less than the expected cost of the harm.[64] The basic idea is that this test would only be applied when PL falls within the normal range of acceptable risks associated with the pattern of interaction in question. As on the standard economic model, all persons (acting within the pattern) would have to apply the test to their own interests as well as to the interests of others. This understanding of the role of the Learned Hand Test is immune to one of the criticisms standardly levelled against it, to the effect that it permits a defendant to trade benefits to himself against possibly quite substantial risks that he is imposing on someone else.[65] On the present interpretation, the test functions only within a range of risks that have already been determined to be acceptable and that are properly regarded as jointly created, not unilaterally imposed.

Far from having to view cost–benefit analysis as involving unilateral risk-imposition, we can in fact view its constrained use as a form of cooperation.[66] Even within an otherwise acceptable range of risks, there will be opportunities to reduce the risk of harm to someone else. If the cost to you is less than the expected cost to the other person, then you should help him out and take the risk-reducing precaution; you can then expect others in similar circumstances to do the same for you. However, the idea that a full marginal cost–benefit analysis is required here is perhaps overidealized, and in practice it might be that individuals are merely expected to take the specific precautions that would occur to the mind of an ordinary person and that would, at no great inconvenience to themselves, reduce the risk that someone else faces.[67] But whether a full marginal cost–benefit analysis is required (within the specified constraints of risk), or merely the specific precautions that would occur to the mind of an ordinary person, failure to reduce the risk in the appropriate way would constitute fault and result in a prima facie case for liability.

This analysis offers a fairly decent fit with the positive law of negligence. In all common law jurisdictions the formulation of the negligence standard seems to call for *some* form of cost–benefit analysis, yet at the same time the courts do not apply it across the full range of risks to which human interaction gives rise. The English law offers a good testing ground, particularly since determinations of negligence are made not by juries but by judges, who must justify their decisions. In the Privy Council's decision in *Wagon Mound (No. 2)*, Lord Reid said that in the case of a foreseeable but non-substantial risk a reasonable man "would weigh the risk against the difficulty of eliminating it" (*Wagon Mound [No. 2]*, 642). But that case was actually a gloss on the earlier decision of *Bolton v. Stone*, where Lord Reid had said:

What a man must not do, and what I think a careful man tries not to do, is to create a risk which is substantial. In considering that matter I think that it would be right to take into account not only how remote is the chance that a person might be struck but also how serious the consequences are likely to be if a person is struck; but I do not think it would be right to take account of the difficulty of remedial measures. If cricket cannot be played on a ground without creating a substantial risk, then it should not be played there at all. (*Bolton* at 867)

In this passage Lord Reid seems to say that the court will take account of PL in the Learned Hand formula, but not B. In other words, it will not weigh costs against benefits. But the qualifier is that cost–benefit analysis is not to be undertaken in cases where the defendant has created a *substantial* risk. On the reading of negligence law I am offering, a substantial risk is one that exceeds the normal range of risks associated with the pattern of interaction in question, and does so for reasons that can be traced to the defendant's conduct in particular. An example might be building a cricket pitch on a small lot in an urban area, where cricket pitches are ordinarily found in rural areas or, if in cities, on good-sized pieces of land.[68] Normatively speaking, we can properly regard this as a case of unilateral risk imposition. We can do so, moreover, even if creation of the risk might be warranted by an unconstrained cost–benefit analysis.

Of course, not all risks arise within the context of accepted patterns of interaction, or can be regarded as illegitimate departures from such patterns. Non-pattern cases will arise when the defendant's activity is very uncommon, or when the likely victim is simply not in a position to know about the risk or to take any steps to avoid it if he does know about it. Blasting might be an example of the first kind,[69] the danger from falling airplanes an example of the second.[70] In such cases the objective risk is still jointly created, but often only one party will know about or be in a position to control the epistemic risk. There is thus a sense in such cases in which we can speak of the party in control as having creating the risk, and we might expect to see liability imposed simply for engaging in the activity and causing harm. Here, too, we can meaningfully speak of a normative notion of unilateral risk imposition. In such cases outcome-responsibility is determined from the perspective of the activity as a whole, rather than from the perspective of specific precautions that might be taken. This is not to say that the defendant has necessarily done anything wrongful in engaging in the activity, and indeed in absolute terms the risk might not even be very high. The point is that the defendant can be regarded as having unilaterally imposed the risk on another person. As we might expect, such activities are often subject to strict liability under the abnormally dangerous activities rule,[71] the rule in *Rylands v. Fletcher,*[72] or some similar doctrinal rubric.[73]

The theoretical analysis of tort liability just offered seems to capture the kernel of truth in George Fletcher's proposed principle, that liability in tort should be imposed for non-reciprocal risk imposition. Fletcher maintains that "[t]he paradigm of reciprocity holds that we may be expected to bear, without indemnification, those risks we all impose reciprocally on one another" (Fletcher 1972, p. 543). At points in the article Fletcher suggests that reciprocity is a matter of the risks that the individual defendant and plaintiff independently impose on one another, but this approach has little moral warrant and bears no relation whatever to the actual doctrines of tort law. It is thus not surprising that Fletcher tacitly begins to describe reciprocal risk imposition as a matter of *background* risk within a particular activity or across an entire community: "reciprocity in strict liability cases is analyzed relative to the background of innocuous risks in the community, while reciprocity in . . . negligence cases . . . is measured against the background of risk generated in specific activities like motoring and skiing" (Fletcher 1972, p. 549). There is something to this analysis, but only if we understand background risk in terms of the epistemic risks that are jointly created within certain patterns of interaction, rather than, as Fletcher himself suggests, in terms of the risks – meaning, apparently, risks in the objective sense – that we habitually impose on one another in various kinds of contexts. If this is right, then the risks Fletcher says are subject to negligence analysis are those that arise within accepted patterns of interaction, while those that give rise to strict liability are those that arise outside such patterns. The proper context for applying negligence law is thus not homogeneous activities like driving or skiing – such an account cannot, for example, account for accidents between cars and pedestrians – but rather patterns of interaction either within or between such activities.

## VIII.  Is Outcome-Responsibility Redundant?

I have argued that finding a defendant outcome-responsible for a given harm is only the first step in a two-step process that must be followed before a moral obligation to compensate can be established. The second step involves either a finding of fault or a conclusion that the defendant's outcome-responsibility involved a unilateral imposition of risk on the plaintiff. But my argument might now seem to be vulnerable to the following objection.[74] If fault or some analogue of fault such as unilateral risk imposition is a necessary condition of liability, why is it not the *only* such condition? Why do we have to insist as well that the defendant could also foresee and avoid the harm? Why, in other words, is it not sufficient that the defendant did something faulty and in consequence harmed the plaintiff? This is the challenge of Judge Andrews' dissent in *Palsgraf v. Long Island Railroad*.[75] Andrews argued that it was enough to establish liability in tort that the defendant fell below the standard of care (i.e., behaved faultily), as a result of which behavior the plaintiff suffered sufficiently proximate (i.e., direct) harm. It did not matter, according to Andrews, that the plaintiff was not within a reasonably foreseeable class of possible victims; to the extent that it makes sense to speak of a duty of care, the defendant owes his duty to all the world and not just to those who might foreseeably be harmed by his actions. What, if anything, is wrong with this argument?

The gist of Andrews' challenge is the claim that fault alone is enough to establish a moral obligation to compensate. The response to the challenge begins with the observation that, in the absence of outcome-responsibility, all we have in fault is the violation of a norm. In the present context the relevant norm is the negligence standard of due care, but if this is not systematically related to and constrained by a requirement of outcome-responsibility (as embodied in the defendant's duty of care), then there is nothing to distinguish this particular norm of conduct from any other. If an obligation to compensate is the appropriate moral and legal remedy here, why is it not the appropriate remedy in the case of any other norm violation that causes harm? Consider the following hypothetical, based on an example of Warren Seavey's (1939, p. 33). The defendant kidnaps someone, and in the course of his felonious activity quite unforeseeably and non-negligently injures a third party. Does the injured third party have a morally justified claim in tort against the defendant, just because her injury would not have occurred but for the defendant's violation of the moral and legal norm against kidnapping? The intuitive response of most people, both lawyers and nonlawyers, is no.

Conversely, if the negligence standard of care is to be treated as a free-standing norm, then why should we think that the appropriate normative response, when the defendant's negligence causes harm, requires compensation? Why is not the appropriate response punishment, or a distributive approach to the loss, or both? The thesis that punishment is the appropriate remedy leads quite naturally, at least if we take up a non-retributive attitude to punishment, to a deterrence-based theory of tort law. This is probably the most straightforward reading of Andrews' own judgment in *Palsgraf;* it is not at all difficult to see him as a precursor of, say, Richard Posner. But to take the deterrence route is obviously to reject out of hand a corrective justice-based, responsibility-oriented view of tort. A distributive reading of Andrews' judgment, on the other hand, was offered by William Prosser: "Essentially the choice is between an innocent plaintiff and a defendant who is admittedly at fault. If the loss is out of all proportion to the defendant's fault, it can be no less out of proportion to the plaintiff's innocence" (Prosser 1953, p. 17). This suggests that fault should be used as a criterion of distribution to allocate the loss between the two parties to a harmful interaction; the determination of liability is treated, in effect, as a problem of localized distributive justice.[76] Whether or not the defendant could foresee the type of harm that actually occurred, she was at fault and injured an innocent plaintiff. As between the two, it is the faulty defendant who should bear the loss.

The difficulty with the distributive argument just sketched is that it is too powerful, in at least two respects.[77] First, it cannot be arbitrarily confined to fault in the sense of negligence, nor to fault on the defendant's part only. The approach thus leads fairly quickly to a comparative assessment of the parties' relative moral worth.[78] It would seem to call, for example, for liability in the kidnapping case discussed earlier, if we assume that the kidnapper is morally less innocent than the injured plaintiff. Second, there is no basis for confining the distributive argument to the two parties who were causally involved in the harmful interaction; relatedly, there is no reason for insisting that causation of harm is a necessary condition of liability. This point is illustrated by the at-fault pool, which Jules Coleman once proposed as one possible instantiation of the annulment conception of corrective justice that he defended for many years. (As Coleman later came to acknowledge, the annulment conception was really best understood as a theory of distributive, not corrective, justice.)[79] The at-fault pool would require all persons found guilty of, say, faulty driving, to pay into a central pool in amounts proportional to the degree of fault shown by each and regardless of whether he or she had actually caused an accident; persons injured on the highway would then claim compensation directly from the pool (Coleman 1974, pp. 484–8). The at-fault pool illustrates where the logic of the distributive argument seems inevitably to lead, namely, away from tort law and the liability of specific persons for specific harms, and toward a more general distributive scheme of some kind.

George Fletcher has, in the article discussed in the preceding section, defended a variation of the distributive argument. Fletcher claims that the moral basis of corrective justice is the following, Rawls-inspired principle of equal security: "[W]e all have the right to the maximum amount of security compatible with a like security for everyone else" (Fletcher 1972, p. 550). As the analogy with Rawls suggests, this is best understood as a principle of distributive justice (distributing the good of security). Someone who imposes on another person an excessive level of risk – as determined by the principle of reciprocity, which was discussed earlier – comes under an obligation to compensate for any loss that results because "[c]ompensation is a surrogate for the individual's right to the same security as enjoyed by others" (Fletcher 1972, p. 550). Fletcher thus appeals, in effect, to a subsidiary distributive principle that reassigns losses so as to maintain the expected level of well-being guaranteed by the initial distribution of security. Since Fletcher assumes that a loss can only be reassigned to the particular excessive risk-imposer who happened to cause it, he is implicitly relying on a localized conception of distributive justice. But the underlying logic of the distributive argument offers no basis for this restriction. As with the at-fault pool, it seems more sensible and fair, from the perspective of distributive justice, to require a given victim's loss to be shared among *all* persons who engaged in excessively risky behavior, without regard to whether they caused injury (and thus, *a fortiori,* without regard to whether they caused *this* injury). This logic is in fact partially reflected in Fletcher's claim that a victim's right to recover will survive even where a risk-creator's behavior is excused, thereby relieving the latter from the obligation to compensate: Such victims might, Fletcher says, have a claim of priority in a social insurance scheme (Fletcher 1972, pp. 553–4).

Outcome-responsibility, in the theory of tort law I wish to defend, normatively ties an actor to the outcome of his action in a way that is specifically capable of grounding an obligation of compensation. The normative tie exists because the actor was outcome-responsible: he was in a position to foresee and avoid the harm. If in addition he *should* have avoided the harm – if, in other words, he was also at fault – or if his outcome-responsibility can be regarded as a unilateral imposition of risk, then he is morally required to undo the outcome, to the extent that this is possible to achieve by a transfer of money or other resources. It is important to notice, however, that in fault-based cases the obligation to compensate does not depend on the simple coexistence of outcome-responsibility, fault, and sufficiently proximate causation. Consider Seavey's kidnapping example again. Suppose that the third party is injured by the kidnapper while the latter is carefully driving the kidnappee to a hiding spot. As was explained in the preceding section, driving accidents of this kind seem to involve outcome-responsibility on the part of the driver. But even though outcome-responsibility, fault, and causation of harm are all compresent here, our intuitions argue very strongly against liability. This is because the element of fault is not related in the right way to the antecedent element of outcome-responsibility.

Outcome-responsibility involves the perception of risk, where risk is to be understood in an epistemic rather than in an objective sense. As Cardozo put the point in his majority judgment in *Palsgraf* (p. 100), "[t]he risk reasonably to be perceived defines the duty to be obeyed, and risk imports relation; it is risk to another or to others within the range of apprehension." If we are to avoid such unintuitive results as liability in the kidnapping example, the fault that will justify an obligation to compensate must be defined by reference to the risk that gave rise to the defendant's outcome-responsibility (and hence to her duty of care). In other words, the fault must grow out of the defendant's outcome-responsibility. It is the failure to take the steps that she should have taken to avoid the very type of harm that occurred that justifies the imposition of an obligation to compensate.

## IX. Conclusion

I have argued in this article that there is a conception of responsibility for outcomes that is distinct from, although related to, the concept of responsibility for one's actions. According to the avoidability-based theory of outcome-responsibility that I have been defending, a person cannot be held responsible for an outcome of one of her actions unless she had the general capacity to foresee the outcome and the ability to take steps to avoid its occurrence. This conception of outcome-responsibility involves a different understanding from both the libertarian and the advertence-based theories of what it means to have control over an outcome. The capacity-based understanding of control is, I have suggested, a fundamental aspect of our self-understanding as moral agents. Consequently it has important connections to other types of responsibility judgments, such as judgments that an agent successfully achieved an intended outcome, or judgments allocating blame. The avoidability conception also differs from libertarianism and the blame-based advertence theory in that it does not treat outcome-responsibility as equivalent to a prima facie obligation to compensate. Rather it constitutes a more general conception of moral authorship that, again, figures pervasively in our understanding of our own agency.[80] Outcome-responsibility in the avoidability sense is nonetheless a necessary condition for the existence of a moral obligation to compensate, and as such is also a necessary condition for the imposition, in the most central cases, of a legal obligation to pay damages in tort.

Outcome-responsibility on the part of an agent for a harmful outcome entails that he had the capacity at the time he acted to perceive a risk, characterized in appropriate epistemic terms, that such an outcome would eventuate. The appropriate characterization of risk is based on the level of knowledge and ability to assess probabilities that an ordinary person in the defendant's position could be expected to possess. From a normative perspective, some risks can be viewed as unilaterally imposed and some as jointly created. In the case of unilaterally imposed risks, outcome-responsibility alone will ordinarily suffice to establish a moral obligation to compensate: when such an obligation is translated into law, the result is a foresight-based standard of strict liability. By contrast, outcome-responsibility for the materialization of a risk that was jointly created will only give rise to an obligation to compensate if we can say that the agent not only could have avoided the outcome, but should have done so. This imports a conception of fault, which in legal terms is represented by the standard of care in negligence law. In contexts where negligence is the appropriate standard of liability, the mere fact that one contributed to the existence of a risk does not mean that one acted faultily; thus the materialization of a risk that is normally incident to an accepted pattern of social interaction will not give rise to liability. Fault will only exist in those cases where the defendant acted so as to increase the risk substantially, or else could have reduced or eliminated the risk at a relatively low cost to himself.

In this way, then, outcome-responsibility in the avoidability sense helps both to explain and justify some of the central doctrines of tort law. It constitutes the core of a corrective justice-based account of tort, and for that reason is not just an important concept in moral theory, but in legal theory as well. It seems plausible to think that outcome-responsibility also has a role to play in other areas of legal theory. I believe, for example, that it can help to show why the theory of criminal law cannot take a purely subjectivist form, by justifying the widely held intuition that the punishment for murder (say) should be greater than that for attempted murder. But that is a complicated inquiry in its own right, and one that must be left to another occasion.

## Notes

*   John J. O'Brien Professor of Law and Professor of Philosophy, University of Pennsylvania. Earlier versions of this essay – in some instances, a distant ancestor – were presented at workshops at the following law schools: Berkeley, Boston University, Hebrew University, Texas, Toronto, and University College London. Versions of the essay were also presented to the Colloquium in Law, Philosophy and Political Theory at New York University, the Seminar in Ethics and Public Affairs at Princeton University, and the Research Group on the Nature and Limits of Moral Responsibility at Stanford University. I am particularly grateful to the following persons for their comments: Jules Coleman, Meir Dan-Cohen, Ronald Dworkin, Claire Finkelstein, Frances Kamm, Andy Koppelman, Jody Kraus, Brian Leiter, Liam Murphy, Thomas Nagel, Arthur Ripstein, Samuel Scheffler, Scott Shapiro, Ken Simons, Jeremy Waldron, and Ben Zipursky.

[1]   Honoré (1988). My understanding of outcome-responsibility differs in several important respects from Honoré's. See further Perry (1992b, pp. 488–512) and Perry (1993, pp. 38–47). I should note that my views have changed in some respects since the publication of these articles.

[2]   Cf. *Restatement (Second) of Torts,* § 8A, which defines "intent" as either desiring to cause the consequences of one's act, or else believing that those consequences are substantially certain to result from the act.

[3]   Hurd (1996, p. 250). In *United Sates v. Carroll Towing Co.,* 159 F. 2d 169, 173 (2d Cir. 1947), Judge Learned Hand defined negligence as failing to take precautions whenever $B < P \times L$ (where B stands for the cost of preventive measures, P the probability of an accident occurring, and L the magnitude of the loss that the accident would cause).

[4]   Further problems, in addition to those I discuss, are pointed out in Simons (1996).

[5]   Robert Nozick is clearly contemplating a theory of wrongdoing along these lines when he discusses the thesis that risking a rights violation might itself be a rights violation (Nozick 1974, pp. 73–8). Nozick's discussion, which points to serious potential problems with this thesis, is inconclusive on the substantive point. However, he is plainly not guilty of overlooking a vicious circularity that would settle the issue on simple logical or conceptual grounds.

[6]   Hurd's ultimate category of wrongs in fact consists of acts that constitute rights violations, rather than acts that causally implicate harm. While she thinks that most rights violations

involve harm, she concedes that there can be both harmless wrongs and wrongless harms. See Hurd (1994, pp. 209–15). Given this concession, is it so clear that some risky but non-harm-causing acts cannot be rights violations falling into the category of harmless wrongs?

7  That is one reason why I have not felt it necessary to discuss the details of the four theories here. Hurd attributes one of the theories she discusses to me, namely, the view that negligence consists of the imposition of substantial risks, and says that I fail to distinguish that view from the theory that negligence consists of the imposition of unjustly enriching risks (Hurd 1996, pp. 257–61). I did at one time hold something like the former theory (Perry 1988), but, as will become clear in Section VII, I no longer do. As for the unjust enrichment idea, my view has always been that, because it focuses on wrongful gains rather than on wrongful losses, it is a non-starter in tort theory. However, I think that an argument superficially similar to the unjust enrichment approach has been advanced by Richard Epstein, among others, not as an independent substantive theory of what constitutes acceptable and unacceptable risk imposition, but rather as a justification for the substantive libertarian thesis that persons should in general be held absolutely liable for the harms that they cause. The argument that superficially resembles the unjust enrichment idea is the claim that, just as people are morally entitled to the fruits of their labor, so they are morally responsible for the harms that their actions cause others. But it is not the fact that someone benefited or stood to benefit from his action that is thought to justify the imposition of liability for any losses that that action causes. The argument is, rather, one of analogy: just as people morally own what they produce, so too do they morally "own" the losses they cause others. I briefly discuss this argument in Section III. See further Perry (1997, pp. 363–73).

8  See Dworkin (1978, pp. 98–100); Dworkin (1986, pp. 276–312); Weinrib (1983, pp. 49–54).

9  Compare Nozick's repudiation of the apparently redistributive function of the night-watchman state, on the grounds that "the term 'redistributive' applies to types of *reasons* for an arrangement, rather than to an arrangement itself" (Nozick 1974, p. 27). Thus we might similarly say that an apparently consequentialist interpretation of the negligence standard is not consequentialist after all, if the reasons for adopting that interpretation are themselves non-consequentialist.

10  Suppose Hurd's conceptual argument that negligence is not deontological wrongdoing succeeded, but her moral argument that it cannot be a matter of deontological culpability failed. What would follow from this, in either theoretical or practical terms?

11  For Hurd, a theory of wrongdoing is centrally concerned with causally complex acts that include, in core cases, harmful results. "Results," in the technical sense defined earlier, are a species of outcome, so it might be thought that her theoretical approach to tort law indirectly takes responsibility for outcomes into account to whatever extent that deontological considerations require that it be taken into account. This is a variation of the suggestion I considered at the beginning of this article, to the effect that outcome-responsibility is equivalent to, or subsumed under, action-responsibility, and the response I offered there applies here as well. It should further be noted that, while Hurd is somewhat unclear about what theoretical or practical difference she thinks it would make to treat negligence as deontological culpability rather than as deontological wrongdoing, her view seems to be that an account of negligence-as-culpability would hold a legitimate place in deontological theory generally, so long as the conceptual and moral objections that she offers to such accounts could be overcome. The focus of a deontological theory of negligence-as-culpa-

bility would, I assume, be on acts that were culpable because they were risky but that did not necessarily issue in harmful outcomes (i.e., they produced neither harmful results nor harmful consequences). I think it is clear that underlying such a theory would be a conception of action-responsibility rather than a conception of outcome-responsibility.

[12] It might be suggested that the relevant deontological norm is a categorical obligation to compensate after the fact. But if that was the relevant categorical norm under strict liability, there would be no reason why the same should not be true under a negligence rule.

[13] I say "potentially" because a particular theory might make outcome-responsibility a necessary but not a sufficient condition for the existence of a moral obligation to compensate. This is true, as we shall see, of the avoidability conception. Note also that while violation of a norm is not conceptually necessary for outcome-responsibility, some theories might insist on normative grounds that a person cannot be held outcome-responsible for a harm unless she violated a norm in causing it. This is true, for example, of the blame-based theory we will examine later.

[14] Character theories of responsibility in criminal law, which are generally contrasted with choice theories, appear to be an exception to this proposition. Orthodox character theories hold that a person is responsible for those well-established traits and dispositions that reflect or express the sort of person she really is, whether or not she can have any meaningful degree of control over these traits and dispositions. See Lacey (1988, pp. 65–8). As we shall see later in this section, Arthur Ripstein has recently argued that responsibility for harmful outcomes, of the kind that figures in tort law, does not depend in any way on a notion of control.

[15] When the perceived probability of success becomes too remote, I do not have control over the outcome, regardless of what I intended: Even if I enter the lottery "intending" to win, and in fact do win, I cannot be said to have had control over that consequence.

[16] The notion of "what I should have expected as normal" is to be explained in terms of the account of foreseeability, to be given in Section V.

[17] The fact that I might not be outcome-responsible in the achievement sense does not, however, preclude the possibility that I might be outcome-responsible in the avoidability sense. Suppose there is some good reason why the snooker balls should not go into the pockets at all. Perhaps the netting is broken, and the owner has told me not to let balls roll into the pockets where they will drop onto the floor. Now it is perfectly foreseeable to me that idly batting balls around on the table, let alone actually playing a serious game of snooker, could result in the undesirable outcome of a ball going into a pocket. So I am outcome-responsible in the avoidability sense for the outcome of some ball going into some pocket, even though I am not outcome-responsible in the achievement sense for the outcome of the black ball going into the far corner pocket.

[18] *Vincent v. Lake Erie Transportation Co.*, 109 Minn. 456, 124 N.W. 221 (1910).

[19] The central figure in this regard is Oliver Wendell Holmes, who is very naturally read as criticizing versions of the advertence-based and libertarian theories of outcome-responsibility, and defending the avoidability conception (Holmes 1963, pp. 63–103). Holmes attributes (pp. 66–7) what I have labelled an advertence-based theory – he calls it "the theory of a criminalist" – to Austin. See p. 68 for Holmes' formulation of the libertarian theory, which he does not attribute to anyone in particular. I have discussed Holmes' critique of the libertarian theory in Perry (1997, pp. 392–4).

[20] Coleman and Ripstein argue, on apparently purely conceptual grounds, that we can only have control over "intended or actually-foreseen consequences," and that tort liability

therefore cannot be premised on control. Coleman and Ripstein (1995, p. 127). They argue, in effect, that outcome-responsibility must be understood in terms of a strong advertence theory, and that for that reason corrective justice and tort law cannot be based on outcome-responsibility. I have argued elsewhere that this argument turns on too narrow a construal of the concept of having control over an outcome (Perry 1998a, pp. 156–7).

21   I owe this example to Jeremy Waldron.

22   Moore (1990, p. 33). In the literature, theories of what I am calling action-responsibility are generally referred to as choice theories of responsibility. These are contrasted with character theories, which make blame and punishment turn on possession or manifestation of a bad character rather than on the culpable choice to perform a wrong action. See note 14 above.

23   This is true in the case of the blame-based theory because of the manner in which I defined it. But that definition makes philosophical and moral sense, because we have a strong intuition that intentionally or knowingly harming another person places one under a moral obligation to compensate.

24   The arguments in this and the following paragraph are elaborated in greater detail in Perry (1998a, pp. 147–54).

25   Strictly speaking, what matters is not the ability to avoid the outcome, but rather the ability to avoid causally contributing to it. This modification of the definition of outcome-responsibility is required to deal with cases of causal overdetermination, as for example when either of two independently set fires would have been sufficient to burn down a house. So far as the theory of corrective justice and tort law are concerned, however, the modification makes little or no difference, since ordinarily one can only have an obligation to compensate for a loss if the loss would not have occurred but for one's action. If a person causally contributed to a loss that would have occurred anyway, even if she had not causally contributed to it, generally speaking she comes under no such obligation.

26   It should be noted, however, that nothing prevents more than one person from being outcome-responsible in the avoidability sense. Often two persons will be outcome-responsible for a harm that befell just one of them. See further the discussion in Section VII below.

27   One relevant factor is Bernard Williams' notion of agent-regret. See Williams (1981, p. 20). Williams gives the example of a lorry driver who, through no fault of his own, runs over a child. As an agent who was causally implicated in the injury, he will properly regret the outcome even though he cannot blame himself for its occurrence. Williams says that, as a result, the driver may be moved to apologize, offer symbolic recompense, or take some other kind of action. This example is sometimes presented to me as showing that agent-regret, rather than outcome-responsibility in the avoidability sense, might be doing the real work of creating new reasons for action. However, Williams clearly does not think, nor is it plausible to think, that agent-regret alone could give rise to anything other than relatively weak reasons; thus it could not serve as the basis for a moral (and ultimately legal) obligation to compensate. Moreover it is far from clear, at least from this example, that agent-regret is attributable to causal involvement alone, since even though the driver was not at fault in injuring the child, he was nonetheless outcome-responsible for what happened. From the general perspective of the activity he was engaged in, namely, driving, an accident of this kind was clearly foreseeable, and it also could have been easily avoided (by not driving). It is true that the driver did not have control over the situation in terms of specific precautions he might have taken, and for that reason, as we shall see be-

low, he does not have an obligation to compensate. But he still had control in a sense that gives rise to outcome-responsibility, and that is why we can say of him, I want to suggest, that he *did* this thing. Perhaps it is because he is outcome-responsible that the driver properly experiences greater regret than a bystander. Driving is an accepted and normal activity, but we are aware of its great risks and have every reason to feel regret when we voluntarily engage in the activity and one of those risks materializes. (On the distinction between two perspectives from which foreseeability can be assessed, see note 31. The distinction is further developed in Sections V and VII.) To determine the precise basis of agent-regret, it seems to me, we would have to look at cases involving truly unforeseeable harm. In such situations, in which the agent could have done absolutely nothing to avoid a harmful outcome, perhaps the appropriate attitude of the agent is not so very different from that of someone who merely comes upon the scene of an accident. I should add that at one time I believed that agent-regret was the basis of outcome-responsibility. See Perry (1992b, pp. 492–3) and Perry (1993, pp. 40–3). As the preceding discussion makes clear, I now think that view is mistaken.

[28] Both Ken Simons and Arthur Ripstein have emphasized these points to me.

[29] In negligence law, this proximity is captured (in part) by the notion of duty of care: "The rule that you are to love your neighbour becomes in law, you must not injure your neighbour; and the lawyer's question, Who is my neighbour? receives a restricted reply. You must take reasonable care to avoid acts or omissions that you can reasonably foresee would be likely to injure your neighbour. Who, then, in law is my neighbour? The answer seems to be – persons who are so closely and directly affected by my act that I ought reasonably to have them in contemplation as being so affected when I am directing my mind to the acts or omissions which are called into question." *Donoghue v. Stevenson,* [1932] A.C. 562, 580 (H.L.), per Lord Atkin. Cf. *MacPherson v. Buick Motor Co.,* 111 N.E. 1050 (N.Y. 1916).

[30] Judith Jarvis Thomson has argued that causation matters in the justification of an obligation to compensate "because if B did not cause . . . A's injury, then B's freedom of action protects him against liability for A's injury." Thomson (1986, p. 202). We thus cannot call upon someone at random to pay B's costs because that would be to interfere without reason with that person's freedom of action. From this Thomson apparently concludes that if B *did* cause A's injury then she *can* be held liable for A's costs, at least if B was also at fault. But it does not follow from the proposition that without causation you cannot impose liability, that with causation you can. While it is true that if the argument were successful it would establish that causation is, in a formal sense, a necessary condition of liability, this is compatible with the complete nonexistence of liability: The argument does not establish a substantive link between liability and causation. Thomson uses freedom of action to try to forge a link between non-harm-causers and nonliability, when it is a link between causers of harm and liability for the harm that is needed. My argument is that outcome-responsibility provides such a substantive link, in a way that mere causation cannot.

[31] This statement needs to be qualified, in ways not at present relevant, to deal with causal overdetermination and certain other problematic circumstances. See note 25. The following point should also be borne in mind. There are, as we shall see in Sections V and VII, two different perspectives at which foreseeability, and hence outcome-responsibility, can operate. These are, first, the perspective of the action or activity itself, and second, the perspective of precautions that might be taken as part of the overall activity. From the perspective of the activity, the only step that could be taken to avoid the outcome would be

cessation of the activity (or reduction in its level to the point where the harm would not have occurred). In that case, it is the action or activity as such (or at least engaging in a certain level of the activity) that must be regarded as the cause of the harm. At the second level, the steps that could be taken to avoid the harm are precautions that could be taken as part of the ongoing activity. In that case, it is not the action or level of activity as such that is the cause of the harm, but rather the failure to take the relevant precautions.

32    Of course, we never have complete control over our mental lives, including in particular our intentions, either. As Joel Feinberg has pointed out, an opportune sneeze might prevent me from forming the intention to kill that I otherwise would have formed (Feinberg 1970, pp. 25–37). Cf. Moore (1994, pp. 270–80). Presumably the philosophical specification of what it means to say that someone could have acted otherwise, which is part of a comprehensive theory of action-responsibility, will take this fact into account.

33    Thomas Nagel, in his original characterization of the problem of moral luck, described the role of control in the following way: "Where a significant aspect of what someone does depends on factors beyond his control, yet we continue to treat him in that respect as an object of moral judgment, it can be called moral luck" Nagel (1979, p. 26). As a number of commentators have suggested, Nagel seemed to have in mind a criterion of *complete* control over all aspects of the relevant action or outcome. Michael Moore persuasively argues, however, that the fact that control is never complete, together with the fact that our ordinary moral notions do not expect it to be complete, means that there is after all no puzzle of the kind Nagel envisages (Moore 1994, pp. 253–8). For a broadly similar approach to moral luck, see also Walker (1992, p. 19). Walker argues that, because control is never complete – because our agency is in that sense impure – "responsibilities outrun control."

34    See particularly Judge Cardozo's majority decision in *Palsgraf v. Long Island Railroad Co.,* 248 N.Y. 339, 162 N.E. 99 (1928). See also *Donoghue,* [1932] A.C. 562, and *Macpherson,* 111 N.E. 1050. The notion of a foreseeable *type* of harm will be discussed in Section V. Note that outcome-responsibility is not the only normative consideration that figures in the doctrinal element of duty of care. Other considerations include the following. First, outcome-responsibility applies to harm of all types, but the law of torts only protects certain interests. The duty of care filters out the protected interests from the nonprotected. Second, the considerations that determine when one party owes an affirmative duty to another are also taken into account at this stage of analysis. As I shall suggest below, the breach of an affirmative duty typically gives rise to non-causal liability and should not, therefore, be regarded as an instance of outcome-responsibility. Third, in modern American tort law, policy-based considerations – meaning, essentially, consequentialist considerations – are often employed either to limit or to extend a duty of care, where the underlying moral foundation for that duty is either foreseeability (i.e., outcome-responsibility) or, in the case of an affirmative duty, a special relationship. On the conceptual importance of the requirement of duty of care in a non-consequentialist understanding of tort law, see Goldberg and Zipursky (1998).

35    *The Wagon Mound (No. 1),* [1961] A.C. 338 (P.C.).

36    Thin-skull cases in which injury of a foreseeable type leads to injury of another, quite unforeseeable type – as, for example, when a burn causes subsequent cancer – are a possible example. See, e.g., *Smith v. Leech Brain & Co.,* [1962] 2 Q.B. 405.

37    See, e.g., *Hymowitz v. Eli Lilly & Co.,* 73 N.Y. 2d 487, 539 N.E. 2d 1069 (1989).

38    This is perhaps too strictly stated, because it is conceivable that the correct understanding

of positive agency does not coincide exactly with the act/omission distinction. See, e.g., Quinn (1993, p. 149). This is not an issue that can be explored here.

39 In cases in which harm flows from an omission that takes place within the context of an undertaking or special relationship, can the person who failed to take action be said to be outcome-responsible for the harm? I believe that the answer is a qualified yes. Such cases are best regarded as involving a conceptual extension of the core notion of outcome-responsibility, as I have described that core notion in this article. Usually, in tort actions based on an undertaking or a special relationship, there is prior causal involvement, as when I induce you to go swimming by undertaking to rescue you if you get into trouble. But my actual failure to rescue is best understood as playing no causal role in your drowning. See, e.g., Moore (1999, pp. 31–4). In this example it is my (negligent) omission to rescue that triggers legal liability, and while it is true that the omission was neither an action nor a cause of your drowning, it seems correct, because of my prior causal involvement in inducing you to go swimming, to regard that omission as an upshot of my agency. Hence the extended notion of outcome-responsibility. It is an interesting question whether this extended notion can be extended further, so as to apply when there was no prior causal involvement. Consider, for example, the case of a professional lifeguard who has taken on a general obligation to rescue persons who get into difficulty in the water. Is there outcome-responsibility when he fails to try to rescue someone who was not aware there was a lifeguard on the beach, and hence was not induced by that fact to go into the water? Frances Kamm would go further still. She suggests that there could be legal liability in cases in which one has the de facto ability to control an active force which one did not create and for whose existence one has no special responsibility (e.g. oneself turned into a missile by a force of nature). See Kamm (1996, pp. 95–6). I agree with Kamm that someone finding himself in such a situation might be morally required to exercise the control, just as a non-lifeguard who played no causal role in inducing a drowning swimmer to go into the water might be morally required to effect an easy rescue. But it does not follow in either case that there would be outcome-responsibility for the harm, let alone legal liability.

40 I discuss the distinction between objective and epistemic probability at greater length in Perry (1995, pp. 322–9).

41 We can now easily formulate concepts of objective and epistemic *risk*. First, we define "risk" as $P \times L$ (the mathematical expectation of harm). L represents the magnitude of the loss that would be suffered if harm were to occur. P represents the probability of harm occurring. Objective risk is then just the mathematical expectation of harm where "P" is understood in terms of the objective account of probability given in the text. Epistemic risk is defined similarly.

42 In the context of tort law, it was Clarence Morris who originally drew attention to this problem. See Morris (1952). The example in the text is based on a hypothetical of Morris's.

43 See Perry (1995, p. 335). "Possible" entities, it should be noted, are not to be accorded ontological status in their own right; they are simply placeholders for varying configurations of other properties – i.e., properties other than the one whose relative frequency we wish to measure – that actual entities might have.

44 I have argued elsewhere that it follows from this conclusion that risk is not properly regarded as a form of harm in its own right. See Perry (1995, pp. 330–6).

45 Hart and Honoré (1985, p. 258). Hart and Honoré give the following example: "If we have learned from experience to expect a 'rainstorm' on seeing dark clouds, then the rainstorm

was foreseeable even if, when it occurs, it has other characteristics (e.g., lasted two hours, covered an area of 40 square miles) which we could not foresee but which might appear, *ex post facto,* in a more specific description of it. Conversely, if we have learned to anticipate a *rainstorm* we cannot be said to have foreseen a hailstorm because it shares the same generic description, i.e. 'storm'."

46 Hart and Honoré (1985, p. 80). At this point in *Causation in the Law,* Hart and Honoré are considering the notion of a coincidence. A coincidence is, roughly, a very unlikely conjunction of independent events. The multiple description problem arises in the characterization of coincidences just as much as it does in the determination of what is foreseeable, and Hart and Honoré adopt exactly the same solution: they appeal to the knowledge and experience of the ordinary person to determine the appropriate description and probability of the event. This "typology of the ordinary" is thus incorporated into their own "directness" account of causation, according to which "a voluntary act, or a conjunction of events amounting to a coincidence, operates as a limit in the sense that events subsequent to these are not attributed to the antecedent action or event as its consequence even though they would not have happened without it" (p. 71). It is worth noting that Moore seems to favor a theory of proximate causation based on Hart and Honoré's notion of directness. See Moore (1994, p. 255). This is significant because, as Hart and Honoré formulate that account, it is both vulnerable to the multiple description problem and dependant on the very solution – namely, the typology of the ordinary – that Moore repudiates.

47 With respect to the problems of proximate causation that particularly vex Moore, Hart and Honoré would advocate, for the foreseeability-based theory that they do not themselves favor, a "harm-within-the-risk" solution: "[T]he class of harm or accident which must be foreseeable . . . can be determined by reference to the generalizations which one would have recourse to in describing conduct as negligent" (Hart and Honoré 1985, p. 258). (I would prefer to say that the same description of the harm-type must be used at both the duty and the proximate cause stages of the analysis.) Moore rejects the harm-within-the-risk solution because devotees of that analysis "[usually] do not seek to salvage foreseeability but to eliminate it entirely" (Moore 1993, p. 153). But, at least in the negligence context, harm-within-the-risk must refer to *epistemic* risk, and for all present purposes foreseeability and epistemic risk are nearly interchangeable concepts.

48 On the different roles in tort law of the ordinary person and the reasonable person, see note 53.

49 Dennett (1985): "[A] particular *type* of deliberator-agent – a species, for instance – will always be equipped with a somewhat idiosyncratic way of gathering information about the world; it will have its way of "conceiving" the world so it can act effectively in it. Extending somewhat a concept of Sellars', we may call this 'conceptual scheme' of a species its *manifest image.* . . . In its manifest image some features are standing, background conditions, and some are 'possible' states of things in the world. Among these possible states of things, some are simply unpredictable, some are reliably predictable by their harbingers, some are indirectly controllable by (the effects of) actions of the deliberator, and some – the actions themselves – are directly controllable by the deliberator. . . . The point of all this prudent information management is to enable the deliberator to make good (reliable, useful) control decisions. . . . And these decisions must be based not only on the deliberator's goals (or desires), but also on reliable expectations of several sorts" (p. 111, emphasis in original).

50 This distinction is modelled *very* roughly on a distinction formulated by Steven Shavell

for quite different purposes, relating to an economic understanding of tort law. Shavell's distinction is between activity level, understood as the extent of the activity engaged in, and precaution level, understood as the extent of precautions taken (Shavell 1987, pp. 21–30).

[51]  Cf. Tony Honoré (1964, p. 463); Honoré (1988); Dennett (1985, ch. 6).

[52]  An objection along these general lines was put to me by Arthur Ripstein.

[53]  That is why I prefer to speak, at this stage of the analysis, of an ordinary rather than a reasonable person. The term "reasonable" suggests the norms of reasonable care, which enter into the analysis at a later stage, when the determination of fault is at issue. At that point it is appropriate to ask what the reasonable rather than the ordinary person would do. The ordinary and reasonable persons are both normative constructs, but the latter involves action-guiding norms in a way that the former does not.

[54]  See note 3 above.

[55]  This objection was put to me by Ronald Dworkin. Arthur Ripstein makes an argument along similar lines in Ripstein (1994, pp. 11–12).

[56]  I owe this point to Paul Litton.

[57]  Some courts accept that a defendant should be relieved of liability if he suffers from a mental disability serious enough to interfere with his capacity to foresee harm (or, what comes to the same thing, his capacity to appreciate his duty of care). See, e.g., *Canada (Attorney-General) v. Connolly*, 64 D.L.R. (4th) 84 (B.C. S.C. 198); *Breunig v. American Family Insurance Co.*, 173 N.W. 2d 619 (Wis. 1970). Other courts take a different view, and this is in fact the predominant trend in modern tort law. See, e.g., *Wenden v. Trikha*, 8 C.C.L.T. (2d) 138 (Alberta Q.B. 1991); *Preferred Risk Mutual Insurance Co. v. Saboda*, 489 So. 2d 768 (Fl. 1986); *Roberts v. Ramsbottom*, [1980] 1 All E.R. 7 (Q.B. 1979). Typically these are driving cases, and the court is clearly concerned to ensure that the plaintiff is compensated by the defendant driver's liability insurance. This is, evidently, a consequentialist rather than a non-consequentialist consideration. It is, moreover, a consequentialist argument that proves too much: if loss-spreading is that important, it should justify a standard of strict liability for motorists, and not just an objective requirement of capacity in negligence cases. Policy concerns of course have a place in the law of tort, even on an understanding of tort law that is fundamentally non-consequentialist. In the context of such an understanding, however, it seems wrong to displace the usual requirement of outcome-responsibility on such relatively superficial grounds.

[58]  See the discussion of moral luck in Section IV.

[59]  *Donoghue,* [1932] A.C. 562, at 580.

[60]  I develop the ideas sketched in the remainder of this section at much greater length in Stephen Perry, "Risk and the Meaning of Negligence," (unpublished manuscript).

[61]  The only situations in which it is not true that both parties create the objective risk are situations in which the Coasean point would not hold either, if harm were to occur. For example, George blankets the entire world with poisonous gas and in consequence kills Paul (along with a lot of other people). Of course, some *attribute* of Paul is causally implicated in his death, namely, his susceptibility to poisonous gas. But no *action* he took was causally implicated (unless we treat his propensity to remain on the planet as somehow involving an action).

[62]  The classic discussion of this issue is Learned Hand's judgment in *The T.J. Hooper,* 60 F. 2d 737 (2d Cir. 1932) (rejecting defendant's allegation that there existed a custom on ocean-going tugs of not having a radio aboard).

[63] *Bolton v. Stone,* [1951] A.C. 850 (H.L.). At one time I accepted that the level-of-risk idea was the appropriate formulation of the negligence standard. See Perry (1988, pp. 168–71). Other theorists still accept this view. See Weinrib (1995, pp. 148–52); Wright (1995, pp. 261–3).

[64] *Carroll Towing,* 159 F. 2d 169, 173.

[65] See, e.g., Epstein (1985a, p. 40).

[66] Ronald Dworkin views cost-benefit analysis in tort law along somewhat similar lines Dworkin (1986, pp. 302–8). Dworkin notably assumes that the use of cost-benefit analysis must be constrained in various ways, such as by rights or fundamental interests, but does not say very much about how that would work. He also relies on the assumption that what he calls the test of comparative cost will work out fairly for everyone in the long run. The account of constraint that I give here, which is based on the idea that cost–benefit analysis will not apply in the case of non-normal risks, lends that assumption some plausibility. Dworkin's theory of torts, it should be noted, differs from mine in that its staring point is a conception of distributive, not corrective, justice. I criticize this aspect of his theory in Perry (2000).

[67] Cf. Judge Cardozo's decision in *Adams v. Bullock,* 227 N.Y. 208, 125 N.E. 93 (1919): "Chance of harm though remote, may betoken negligence, if needless. Facility of protection imposes a duty to protect." See also *Wagon Mound (No. 2),* 1967 A.C. 617, 643–4, in which Lord Reid said that a reasonable man would not neglect a "real" risk (i.e., a non-substantial risk which would nonetheless occur to the mind of a reasonable man in the defendant's position) "if action to eliminate it presented no difficulty, involved no disadvantage, and required no expense." On the idea that negligence involves specific untaken precautions rather than a full-blown cost–benefit analysis, see Grady (1989).

[68] In the actual case, the House of Lords held that the defendants were not liable. But all the judges said that the case was very close to the line, even though the risk in absolute terms of being hit by a cricket ball was clearly quite low. This supports the thesis that what matters is not level of risk as such, but rather the normality of the risk relative to an accepted pattern of interaction.

[69] See, e.g., *Spano v. Perini Corp.,* 25 N.Y. 2d 11, 250 N.E. 2d 31 (1969).

[70] *Restatement (Second) of Torts,* § 520A.

[71] *Restatement (Second) of Torts,* §§ 519, 520.

[72] *Rylands v. Fletcher,* L.R. 3 H.L. 330 (1868). Recently the House of Lords has made clear that the rule in *Rylands* requires that the plaintiff's harm have been reasonably foreseeable, which means that the rule is an instance of foresight-based strict liability rather than, as has sometimes been thought, causation-based absolute liability. This understanding of *Rylands* is in accordance with the avoidability conception of outcome-responsibility. *Cambridge Water Co. v. Eastern Counties Leather PLC,* [1994] 2 A.C. 264.

[73] Claire Finkelstein criticized an earlier version of the theory of outcome-responsibility I defend on the grounds that it should, under certain circumstances, permit liability to be imposed for outcome-responsibility alone, even in the absence of fault. See Finkelstein (1992, pp. 956–62), criticizing Perry (1993). I think this is basically correct, although the number of instances of liability for outcome-responsibility in the absence of fault will be fewer than Finkelstein suggests. This is because outcome-responsibility does not give rise to a duty to compensate when it arises within the context of an accepted pattern of interaction. It only gives rise to such a duty when it amounts to an instance of unilateral risk imposition.

[74] This argument is, in a sense, the converse of the argument discussed in the preceding section, according to which outcome-responsibility should be considered as necessary and sufficient for tort liability, and not just as necessary.

[75] 248 N.Y. 339, 162 N.E. 99 (1928).

[76] On the more general issue of the relationship between corrective and distributive justice, see Perry (2000).

[77] The criticisms of the distributive approach that are summarized in this paragraph I have set out in more detail in Perry (1992b, pp. 467–74).

[78] Cf. Keeton (1963, p. 21).

[79] Coleman (1992a, pp. 306–18). The "mixed" conception of corrective justice that Coleman defends in *Risks and Wrongs* is, in many respects, similar to the account of tort law, based on outcome-responsibility, for which I have been arguing here. See Perry (1992a). Recently, in an article coauthored with Arthur Ripstein, Coleman has adopted an apparently different, more politically-oriented, conception of responsibility for harmful outcomes (Coleman and Ripstein 1995).

[80] Recently Jules Coleman and Arthur Ripstein have argued, jointly as well as severally, that the underlying form of responsibility in tort law is not, as I have suggested, an aspect of our most fundamental understanding of moral agency, but rather a free-standing, sui generis, and ultimately political concept that does not involve a notion of control at all. Ripstein (1994); Coleman and Ripstein (1995). I have responded to Ripstein's article in the discussion at the end of Section III, and to Coleman and Ripstein's jointly authored article in Perry (1998). I hope to respond to their most recent work, and in particular to their interesting criticisms of my own approach to these matters, in future work. See Ripstein (1999, pp. 97–104); Coleman (1998b, pp. 310–16) and Coleman, "Tort Law and Tort Theory: Preliminary Reflections on Method," (this volume).

# 4

# The Significance of Doing and Suffering

## MARTIN STONE*

### I. Introductory: Understanding Tort Law

Nor should we make the same demand for an explanation in all cases. Rather, it is sufficient in some cases to have "the that" shown properly. This is so where "the that" is a
first thing and a starting point.

Aristotle, *Nicomachean Ethics,* 1098b1

Negligence cases constitute the largest item of business on the civil side of the nation's
trial courts. Yet we lack a theory to explain the social function of the negligence concept.

Posner, *A Theory of Negligence*

Modern tort law looks out on a situation which is ubiquitous in human affairs
and inherent, as a possibility, in the fact of human action: a situation in which
the actions of one person are connected to the misfortune of another. Nowhere
does the law attach significance to this just as such. Rather, throughout the
world today, tort law asks: Is the plaintiff's suffering a consequence of some
impropriety on the defendant's part, or is it a mere misfortune, a case of bad
luck?[1] As "mere misfortune," the plaintiff's suffering would be without legal
significance, something on par with a natural event, like a destructive turn in
the weather. But if there is impropriety – if, for example, the likely prospect of
the plaintiff's suffering makes it "negligent" for the defendant to have acted as
she did – then the plaintiff is entitled to receive, and the defendant obligated to
pay, compensation.

This paper concerns the terms in which we might understand tort law – that
is, make sense of it by exhibiting the reasons in play in it.[2] I argue (1) that contemporary functionalism fails to make sense of central features of the law, and
(2) that the significance of what Aristotle calls "corrective justice" can come
into sharp focus against the background of an understanding of the way functionalism fails.[3] To grasp the source of the trouble with functionalism is to see
the need for an account of tort law which attaches direct normative significance
to the relation that exists between two persons whenever it appropriately can be

said, concerning a certain injury, that one person "did it" and the other "suffered it." The doing and suffering of wrong is the key element in the situation which brings a concern for corrective justice into play.

Bound up with these claims about how to understand tort law is a further methodological issue concerning the relation we should expect to find between a reason-exhibiting account of the law (which may innocuously be called a "theory" of it) and the substantive conceptions present in the law itself. Recent tort theory offers a number of partially overlapping discussions of corrective justice. Part of my motivation for giving special attention to Aristotle's discussion is that it brings this methodological issue (concerning the relation between the law and its theory) into especially sharp relief.[4]

The issue arises, it may be said, because tort law is not just a set of results concerning who wins and loses in particular cases, but also a discursive or concept-involving practice purporting to justify those results. As Posner says, it is the "negligence concept" concerning which a theory is wanted. This means that an understanding of tort law must be an understanding of certain legal understandings: of the concepts through which the law is self-consciously organized and which figure in its everyday application. However, someone seeking to understand tort law, in the present sense, is obviously not merely wanting to learn *that* the present legal understandings are such-and-such; she is not going to be satisfied (nor should she be) by a mere recitation of legal doctrine, say along the lines of Prosser's famous hornbook (Keeton 1984). If it is sometimes enough in ethical inquiry, as Aristotle puts it, properly to exhibit *the that,* still, we might stress (what is part of the same thought), "the that" needs to be exhibited *properly.* The question is: What do we lack when we lack an appropriate theoretical understanding of a concept like negligence? Also: Is there a misunderstanding of this (a demand for explanation which misconstrues what we lack) to which we are, in such inquiries, sometimes prone?

I take it that, for anyone seeking to understand tort law, at least two things will be insufficiently perspicuous in a Prosser-like restatement. First, what good, if any, the practice touches on; second, what unity it has – is there a way of grasping which instances or strands are in keeping with it and which are mistaken departures? These two aspects of understanding the law are related. In Prosser, we have merely a kind of useful sociological report concerning everything jurists typically take the law to comprise.[5] If, however, we can see how these juridical "takings," or some main core of them, touch on some good, we become entitled to reject some purported instances of the practice as deviations (misunderstandings or mistakings) – namely, those that do not further this good. To understand tort law is thus to grasp its unity in a distinctly practical (and not merely sociological) way.[6]

How does functionalism endeavor to further an understanding of tort law in this sense? Essentially, the functionalist proposes to exhibit tort law as a means of advancing one or more independently defined goals – e.g., "deterrence" or "compensation" – each subsumable under the more general aim of reducing accident costs.[7] Allowing that this general aim is worthwhile,[8] part of the attraction of this proposal is that it offers a standpoint for assessing the law which is independent of the law itself. That is, the goals which suit the functionalist's theoretical purposes are such that: (1) What it is to achieve them can be fully spelled-out without reference to the concepts through which the law is self-consciously organized; and (2) they can (therefore) function as part of a demonstration of the goodness (or otherwise) of particular legal doctrines, without relying on the sort of practical thinking which figures in the law's everyday application.[9] In positing goals which meet these requirements, functionalism is congruous with a familiar picture of the division of labor between the law and its theory. In this picture, theory plays a "grounding" role; it is called upon to supply an independently standing measure to which the law, if it is genuinely reason affording, will conform.

Given the independent standing of his goals, there is an intelligible tendency for the functionalist to conclude, when confronted by the ways the law might actually frustrate rather than advance such goals, "So much the worse for the law, if, by such theoretical lights, it doesn't measure up." In fact, many functionalists today embrace this conclusion. Tort law, they say, should be "repealed" in favor of other legal arrangements for deterring wrongdoing and compensating accident victims: "There is a widespread social consensus in favor of deterring wrongdoing and compensating accident victims. But . . . it is difficult to argue that tort law well serves these . . . goals. [W]ere tort law for accidents repealed, society as a whole would gain."[10] My argument aims at least to make plausible a different conclusion. Partly by understanding why functionalism is apt to become a brief for the abolition of tort law, we might come to see tort law as the expression of an ethical idea (corrective justice) which is original to it but whose content is not fully graspable in a way which will satisfy the functionalist's demand for an independent measure.

Corrective justice, I argue, can serve to identify the aim of tort law and thus provide a way of grasping its practical unity. One might even say that tort law is a means of advancing corrective justice, as long as one is clear on the essential point, viz., that no reference is made here to any goals or purposes which satisfy requirements (1) and (2) above. Rather, understanding tort law, on this account, traces a circle: the law's aim is to express the requirements of corrective justice; but fully grasping the content of corrective justice calls for the same sort of jurisprudential thinking as occurs in the elaboration of legal doctrine in the circumstances of particular cases. As will emerge, there is a tendency to object that, so construed, corrective justice does not really comprise an explanatory alternative to the functionalist's notion of cost reduction in a theory of tort. That is half-right and half-wrong. For so conceived, corrective justice comprises an alternative to the functionalist's notion of what a theoretical explanation of the law has got to be.

To develop these claims, and to consider the objections, it will be helpful to begin by sketching the main concepts of tort law. Doing so naturally risks begging the questions of someone who has a theory of these concepts. But if that meant that we could not describe tort law, would it make sense to speak of a theory which grounded it, much less to ask whether we ought to abolish it? (Coleman, 1988, pp. 1251–3). The main point to be grasped from the following sketch will be that in tort, one person has done wrong (and is therefore obliged to make compensation) if and only if another person has been wronged (and is entitled to compensation). As befits a pretheoretical description of the law, this appears merely to state a commonplace: tort law connects two particular parties through an adjudication of liability. However, the significance of this apparent commonplace will come out by way of contrast to cases in which the appropriate conception of wrongdoing involves no such bi-conditional. Functionalism, to anticipate the argument, leaves no room for such bi-conditionality; and since such bi-conditionality is basic to (what we understand as) tort law, it may be said (given that the thing to be understood here is not present apart from such basic understandings) that, in a functionalist account, tort law itself goes missing.

What then are the basic legal understandings which someone seeking to understand tort law is seeking to understand?

## II. The Basic Rule

Another topic is derived from correlatives. If to have done rightly or justly may be predicated of one, then to have suffered similarly may be predicated of the other. Similarly with ordering and executing an order. As Diomedon the tax-contractor said about the taxes, "if selling them is not disgraceful for you, buying them is not disgraceful for us." And if rightly or justly can be predicated of the sufferer, it can equally be predicated of the doer, and if of the doer, then also of the sufferer. (Aristotle, *Rhetoric,* 1397a23–7[11])

### *II.1*

In tort, the plaintiff complains that she has been injured by the defendant's wrongdoing. Such wrongdoing may consist in the defendant's having acted with the intention of injuring, or having acted recklessly or negligently, or sometimes simply having engaged in an activity that, even when carefully conducted, carries a high risk of injury to others. In fact, most tort cases involve negligence, and that is the sort of case I shall focus on here.[12]

In America, whenever the answer is subject to reasonable doubt, it is almost always a jury, not a judge, which ultimately decides the question of whether the defendant acted negligently. This division of functions evinces an aspect of the law's self-understanding. It marks a distinction between questions concerning the general legal standard to be applied and questions concerning the judgment to be made in the particular case (something about which the law, in leaving the case to the jury, appears to say that it has, appropriately, nothing to say).[13] As it turns out, the standard which the law supplies is rather general and abstract. Here is the instruction typically read to the jury:

Negligence is the doing of something which a reasonably prudent person would not do, or the failure to do something a reasonably prudent person would do, under circumstances similar to those shown by the evidence.

It is the failure to use ordinary or reasonable care.

Ordinary or reasonable care is that care which persons of ordinary prudence would use in order to avoid injury to themselves or others under circumstances similar to those shown by the evidence.[14]

Two points are especially apt to be underscored by the judge in explaining this instruction to the jury.

First, negligence *is the doing of something.* It is an assessment of the quality of the defendant's *conduct,* not his state of mind, much less his intentions, motives, or character. Naturally, inadvertence or indifference to the consequences of one's actions tends to result in dangerous acts. But no particular mental shortcoming is necessary (nor, of course, ever sufficient) for conduct to be negligent; negligence is consistent with concern for the plaintiff or with anxious attention to the surrounding circumstances.

Second, negligence is the doing of something which a *reasonably prudent person* would not do. The defendant's conduct is to be measured by reference to the conduct of a standard person located in the same or similar circumstances and knowing at least what the defendant knows (e.g., that a particular glass is filled with poison), if not in fact more. Such a general or non-individualized standard notably leaves out of account many aspects of the defendant's *capacity* to act without creating dangers to others – for example, his intelligence, powers of discernment, physical adroitness, or ability to appreciate risk.[15]

Summarizing these two features of the negligence standard, it is common to say that negligence is an objective standard of conduct.

There is a sense in which negligence is also a fault-based standard. Generally this means that conduct which injures another, but which is reasonable in the relevant sense, is without legal significance. Given the objectivity of the standard, however, talk of negligence as a kind of "fault" displays important asymmetries with what we might think of as distinctively moral notions of fault. To say that something is someone's fault, in that distinctive sense, is usually to say something not just about what they did but about *them* as well, for example, that they are open to blame for not doing better; and this implies the availability of blame-deflecting or mitigating excuses that speak to the individual's capacities, intentions, or motives. The objectivity of the negligence standard functions precisely to make unavailable all but a narrow class of such excuses. So one might say that if negligence involves a kind of fault, this need not be any fault in the actor, only in the act itself.

A further feature of the tort plaintiff's complaint is implicit in all of this. The defendant's wrongdoing and the plaintiff's injury are legally significant not as two discrete, coexisting items, but only as they stand in the relation of cause and effect. It follows that two actors, identical in point of their carelessness, will have different legal obligations if only one has the misfortune of causing injury, just as two victims, identical in point of their injuries, will have different entitlements to compensation if only one has the good fortune, such as it is, to identify some wrongdoing in the chain of events leading up to her injury.

In fact, the requisite liability-creating relation between wrongdoing and injury is even more stringent this. To see why, consider a now famous story. An employee of the Long Island Railroad pushes a passenger in order to help him board a train that has already started to depart.[16] In doing this, the employee dislodges a plain brown package that the passenger is carrying, a package giving no notice of its contents – fireworks. The package explodes when it hits the ground, causing a heavy scale to tip over and fall on a woman who is standing at the other end of the platform. Now assuming that the employee has done something that the 'reasonable person' would not have done,[17] a story like this exhibits something about the (tragic) nature of action[18] that is apt to suggest the following thought: If civil liability is not to be unduly extended, say, to all the upshots of faulty action, and if it is not to be unduly restricted, say, to actions only in their intended or foreseen aspects (restricted, thus, in a way that would belie the objectivity of the negligence standard), then there is bound to be a recurring question in the civil law that is not yet answered simply by placing an instance of wrongdoing and injury in the same chain of events. For lawyers, this is the question of whether the defendant's wrongdoing was a "proximate cause" of the plaintiff's injury.

Attempts to say exactly what relation the term proximate cause is looking for notoriously engender controversy – which is not to say, of course, that there are not clear or agreed-upon cases. But more important than having a particular formula is simply to see more precisely what work this concept is needed to do. A common judicial gloss says, in effect, that an appropriate specification of the type of injury (say, a concussion), of its manner of occurrence (a falling scale) and of the class of person to whom it occurred (someone standing on the platform) must be such as to exhibit the action creating the risk of just such injury as wrongful. In short, the risk or prospect of the plaintiff's injury must be part of the account of why the defendant, in acting as he did, was taking an unreasonable risk.

The meaning of this may be brought into clearer focus by seeing how the court applied it in the case at hand. The majority held that the plaintiff had not been wronged at all – there was no tort. For what made the railroad employee's conduct wrongful, in their judgment, was at most the prospect of injury to the boarding passenger or his property, not the prospect of injury to the plaintiff, the woman on the platform. To use the foregoing terms: The prospect of someone on the platform being injured by falling scales in an explosion was not the sort of thing that could figure in an appropriate specification of what made the defendant's action unreasonable, however unreasonable it may have been.[19]

To complete this survey of basic tort concepts, it should to be added that there is, in general, no legally wrongful conduct unless the defendant *acted* in a way that caused injury; it is not enough that he merely failed to confer a benefit on the plaintiff. The point of this distinction – classically, between nonfeasance and misfeasance – is sometimes described in terms of the value of choice associated with the law of contract. It marks a boundary beyond which the duties of tort law (to modify one's activity for the sake of others) do not reach, hence a sphere in which a legal entitlement to enlist another's assistance in one's own projects can come only by way of securing their consent (Epstein, 1973, p. 199). Failing to help a drowning swimmer you happen to come upon is the classic case of nonfeasance, whereas failing to assist the injured driver of a vehicle you even quite innocently crash into is apt to be considered misfeasance, an act bringing about further injury. What is the difference? The relevant distinction is not given by the grammatical distinction between doing and not-doing, as the jury instructions on negligence quoted above show. Nor obviously is the pertinent idea of an act simply that of a doing or not-doing that leaves another person worse-off than they would otherwise have been; in both of these cases, someone's failure to do something does that. Apparently what is needed here is the idea of a doing or not-doing that is causally relevant to the creation of injury by creating also the risk that materialized in injury. On this basis, we may distinguish the case of the drowning swimmer as nonfeasance by the fact that the risk of injury already exists independently of the person who merely fails to head it off.[20] This explanation represents the idea of a tortious act as part and parcel of the core idea present through the concepts of negligence and proximate cause: the idea of an agent's conduct as wrongful in virtue of the nature of the risk it creates of injury to another.

## II.2

We might now draw together the elements in this discussion in the form of a rule, as follows:

*Basic Rule of Negligence Liability:* If D (1) acts (2) negligently (without taking the care of a reasonable person under the circumstances) and thereby (3) causes, (4) and proximately so, (5) P's injury, then P is entitled to compensation from D and D has an obligation to pay compensation to P.[21]

Still sticking close to the surface of things, two basic features of tort liability might be surmised from this rule.

1. *Correlativity.* Tort liability involves exactly two persons (it is bi-polar) who have come to stand, through previous events, in the following relation: One

has acted wrongfully and the other has been wronged by suffering the wrongful aspect of the first's action. To establish, in tort, that one has been wrongfully injured is thus to establish that another has done wrong (and vice versa); each of these – the doing and suffering of wrong – entails the other.

If doing and suffering wrong are correlatives in tort law, that would seem, however obvious, to be a not insignificant fact. For just as obviously, much of the vocabulary of human conduct, even wrongdoing, doesn't fit the pattern. To say that A insults B is not to say, or need not be, that B suffers insult from A; if A poisons the drinks, it obviously does not follow that anyone has been poisoned. Moreover, outside the scope of civil law, the expression "doing wrong" itself does not invariably fit the pattern. Many of the duties laid down by criminal law, for example, can be breached without injuring another (e.g., reckless driving) or without injuring any other person in particular (e.g., tax evasion). And so-called wide obligations – like those of benevolence or charity, or those falling upon public agencies (to act for the public benefit) – also break the pattern. Since such obligations are owed to everyone, they are not, except under special conditions, owed to anyone in particular. So the breach of such obligations sometimes presents a case in which it is correct to say that someone does wrong without anyone else *being* wronged.[22]

Doing and suffering wrong are, moreover, not the only manifestation of correlativity in tort law. At the remedial stage of the lawsuit, the defendant is obliged to pay damages just when the plaintiff is entitled to *be paid* damages.[23] Such correlativity is so familiar in civil law as to be much of the time practically invisible. But its significance appears, as will emerge, when one begins to theorize about the law.

2. *Reasonableness.* The second basic feature of tort law is its use of a norm of reasonableness, something seen not only in the explanation of negligence given to the jury (the reasonable person) but also in the idea of an appropriate specification of action (reasonable foreseeability) which, as I shall note later (Section IV.4), often informs the arguments of lawyers and judges about the application of proximate cause in the circumstances of particular cases.

So in sum: It looks as if correlativity describes the *form* of tort liability, while reasonableness, at least in the predominant case of the Basic Rule, describes its content. If one wanted a single formula, it might be this: Tort law is reasonableness as it bears on two-party transactions. As I shall argue (in Sections III and IV), to see tort law as an embodiment of corrective justice is to see its content as an expression of the formal requirement that any grounds for describing one party's doing as wrongful must also be appropriate grounds for so describing another's suffering; hence any grounds for the defendant's liability must also be appropriate grounds for the plaintiff's entitlement to recover. What is meant by this – and how it is something more than a description of any interpersonal liability rule – can begin to appear by seeing how such a formal requirement is in fact flouted in the functionalist understanding of the Basic Rule; how the law's content comes to chafe, on such an understanding, against its form.

### III. Tort Theory: Functionalism

Law is a human construct designed to accomplish certain goals.
Guido Calabresi, "Concerning Cause and the Law of Torts"

*III.1*

How does the issue raised in Section I about how to "understand" the Basic Rule come about? Some brief remarks will suffice here to motivate the endeavor of tort theory.

Necessarily, in any legal culture that has negligence law (and, as it happens, in every legal culture that has tort law), the Basic Rule is treated as reason affording, at least by legal officials in their official actions. To the question, "Why does this person have to pay compensation to that one?" an appropriately official answer would be: "Because his negligent conduct was a proximate cause of the other's injuries." But even in officialdom, there are doubts today about whether the legal rule cited in such an answer captures any genuine reasons at all.

The doubt comes out in a number of questions. First and foremost, why have a system of interpersonal liability? Why not allow all unintended losses either to lie where they fall or to be redistributed by mechanisms of social insurance? Second, if interpersonal liability, why liability on the terms the Basic Rule prescribes? Why require proof of a causal connection? Shouldn't it be enough, where such proof is hard to come by, that the defendant is a wrongdoer and the plaintiff innocently injured?[24] If not, how are we to defend the double moral luck that must apparently follow: the fact that some wrongdoers benefit (and some victims suffer) from the contingency that some unreasonable actions do not (and some reasonable actions do) complete themselves in injury? Or, leaving causation aside, consider the Basic Rule's definition of wrongdoing. In one way, the standard of reasonable care seems too permissive. Shouldn't everyone who causes injury be answerable for it? (Epstein, 1973, pp. 158–60) Yet insofar as the standard is objective, it might also seem too harsh. Is it fair to judge the defendant by a standard he may be incapable of meeting? Perhaps our reason for doing so lies in the victim's need for compensation.[25] But then doesn't that need also argue against reasonable care in favor of some stricter standard of liability? Perhaps our reason for rejecting a stricter standard is the moral unfairness of liability without fault. But then isn't that also a reason for taking into consideration a person's particular capacities in acting?[26]

In speaking of "reasonableness as it bears on two-party transactions," it may sound as if tort law is basically sound. The preceding questions suggest that nothing about it is obviously sound. That is the moment of the theorist's call for an understanding of tort law, an account of its aim and unity (Section I).

## *III.2*

Functionalism, as Section I suggested, presents not just a theory of tort law but also a particular kind of theoretical project. Against the background of the foregoing questions, the tendency of this project might be expressed as follows. Reasoning toward conviction in answers to these questions is not exactly lacking in tort law as we now find it. But, generally, the juridical procedures for attaining such conviction – e.g., the specification of abstract concepts ("fair," "just") through the analogical comparison of hard cases to clear or settled ones – treat the law as if it already captured, however imperfectly, reasons for action; as if it expressed genuine (and not merely purported) requirements of fairness or justice. The functionalist is apt to regard such juridical procedures as rationally second best. In Posner's call for a theory of negligence (Section I), the work to be done by theory contrasts with practice in two related ways. First, by referring to independently defined goals, a theory would connect the law to something we take (at least more easily, apparently, than we take the law) to be normatively genuine or real.[27] Second, once we accept that the law's aim is to advance such goals, then, in principle, only empirical problems (requiring for their solution only information about the effects of various legal rules), and not any traditional problems of jurisprudence (requiring the forgoing sort of juridical thinking) would stand in the way of attaining conviction in the appropriateness of this or that legal rule or judgment. On the basis of the sort of theory Posner says we lack, the appropriateness of the Basic Rule could thus be exhibited as the conclusion of an argument involving (1) independently standing normative premises, and (given sufficient information), (2) only such further steps of reasoning as do not require, for their cogency, any of the law's distinctively practical procedures.

Before turning to the details of the functionalist theory of tort, it is worth asking: Why should it be thought that rational conviction in the appropriateness of the law requires something so distinct from the kind of thinking which informs the law's everyday application? The functionalist himself does not usually see a question here. Rather, he is apt to speak as if it were obvious that an account of the law's functions is just what one has when one has something more than a merely habitual or superstitious acceptance of it. Here, for example, is Guido Calabresi toward the end of a virtuosic analysis of what he calls "the functions of causal language" in tort law:

Causal requirements, like all other legal requirements must ultimately justify themselves in functional terms. Law is a human construct designed to accomplish certain goals. Often – perhaps most of the time – the goals are terribly complex and hard to analyze clearly, and one is properly suspicious of analysis and prescription that would discard time-honored legal terms because one cannot find immediate, clear policy justifications for them. Still, the object of law is to serve human needs, and thus legal terms (which in other contexts may have other deeper meanings) must sooner or later be linked to the service of human needs. (Calabresi 1975, p. 105)

This is meant to sound like common sense. Surely one wouldn't want to deny that law is something we make for a purpose or that its object is to serve human needs![28] Yet as an account of what compels the functionalist's program it seems quite dogmatic.

1. "Law is a human construct," to be sure. But here it seems worth bearing a distinction in mind. Some things we might call human constructs are such as to distinguish our human form of life from other things which are not human or even forms of life: counting, drawing, giving reasons, the teaching of correct ways of using words, the recognition of certain bodies as the presence of other minds, or the idea of another's suffering as something demanding acknowledgment, to name a few.[29] Whereas other things we call human constructs are such as to distinguish the life of a particular society at a particular time: an economy based on commodity exchange, the death penalty, television, and so on. The two categories are not substantively exclusive; items in the first are bound to appear, under more specific descriptions, in the second.[30] But we naturally do not expect things described by the first category to be intelligible as instruments, for the simple reason that no human goal is any more fundamental than these things; to cease to understand them, one wants to say, is no longer to find intelligible the fact of human life – everything that human beings say and do – as such.[31] Now is it so clear that there is no aspect of law which this category describes? Even granting H. L. A. Hart's suggestion that legal systems may be understood as special constructs, involving second-order rules, introduced to remedy defects (related to the needs of shared existence) in pre-legal societies that lack such rules (Hart 1961, pp. 89–96), is it so clear that all of the first-order norms that have figured in such systems (e.g., norms against intentional destruction of others, or norms of reciprocity and compensation) might similarly be explained as mere instruments (for which there might as well be other instruments) in the service of more basic human needs?[32] None of this is to imply, at any rate, that all things in the second category of human constructs *are* instruments. Calabresi must somehow be forgetting all the aspects of human culture which (though certainly "constructed by us" – who else?) do not obviously invite explanation in terms of their functions, much less a reductive account of the meanings of their central concepts.

2. "The object of law is to serve human needs," to be sure. But why suppose that a functionalist analysis is required if the law is not to appear disengaged from this object? In the context of a certain philosophical tendency to say *fiat justita, pereat mundus,* one may wish to stress a good point in what Calabresi says: If the perpetuation of the law in social institutions is rationally to commend itself to us, it ought to be possible to see the law as making human life

fare better rather than worse. But one need not question such a broad welfarist constraint as this in order to see that Calabresi has offered no reason to accede to the further requirement that it must always be possible to say *how* human life fares better in terms that make no reference to the conceptions of the law itself – e.g., to its way of expressing ideas of right and wrong. I take it that even a so-called deontologist like Kant may be understood as respecting such a welfarist constraint (rather than expressing the above mentioned philosophical tendency) when he says such things as:

> By the well-being of a state must not be understood the *welfare* of its citizens and their *happiness;* for happiness can perhaps come to them more easily and as they would like it to in a state of nature (as Rousseau asserts) or even under a despotic government. By the well-being of a state is understood, instead, that condition in which the constitution conforms most fully to principles of Right.[33]

The object of civic association, this says, is well-being, only not that kind of well-being (viz., "welfare," "happiness") which is already in reach in a state of nature. Civic association brings about a new kind of human good that is not just an operation (maximizing, equalizing, etc.) on more basic goods; it makes it possible for persons to live in a new way – in conformity with "principles of Right." The functionalist, in the present passage, appears as someone who dog-matically assumes that to keep one's common sense is to incur a commitment to exhibiting the latter good as just more of the same cloth. And so – ironically in the name of what passes today as "realism" about law – he lays down a new philosophical requirement: To understand the law must be to see it as bringing into reach such basic goods as every human society, independently of its de-veloped legal and ethical forms, may be presumed to want, hence goods that re-quire none of the law's distinctive conceptions to be concretely in view. (Of course, that is just the sort of good that is suited to function as part of a prem-ise in the sort of theoretical argument the functionalist feels we lack.)[34]

### III.3

Calabresi's principal nominee for such a basic good is "optimal accident cost-reduction." The goal that figures in Posner's theory of negligence – efficient de-terrence – is in fact one component of this general idea. The main point to be argued now is that no theoretical conjuring can pull an understanding of tort law out of a hat containing only the components of this general idea (Sections III.4–III.8). But to begin with, what exactly does reducing accident costs in-volve?[35]

One naturally thinks first of the loss resulting from accidents themselves, their toll in human misery. But a program of minimizing just this sort of cost would paralyze human activity; it would be too expensive. Safety may be the first but it is never an absolute demand on any activity. What is needed is the idea of a safe enough activity, or rather – since, from an optimizing point of view, an activity can be either too risky or too safe – a reasonably safe activity. An activity is reasonably safe when it is carried on in such a way as to minimize the sum of both accident costs and prevention costs, the later including the cost of specific precautionary measures as well as the cost, in pleasure or profits foregone, of eliminating certain activities entirely.

If the law's aim is to reduce accidents costs, one of its main goals must thus be to deter activities that are not safe enough without over-deterring them (i.e., creating prevention costs not worth the savings in accidents they bring). Contemporary functionalists disagree about the efficacy of various legal rules in furthering this goal. But in the case of negligence liability (the Basic Rule), the general story is this. By compelling the unreasonable actor to pay damages equal to the cost of the accident, the law creates an incentive for self-interested agents to behave in a socially efficient way, that is, to take preventative measures whenever their cost is less than the expected cost of an accident.[36] The theory of negligence thus translates the legal idiom of reasonableness into economic rationality. Reasonable care stands for the requirement that persons conduct themselves so as to maximize the value of social resources by taking cost-effective measures against accidents.

Achieving such an ideal mix of accidents and safety is not yet sufficient, however, for the broader goal of optimal accident cost reduction. For given certain economic postulates (viz., the diminishing marginal utility of money or the increasing marginal utility of accident losses), accident costs may be reduced even *after* an accident has occurred by distributing the resulting loss either more widely or into deeper pockets (Calabresi 1970, p. 39ff). Hence some functionalists say that in addition to its deterrence goal, tort law has a compensation (or loss allocation) goal as well – it aims to make accident losses easier to bear by spreading them through the price system or through liability insurance.[37] In this way, the functionalist purports to give normative underpinnings to at least one of two judicial commonplaces about tort law, namely, that its purpose is to deter accidents and to compensate the victims of accidents.

### III.4

So much for the general idea of accident cost reduction. A good place to begin thinking about the prospects of this program is with one of the questions disputed among functionalists themselves, namely, whether tort law has, besides a deterrence goal, a compensation or loss allocation goal as well. No one supposes that tort law is merely a compensation system; if the overall aim is cost reduction, it can hardly make sense to reallocate accident losses without trying to prevent them as well. But given that reallocating accident losses is one way of reducing accident costs, why would anyone deny that tort law might *at least* be assigned a compensatory aim?

The answer is not hard to see. Rather than advancing compensation for accident victims, tort law mainly frustrates it: The Basic Rule restricts compensation to losses proximately caused by another's wrongdoing. Of course, given that compensating or reallocating accident losses is one way of reducing accident costs, this severe restriction bears not just on the issue dividing functionalists (concerning whether tort law has a compensatory aim), but also on the prospects of functionalism (as an account of tort law in terms of accident cost reduction) *tout court.* In denying compensation, tort law systematically forgoes opportunities to reduce accident costs by diffusing the losses of individual victims.[38]

It is possible to miss the depth of the problem here. The functionalist might grant that the ground he supplies for tort law (accident cost reduction) requires more loss reallocation than the law – given its restricted focus on wrongful losses – can deliver. But, he will say, that doesn't impede our thinking that cost reduction is an appropriate ground for tort law's treatment of *this* class of losses. Because tort law says nothing about how other losses should be dealt with, it does not frustrate compensation; it leaves open that losses falling outside its own domain might be dealt with by other mechanisms such as social insurance.

But anyone contemplating this response needs to explain why there should be a special legal domain centered on *wrongful* losses when the significance she attributes to suffered losses (an ameliorable social cost) cuts across any such qualifier.[39] The task, moreover, is not merely to give some point to a qualifier restricting the class of compensable losses; it is to explain the law's use of a qualifier that, in restricting the class of compensable losses, thereby also restricts the sources of compensation for those losses. The qualifier "wrongful" links the plaintiff's entitlement to repair to a specific defendant's obligation to make repair; no claim arises in tort against members of society at large. But nothing in the thought that what makes even a *wrongful* loss compensation-worthy is its status as an ameliorable social *loss* gives a reason for thus limiting the many ways of ameliorating it.[40] In general, the problem is that the goal of reducing accident costs by reallocating loss creates reasons of a much too unspecific sort. Even limiting the domain to wrongful loss, it creates reasons for a certain ameliorative outcome to be brought about, rather than reasons why one particular person, the properly identified defendant, should be the one to bring about that outcome.[41]

These considerations make it understandable why some functionalists should view tort law as a system of pure deterrence. In accounting for the defendant's obligation to pay damages, deterrence would presumably also account for the law's use of the qualifier "wrongful" to limit the class of compensable losses: The sort of losses singled out for compensation would be precisely those caused by activities which are worth deterring – activities which are not cost efficient from the point of view of safety. Such an account of tort obligation is only weakened, it might be supposed, by attributing to the law a compensatory aim which it either frustrates or, at best, advances haphazardly. Reallocating accident losses may be an important strand in a scheme of social welfare, but a welfare scheme that withheld benefits whenever a loss did not fall under the Basic Rule would seem rather anomalous (Posner 1972, p. 31).

## III.5

At first blush, deterrence looks promising in this explanatory role. For an agent-specific obligation to pay damages looks like an indispensable requirement of deterrence itself. If the obligation were anything less than agent-specific, the *ex-ante* incentive each agent has to take appropriate precautions – the very mechanism of deterrence – could not operate.

But, in fact, the idea of tort law as pure deterrence is not very promising at all. For the agent-specific obligation which deterrence is supposed to explain is not merely the obligation to pay, under certain conditions, an amount sufficient to motivate an economically rational agent, facing the future prospect of incurring such an obligation, to take steps to ensure that such conditions are never satisfied. This is the core idea of a deterrence function. But clearly what this describes – and all that deterrence, strictly speaking, requires – is a legally imposed obligation to pay an appropriately set penalty (a fine or tax), not an obligation to compensate another person, much less to compensate one particular person for the exact value of a particular loss. An agent-specific obligation to pay a penalty when future conditions are satisfied is indeed an indispensable element of any regime of deterrence; but an obligation, of the sort tort law creates, to pay compensatory damages is not. Between these two kinds of obligation there are in fact several significant asymmetries.[42]

First, and most obviously, the reasons for imposing a deterrent penalty are not reasons, just by themselves, for giving the proceeds to any particular person. Indeed, given the economic postulate that represents accident costs as greater or less depending on how they are allocated (Section III.4), it seems reasonable to think that the proceeds of deterrent penalties should be collected by the state (as happens with criminal fines) and allocated to those who need them most. In any case, there is an explanatory gap here. If deterrence is supposed to explain why tort law involves an agent-specific obligation to pay damages, the problem now is to explain why it also creates a victim-specific entitlement to collect the proceeds.

This gap provides a motivation for thinking that tort must have a compensatory aim. But among functionalists who (for the foregoing reasons: Section III.4) deny this, the basic explanation of the payment of damages to the plaintiff is that such damages are "the price of enlisting [the plaintiff's and his lawyer's] participation in the operation of the system" (Posner 1972, p.33) – in short, they are a bribe. The "system" envisioned here is one which regulates social activity on the basis of a norm of efficiency. But it is a system of private, not public, regulation. Instead of engaging executive and administrative agencies to enforce the norm, an incentive is created for private persons to identify substandard conduct and bring the requisite penalties to bear. The incentive is that a private person who takes on this job (of ersatz public prosecutor) may, if he wins the case, pocket the proceeds of the penalty collected from the defendant. Deterrence continues here to play a solo explanatory role. Making lawyers and their clients financially better off is not a *goal* of tort law; it is simply the means the state has chosen to put a system of deterrence into effect. (Another means might be to offer the financial incentive in question to lawyers only; see below.) Thus Posner: "That the damages are paid to the plaintiff is, from an economic standpoint, a detail" (Posner 1977, p. 143). Is this a good picture of tort law? Does it close the gap between an obligation to pay a deterrent penalty and an obligation to pay compensatory damages?

As a first point, it may be noticed that, on this "private regulation" picture, the tort plaintiff has not suffered a "wrong" in any sense which allows us to see his legal entitlement to damages as vindicating any prior claim – i.e., one arising in virtue of his prior relation with the defendant – to redress. His entitlement to damages has no deeper or firmer ground than this: the state has decided to make him a conditional offer of money in order to induce him to play a regulatory role. In accepting this offer, the plaintiff seeks, in effect, to collect a bounty after fulfilling its conditions by apprehending a wrongdoer.[43] Should it matter to our acceptance of this picture that the plaintiff and his lawyer are apt to view the matter otherwise? Or that the argument before the jury will imply, on both sides, that if the plaintiff is entitled to damages, it is by virtue of what has occurred between him and the defendant, and not merely his being a useful accessory for enforcing the norm of efficiency?[44] One need not deny the possibility Posner is exploiting – viz., that a society might create private rights of action as a means of regulation[45] – in order to suspect that the possibility pictured here, missing as it does the major participant's understandings, is not a good picture of tort law. But even leaving this aside, and attaching no disadvantage to pictures of a practice that portray its participants as entirely misconceiving what they are doing, the present picture would not – for at least two reasons – close the gap between a deterrent penalty on the one hand and tort law's obligation/entitlement to repair on the other.

1. The first reason has to do with the qualifications a person must meet to play the role of plaintiff-prosecutor in a torts case. It is in the nature of bounties and other incentives to act for a public purpose that they may be offered to a wide range of persons; generally, they are thought to be most effective in that form. It may indeed be true that the needs of deterrence are well served by giving *some* private party standing to prosecute violators and collect a reward if he is successful. But why should that standing be limited exclusively to someone injured at the hands of the defendant? Here we must imagine that the regula-

tory authority has determined that it would not be efficacious to bribe any other person – just as if the authorities in a Western movie were to offer a reward for the apprehension of the villain, but then limit (say, to the immediate family of his victims) the right to collect it. It may be that, for certain contingent empirical reasons, this has become (in the modern accident context) a rational thing to do. But this is hardly apparent. Granted, victims are in a relatively good position to know about potential violations of the norm of efficiency. But are others never in a better position to know or find out? (Is there no use, from the point of view of efficiency, for the resources of the professional bounty hunter?) And because lawyers are always involved in bringing the actions which enforce a legal norm (and best positioned to do so), might not the state do as well or better by offering the relevant incentives in the first place to lawyers who would then hire injured plaintiffs in much the way that they currently hire expert witnesses?[46] Besides severing the connection to participant understandings of the practice, the present picture leaves the rationality of tort liability hanging by a thin empirical thread.

2. A further difficulty with this picture centers not on the tort plaintiff's exclusive entitlement to collect, but on his exclusive entitlement to collect *damages*. The reward offered to the plaintiff is supposed to comprise a sufficient incentive to sue. But we might ask: (A) What is the relation between the idea of a sufficient incentive to sue and that of an appropriate deterrent penalty? (B) Are *either* of these ideas sufficient to bring the idea of a damage payment into view? All three ideas are commingled in the present picture: The *penalty* facing the defendant who does not take cost-justified precautions is to pay a *reward* offered for his apprehension, the value of which is determined by his victim's *actual loss*. But regarding (A): The idea of a sufficient incentive to sue (or to perform any other action for a public purpose) is only externally related (as again the practice of bounties will suggest) to the idea of an appropriate penalty to be brought against an offender. A sufficient incentive certainly need not involve an offer of the entire amount required for deterrent purposes; half that amount should do as well. And regarding (B): It appears that both categories – appropriate penalty and sufficient incentive – are themselves external to the measure of damages that tort law employs and that is natural to the idea of compensation or repair, viz., the victim's actual loss.[47] Thus, Posner has stated the matter only half correctly. It is not just the fact that "damages are paid to the *plaintiff*" which is, in the private-regulation picture, "a detail" (Posner 1977, p. 143). Equally insignificant is the fact that "*damages* are paid to the plaintiff."

A system of private regulation now might be imagined in which the qualifications for becoming a quasi-public prosecutor need not involve having suffered a recent injury or being involved in any causal transaction with the defendant; in which the qualified plaintiff or attorney who succeeds in her case would be paid, according to some established formula, an amount sufficient to insure that there will be a steady stream of similar persons willing to play this public role; and in which such payments are funded out of deterrent penalties assessed against defendants, with the difference collected by the state and used for public purposes. The tendency of current tort plaintiffs and their attorneys to think that the law vindicates entitlements to the repair of wrongful losses in some stronger sense than appears in this picture might at least be understandable when one reflects that, however worthwhile what is imagined here might be, no one would be in danger of confusing it with tort law.

### III.6

The argument so far against the thesis that tort law has a deterrence goal is essentially that this thesis renders tort law unrecognizable by leaving out of account the significance which the law gives to the notion of a victim entitled to be compensated for her loss. Despite this, it might be thought that, with the idea of deterrence, at least half the equation is solved: If an account is still owing of a victim's entitlement to compensation, we have at least a good account of an injurer's liability. But this is not so. A failure to account for the way tort law compensates victims must reflect negatively on the present account of the interest it takes in the activities of injurers. The reason is that while the idea of deterrence is essentially prospective (tort liability deters insofar as the prospect of incurring it under certain conditions creates an incentive to prevent those conditions from being realized), the category of an injurer (as opposed to someone who engages in injurious activity) is a retrospective one, the salience of which falls away when the corresponding idea of a victim (one who has suffered injury) comes to look like a mere detail.

The point may be explained like this. The obligation to repair an injury one has caused is naturally an obligation possessed by an injurer, someone retrospectively identified by reference to that injury. But since obligations to pay deterrent penalties need make no reference to the person who may turn out to suffer a particular course of conduct, by the same token, the conditions which trigger such obligations need not refer to the retrospective category of an injurer. Any substandard injurious conduct is, in principle, a suitable target of deterrent penalties, regardless of whether it happens to cause injury or not. Indeed, since the foundational idea of reducing accident costs is, by its very nature, both prospective and global (the relevant costs ranging over all future accidents and all preventative measures), deterrent penalties are ideally addressed to whomever can most cheaply, through modification of their own activity, avoid certain categories of accident costs (Calabresi 1970). There is no reason to expect that person to be an injurer in the conventional sense of one who has caused an accident. Except perhaps by way of functionalist stipulation, the best prospective accident-preventer may never have been a party to an accident at all.[48]

*III.7*

It is time to take stock. It appears that neither the idea of a compensation nor a deterrence function (the main components of the idea of accident cost reduction: Section III.3) makes sense of the way tort law pairs injurers and victims. What is more, these functions fail in symmetrical ways. The idea of compensation affords no reason why repairing the plaintiff's loss should be the obligation of a particular injurer; the idea of deterrence affords no reason why collecting damages from the defendant should be the entitlement of a particular victim. For compensation, the problem is why losses should be singled out only in terms that connect them to a particular injurer; for deterrence, it is why injurers should be singled out only in terms that look backward from one particular person's loss. Compensation makes an enigma of the Basic Rule insofar as it singles out *this* defendant for liability; deterrence, insofar as it singles out *this* plaintiff for recovery. The common problem is this: How could a rule governing the compensatory response of one party to another emerge from considerations attaching normative significance directly to *losses* as such, and to the two-party transactions on which the law focuses only derivatively? The common problem, simply put, is the bi-polarity (Section II.2) of tort law.

Someone might be tempted to think, however, that these symmetrical failures offer the interlocking materials for explanatory success. Since no one proposes that tort law's only aim is compensation, it might be said, the foregoing argument establishes only that it is something more than a system of pure deterrence. But why should it be assumed – the thought would continue – that at most one function should account for all of tort law's features? That is to ignore an obvious alternative, namely, that deterrence affords a reason for fixing liability on the defendant, compensation, a reason for paying the proceeds to the plaintiff. Striking the one-function assumption, isn't each of these goals, given the shape of its failure in a solo role, well-suited to remedy the defect of the other?

In fact, the answer is "no" – though it might appear otherwise on an understandable misdiagnosis of how each function fails when considered alone. The present (pluralist) proposal treats each function as if it gave merely incomplete reasons. For example: Specifying the function of the kitchen – the requirements of cooking – is not yet sufficient for designing the rest of the house. And if, in completing the house, we find we need to trade-off the optimal configuration of the kitchen against that of the common rooms, no special problem need arise. For it is perfectly clear why these rooms, these functions, are to be brought under the same roof. After all, it is a house we are designing. But of course it is not like this with tort law. Under the present proposal, tort law appears as a structure in which compensation occurs only when this also serves the requirements of deterrence (and vice versa). But why bring these functions together under the same roof where the requirements of each must check the pursuit of the other? Clearly, it only begs the question to suggest that tort liability represents a kind of optimality given the requirement that these goals be pursued in tandem. For what is wanted is precisely some way of rationally motivating this requirement.

Absent such a motivation, assigning one function to the defendant's liability and another to the plaintiff's recovery can hardly make for a pragmatically agreeable pluralism as opposed to a compounded explanatory crisis. In fact, it is not hard to see that what the pluralist has done is simply to start with the bi-polar form of tort law and then to ask what combination of welfare functions would roughly reproduce its contours. But bi-polarity cannot thus be pulled out of a hat. Because the rationality of compensating does not vary with presence of opportunities for deterring (nor vice versa), it seems implausible to think that someone starting with these goals would seize upon the bi-polar form of tort liability as a good way to implement them; that a legal structure that placed liability and recovery on the same grounds would commend itself when no such connection exists between the goals that liability and recovery are independently supposed to advance. So to be pulled out of this hat, bi-polarity must have been in it from the beginning. Which means that the first question of tort theory – What reason is there to join two parties? (Section III.1) – goes unanswered.

### III.8

If the form of tort law resists the substantive grounds that functional analysis would supply for it, what conclusion should be drawn from this? If, like Calabresi, one lays it down that "all legal requirements *must* ultimately justify themselves in functional terms" (see Section III.2), then it might seem to follow that tort law is rationally indefensible. That is in fact the conclusion drawn by many functionalist critics of tort law today. Tort law, they observe, frustrates the goals of compensation and deterrence, or frustrates their rational pursuit, by linking them together.[49] So tort law, these critics conclude, should be abolished and replaced by institutions that have compensation (e.g., social insurance) and deterrence (e.g., administrative regulation) as their straightforward aims. "The key to reform," as one critic understandably puts it, "is the complete uncoupling of compensation from deterrence" (Sugarman 1985, p. 664).

But here we ought to distinguish two versions of the claim that functional analysis is inhospitable to tort law. The functionalist can agree with one version of the claim (while still professing to have a correct understanding of tort law) because inherent in his theoretical project (Section III.2) is a particular way of conceiving the object of his theory. That object is not (or at least not in the first place) tort law, but rather, as it might be called, "the legal response to the problem of accidents," where the normatively salient fact about accidents (which calls for a legal response) is that they affect whatever basic good performs the theory's explanatory work – for example, accidents sometimes involve a preventable squandering of society's collective wealth. With such a basic good in hand, the functionalist takes himself to have the right starting point for an account of accident law,[50] and hence an appropriately external starting point for a certification (or decertification) of tort law, such certification turning ultimately on the empirical question of whether (or when, in what subset of situations) tort law is an appropriate response to the problem of accidents so conceived. Answering in the negative, the functionalist critic of tort law claims precisely to have a correct account of tort law that is also, as it turns out, inhospitable to it.[51]

But even if we are sympathetic to the functionalist's goals, and even if the best empirical information did speak against tort law as an efficacious means of advancing them, we might reasonably hesitate to embrace this claim; or to embrace it, anyway, on the basis of such an argument, whereby not just tort liability but the very idea of it would disappear, like an irrational superstition, without conceptual loss (cf. Ehrenzweig 1953, pp. 869, 871–2). For shouldn't we wonder why tort law had been dealing out judgments while keeping its reasons so secret? Perhaps, as some suggest, such secrecy is a condition of the appearance of judicial legitimacy.[52] But then shouldn't we be curious to know what it is about the law's traditional idiom that gives it so much as even the *appearance* of legitimacy? If even "time-honored legal terms" (Calabresi 1975, p. 105) must eventually be translated into welfare functions, is there not at least a good question, to which the functionalist gives no answer, as to why exactly *these* terms have been so honored by time? A similar question arises with regard to functionalist *defenses* of tort law. If it is true that the bi-polar form of tort law has been put offstage into the theorist's hat (as if tort law were a natural unity, like a house; Section III.7), does this not suggest that the form of tort law deserves a more basic explanation, one that makes perspicuous a reason for its limitations?

There is another possible conclusion which might be drawn from the argument so far, a different way of construing functionalism's apparent inhospitality to tort law. Simply put, in conceiving the object of his theory as the legal response to the problem of accidents, the functionalist never gets (what we understand as) tort law properly into view at all.[53] On the first conclusion, we find we may have good instrumental reasons, stemming from a concern with deterrence and compensation on the one hand, and from tort law's basic formal features on the other to replace tort law with forms of legal obligation and entitlement that involve no relation of interpersonal liability. On the second conclusion, tort law's basic formal features suggest that a practice of interpersonal liability is not to be understood merely as an instrument, even a bad one, for securing compensation and deterrence. Of course, it is only by the functionalist's lights that these conclusions need occlude one another.[54] But to make it plausible that the functionalist misunderstands the practice he seeks either to support or revise, we need of course to say how tort law is otherwise to be understood.

In the remainder of this essay, I shall suggest that, notwithstanding his unfamiliarity with modern negligence law, Aristotle's discussion of corrective justice both motivates the law's time-honored terms and provides a contemporarily relevant diagnosis of what goes wrong in the functionalist translation of them.

## IV. Corrective Justice

The just, then, is intermediate, since the judge is so.
                    Aristotle, *Nicomachean Ethics*

### IV.1

As it bears on the present issues, the key thought in Aristotle's discussion is simply that there are two distinct notions of justice. Both involve a norm of equality or fairness (*to ison*). But the judicial concern with equality in a situation of transactional wrongdoing (the domain of corrective justice) is distinct, Aristotle says, from a concern with equality in the allocation of benefits and burdens from a common stock (the domain of distributive justice):

> For here [in corrective justice] it does not matter if a decent person has taken from a base person, or a base person from a decent person, or if a decent or a base person has committed adultery. Rather, the law looks only at differences in the harm [inflicted], and treats the people involved as equals, when one does injustice while the other suffers it, and one has done the harm while the other has suffered it. Hence the judge tries to restore this unjust situation to equality, since it is unequal. (Aristotle, *NE,* 1132a)

Aristotle's point may be developed like this. In a distribution, two or more parties are related only *mediately,* through some criterion of desert – e.g., "decency/baseness" – which connects them to whatever items are to be shared among them.[55] The equality to be achieved through such connections is thus one of ratios or proportions, expressible by the formula "to each and from each according to his ____." Corrective justice also aims to give each person his due. But what is due, in this case, is a function of an immediate relation between two parties, a relation which is normatively significant even apart from such criteria as would connect persons to social benefits and burdens (and thereby to each other) in a distributive scheme. Hence, rather than attending to features of the situation which such criteria would make salient, the law, as Aristotle puts it, "looks only at differences in the harm inflicted." That is, the departure from equality here is essentially a matter of the difference that wrongful doing and suffering makes – the difference between what a person has before and after a wrongful transaction – as opposed to the difference between what a person has and what is due to them according to criteria which could, in principle, operate independently of the parties' being so related.

Read in the context of the trouble with functionalism (Section III), the special interest of this should be clear. For functionalism exhibits injurers and victims as joined together only mediately, in virtue of their relation to certain social goals rather than to each other. Essentially, it construes tort law as aiming to confer burdens and benefits according to criteria rationally related to such goals: accident losses, conceived as common stock, are to be distributed so as to (1) make them easier to bear, and/or (2) create incentives for cost-effective precaution taking. The trouble is that the criteria, made relevant by these goals, for selecting persons to be benefited and burdened selects much broader classes than those of persons related as victim and injurer; and such classes therefore appear to be arbitrarily limited when the law in fact determines who is to be benefited and burdened by following the lines of particular transactions. But suppose that there are, as Aristotle suggests, concerns of equality or fairness pertaining specially to transactions; and suppose we can make out that tort law expresses such concerns. Then we would have, in the idea of corrective justice, a characterization of tort law that gives content to the thought – the second conclusion of Section III.8 – that, when the material for understanding tort law is limited to the functionalist's goals, a distinct sort of reason that informs the law is not yet in view. Compensation and deterrence, we might say, help answer the question, "How should the costs of social cooperation be distributed among the members of a political community?"[56] Such goals are satisfied – and the reasons they provide are given their full practical weight – whenever the resources of the community are allocated in a certain way; and the reasons provided apply not just to interacting pairs but to everyone in the relevant community. As an expression of corrective justice, tort law would bring a sort of reason into play which contrasts with these features of the functionalist's goals.[57]

I shall develop the claim that tort law expresses corrective justice in three stages: first, by asking how the "equality" pertinent to corrective justice is to be understood (Sections IV.2–IV.3); second, by presenting the Basic Rule as spelling out what such equality requires in a particular type of case (Section IV.4); and third, by answering an objection which arises from functionalist quarters: namely, that because the content of corrective justice is not fully available, on this account, apart from the legal practices which express it, to refer to corrective justice is to do little more than to point out that there are such-and-such legal practices rather than to rationalize or explain them (Section V).

### IV.2 The Equality of Corrective Justice (A)

In the passage quoted (Section IV.1), Aristotle invokes the notion of equality in two seemingly different ways. First, some baseline condition of equality between the parties is restored through a material transfer required by justice. Second, the law treats the parties as equals. The first invocation of equality refers to a state-of-affairs to be achieved, one in which each party is given its due; the second, to an apparently formal constraint on legal judgment. This suggests two different readings of the passage, depending on which of these invocations one takes as primary. Taking "equality as baseline condition" as primary, it seems natural to understand the equality restored by the judge as the proportional equality of distributive shares. On this first reading, in saying that the judge treats the parties as equals, Aristotle means that the judge respects their initial equality as antecedently defined. He respects their equality – and thus treats them as equals – by taking their rightful holdings as the basis for judging wrongful departures. I shall first criticize this reading and then develop the second reading in Section IV.3.

The first reading has two understandable motivations. First, it honors the (for many, attractive) thought that no genuine entitlements to the repair of loss could be held in the first place except in accordance with a just scheme of distribution; the justice of repair depends, in this reading, on the justness of the parties' previous holdings. Second, this reading makes the appropriateness of repair in particular cases available for assessment in light of an independent doctrine of just holdings. It may be felt that the claim to be doing justice in a case of alleged wrongful transaction requires this – in effect, some test, independent of the possible judgments that could be rendered, of when the judge has got it right. A form of justice defined in terms of judgments that respect the equality of the parties, that is, may be felt to require some prior doctrine, capable of functioning as an external touch point, of what that equality consists in.

But however motivated,[58] it is not hard to see that this reading creates a number of insuperable problems for Aristotle's discussion. First, in *Nicomachean Ethics* 1132a quoted above, Aristotle observes that the law pays no attention to (what would elsewhere be) a pertinent distributive criterion (decency/baseness), and he then contrasts the use of such a criterion with attention to the harm inflicted and the application of a norm of equality ("Rather, the law . . . treats the people involved as equals."). How can we credit the most general point of this passage – viz., that there are two distinct forms of justice[59] – unless we are prepared to see the equality infringed by a wrongful transaction as something other than the equality of distributive shares?

In support of this, it may be noted that Aristotle's observation concerning the law's restricted focus remains universally correct. For example, the law never allows a wrongdoer to defend herself on the Robin Hood-like grounds that her actions have in fact brought about a more just allocation. If the normative basis of corrective justice were an independently defined equality of holdings, it is not easy to explain why.

Finally, the present reading seems obscure outside the case of a simple property taking, in which one person literally gains what another loses. If X wrong-

fully takes Y's goods, then, on the assumption that the parties' antecedent holdings were in the right proportion, the law can make the parties equal again by
ordering the return of the goods. But how are we to apply this idea to the case
in which X does not take, but wrongfully damages, Y's goods? If X must compensate Y for the damage, why is this any less disruptive of the antecedently
just status quo than if the damage were to remain (uncompensated) with Y? To
answer this question, we need either to burden Aristotle with the fantastic assumption that every wrongdoer realizes a material gain equivalent to her victim's loss, or else to explain how X's wrongdoing can alter her distributive entitlement. Clearly, however, the later course amounts to abandoning the attempt
to understand the equality of corrective justice along the present lines. If a transaction consisting of X's wrongdoing and Y's loss can alter X's distributive entitlement in the amount of Y's loss, that can only mean that the transaction has
a significance not entirely captured in terms of its upsetting an antecedent proportion of holdings.[60]

A clear view of these matters is doubtless made more difficult by the fact that
Aristotle does portray (1) a wrongdoer as realizing a "gain" or "profit" which is
quantitatively equivalent to a victim's "loss," and (2) the judge as restoring
"equality" by transferring the amount the one has gained and the other lost (Aristotle, *NE,* 1132a5–1132b20). This may encourage the thought that the equality
restored by the judge can be independently identified in terms of the parties' antecedent holdings, despite the unacceptable consequences of this thought: The
scope of corrective justice must either be restricted to cases of property-taking,
or else all other wrongful injuries must somehow be assimilated to that case. The
assimilation is clearly hopeless. Even if there is always a gain in, say, driving
negligently (which is doubtful), that gain would have to accrue whether loss occurs or not; and because the value of any occurring loss depends on various con-
tingencies, its equivalence to the driver's gain in a particular case could only be
fortuitous. Fortunately, Aristotle himself indicates a different way of understanding the sort of equivalence in question here, one which makes property-taking a special – and not the paradigm – case of the transactional departure from
equality: Following a wrongful transaction the victim has "too little" and the injurer "too much" simply in the sense that the injurer has that which, as a matter
of justice, belongs to the victim; in a case of personal injury, the loss inflicted is
his (the injurer's) to bear.[61] On this understanding, we must of course give up
the thought that Aristotle is even purporting to supply an independent test for
identifying legal wrongs; the existence of the relevant losses and gains does not
appear apart from the whole system of legal entitlements which specify the relevant notion of wrongdoing. Talk of equivalent loss and gain is a way of representing a wrongful transaction from the point of view of the remedy offered by
the law; its point is simply to mark a distinction between the way this remedy
vindicates equality (see Section IV.3) and the creation of such proportionate
equivalences of holdings as would comprise a just distribution.[62]

This understanding of the equivalence of loss and gain leaves appropriate room for corrective justice to apply (as Aristotle claims it does: *NE,* 1131a–b) to a range of transactional wrongs. But it still leaves us, of course, in need of an explanation of the sense in which the judge, in a case of corrective justice, either restores equality or treats the parties as equals.

### IV.3  The Equality of Corrective Justice (B)

The second reading reverses the direction between equality as a state-of-affairs to be restored and equality as a formal constraint on judgment. Thus when Aristotle says that the judge "tries to restore this unjust situation to equality" this should be taken to mean that he renders a judgment consistent with treating the two parties as equals; the just equilibrium, the outcome sought, is not given prior to a judgment that meets this formal constraint. So, on this reading, corrective justice would have, as Aristotle suggests, its own norm of equality; it would involve reasons to alter the parties' relation to each other that do not stem from the requirements of equality or fairness in distributions.

If the first reading were acceptable, the equality of the parties would function as an independent benchmark of when the law had got things right: to get things right (to treat the parties as equals) would be to uphold the requirements of distributive justice against transactional interferences. But taken apart from such requirements, doesn't treating the parties as equals now (on the second reading) threaten to look like a mere formalism? The problem is a familiar one. If X is entitled to restitution when Y takes his property, then it may be said that the law treats the parties as equals whenever this rule is applied evenhandedly, without any characteristics of X or Y (e.g., their status or character) modifying its application in favor of either one of them. But the notion of equal treatment does not function here as an explanation of the parties' entitlements; rather, its application presupposes them.[63] The question is: How can the idea of equal treatment comprise, just by itself, something to which legal judgment may (or may fail) to accord? This is what needs to be made out, the discussion so far suggests, if the notion of corrective justice is to find application to transactional wrongs in general and not merely to the taking of property.

The passage quoted provides two sources of help. First, Aristotle associates the relevant sort of legal judgment with a situation of correlative doing and suffering: "[T]he law . . . treats the parties as equals, when one does injustice while the other suffers it, and one has done the harm while the other has suffered it." Second, he presents the law's focus on such doing and suffering as an alternative to its consideration of either party's character: "For here it does not matter if a decent person has taken from a base person." On the reading I propose, the main point is that the law treats the parties as equals when it assesses their transaction in terms that have a correlative significance for each of them, rather than in terms (like "decency/baseness") which pick out their several qualities and are therefore suitable for relating them (both to each other and to others) in a distributive scheme.

Here we should recall Aristotle's explanation of correlativity: If a term "can be predicated of the sufferer, it can equally be predicated of the doer, and if of the doer, then also of the sufferer."[64] The significance of the thought that treating the parties as equals involves correlativity (as an "equality of predication") is easy to miss because the later notion can be construed as merely the general *form* of interpersonal liability. Let $\phi$ be a term describing the nature of a transaction such that when it applies, liability follows. If a liability rule says it is wrong to $\phi$, then – if we really are speaking of interpersonal liability – someone has *been wronged*, in the liability-incurring sense, whenever anyone $\phi$'s; so the requirement of correlativity is indifferently satisfied, it may seem, by any substantive definition of a transactional wrong.[65] However, the notion of correlativity admits of a less formal reading, whereby some instantiations of $\phi$, and hence some liability rules, are more appropriate specifications of the general form of liability than others. To say of the term '$\phi$' that "if it can be predicated of the sufferer, it can *equally* be predicated of the doer" (and vice versa) would not be to say just that, according to some rule, one party is liable and another may recover whenever $\phi$ applies; it would be to say, in addition, that the rule in question, by making liability and recovery a matter of '$\phi$', allows one party to recover only for such *reasons* as are also no less appropriate reasons for another's liability. On the purely formal reading, we have merely the idea that a rule (whatever its content) is of such a kind as to be applicable to one party (as doer) just when it is also applicable to another party (as sufferer); obviously, very iniquitous rules can be of this kind. On the less formal reading, we have the idea that some particular rules of this kind capture a special type of reason, a consideration in favor of the recovery of one party that is equally – neither more nor less – a consideration in favor of the liability of another; the idea of correlativity or equality of predication, in other words, sorts out fair and iniquitous rules of the general kind.[66]

To make this clearer, consider the most basic question that must arise if the law is to assess whether an action complained of is wrongful or not: *What* did he do? Taking the example from Section II.1, the question might be: Did he inflict harm on the person standing on the platform, or did he merely push a passenger, the rest being a matter of the independent course of the world? Insofar as we are interested in action as an expression of a person's character, it would be natural, in answering this question, to focus on the deliberated, intentional or foreseen aspects of action; these aspects exhibit something about the person's character by revealing (i.e., either positively as his aims or negatively as considerations he did not act against) his reasons in acting. Aristotle himself seems to be thinking along these lines when he turns, after the discussion of particular justice, to questions concerning the relation of voluntary action to justice (*NE*, Section V.8). Here the special ethical interest of what is "voluntary" puts the sort of pressure we would expect on the description of a purportedly wrong-ful act, for Aristotle says that an action must be "defined" by features of the practical situation that the agent is aware of – viz., the person harmed, the in-strumentality of harm, and the nature or type of harm (*NE,* 1135a15–30). But now an interesting consequence emerges. Defining action in this way opens a gap, which Aristotle points out, between something "being unjust" and "there being an act of injustice" (*NE,* 1135a15–25). For someone who acts in igno-rance of features of the situation that characterize the action *as suffered* has not – if the action is really to be "defined" by reference to his awareness – done wrong. He has not done wrong because he has not, strictly speaking, *done that* at all. The doing (of what turns out to be a suffered wrong) does not – "except coincidently" – belong to him, Aristotle suggests, as a doing.[67]

Answering the question, What did he do? from the point of view of an in-terest in action as an expression of ethical character will thus defeat the correl-ativity of doing and suffering wrong. For if something can "be unjust" without "there being an act of injustice," then injustice or wrong is there to be suffered without anyone having done injustice or wrong. A gap appears between doing and suffering wrong. Of course, we could easily close this gap if we were pre-pared to say that no one could suffer wrong unless another had done wrong in the presently circumscribed sense (involving awareness, etc.).[68] This would close the gap by making the passive (to suffer wrong) a simple reflex of the ac-tive form, with the later defined in such a way as to confine it to cases in which blame is appropriate. But this seems unfair, for it makes the status of the trans-action depend on a feature of the situation that pertains to one of the parties alone. Why should the one who suffers find the agents' self-consciousness rel-evant at all? He too is a self-consciousness, and his relation to the action is to an injury he has suffered. Just as easily, we could close the gap in the other di-rection. What matters, the sufferer might say, is not whether the agent has done wrong knowingly but whether he has done something that, from the point of view of one who suffers it, is a wrong. Opposing the doer's narcissistic demand to recognize as his action only what he knew as his deed would thus be a no-tion of responsibility that runs at greater or less length along the lines of cau-sation. But clearly this is no less one-sided. It closes the potential gap between doing and suffering by making the active form a reflex of the passive "suffer-ing wrong." Why should the doer find the sufferer's self-consciousness relevant at all? He too is a self-consciousness, and his relation to the act is to something that involves no wrong.

The upshot of these reflections is that, as a matter of corrective justice, wrongdoing cannot be confined to cases involving the actor's awareness that her action might cause injury; and, by the same token, wrongful suffering can-not be extended to cases involving any undeserved misfortune connected to an-other's agency. (This tells us something about legally significant doing and suf-fering; it is not a mere formality.) Under these illegitimate conceptions, cases of wrongful doing and wrongful suffering can be represented as the doing and suffering of the *same* wrong only at the cost of making suffering the reflex of doing or vice versa. Justice – "virtue in relation to another" (*NE,* 1129b32) – opposes these one-sided possibilities of human relation. It requires, in effect, that the transaction be assessed from the point of view of a neutral third party, a representative of the law: "The just, then, is intermediate, since the judge is so" (1132a).

To summarize: The task of judgment, on the second reading of the equality of corrective justice, is to determine when (in what circumstances) two parties stand in the relationship of having done and suffered the same wrong.[69] Insofar as he seeks justice, the judge seeks an answer intermediate between two descriptions of what was done, one making suffering the reflex of doing, the other making doing the reflex of suffering. This is to treat the parties as equals by according equal status to their interests in acting (which includes their interest in being free from injurious interferences). The departure from equality in this situation consists, then, in doings which are wrongful, not because they upset a previously just distribution, or because they threaten a communal goal, but because they are inconsistent with the equal status of other affected agents. Such wrongful doing and suffering comprises an equivalent loss and gain, i.e., a loss which, uncorrected, lies with the victim, but which ought, as a matter of justice, to be borne by the injurer. The thought expressed by such 'equivalence' is not that whenever there are materially equivalent losses and gains, there is reason for corrective action, but rather that the basic reasons for corrective action – unlike those supplied by concerns of distributive fairness or by the goals pertinent to a distributive scheme – are such that any ground for thinking that one person has less than their due is also a ground for thinking that another person has more; any ground for giving to one person is a ground for taking from another. Accordingly, the judicial restoration of equality consists neither in giving the parties the share they had before the transaction (though, in a taking of property, that may result), nor in giving them the share they ought to have as a matter of distributive fairness (or in furtherance of a communal goal), but in annulling the equality-negating wrong by transferring the loss to the party who wrongfully created it. Borne by the victim, that loss constitutes a transactional wrong; borne by the wrongdoer, it constitutes, at most, his misfortune.

Conceived thus, corrective justice might also be described as an abstract framework for arguments about the terms on which one person is responsible for the injurious consequences of her actions. But it will need to be stressed that the notion of responsibility here is one required to do a wider kind of practical work than is reflected in questions about when an agent may be blamed for her actions; it has to do with the answerability of persons, potentially indifferent to one another, living in civic association.[70] There is a philosophical tendency to think of judgments of responsibility as arising with respect to each person considered in isolation. In effect, one imagines the person standing before a god

who, as the perfect judge, will not fault the person for deeds that do not deeply
express her will. But this is to imagine a scene of judgment presenting no other
party whose grievances need to be answered. The notion of responsibility relevant to corrective justice, in contrast, only comes into view when we consider
two persons in relation, each with an equal interest in acting and in being secure against the interferences of others. To consider persons in this way (viz.,
as parties) reflects an ethical concern that is distinct from other moral assessments of action; its home – the practical situation that brings this concern into
play – is the situation of alleged wrongdoing in which a plaintiff and defendant
appear before the law.

## IV.4

How do the elements of the Basic Rule (Section II.2) express the notion of corrective justice?

(A) DAMAGES. Conceived along functionalist lines – either as a deterrent
penalty or as a way of reallocating (and thereby reducing) the burden of accidental loss – the payment of damages seemed puzzling (Section III). Why does
this payment follow the contours of an antecedent transaction, proceeding from
the defendant-injurer to the plaintiff-victim? And why is the loss suffered by
the plaintiff the measure of both what the defendant must pay and what the
plaintiff should recover? Conceived as a way of annulling a wrongful (because
equality-negating) transaction, these features of the standard tort remedy present no special difficulty.[71] If the payment proceeded from a source other than
the defendant, it might address the plaintiff's need but it would not touch the
defendant's wrongdoing. If it were based on a measure other than the plaintiff's
loss, it might touch the defendant's wrongdoing, or it might advance a conception of distributive equality, but it would not redress the wrong as suffered, its
manifestation as loss. The notion of corrective justice can thus help reinforce
our grip on the basic features of the tort remedy, and on the standard judicial
principle governing the award of damages, viz., that their purpose is to "put the
party who has been injured, or who has suffered, in the same position he would
have been in if he had not sustained the wrong."[72] This principle can of course
be expressed by saying that tort law aims to provide compensation for wrongful injury. But this commonplace is apt to be misunderstood, as we have seen,
if we try to derive the significance of compensation in tort from the normative
significance of loss considered just as such, apart from the relation of wrongful doing and suffering.

(B) AGENCY, CAUSATION, AND INJURY. Prior to the question of any damages
to be paid is the question of whether the defendant is liable at all. In making this
conditional on a causal sequence beginning with agency and ending with in-

jury, the Basic Rule ensures that a person's doings are legally significant (a basis of liability) only when they result in another's suffering, and that a person's suffering is legally significant (a basis for recovery) only when it results from another's doing. Hence, in making civil liability possible, the Basic Rule also limits it to just the sort of case – when "one has done the harm while the other has suffered it" – which brings a concern for corrective justice into play. Moreover, the requirement of agency (the distinction between misfeasance and nonfeasance: Section II.1) expresses the notion of equality that gives salience to this case. For if, apart from any action on his part endangering the plaintiff, a civil defendant could, as a rule, be liable for the plaintiff's suffering, then the defendant's entitlement to act in pursuit of his own projects (in potential indifference to those of others) would be determined on the basis of – would be subordinate to – the requirements of the plaintiff's welfare. Although, formally speaking, the grounds for liability would be the same as the grounds for recovery, such a rule would flout correlativity (equality of prediction) in the less-formal sense (Section IV.3). For, in the terms used previously, the plaintiff's claim to have suffered wrong in such a situation could only be construed as a case of doing and suffering the *same* wrong by making the defendant's wrongdoing a notional reflex of the plaintiff's suffering.[73]

(C) THE REASONABLE PERSON STANDARD. Tort law's use of an objective standard of reasonable conduct entails both (1) that undeserved misfortune flowing from the action of another is not, just in itself, legally significant, and (2) that a defendant may wrongfully injure another even when he tries his best to avoid it. The significance of the standard as an expression of the equality of corrective justice can be seen in these consequences. Undeserved misfortune might call for shifting social resources in someone's direction. But if the connection of such misfortune to another's agency were alone sufficient grounds of liability, the boundaries of rightful agency would be determined simply on the basis of how an action affects others. Similarly, that someone tried his best to avoid injuring others may bear upon his moral culpability. But if this could put the effects of action beyond another's entitlement to complain, the boundaries of rightful agency would be determined simply on the basis of agent's self-relation to his own action. Of course, action can appropriately be judged from different points of view. The reasonable person formula aims to express the grounds appropriate to judgments about action in which doer and sufferer weigh equally as agents. Putting this in terms of responsibility, one might say that the formula aims to answer the question, What actions should an agent justly regard as his? in a way that turns neither one-sidedly on the agent's self-conception of his action nor one-sidedly on the suffering of another.

Earlier, in motivating the call for tort theory, the question was specifically posed of how the law's use of an objective standard, its rejection of most capacity-based excuses,[74] could be consistent with liability based on wrongdoing or fault. We might now answer: The objective standard specifies the notion of wrongdoing or fault appropriate to the assessment of action from the point of view of justice (i.e., "in relation to another") rather than, say, as an expression of a person's character or will. Similarly, we can now address the worry that the objective standard and the causation requirement beset tort law with a problem of moral luck (Section III.1). That notorious problem arises in light of the fortuitously different consequences an action may have considered from a point of view where the object of moral assessment is the person considered in isolation. Enlarging the frame – considering the person "in relation to another" – situates a different ethical concern. Whatever the paradox-inducing temptations may be, from the first point of view, to pare down every act to some inner core of pure volitional self-relation (Nagel, 1979, p. 31), it hardly seems tolerable to tell the victim of a person's action that, characterized in terms of her suffering, that action lacks normative significance because all that can appropriately concern us, morally speaking, is the actor's will. Of course, answering the victim's complaint in some other way is bound to be expedient wherever persons need to cooperate,[75] but that is no reason to deny that it also expresses sensitivity to an aspect of justice.

(D) PROXIMATE CAUSE. Whatever applicative difficulties may arise in particular cases, the basic idea of proximate cause is clear enough: not everyone who suffers the effects of someone's (otherwise) wrongful action has, in the sense relevant to tort liability, been wrongfully injured. In the case cited earlier (Section II.1), Cardozo described the requisite liability-creating relationship by saying that the plaintiff's injury must be (from the point of view of the defendant's action) reasonably foreseeable. The notion of corrective justice provides a way to understand the appropriateness of this judicially commonplace formula.

The key is to see that asking whether the plaintiff's injury was reasonably foreseeable makes the question of liability sensitive to different descriptions of that injury and hence to different descriptions of the risk created by the defendant.[76] At one end of a spectrum, it might be said that, in acting as he did, the defendant created a risk that *an* injury might occur in *one manner or another* to *someone or other.* Under such a description, we are bound to regard the plaintiff's injury as a foreseeable consequence of his action (for every action carries such a generally describable risk). At the other end of the spectrum, it might be said that the defendant created a risk of a cut with such-and-such microstructure occurring in such-and-such manner to Mr. so-and-so; and under some such fine-grained description, we shall naturally be compelled to say that the plaintiff's injury was not a foreseeable consequence of what the defendant did. Conceived, then, as a question of reasonable foreseeability, the question of proximate cause becomes essentially this: Is an appropriate specification of what makes the defendant's action wrongful – a specification of the risk he created in terms of features that pertain to any practical situation (i.e., risk of what, occurring in what manner, to whom) – such as to describe the (type of) injury that befell the plaintiff. If it is – if the plaintiff's injury is the materialization of a risk that makes the defendant's conduct wrongful – then the plaintiff has been wrongfully injured. (She has been injured, in other words, by an action which is wrongful not in general but specifically in virtue of the prospect of her suffering it.) So conceived, the requirement of proximate cause makes one person's doing and another's suffering legally significant – i.e., a basis for liability and recovery – just when they are the doing and suffering of the same wrong.

Of course, the appropriateness of liability in any particular case will depend, on this account, on an appropriate description of the defendant's creation of risk. The notion of reasonable foreseeability does not function, independently of such a description, as a decision procedure for liability;[77] it simply exhibits the sort of judgment the law, as matter of justice, must make: a judgment about the appropriate description of one's person's doing in light of complaints from another for whom it is a case of "being done to." In arguments about a particular case, we can naturally expect the plaintiff to describe the defendant's risk-creation in the most general terms consistent with the action's continuing to seem wrongful (unreasonable); and we can expect the defendant to emphasize any unusual details of the situation.[78] Insofar as it is just, the law seeks a judgment that privileges the point of view of neither plaintiff nor defendant, a judgment that describes what happened neither too generally (at the limit, identifying wrongdoing with all of its fortuitous consequences) nor too specifically (at the limit, making omniscience a condition of identifying wrongdoing with any of its consequences); hence a judgment that, in the sense pertinent to transactions, treats the parties as equals.[79]

## V. Theory and Practice

> But let us take it as agreed in advance that every account of the actions we must do has to be stated in outline, not exactly.
>
> Aristotle, *Nicomachean Ethics,* 1104a

### V.1

On the foregoing account, the concept of corrective justice stands to the Basic Rule of tort liability (1) as the Basic Rule stands to such judicial elaborations as "reasonable care" and "reasonable foreseeability"; and (2) as these elaborations stand to the judgments which either further articulate the law or determine liability in particular cases (e.g., "reasonable care requires so-and-so in such-and-such circumstances" or "the defendant failed to exercise reasonable care"). In short, one gets from corrective justice to liability verdicts through applicative judgments which spell out what corrective justice requires in various (types of) circumstances. Since the Basic Rule spells this out in one type of circumstance (personal injury),[80] and since the judicial elaboration of this Rule spells this out further in particular cases of this type, it may be said that judges who elaborate the Basic Rule attempt to discern the significance of the facts of particular cases in light of a correct grasp of what justice requires. But it is no part of this account that what justice requires must be fully graspable apart from the sort of practical thinking which informs the juridical consideration of particular cases. Hence, there need be no "principle" of corrective justice which is sufficiently spelled out so as to be serviceable in a validation of legal requirements without relying on such jurisprudence.

Contemporary scholarship tends to represent efficiency and corrective justice as the central concepts in competing theories of tort law; and, in a general enough sense of "theory," that is true enough. Each account endeavors to exhibit tort law's unifying aims, and so might innocuously be called a theory, without prejudice to questions concerning the relation between such theoretically posited aims and the understandings which inform the law's everyday application. But efficiency belongs to a call for theory in a more specific sense, viz., an external grounding of legal understandings (Sections I, III.2). So the now familiar alignment of these accounts (as alternatives within a common theoretical project) is apt to make us suppose that corrective justice should play an analogous grounding role.[81] And that is apt to obscure certain possibilities concerning the way the law's self-understandings might be related to an understanding of its aim.

In this context, Aristotle's discussion seems notable because it is implausible to suppose, given its abstractness, that the relation it contemplates between corrective justice and everyday legal thinking could be anything other than a casuistic specification: A specification, in that the law's advancement of corrective justice consists not in devising means to an already understood end, but in saying how, in various circumstances, the end of justice is to be understood; and casuistic, in that this endeavor (like the application of concepts such as reasonable care or reasonable foreseeability) calls for practical thought, the appropriateness of which cannot be demonstrated simply as a matter of deductive rationality.[82] So conceived, corrective justice is really only misleadingly described as an explanatory alternative to the functionalists' notion of efficiency in a theory of tort law; for if it is that, it must be no less an alternative to the functionalist's idea of what an appropriate theoretical explanation of the law must be.

Not surprisingly, there is a tendency among functionalists to dismiss summarily, if not simply to overlook, this sort of possibility for understanding tort law. Underlying this tendency are two related objections. The first is that we are not entitled, on such an understanding, to see legal rules and judgments as normatively constrained by corrective justice, as items that can be in accord with it (or not). The second objection is that such an understanding of tort law fails, in any case, to give us what we need from a theory, namely, reasons for continued commitment to the institution of tort law in the face of other possibly attractive ways of allocating accident losses. These objections deserve a more careful treatment elsewhere. But the present discussion would be incomplete without at least a brief consideration of them.

### V.2 First Objection: Lack of Constraint

Circling Aristotle's representation of equality as something intermediate between wrongful gain (doing at the expense of another's wrongful suffering) and wrongful loss (suffering on account of another's wrongdoing), Hans Kelsen takes this to mean that a judge who grasps the concept of corrective justice has a decision procedure for determining what is owed by one party to the other, just as (to extend Aristotle's own analogy) the geometer has a procedure for determining the midpoint of a line (Kelsen 1957, p. 130; *NE,* 1132a). Kelsen correctly sees, however, that Aristotle does not afford materials for such a procedure. Before the idea of wrongful gain and loss can find application, some further specification of the party's entitlements (e.g., of what constitutes a wrongful transaction, of who owes who what, etc.) is needed. Yet once such entitlements are specified, everything relevant to settling the case is in place, Kelsen reasons, so the further characterization of such transactions as involving a departure from "equality" can fall away as an unconstraining formalism (Kelsen 1957, pp.132–6). On this view, Aristotle offers merely the "tautology" (Kelsen 1957, p. 132) that justice requires giving each person his due without the normative materials for determining what, in any particular case, is due.

Posner has recently filed a similar complaint: "The definition of wrongs is prior to the duty of corrective justice, [so] society is always free, at least as a matter of corrective justice, to alter the definition of wrongful conduct."[83] This means that a concern to realize corrective justice does not by itself constrain society's options; additional normative considerations are needed if one legal definition of wrongful conduct is to be considered better than any other. It follows that Aristotle's discussion is useless, as it stands, for understanding tort law. If one legal regime really has, absent the requisite normative supplement, no better claim to accord with corrective justice than any other, talk of the duty of corrective justice can only refer to the existing regime of positive law, not to anything that appropriately explains it:

Aristotle did not explain *why* he thought there was a duty of corrective justice, he merely explained what that duty was. [Posner's footnote: 'In fact . . . it is unclear to what extent Aristotle thought he was doing more than describing legal concepts that happened to be prevalent in his society.'] Economic analysis [*i.e., an analysis of what the regime of legal duty needs to be if it is to promote wealth or reduce costs – my note*] supplies a reason why the duty to rectify wrongs . . . is (depending on the cost of rectification) a part of the concept of justice. Corrective justice is an instrument for maximizing wealth and in the normative economic theory of the state . . . that I espouse[,] wealth maximization is the ultimate objective of the just state. (Posner 1981, p. 206)

This complaint, like Kelsen's, has two prongs. First, Aristotle lacks a principle from which any legal conceptions of wrong can autonomously be derived (rather, "the definition of wrongful conduct is prior . . ."). Second, his discussion is (therefore) explanatorily empty: At best, a statement *that* – not an answer to the question *why* – such conceptions are valid legal duties. The sort of explanatory materials Aristotle lacks, on this view, is shown by Posner's offer to supply them via the principle that legal intervention should maximize wealth.[84] From this principle, one might deduce the appropriate legal duties without relying on understandings or procedures which are juridical in any distinctive sense; all that is required is an application of empirical information about the effects of this or that legal intervention.

Is this complaint compelling? The first prong surely contains an accurate perception. But must we really accept the explanatory options offered in the second? Why should it be supposed that the explanatory usefulness of "corrective justice" depends on our being able to construe it as the answer to a "why" question, conceived as a demand for reasons for the law which can appear apart from the juridical conception of the situation (viz., unreasonable conduct, foreseeable harm, etc.) which brings such reasons into play? Why should it be supposed that "corrective justice" fails normatively to constrain such juridical conceptions unless (like, e.g., "wealth-maximization") it affords an independent test of whether, in point of application (in the way such conceptions sort out particular cases), they are correct?

Someone might think that these suppositions are simply the prerequisites of any entitlement to speak of corrective justice as an aim which the law might (or might not) get right. Application of this notion requires that there be a kind of conceptual distance between anything we take as the aim of legal practice and identifiable instances of the practice that are supposed to advance it.[85] If our concept of corrective justice is such that its specific requirements are to be grasped only through the kind of thinking which, in the circumstances of particular cases, engages such juridical notions as the reasonable person and proximate cause, then – the thought goes – the distance needed to get the notion of practical correctness into play is lacking. To purport to explain the law by reference to a concept of justice that is practice-dependent in this way is thus really only to explain the law in terms of itself, and so to work an empty tautology – the law is the law.[86]

But this argument proves too much. Whatever grounds may exist for thinking that tort law is merely an instrument, it can't generally be that practical aims are distant (in the way required for them to bear explanatory weight) only when they are fully specifiable independently of the circumstantially specific actions that advance them; otherwise, there could be no rationalizations of action other than the instrumentalist kind. What should be said here is simply that corrective justice is not instrumentally distant from the law, but distant in a different way. Instrumental distance would consist in this, that, while there is no special problem saying what it would be for the law to realize a given aim, positing the aim (e.g., compensation, deterrence, or more generally accident cost reduction) does not yet single out any of the various measures (e.g., liability rules, criminal penalties, taxation, insurance schemes, etc.) that might feasibly be adopted as a means. Here, the notion of the law's getting things right is basically that of the expected efficacy of the means adopted in bringing about the relevant aim. The present notion of corrective justice is no less distant. Positing this aim does not yet single out the appropriate legal measures because (once again) a further question needs to be answered – not about the efficacy of various measures in realizing this aim, but, in this case, about what it would be, in this or that situation, for the aim to be realized. The law gets things right not when it efficaciously brings about corrective justice (that idea has no application here), but when its particular determinations express and make known its requirements.[87]

The present objection (concerning the unconstrainingness of corrective justice) follows, it seems, only on the basis of an unsupported assumption, namely, that we can't rationally regard one legal determination as more appropriate to corrective justice than another unless the notion of corrective justice comes sufficiently equipped (e.g., with the wealth-maximizing principle) so as to afford (given only some further knowledge of the facts) an independent procedure for deciding among such determinations.[88] One way to see why this assumption is questionable (and therefore in need of support) is to remember that the basic legal conceptions – e.g., proximate cause and reasonable care – do not themselves afford such a procedure for deciding particular cases. So on the basis of the present assumption, the threat of emptiness confronting corrective justice would be invidious, affecting the law at every level except the singular judgments – which create no law and have no analogical force as precedent (Section II.1) – concerning the liability of a particular party in a particular case. Leaving the assumption unquestioned, we must either deny that we can regard some judicial elaborations and applications of proximate cause or reasonable care as being genuinely in accord with those notions, or we must expect to find some utilitarian or other normative supplement in the offing which would furnish the requisite validating procedure.

Given these alternatives, one might view the present assumption (that there must be a decision procedure) as part of the tendency of thought that can make it seem more or less obvious that "all . . . legal requirements *must* ultimately justify themselves in functional terms" (Calabresi 1975, p. 105). Not questioning the assumption, the functionalist is someone who, correctly conceiving the law as a normative practice directed toward "getting things right," feels that our entitlement to applications of this notion can come only by way of an analysis that would, at least in principle, (1) represent the law's time-honored terms as the outcomes of independently compelling reasoning (e.g., maximizing operations on wealth), and, by the same means, (2) validate determinate applications of them in particular cases.[89] However, the trouble with functionalism (Section III) indicates that the argument should run in the opposite direction. The normativity of the law, taken together with an appreciation of its resistance to functional analysis, should provide a reason for questioning the underlying assumption that is apt to make such analysis seem like the only alternative to an uncritical acceptance of the law. Dropping the assumption, one need not feel compelled to choose between mere acceptance of "the that" (without rational entitlement to the idea of the law sometimes getting things right) on the one hand, and an answer to the question "why" (as the functionalist conceives it) on the other. (Of course, accepting "the that" as it figures in this contrast is not a serious option.)

To say that functionalism is not obligatory is not, of course, to say that the wish for an external grounding of the law – and hence disappointment with a representation of corrective justice which leaves this wish unfulfilled – is not intelligible. (The law coercively structures our everyday life, so a derivation of it from principles which carry more immediate conviction would be a good thing, in whatever doctrinal areas this is possible.) The present point is simply that a dogmatic assumption blinds the functionalist to another possibility: An explanatory role for a notion of justice can be one which does not lead but simply supports – by continuing in a more abstract way – the sort of practical thinking instinct in the law's everyday elaboration. Cast in this supporting role, corrective justice would afford a reflective awareness of the configuration of a legal practice in which a certain kind of case (involving doing and suffering and claims of right) is central, and in which a distinctive type of ethical concern, special to that case, is in play. Reflecting on the legal understandings that describe this case (action, wrongdoing, causation, etc.) brings the relevant ethical concern into focus; and it is by grasping that concern (as distinct from other concerns, e.g., distributive justice or the moral assessment of character or conduct)[90] that we can understand – i.e., grasp the aim and unity of (Section I) – the practice.[91] Such an understanding does not float free of the jurisprudential endeavor to make the content of corrective justice explicit in particular cases, so conviction in the appropriateness of particular legal requirements is advanced here only by means continuous with the internal reflection that is a source of the law's development. But that is no reason to say that corrective justice affords *no* understanding or that "all legal requirements must be analyzed in functional terms." Such felt necessity might simply remind us of the freedom we stand to gain by taking seriously an old philosopher who does not share – and can therefore help make visible – the assumptions we have come to take for granted.[92]

## V.3 Second Objection: Competing Concerns

Someone who agreed that corrective justice, as presently conceived, *does* normatively constrain the legal specification of duty might still wish to object that this conception leaves us without an answer to the question, Why are there such duties? understood in a different sense. The question, it will be said, is not why the requirements of corrective justice are to be specified *thus* (reasonable care, foreseeability, etc.); it is why, in a situation of transactional loss, the sort of fairness pertinent to corrective justice, however specified, should engage our concern at all. (Posner's remark in Section V.2 can be understood as raising both of these questions.[93])

Fueling the second question is the contemporary feeling that no injustice or other evil need be involved if a society were to treat some of the natural events which currently trigger tort liability as matters of distributive justice – triggering, e.g., contributions to, and withdrawals from, a social insurance scheme – instead. So in characterizing tort law as an expression of corrective justice, the objection goes, one has not yet given a justification of the *institution* of tort law, a reason for preferring it to other institutions for allocating loss.

This second objection exhibits a different source of the functionalist's motivation. By presenting tort law as an efficacious means of reducing accident costs, functional analysis, it might be said, answers the first "why" question (why fairness between two parties should be specified *thus*) by way of addressing the second (why be concerned, as an institutional matter, with fairness between *two* parties). No special animus to practical jurisprudence need be involved here, only the competition of other practical concerns. A procedure for deciding whether the law's specification of "corrective justice" is getting things right then emerges from the need for some procedure for deciding whether "corrective justice" or some other concern should govern the law's response to transactional loss.

Something is right in this objection, but, as a motivation for functionalism, it is confused. To begin with, certain regulatory and compensatory institutions, not involving two-party liability, are correctly described as "alternatives" to tort law; and this is so even if one understands tort law as an expression of corrective justice and not merely as one instrument (among others) for deterring and compensating. The reason is that tort liability has an effect on the allocation of loss, and moreover, would seem to have a point only where the welfare of persons is vulnerable, given the scarcity of resources, to the occurrence of loss.[94] If there were no other social mechanisms for reallocating loss, then to show that tort law applies a norm of transactional equality might be to exhibit sufficient reason for it. But as things are, tort law realizes only one possibility for allocating transactional losses among many. And since these losses engage concerns of welfare (as do nontransactional misfortunes like illness or natural disaster), it seems right that the present argument still leaves an open question: that some losses stem from transactions does not, on this argument, itself determine that the only appropriate institutional concern, when this occurs, is with the rightness of the transaction rather than, as in other cases, with the fact of the loss.

Still, why should the persistence of this question incur any commitment, of the sort Posner avers, to manufacturing the norms of corrective justice out of more basic considerations of welfare, or to finding a justification which would make the value of tort law commensurate with that of other loss-allocating institutions? Such reductive commitments *would* follow from the thought that there must be a neutral decision procedure for choosing between such institutions. But what reason is there to think so? Moreover, if one accepts that the concern with corrective justice is a genuine concern (constraining and not empty: Section V.2), and if one accepts that tort law expresses such a concern, it can't simply be assumed that one could help oneself to such a (commensurate-making) justification of tort law and still be making contact with *that* concern. In the passage quoted, Posner speaks as if "corrective justice" described merely the formal (bi-polar) structure of an institution, leaving the question, Why have an institution with *that* structure open to whatever (other) reasons might be found.[95] But that is just to suppose that "corrective justice" merely represents the fact that the Basic Rule of a certain institution is an interpersonal liability rule ("X must compensate Y for wrongfully causing him harm"). And this fails to capture – clearly it misses – the point of the claim that tort law expresses corrective justice. Anyone passingly familiar with tort law knows that, under the institution's Basic Rule, X must compensate Y for wrongfully causing him harm. The claim is that X must do so *because* she has wrongfully caused Y harm.[96] That is a claim, not just about what the rules of an institution are, but about a distinctive kind of reason captured in those rules. It may not follow from this claim that there must be a legal institution embodying such rules (other concerns may compete), only that when there is, the reasons for interpersonal liability derive from the requirements of transactional equality and not merely from the significance of loss (such as that may be), independently conceived.

### V.4

Hence, understanding tort law as an expression of Aristotelean corrective justice does not oblige us to think that it should not be abolished; the theoretical gain is simply an appropriate understanding (which is not merely a sociology or history of legal rules: see Section I) of what it is we may have reasons to abolish. (On a functionalist view, the abolitionist proposal is essentially a proposal to abolish a practice for which no good reason can be found at all – a superstition.) On the other hand, nothing in the foregoing argument rules out the possibility that the Aristotelean notion of corrective justice could be elaborated in ways that, without reducing it to operations on some lowest common denominator of loss, would offer more positive support to tort law where it occludes other ways of allocating the burdens of accidents. My present purpose, however, has not been to make a positive case for (or against) tort law, but to bring certain issues concerning what it is to understand it (issues apt to be obscured in the standard contrast between efficiency and corrective justice as alternatives within a theory of tort) into sharper focus. To do so, my strategy has been to take the notion of corrective justice in its original and most anemic form, and to argue for its superiority, even in that form, over functionalist goals in understanding tort law. This seems especially significant in an intellectual environment where feelings of necessity accompany the later understanding.

Wittgenstein said: "In ethics we have to keep from assuming that reasons must really be of a different sort from what they are seen to be."[97] By "ethics," Wittgenstein meant the endeavor to bring the reasons for our practices to mind. Part of what makes this endeavor difficult for us, he was suggesting, is that we are apt to see what our reasons are but then to discount what we see by thinking that those simply couldn't be our reasons: Our reasons must really be of a "different sort." This implies that we have a preconceived idea of the sort of reasons we are looking for in ethics, and that we are disappointed when what we find does not fit our idea. What sort of preconception might this be? The remark I have quoted from Book I of *Nicomachean Ethics* suggests a possible answer: "Nor should we make the same demand for an explanation in all cases. Rather, it is sufficient in some cases to have 'the that' shown properly. This is so where 'the that' is a first thing and a starting point" (*NE,* 1098b1). Aristotle calls attention to a temptation, in studying ethics, to make a certain demand for explanation. Having seen that such-and-such are reasons for our practice, we are apt, he implies, to demand an account of why our practice proceeds on such grounds. At first blush this looks like a different point than Wittgenstein's. But the two remarks come together when we see that this call for theory amounts to a demand for further reasons or grounds – some antecedent or more primordial starting point. If we make such a demand, then we are inclined to think that the real grounds of our practices lie somewhere beyond the ones we have managed to bring into view; and this involves the idea of a different sort of reason in the sense of a distinction between reasons that strike us as sufficiently explanatory of our practice and those that do not. We might express the intimacy between Aristotle's and Wittgenstein's remarks by saying that the explanatory demand against which Aristotle cautions is expressed in – it is the source of – our thinking that "our reasons must really be of a different sort from what they are seen to be." The trouble with thinking this, both authors imply, is that we thereby fail to see the significance of the grounds which lie before us.

Is the contemporary endeavor to understand tort law sometimes impeded by a form of the trouble which Wittgenstein and Aristotle had in mind? If it is, Aristotle's presentation of corrective justice is exemplary, both in its relative clarity about the limited sense in which it comprises a theory of the law, and, by the same token, in its capacity to appear disappointingly empty, perhaps even somewhat mysterious: How could such a "spare and seemingly platitudinous concept of justice be thought an advance and . . . echo down through the centuries?" (Posner 1990, p. 316). For those who consider themselves free of the assumptions that produce this mystery, Aristotle's discussion may be exemplary in a further way. Instead of having to suppose that what that discussion provides could be "little more than a skeletal description" of corrective justice,[98] theorists of corrective justice might be challenged to consider whether Aristotle didn't in fact grasp the essential point to be made about it; namely, that corrective justice is what one grasps when one sees the law's treatment of doing and suffering as reason-involving. Of course, Aristotle's account was bound to be only an outline (*NE,* 1104a). But one might ask: Can it really be supposed that the work of fleshing out its more specific content was begun by philosophers in the last decade or two and not carried out by jurists for centuries?

## Notes

* This paper is indebted to conversations with Ernest Weinrib, and to comments on earlier drafts by Jules Coleman, James Conant, Alon Harrel, Jody Kraus, Liam Murphy, Jerry Postema, Stephen Perry, Arthur Ripstein, Scott Shapiro, Ralph Wedgwood, Edward Witherspoon, and Ben Zipursky. I am grateful to Eric Baim for helpful research assistance.

[1] See Coleman and Ripstein (1995), which suggested this formulation.

[2] The rest of this introductory section sketches the main claims I shall be developing later.

[3] On both points, I am indebted to similar arguments by Jules Coleman and Ernest Weinrib. See esp. Coleman (1992a) and (1988); Weinrib (1989c and 1995).

[4] Many legal theorists find Aristotle's discussion of justice to be disappointingly empty. See e.g., Kelsen (1957); Posner (1990, pp. 313–34). As will emerge in Section V, I take the exemplarity of Aristotle's discussion to lie partly in its capacity to provoke this sort of response.

[5] In a sophisticated legal culture these understandings are themselves typically shaped by reflection on the goodness and unity of the practice. Hence, a compendium like Prosser's reflects an attempt at understanding which is at work in the practice itself; it does not merely enumerate what, say, any judge in a torts case has ever said. This does not affect the present point.

[6] Of course, it may be that tort law touches on no good at all. In that case, there is no "understanding" it except – in the way we might understand a superstition – through a sociology or psychology of "takings." This general description of "understanding" resembles Dworkin's idea of a "constructive interpretation of legal practice," but (as suits my present purposes) it is much less specific. See Dworkin (1986, p. 225).

[7] The classic analysis is Calabresi (1970).

[8] Most functionalists appear to take this for granted. Pending further argument, the most that can be said, I think, is that having fewer accident costs is a worthwhile aim, *other things being equal.* It hardly seems obvious that even some efficacious means to cost-justified accident prevention couldn't be unattractive from the standpoint of values not well described in terms of 'costs.' See also note 27.

9   Correlatively, the functionalist's purposes would be frustrated if the goals invoked were
    such as to require the law to specify their content – e.g., "the function of tort liability is to
    protect a person's projects against *wrongful* interference" (either leaving it at that or con-
    necting the idea of wrongful interference to such abstract values as equality, liberty, or au-
    tonomy).

10  Sugarman (1985, pp. 616–17). See also Franklin (1967) and Ison (1967).

11  Quoted in Weinrib (1994, p. 284 n. 15). In speaking of "correlativity" in this section, I am
    following Weinrib.

12  A complete account of tort would require discussion of other grounds of wrongdoing (e.g.,
    intentional harm and strict liability), as well as special causes of action (e.g., trespass and
    nuisance). For my present purpose – viz., to suggest how corrective justice might function
    as a reason-revealing (but internal) characterization of the law – it is sufficient to focus on
    negligence. For discussion of other aspects of tort in relation to corrective justice, see
    Weinrib (1995, pp. 171–203).

13  Generally, whenever there is room for reasonable disagreement, the law instructs the jury
    in the concept to be applied and tolerates its decision. See *Illinois Pattern Jury Instruc-
    tions Civil* §10.01 (3rd ed. 1990): "The law *does not say* how a reasonably careful person
    would act under [the] circumstances. That is for you to decide."

14  *California Model Jury Instructions* §3.10 (8th ed., 1994).

15  See *Vaughan v. Menlove,* 2 Bing. (N.C.) 468, 133 Eng. Rep. 490 (1837).

16  *Palsgraf v. Long Island Railroad,* 162 N.E. 99 (NY 1926).

17  Or assuming, at least, that there is a reasonable question (one appropriate for a jury, see
    Section II.1) about whether the reasonable person would have done that sort of thing.

18  "Tragic" in Aristotle's sense (*Poetics,* ch. 11), which involves the thought that the conse-
    quences attributable to a person's action exceed intention and expectation.

19  It might be maintained, as it was by the dissenting judge, that since the defendant's action
    was unreasonable in virtue of the risks it created to *someone,* the defendant has done some-
    thing wrong, about which the plaintiff, as someone consequently injured, might legiti-
    mately complain. On this conception, proximate cause appears as a limitation, based on
    judicial "policy," concerning who may recover for wrongful injury. See *Palsgraf,* p. 103.
    On the majority's view, such a conception represents various tort plaintiffs as suing as vi-
    carious beneficiaries of wrongs done to someone else: "Negligence, like risk . . . is a term
    of relation. Negligence in the abstract, apart from things related, is surely not a tort, if in-
    deed it is understandable at all" (p. 101). The significance of this thought (*viz.,* that tortious
    wrongdoing requires an injury falling within the ambit of the defendant's unreasonable
    risk-taking) will become apparent later. I discuss the dissenting view briefly at note 79.

20  Clearly, the distinction between creating risk and merely failing to head one off itself de-
    pends upon certain normative expectations concerning when others may reasonably rely
    on our concern for them. But this shouldn't trouble us. To explain the idea of action by
    reference to creation of risk would be empty if the normative expectations giving content
    to the latter were only determined by positive declarations of law. Such expectations are
    *sometimes* determined by the law, but they also grow out of basic social understandings to
    which the law is responsive.

21  Much is left out for the sake of simplicity, e.g., limitations on duty with respect to certain
    types of injuries, burdens of proof, and defenses that negate or mitigate liability.

22  The wideness of the obligation is in fact one of the standard reasons for the partial tort im-
    munity of municipal and state agencies. See, e.g., *Riss v. City of New York,* 22 N.Y.2d 579

(1968). It also figures in the judicial observation that the duty asserted by the plaintiff in a case of nonfeasance is at best a moral duty of beneficence, not a duty appropriately enforceable by law. See, e.g., *Union Pacific Ry. V. Cappier,* 66 Kan. 649 (1903).

23  Again, this is a distinctive fact about tort, however obvious. With a social security scheme, the conditions under which one person is obliged to pay are independent of those under which another is entitled to benefits.

24  See *Sindell v. Abbott Laboratories,* 607 P.2d 924 (1980).

25  See Holmes (1963, p. 86) for this (mistaken) rationale.

26  See *Breunig v. American Family Insurance Company,* 173 N.S.2d 619 (1970). Besides asking why every defendant must come up to a standard of social ordinariness, one might also ask why meeting this standard is generally sufficient to avoid liability. Shouldn't the law reflect higher ideals? Shouldn't it ask persons to be *caring,* and not leave them free to act with indifference to an imperiled neighbor? See Bender (1988). In addition, isn't it naive to suppose that such notions as reasonable care or proximate cause really determine the status of a person's conduct in a particular case? Doesn't the normative power of these notions arise only courtesy of some interpretation of them, so that, in its settled understandings of what is reasonable, the law must be depending on political considerations which are hidden from view? In Section IV.4, I will suggest how understanding tort law as an expression of corrective justice provides directions for answering these and the other questions presented in the text.

27  There is room for doubt (not to be pursued here) about whether wealth-maximization or Kaldor-Hicks efficiency provides the right sort of item for the role of "undoubted piece of normative Reality." In what sense is "society is better off," as Posner puts it, when (only) cost-effective measures to prevent accidents are adopted? See Posner (1972). If society's welfare is simply defined as the state-of-affairs in which its collective resources are worth more rather than less, one might ask whether it is plausible to think that such a state-of-affairs is an unconditional good. See Dworkin (1980).

28  The suspicion that a substantial assumption is masquerading here as a platitude might be brought out by asking: If the proposition "that the law is made by us to serve human needs" is really undeniable, why should Calabresi think it significantly *assertable?* Why, indeed (starting with Holmes' often-repeated remark that the law is not "a brooding omnipresence in the sky") has it has seemed somehow critical to assert, under the banner of "realism," the connection of law to "*our* purposes"? The implication is that functional analysis rejects a gratifying illusion concerning transcendent sources of law. Cf. Frank (1963, p. 277). Of course, the intelligibility of that implication requires that we at least be able to make sense of the rejected (transcendent) conceptions. Compare: "Cooking and clothing are human constructs," where the word "human" enters into an informative and nonmetaphysical contrast to things which are not human, but not thereby beyond this world.

29  I don't mean that it would be clear what was meant by calling these "human constructs" beyond their involving certain forms of human activity. The point is that the same unclarity is present in applying the term to certain aspects of the law.

30  This suggests a way of understanding one of Aristotle's remarks in his discussion of justice: "With us, though presumably not at all with the gods, there is such a thing as what is natural, but still all is changeable; despite the change there is such a thing as what is natural and what is not." *NE,* 1134b29.

31  "What has to be accepted, the given, is – so one could say – forms of life" (Ludwig Wittgenstein 1958, p. 226). The present discussion of "human constructs" owes a debt to

Stanley Cavell's discussion of what Wittgenstein means by "forms of life." See, e.g., Cavell (1989, pp. 40–52).

[32] Someone might wish to distinguish this question from that of the law's instrumentality by saying such norms are *moral* norms and only legal in virtue of their enforcement by legal institutions. I think of Sections IV and V as offering considerations that may lessen the temptation to say this.

[33] Immanuel Kant (1991, p. 129 [318]; see also p. 123 [311]).

[34] That the felt necessity of functional analysis of tort law is a false necessity, is something best seen after consideration of corrective justice as another possibility. I return to this claim in Section V.

[35] My brief discussion of the two main species of accident costs follows Calabresi (1970). A more complete taxonomy would also include (as Calabresi points out) the expense of administering any system which seeks – through deterrence and compensation – to reduce the first two species of costs.

[36] See Posner (1972). The expected cost of an accident is the value of the loss discounted by the probability of its occurrence.

[37] See James (1948, p. 547): "[W]hile no social good may come from the mere shifting of a loss, society does benefit from the wide and regular distribution of losses." Calabresi calls this "secondary" cost reduction. His version of the theory of accident liability is more pluralistic than Posner's, which focuses merely on reducing "primary" costs (i.e., the sum of accident and prevention costs). The idea that compensation is a way of benefiting society by reducing accident costs is not inconsistent with conceiving the value of compensation in terms of its responding to urgent needs; it merely requires the additional thought that the value of responding to needs derives from a larger concern with social costs. The criticism below of the idea of a compensation goal (Section III.4) applies to *either* conception of it.

[38] Someone might respond that it is not the Basic Rule of negligence but that of strict liability for defective products which best reflects the idea of a compensation or loss-reallocation goal. See, e.g., *Escola v. Coca-Cola Bottling Co.,* 150 P.2d 436, 440 (Justice Traynor, concurring). This (self-consciously functionalist) innovation in products liability law does not affect the present point, however. Even such liability does not eliminate the causation requirement. And the law standardly insists on the Basic Rule in the face of analogous opportunities to shift losses to those who can insure against them and/or diffuse them through market prices. See, e.g., *Hammontree v. Jenner,* 20 Cal. App. 3d 528 (1971).

[39] As one functionalist critic of tort law puts it: "If we put fault aside and concentrate on the need for compensation alone, tort victims who obtain big recoveries are not more deserving than the sick, the congenitally disabled, the elderly, people injured at work, wounded soldiers, and the unemployed, all of whom are compensated through other social mechanisms" (Sugarman 1985, pp. 595–6).

[40] Indeed, since compensation, on this account, is most desirable when its source is wealthy or has access to an insurance fund (or other means of loss-spreading), there should be reason *not* to limit the sources of compensation to a single defendant identified on the basis of wrongdoing.

[41] As Jules Coleman puts it, it looks like to account for the defendant's obligation, we need an agent-specific reason: something analogous to the unshared reason that someone would have to do something she has promised to do. See Coleman (1992a, pp. 309–26).

[42] See generally, Weinrib (1989c, pp. 503–10); Coleman (1992a, pp. 374–84).

[43] On the pertinence here of the idea of a "bounty," see Weinrib (1989c).

[44] It won't do to say that it is by virtue of the transaction that the victim is a useful accessory for enforcing the norm of efficiency. At best, this says that the transaction is *epistemically* significant: it puts the victim in a relatively good position to know of efficiency violations. (See Jules Coleman's contribution to this book.) But participant understandings accord the transaction a normative significance which is not merely epistemic.

[45] I think Weinrib mistakenly denies this. See Stone (1996).

[46] I am indebted to Arthur Ripstein for this thought, which suggests, in effect, a *reductio ad absurdum* of the private-regulation picture.

[47] For this argument, see Weinrib (1989c, pp. 506–9). The appropriate incentive to efficiency is in place whenever the defendant faces a penalty whose present value (i.e., discounted by the likelihood that he will have to pay it) is greater than the cost of efficient precautions. Posner denies that the appropriate penalty could be anything other than the plaintiff's loss, on pain of either over- or under-spending on accident prevention. But it is hard to see why. Suppose that B (the cost of precautions) is 5, L (the victim's actual damages) are 100 and P (the probability of the accident) is 1/10. Since B is less than LP, the defendant is liable for negligence. But what should the penalty against him be? Wouldn't any amount over 50 provide the right incentive to spend the required 5 on accident prevention?

[48] Naturally, such stipulation runs the risk of making the object to be theorized, tort law, disappear entirely. See Coleman (1988, pp. 1250–3).

[49] See Franklin (1967, p. 784). Nowhere is tort law's frustration of these goals more visible than in the contemporary doctrinal pressures to relax the causation requirement when doing so would make it possible to structure a compensation scheme for a needy group of plaintiffs (see, e.g., *Hymowitz v. Eli Lilly & Co.,* 73 N.Y.2d 487, 1989); or in the tendency to apply causal requirements in ways that are sensitive to considerations about which party is a better conduit of loss-spreading (see, e.g., Petition of Kinsman Transit Co., 338 F.2d 708, 2d Cir., 1964). But clearly, there are limits to the extent to which such goals can be accomplished within the bi-polar setting of tort adjudication, and the price of accomplishing them there, as Franklin points out, is haphazardness.

[50] Thus, for Calabresi, it is "axiomatic that the principle function of accident law is to reduce [the cost of accidents]" Calabresi (1970, p. 26).

[51] It should be noted that Calabresi himself tends to remain agnostic on the empirical question of which legal measures are desirable from the point of view of accident cost-reduction. See, e.g., Calabresi (1970, p. 14–15).

[52] See Calabresi, (1975, p. 107): "Terms with an historical common law gloss permit us to consider goals . . . that we do not want to spell out or too obviously assign to judicial institutions."

[53] Consider an analogy: Conceiving of tort law as a legal response to the costs of accidents is like conceiving of honesty, trustworthiness and love as a way of "enhancing an individual's ability to maximize his satisfactions" by reducing the transaction costs of repeated negotiations among parties to the relationship. Posner (1977, pp. 185–6). One wants to say that here these values go missing, that someone who conceives of their appeal entirely in such terms hasn't got the relevant items in view.

[54] For others, a concern with compensation and deterrence could provide a reason for revising a legal practice which turned out to frustrate such goals (conclusion one), even if an appropriate understanding of *what* is to be thus revised is not to be manufactured entirely out of the same cloth (conclusion two). See Sections V.3 and V.4.

55  As I read it, decency/baseness figures in the quoted passage as an example of an allocational criterion, the one appropriate to aristocracies. Cf. Aristotle, *NE,* 1131a25.

56  Note that, alongside the point that society benefits by spreading, the functionalist's compensation goal is often given a second, and more explicitly distributive ("to each according to his _____"), rationale. Fairness, it is said, requires that the costs of a beneficial activity be distributed among all of its beneficiaries. See, e.g., James (1948, p. 550).

57  On agent-neutral reasons as a mark of distributive as opposed to corrective justice, see Coleman (1992a, p. 355). Doesn't tort law, when it requires one person to repair another's loss, also require that the resources of a community be allocated in a certain way? The answer is "no." Tort law is indifferent, for example, to whether the defendant has entered into a contract to insure against such possible liability.

58  I return to the idea that there ought to be a test for the correctness of judgments specifying the equality of corrective justice in Section V.

59  See *NE,* 1130b31–1131a1, 1131b25.

60  There are further problems for the present reading. The focus of corrective justice on wrongful transactions looks inexplicably narrow, since a distributive pattern can be disturbed by transactions that are not wrongful as well as by natural events which are not transactions. For discussion of the objections to the present reading, see Weinrib (1995, p. 79) and Benson (1992, pp. 530–1). These objections are not inconsistent with the thought that practices of corrective justice might loose their moral force against a background of serious distributive inequality. That thought does not require the idea that the justice in "corrective justice" consists in returning to a distributive *status quo ante.*

61  See *NE,* 1132a10–14 ("we speak of profit . . . even if that is not the proper word for some cases") which indicates that in cases of personal injury the victim's loss is used as the measure of the defendant's gain. Aquinas' gloss points out that the "loss is so called from one having less than he should have." Thomas Aquinas, *Summa Theologiae* II–II, A. 62, Art. 5 (Aquinas, 1975). The same may be said about the "gain" in question: By having that which properly belongs to the victim, the injurer has more than he should have. Ernest Weinrib has helpfully shown that this structure holds in a symmetrical fashion in cases of unjust enrichment where the law requires that the defendant's gain be "at the plaintiff's expense." Just as, in a case of personal injury, talk of the defendant's gain can be a way of representing the fact that the defendant has wrongfully inflicted a loss, so, in a case where (say) the defendant profits from the unauthorized use of the plaintiff's property, talk of the plaintiff's loss can be a way of representing the fact that such profit is a wrong to the plaintiff. See Weinrib (1995, pp. 140–2). The idea that in a case of wrongful injury, the defendant gains by having that which belongs to the plaintiff is reversed in Ripstein and Coleman's account of corrective justice: the loss suffered by the victim, they say, properly belongs to the injurer. See Coleman and Ripstein (1995); Ripstein (1999, pp. 24–58). These seem to me to be equivalent ways of representing what one person owes another in a case of wrongful transaction. Heavy weather is often made of the fact that equivalent losses and gains could only be fortuitous in a case of personal injury. See, e.g., Fletcher (1993, p. 1668); Perry (1992b, pp. 457–61). But given the alternative reading favored by Aristotle, this is misconceived as an objection.

62  Rejection of this reading of the equality of corrective justice is not inconsistent, I think, with Jules Coleman's thought (see his contribution to this volume) that corrective and distributive justice share a common concern with the allocation of losses. See also Ripstein (1999). The present point – not disputed by these authors – is simply that the norms per-

[63]     tinent to loss allocation in cases of transactions are not to be established on the basis of allocational entitlements given prior to reflection on what justice requires in such cases.

[63]     Cf. Kelsen (1957); Posner (1981). I take up Kelsen's and Posner's view of Aristotle's discussion more explicitly in Section V.

[64]     See p. 134 above.

[65]     This captures, I think Posner's way of construing Aristotle in Posner (1981). See esp. pp 190–2, 193, 203.

[66]     On this less formal reading, one might say that the problem of just transaction is related to the problems of "speaking justly," where to "speak justly" is to apply – and thus to work out the sense of – the predicates which describe a liability-incurring relation with another in light of a basic norm stemming from the fact that the other is a speaker too.

[67]     I am following Ackrill (1980), esp. pp. 95–7.

[68]     Cf. NE 1134a: "Since it is possible to do injustice without thereby being unjust . . . [someone might fail to be] a thief, though he stole . . . an adulterer though he committed adultery, and so on in the other cases." This seems to me to record the fact that we are not prepared to close the gap in the way presently contemplated. As I read it, the point of Aristotle's reference to something that "will be unjust without thereby being an act of injustice, if it is not also voluntary" (1135a) is not that the only sort of wrongdoing there could be is voluntary wrongdoing, but that this is the only sort of wrongdoing that appears from the point of view of the special ethical interest in blameworthy action.

[69]     As Aristotle puts it, "when one is wounded and the other wounds, or one kills and the other is killed, the action and suffering are unequally divided" (NE, 1132a5–10) – that is, they appear as wrongful in a legal judgement that treats the parties as equals in the present sense.

[70]     I do not think this is inconsistent with the thought which might be found in Aristotle's earlier discussion of responsibility (starting at NE, BK. III, ch. 1), namely, that the actions for which an agent is responsible are open to praise or blame in a way that exhibits something about the agent's character. See Stone (1996, pp. 248–9).

[71]     "No special difficulty" – save perhaps that of understanding how it is so much as possible for a wrongdoer's provision of compensation not only to repair a loss but (thereby) also to cancel or annul a wrong. That this is possible, I would tentatively hazard to say, is a matter of the basic social significance of compensation, though certain ways of thinking about wrong may lead us to think that it is in fact impossible. I touch on this in Stone (1996).

[72]     *Livingstone v. Rawyards Coal Co.,* 5 A.C. 25, 39 (1880, Lord Blackburn).

[73]     To be sure, tort law does recognize special circumstances which constitute exceptions to the general rule that, apart from not injuring others, there is no duty to act for their benefit. These circumstances bring into play special justifications which cannot adequately be discussed here. The opposite case – liability for doing apart from suffering – is, of course, familiar to the criminal (but not the civil) law.

[74]     Here again, the reasons for certain established exceptions – principally in cases involving physical incapacity, children, sudden derangement, and (more controversially) emergency – cannot adequately be discussed here.

[75]     Cf. Holmes' (1963, p. 89) suggestion that expedience is the basis of the objective standard.

[76]     In describing the plaintiff's injury (as one of such-and-such type, occurring in such and such manner, etc.) one is specifying at some level of generality the nature of one the risks created by the defendant's conduct (namely, the one which materialized in injury to the plaintiff).

77 Cf. Prosser (1953) for the mistaken impression that it should function as such a decision procedure.

78 See Morris (1952, pp. 196–8).

79 The dissenting judge in *Palsgraf* proposed a different formulation of the requirement of proximate cause, one which is also widely used today: the plaintiff's injury must be a direct consequence of the defendant's wrongdoing, not too remote. Cardozo's preference for the idiom of "foreseeability" stems, I think, from the fact that it is naturally sensitive (in a way the idiom of "proximity" or "remoteness" is not) to just the sort of descriptions of action or risk that interest us when we are characterizing wrongdoing. Cardozo sought to represent the law's duty-limiting judgments as something more than an expedient limitation on the set of injured persons who may complain about wrongdoing; and to this end, he exploited the fact that such a limitation seemed already implicit in the way the law spoke about "negligence" itself. See, for example, the explanation of negligence in terms of foreseeability by Brett, M.R. in *Heaven v. Pender,* 11Q.B.D. 503 (1883), p. 509. By "taking reasonable foreseeability of injury" as the outer bounds of the basic tort duty to take care – Cardozo realized – no further issue of "proximity" in causation need arise; the question of proximate cause would be internal to the question of the defendant's wrongdoing.

Talk of causal proximity or remoteness is apt to convey an inappropriate image of an action as an arrow traversing an infinite space. Given the defendant's wrongdoing, the problem is to divide the space into a proximate part (the proper consequences of the action) and a more remote part (the action's fortuitous upshots). As a representation of the sort of judgments the law makes, this is not exactly wrong. But it is apt to make us think that in identifying an act of wrongdoing we have not yet mentioned any reason for drawing the line between the two spaces in one place rather than another; so it is apt to invite an inquiry into why it might be a good idea, or a good policy, either to enlarge or diminish the space of the "proper consequences" of a wrongdoer's action: "What we do mean by the word 'proximate' is, that because of convenience, of public policy, of a rough sense of justice, the law arbitrarily declines to trace a series of events beyond a certain point. This is not logic. It is practical politics" (*Palsgraf,* p. 103, Andrews J., dissenting). That every case calls for a judgment that is not deductively determined by *either* formulation of proximate cause (hence is not a matter of "logic") must be granted. But Andrews' impression that such a judgment is therefore "arbitrary" or "political" seems to be partly an effect of the way the idiom of directness has clouded the issue. That idiom makes it natural to think that some reason *over and above* the defendant's wrongdoing and the plaintiff's consequent injury is needed for holding the defendant liable and allowing the plaintiff to recover. One may say that Cardozo, in representing proximate cause as internal to the question of the defendant's wrongdoing represents it as a specification of the question of whether the defendant is responsible (in a way others are not) for the misfortunes of the plaintiff; whereas, for Andrews, the question becomes one of whether it would be a good idea to *hold* the defendant responsible (where to "hold responsible" means simply "to make liable").

80 The focus on negligence in recent discussions of corrective justice shouldn't lead one to forget that the law's treatment of other situations (e.g., contract and unjust enrichment) might also be understood as expressing requirements of corrective justice. On contract, see Benson (1989).

81 Thus, it has become common to contrast functionalist theories which ground the law in the principle of economic efficiency with theories which endeavor to ground the law in

some principle of corrective justice. See, for example, Coleman (1982, p. 421). Coleman is reciting a commonplace here, but I think his current view – which emphasizes the role of practice in specifying the content of corrective justice – is not in fact well described in the terms of this commonplace. Stephen Perry's view – insofar as it presents tort law as an expression of an independently-standing moral principle of "responsibility for outcomes" – could much better be described as an attempt at grounding. See Perry (1992b). In other cases, talk of a "theory" of tort which "grounds" it in a principle of corrective justice simply uses these words without the specificity they have for the functionalist.

[82]  Clearly, the forgoing account of the Basic Rule (Section IV.4) was not a deduction of it from a principle of corrective justice. The argument relied on the recognition that alternatives to the Basic Rule (e.g., leaving losses where they fall, shifting losses regardless of fault or foreseeability, or excusing the injurer on the basis of his intentions) comprise forms of transactional unfairness.

[83]  Posner (1990, p. 322). See also Posner (1981, pp. 190, 193, 203).

[84]  Kelsen himself offers no positive fix; but he suggests that absent a procedure for concretely determining each person's due, any practical content which Aristotle discussion may seem to have must stem from its implicit reliance on positive law. See Kelsen (1957, pp. 128–36).

[85]  See Jules Coleman's essay in this volume.

[86]  For the complaint of tautology see Kelsen (1957, pp. 131, 132, 139); Posner (1990, p. 322). Cf. Weinrib (1995, p. 21): "[T]he purpose of private law is simply to be private law." Although such a formulation seems (against Weinrib's intentions) better designed to express the misunderstandings present in Posner's and Kelsen's reading of Aristotle than to avert them, it bears remembering that it is not compulsory to understand even the statement "the law is the law" as a "tautology." Compare: "War is war." What is intended might be something of the form "$\forall x(Fx \longrightarrow Fx)$" (identity of concepts), or perhaps "$a=a$" (identity of objects); but, of course, it is often, familiarly enough, of the form "$\forall x(Fx \longrightarrow Gx)$". Uninformative as they may be, one misunderstands such utterances if one takes them as tautologies.

[87]  Cf. Hegel (1991, §211): "The principle of rightness becomes the law when . . . it is posited, i.e., when thinking makes it determinate for consciousness and makes it known as what is right and valid; and in acquiring this determinate character, the right becomes positive law in general."

[88]  The assumption seems especially clear at various points in Kelsen's discussion: "[W]hat else could a 'theory' of morals present but general rules indicating that under certain conditions a certain human behavior ought to take place? And how can an acting individual know how to act morally in a concrete case if he does not know a general rule prescribing a definite conduct under definite conditions, identical with those under which he is acting? What the acting individual has to decide for himself is only the question as to whether the conditions determined by the general norm exist in his case – he has to decide the *questio facti*, not the *questio juris*" (Kelsen 1957, p. 382, note 37). The implication seems to be that moral thought moving from the general to the particular must take the form of applying rules which are sufficiently articulated in relation to particular situations such that the appropriateness of a particular action can be deduced from the rule once one sees what the facts of the situation are. (If the rule were such that the question of whether "the conditions determined by [it] exist" called for practical discernment beyond the mere recog-

nition of what the facts are, the *questio facti* and the *questio juris* would loose their distinctness.)

89 "At least in principle": Lack of empirical information about the effects of various legal rules may stand in the way of actually carrying out such an analysis. Note, in this regard, the following from Posner's review of Calabresi's *The Costs of Accidents:* "The book . . . furnishes a useful perspective on the problem of accident control but not a predicate for deciding between competing solutions" (Posner 1970, p. 646). Two thoughts appear here: first, a theory ought to supply a decision procedure; second, it furnishes a "useful perspective" even when it does not actually (given informational limitations) assist practical decision. More recently, in declining to replace a jury's judgment concerning "reasonableness" with a judgment derived from his own theory of negligence, Judge Posner observed:

> Ordinarily, and here, the parties do not give the jury the information required to quantify the variables that the Hand Formula [i.e., the cost of precautions and the expected cost of the accident], picks out as relevant. That is why the formula has greater analytic than operational significance. Conceptual as well as practical difficulties in monetizing personal injuries may continue to frustrate efforts to measure expected accident costs with the precision that is possible, in principle at least, in measuring the other side of the equation – the cost or burden of precautions. . . . For many years to come juries may be forced to make rough judgments of reasonableness, intuiting rather than measuring the factors in the Hand Formula; and so long as their judgment is reasonable, the trial judge has no right to set it aside, let alone substitute his own judgment. *McCarty v. Pheasant Run, Inc.,* 826 F.2d 1554 (7th Cir.1987).

"Judgments of reasonableness," Posner implies, are really second best to judgments arrived at through an informed economic analysis. But because the law must continue to rely on the former, the economic theory of negligence "has greater analytic than operational significance." I take this to mean: It gives us an independent description of what makes such judgments correct. (The correct judgment is the one which would be reached on the basis of perfect information together with the premise that the objective of legal intervention is to maximize wealth.) Critics are sometimes surprised that functionalists are not more concerned with empirical questions. The speculative motivation for functionalism described here might help make this less surprising.

90 Aristotle locates the distinctiveness of corrective justice by first distinguishing a special sense of justice (from justice as the whole of virtue), and then, within this special sense, distinguishing corrective from distributive justice. For this reason alone, it is incorrect to characterize his discussion of corrective justice as the "tautology" that each should be given his due (Kelsen 1957, p. 131). For both justice in the general sense and distributive justice also bear on what is due to persons. The contentfullness of Aristotle's discussion lies partly in these conceptual contrasts.

91 This sentence has benefited from the discussion of related problems in McDowell (1998, p. 10). The possibility of understanding a legal practice in this way suggests one way of construing the jurists' talk of the "autonomy" of the law. The idea is not that the law is beyond human making and remaking (see Calabresi, Section III.2), but simply that its rational development might proceed in terms of an idea of justice that it already partially expresses and which is distinctively engaged by the situation with which it deals.

92 This sentence reflects the fact that the demand for a decision procedure ought to have been

seen as especially questionable in the context of a reading of Aristotle, for it begs his questions concerning both the sort of "exactness" possible in ethics and the need for an external grounding. For Aristotle's relation to such a demand, see John McDowell, "Some Issues in Aristotle's Moral Psychology," in McDowell (1998). My discussion in the present section is especially indebted to McDowell's exploration of these issues.

[93] Because Posner takes his economic utilitarianism to answer both questions, he does not always clearly distinguish them. Hence: "If there are good reasons, grounded in considerations of social utility, for abolishing the wrong of negligently injuring another [in favor of a no-fault compensation plan], then the failure to compensate for such an injury is not a failure to compensate for *wrongful* injury. . . . [C]orrective justice is a procedural principle; the meaning of wrongful conduct must be sought elsewhere" (Posner 1981, p. 203). In calling corrective justice a "procedural principle," Posner seems to mean that it describes merely the general form of an interpersonal liability rule (see Section IV.3).

[94] See Ripstein (1999). It is not hard to understand, in this light, why a common feature of no-fault social insurance schemes (such as workman's compensation) is that the beneficiary surrenders the right to bring an action in tort.

[95] I suspect that ambiguities in terms like "institution" and "practice" in describing tort law makes it difficult to see the present issue clearly. It may be that an institution can be identified without understanding its aim or practical unity; that is not so with much of what we call "practices." These issues would need to be explored elsewhere.

[96] The claim, in effect, is that the "for" in "X must compensate Y for wrongfully causing him harm" introduces a reason and not merely a rule. Cf. Section IV.3. This is related to a point Peter Winch makes about punishment in Winch (1972, p. 218).

[97] Quoted in Rhees (1970, p. 103).

[98] Owen (1995, p. 1). Nothing in this paper should be taken to say that Aristotle's discussion of corrective justice leaves no room for useful elaboration. But it shouldn't be assumed that such elaboration must necessarily search, as Owen puts it, "for more specific content" (p. 1); the law itself, on the present argument, already does that. Such elaboration might rather relate Aristotle's notion to other abstract notions, such as ideas of personality (see Weinrib 1995), or ideals of liberalism (see Coleman and Ripstein 1996).

# 5

# Tort Law and Tort Theory
## Preliminary Reflections on Method*

JULES COLEMAN

There is a familiar and clear, if not always clearly understood, distinction between explanation and justification. Explanations seek to illuminate, or to deepen our understanding, whereas justifications seek to defend or legitimate actions, rules, institutions, practices, and the like. This could invite the mistaken view that explanation is a descriptive activity, whereas justification is a normative one. In fact, both are norm-governed activities, regulated, however, by different kinds of norms. The norms that govern explanation are theoretical ones like simplicity, coherence, elegance, and consilience, whereas the norms that govern justification are moral – norms of justice, virtue, goodness, and so on.

Some legal theorists, like Ronald Dworkin and Stephen Perry,[1] and especially the natural lawyers, believe that in the case of law, the projects of explanation and justification are deeply interdependent: that we cannot explain the concept of law without invoking at least some moral norms. While I disagree, this does not mean I believe that a philosophical explanation of the concept of law need not answer to norms of any sort. The debate may be framed in terms of the distinction between the following two kinds of claims: (1) Our concept of X depends in part on what our concept of X should be; (2) our concept of X depends in part on what X should be.[2] My view is that our concept of law depends on what that concept should be; it must, in other words, answer to theoretical norms. This does not mean that our concept of law depends on what *the law* should be. I deny, in other words, that the concept of law must answer to norms of justice, rightness, goodness, and so on.

Though the conflict between these two views lies at the heart of the current debate between the (somewhat misleadingly termed) normative and descriptive methodologies of jurisprudence, the conflict is nonetheless easily misunderstood.[3] It is important that it be made clear at the outset of my project, because my central claim in this essay – that our concept of tort law is best explained by appeal to a principle of corrective justice – could otherwise invite a natural confusion. The claim that tort law expresses and is best understood in terms of a conception of corrective justice does not rest on an endorsement of that conception as morally justified. The normative considerations that support the account are (in the first instance) epistemic or theoretical, not moral.[4]

The principle of corrective justice that forms the core of the account presented here states that *individuals who are responsible for the wrongful losses of others have a duty to repair the losses.* The substantive requirements of that principle, I maintain, are embodied in our institutions of tort law. While I do not mount a thorough defense of the corrective justice account, I do aim to articulate its main elements in a way that I hope is also persuasive.

In addition to presenting the account, a second purpose of this essay is to illustrate a method of legal analysis. In traditional philosophy of law, we would approach the topic of torts by first seeking to determine what justice requires when one person injures or harms another, and then we would examine our institutions of tort law to determine whether, and if so in what ways, they produce outcomes that justice, independently of them, requires. I have called this "top-down" legal theory (Coleman 1992a). It represents the prevalent mode of legal analysis, though not mine.

The method of analysis I adopt is exemplified in the following three claims about the relationship between corrective justice and tort law: (1) The content of corrective justice is given in part by the institutions of tort law: What corrective justice requires depends on the practices of corrective justice, including tort law.[5] (2) In the absence of practices of corrective justice, there can be no moral duties of corrective justice.[6] (3) The justification of corrective justice depends in part on seeing its attractiveness in the institutions that express or articulate it.

The first claim rejects the top-down approach by denying that the requirements of corrective justice can be adequately articulated independent of the social practices that realize corrective justice. The second claim asserts that even if corrective justice could be independently articulated as a "true," "justified," or "valid" principle of morality, that principle would still require practiced instantiations of it in order to impose moral duties of repair. The third claim emphasizes that the attractiveness of corrective justice as a principle of morality depends (in ways that need further clarification and development) on the moral attractiveness of its practiced realizations.

This essay explicates and further develops these claims. Corrective justice articulates the concept of fairness in a certain domain of human activity, namely, keeping track of the costs of those of life's misfortunes owing to human agency.[7] It articulates fairness in terms of other concepts, for example, "wrong," "loss," "responsibility" and "repair." Tort law makes corrective justice more explicit by filling out the content of these concepts. In developing this line of argument, my goal is not only to articulate a coherent view of the relationship between tort law and corrective justice, but also to suggest a general conception of the relationship between legal theory and practice.

Understanding tort law as animated by corrective justice allows us to see it in a particular way: if we explain tort law in terms of the values that it expresses or captures, the question of its justification becomes a question of the place those values ought to occupy in our public life. Even if corrective justice is an independent and independently defensible principle of justice, other concerns of fairness, decency, and beneficence may dictate that many of life's misfortunes – both those owing to human agency and those that are no one's responsibility – should be held in common, their costs distributed among us all, for example, through the tax system.[8] Thus, one of the broader purposes of the corrective justice account is to enable clearer debate about these matters.

## I.

Anyone who claims that tort law embodies certain ideals or principles must provide a conception of tort law and of the relevant principles or ideals, as well as an argument to the effect that tort law, so conceived, is best understood in the light of those principles or ideals. The core of tort law is composed of structural and substantive elements. The substantive core is represented by its basic liability rules: fault and strict liability.[9] Any plausible theory of tort law should explain both and the difference between them, provide a defense, if possible, of each, and an explanation of why fault liability provides the appropriate standard of liability and recovery in some cases, while liability in other cases is appropriately strict.[10]

Tort law's structural core is represented by case-by-case adjudication in which particular victims sue those they identify as responsible for the losses for which they seek redress. In the event a victim's claim to recovery is vindicated, her right to recover takes the form of a claim against the defendant (a claim which the defendant can discharge either directly or by some contractual relation, e.g., insurance). The victim is not, in contrast, awarded a claim against society as a whole or against a pool; and, in the event a defendant is judged liable, she is not required to pay into a general pool, or to compensate some randomly chosen victim, but must instead make good her own victim's compensable losses. Any plausible account of tort law must explain why claims are taken up in this case-by-case fashion, and especially the bi-lateral nature of litigation.[11]

Economic analysis provides a forward-looking account of tort law.[12] The costs of any particular tort are sunk. There is nothing to be done about them, no way of annulling or annihilating them. All that is left is to determine their incidence. Should the loss be left the burden of the victim or shifted to someone else, such as the injurer? Because the past cannot be undone, the decision to shift the loss or to leave it where it lies must be informed by a view to the consequences of the choice. Thus, we should ask what social good can be secured by imposing the costs on one person rather than another. With a body of law devoted to accidents and their costs, the natural consequences to which one ought to attend are the effects of loss-shifting rules on the costs of accidents. The rel-

evant social good is thus the reduction of accident costs, and the economic analyst concludes that the correct liability rules are those likely to lead to the optimal reduction in the costs of accidents.

Of course, any theory of tort law that ignores the costs of accidents and the
need to reduce those costs would miss something both obvious and important.
Showing that this important feature of our accident law is also an explanation
of its existence, endurance and shape is the burden of the economic explanation. The problem that confronts economic analysis, or any entirely forward-
looking theory of tort law, is that it seems to ignore the point that litigants are
brought together in a case because one alleges that the other has wrongfully
harmed her. Litigants do not come to court in order to provide the judge with
an opportunity to pursue or refine his vision of optimal risk-reduction policy.
Rather, they seek to have their claims vindicated: to secure an official pro-
nouncement concerning who had the right to do what to whom. The judge is
there, in some sense to serve them – to do justice between them; they are not
there to serve the judge in his policy-making capacity. Or so one might think
prior to theorizing about tort law.

Under economic analysis, the litigants to a tort suit bear no normatively significant relationship to one another. What is important is the relationship of each
to the goals of tort law, in particular, optimal risk reduction. From that point of
view, the important questions include: How good is the injurer (or injurer class)
at reducing accidents of this type, and at what cost? How good is the victim (or
victim class) at reducing risk, and at what cost? Need incentives be placed on
both of them to achieve optimal deterrence? If so, how should that be done? In
contrast, tort law is structured so that the important questions it asks are ones
about the relationship between the injurer and victim, not ones about the relationship of either or both to the goals of tort law.

There is simply no principled reason, on the economic analysis, to limit the
defendant or plaintiff classes to injurers and their respective victims. The
classes of victims and injurers are identified entirely by backward-looking features (the harmful event); yet those best able to reduce the costs of accidents are
identified by their relationship to the forward-looking goal of cost reduction.
The class of optimal cost reducers is not selectable by any event in which
*either* participated, much less by an event in which *both* participated – and certainly not by an event in which they both participated *in a particular* way
(namely, as victim and injurer). There may be some overlap between the class
of injurers and that of optimal cost reducers, but any such overlap can only be
accidental. To put it quite simply, in any case in which A hits B, it is an open
question whether A, B, C, D, or E . . . is in the best position to reduce the
future risks at the lowest cost.[13]

How then does the economist account for the fact that in the typical tort suit
the victim sues the alleged injurer and not the alleged cheapest cost-avoider?
How does one square the forward-looking goal of tort law (on the economic

model) with the backward-looking structure of tort law? The economist cannot appeal to the obvious answer that the victim believes the injurer harmed him wrongfully and, in doing so incurred a duty to make good the victim's losses. In the economist's account, the victim sues the injurer because the costs of searching for those in the best position to reduce the costs of future accidents is too high.

Next, how does the economist explain the fact that if the victim makes out his case against the injurer, he is entitled to compensation for damages *from the injurer?* Again, the economist cannot call upon the fact that the injurer incurs a duty to repair the victim's loss because he has wrongfully harmed him. It is one thing to ask whether there are good economic reasons for holding the injurer liable to certain costs. It is another question whether similar economic considerations require that *the victim* be compensated for his loss. It is yet another question – assuming that the injurer should be liable and the victim compensated – whether the victim should be compensated *by the injurer.*

The economic explanation cannot avail itself of the natural answer; instead, matters of liability and compensation are to be resolved in the light of their expected impact on the precautions each party – considered separately – will be induced to take. In order to deter the injurer, it is enough that he be made to bear costs sufficient to induce his taking cost-effective precautions. These costs may turn out to be more or less than the damages the victim actually suffers. Moreover, producing this incentive for the injurer does not require that the injurer pay the victim – only that he pay someone an amount sufficient to induce his compliance with the optimal risk-reducing strategy.

It is an open question in every case whether the victim should be encouraged to take precautions and if so, which ones. That will determine whether, on the economic account, he should be compensated; and if so, how much. Therefore, whether the victim is entitled to recover, and how much he should recover, does not depend on whether he was injured wrongfully or the extent of his injury, but on whether compensating him is necessary to avoid over-deterrence (that is, to avoid giving the victim and those in the victim's circumstances incentive to take overly costly precautions), or whether fully compensating him leads to too little deterrence (that is, fails to incite the most effective level of precaution-taking by the victim and those in the victim's circumstances).

There are other, more general, economic reasons for compensating victims – or at least for holding out the prospect of compensation. In any torts case, the victim acts as a private prosecutor bringing an action not only on his own behalf but also as an "agent" of the state. The state has an interest in discouraging economically inefficient behavior, but has only limited resources for doing so. By providing an avenue through which victims can secure recourse for harm done to them, the state creates an institution of "private enforcement." The expectation (or hope) of compensation induces private prosecutions, necessary to secure the optimal mix of private and public enforcement. However, on the economic analysis, it is no part of the victim's case for compensation that he has absorbed a loss as a result of another's wrongdoing. Rather, compensating him is to be explained as the result of the mix of the goals of inducing victims to litigate, and inducing both victims and injurers to take optimal precautions.

Consider, further, the economic explanation of the fact that in the typical case the victim sues the person she alleges wronged her. Because the point of tort law is (forward-looking) cost avoidance, we need to explain why the victim sues the injurer rather than seeking out the person who is in fact in the best position to reduce accidents at the lowest cost. It is always an open question whether that person is the injurer or someone else. The standard economic explanation is that the costs of searching on a case-by-case basis for the person who might be the better cost avoider is too high; and so, to follow a familiar strategy, a general rule in which the victim sues the alleged injurer is the second best alternative.[14]

This is not a particularly good argument. Because valid causal explanations support counterfactuals, the claim that victims sue injurers only because search costs require them to do so as a second-best alternative implies that, in the absence of search costs, victims who wish to sue would have the responsibility of seeking out the cheapest cost avoiders. In other words, were it costless or very cheap to locate the person in the best position to reduce costs, then it would be the duty of the victim who wishes to sue to find that person.

Indeed, it would appear that if search costs are trivial and if the goal is to provide incentives to those in the best position to reduce costs, then not only should the victims who want to sue have a duty to seek out the cheapest cost avoiders, but victims in general should have those duties – whether or not they are personally disposed to litigate.[15] This is in startling contrast to the fact that tort law provides victims with a right of recourse, an opportunity and a power to seek redress if they are so inclined – not a duty to do so. The point of conferring a power rather than imposing a duty is, of course, that powers are left to the control of those who have them.[16]

To generalize about these features of the economic account: Every core feature of the structure of tort law is explained by first disconnecting the injurer from the victim. The injurer and the victim are brought together for no reason having to do with an event that allegedly occurred between them. That is merely accidental (pardon the pun) to the structure of litigation. The victim is involved for reasons having to do with the various goals of tort law (understood from an economic perspective); and the same is true of the injurer. The importance of the fact (if it is one) that the injurer wrongly harmed the victim is epistemic, not normative. It may provide grounds for thinking that the injurer may be a good cost avoider, but is irrelevant beyond that. The economic account has the overall effect of making tort law appear mysterious.[17]

Tort law, I maintain, is not a mysterious social practice. It has a bilateral structure that is pretty well understood and it has a body of liability and procedural rules that are well known and largely unproblematic. In offering an explanation of tort law, we are not seeking to get a handle on a social practice that we find mysterious or difficult to grasp. Quite the contrary, we are trying to deepen our understanding of something we already comprehend.

Prior to theorizing about tort law, most of us believe all of the following: (1) the victim sues the injurer, and not somebody else; (2) the victim presents arguments and evidence to the effect that the injurer acted wrongfully towards him and that, as a result, he (the victim) suffered harm; (3) the wrongfulness of the act, the fact of the harm, and the causal relation between the two are all pertinent to the outcome of the lawsuit; (4) the jury decides – in accordance with instruction by the judge as to what duties, if any, the injurer owed the victim and the relevant standard of compliance with those duties – whether the victim has made out the relevant case in the light of the evidence introduced; and (5) if the victim is found to have made out his case successfully, he is awarded a claim against the injurer, who is in turn required to make good the victim's losses.

These features of tort law are plain to anyone without the benefit of theory, and the purpose of these features seems transparently evident in the light of our ordinary intuitions about corrective justice. The problem with economic analysis is that it renders these obvious and intuitively transparent features of tort law mysterious and opaque. In the absence of any explanatory theory, our intuition is that a victim is entitled to sue *because* he asserts that the injurer has wrongfully harmed him; that the victim must present arguments to that effect *because* the harm and the wrong are recognized by the law as pertinent to the outcome of the lawsuit; and that if the victim's claims are vindicated, he recovers against his injurer *because* the law recognizes wrongful harm as grounds for such recovery. The economic theory tells us, however, that each of these intuitions is wrong; that the apparently transparent purpose of the tort law in each case is not the real purpose; and that the real purpose, efficiency, has nothing at all to do with the fact that the injurer may have wrongfully harmed the victim. If the fact of the harm has any significance at all, it is epistemic.[18] Thus, while the corrective justice account of tort law seeks to show how the structural components of tort law are independently intelligible and mutually coherent in the light of a familiar and widely accepted principle of justice,[19] the economic analysis asserts that in the absence of search, administrative and other transaction costs, these structural features of tort law would be incomprehensible.[20]

## II.

As we have seen, one consequence of the economic analysis of tort institutions is that its participant individuals – including all those responsible for the development over time of the institution, its structure and constitutive concepts – have a false understanding of their practice.[21] Explanations of this sort carry a special burden. If the institutions really do serve some goal or end the participants do not consciously serve, then some further explanation is needed to explain the sense in which the hidden (from view) goal is really the institution's purpose. Only then can the outcome or effect of the institution serve as part of a formally adequate functional explanation.[22]

In order to see how the economic analysis fails to provide a formally adequate functional explanation, compare it, first, to the most straightforward kind of functional explanation of a social practice: one that explains a practice in terms of the purposes or goals of those who developed or designed the practice. Not every user of clocks knows why the time is set back an hour each fall, but presumably the drafters of the daylight savings time legislation had some goals in mind, and those goals, in a perfectly understandable sense, explain the practice. Clearly this is not the nature of the economic explanation, because no one wishes to claim that the many individuals who contributed to the development of our tort institutions were aiming at economic efficiency.

Of course, many functional explanations are not like the explanation of our clock-using practices. In many cases an outcome can explain a practice despite the fact that the practice was developed, and continues to be engaged by, individuals who do not regard the outcome as their goal in engaging in the practice. But where an outcome is not a conscious goal of those who designed or participate in some practice, the outcome can be of explanatory relevance only if it identifies a causal mechanism capable of supporting a range of theoretically interesting counterfactuals. It must be the case that were the outcome substantially different, the practice would not exist, or its central elements would be different. Barring some appeal to the intentions or goals of an agent, only a causal relation can support such counterfactuals, and thus warrant the claim that the outcome is the practice's purpose or function.

The idea is usefully illustrated by the familiar example of the leopard's spots. These have the effect, or produce the outcome, of camouflaging the leopard, thereby increasing its success as a hunter. We might then conjecture that the existence of the leopard's spots is explained by reference to this effect or outcome; that is, we might regard camouflage efficiency as the purpose or function of the spots. But so far, this conjecture remains a "just-so story" and not a genuine functional explanation. Missing is the causal mechanism, or intentional agency, that would support the counterfactual, "if they were not camouflage efficient, the leopard's spots would not be" (or, "would not be as they are"). Random mutation and natural selection (jointly) suffice as a plausible causal mechanism supporting that counterfactual; God's will would also do the trick, were the intentions of a purposive agent called for. Either the mechanisms of evolution or God's plan would suffice to turn a just-so story into a formally adequate functional explanation.

The problem for economic analysis should be apparent. It begins by rejecting the self-understandings of the developers and participants in the practice. That is, it rejects at the outset any intentional agency that might support the relevant counterfactual claim that "were the outcome not efficiency, the institutions of tort would be otherwise." Yet economic analysis of tort law (or of any other body of law, for that matter) offers no causal mechanism either – no analogue of random mutation and natural selection. It thus appears to present us with a classic just-so story.

The claim is not that there can be no economic explanations of the law that would satisfy the causal mechanism requirement. A good example of functional economic explanations of the law is the evolutionarily based litigation-and-settlement models offered by Priest and Klein, among others (Priest and Klein 1984). Their idea is that the efficiency of the common law is an unintended byproduct of rational litigation strategies. The litigation and settlement factors do, however, provide a causal mechanism (albeit one that affects intentional behavior) that could support the relevant counterfactual claim. If this account were true in its particulars, the outcome of efficiency could thus explain some aspects of the law, even if no involved individual's actions have ever aimed at efficiency.

But while these accounts might explain some parts of the law, they cannot serve as a functional explanation of the core tort law. The litigation-and-settlement models purport to work by emphasizing the way efficiency can guide litigants to adopt certain strategies of litigation and settlement. This might (if factually supported) explain the behavior of litigants confronted with the institutions of the common law. But this cannot even purport to explain the shape of those institutions; it cannot explain why tort law is distinct from the other parts of the private law, nor why any of these parts have the characteristic features and central concepts that they have.

If these features – and not just the behavior of litigants – are to be explained by efficiency, then litigation-and-settlement theorists must show a causal link between efficiency and the features to be explained. This they do not seem prepared to do, and one would indeed be hard pressed to defend the claim that the common law has been crafted over time by generations of judges and legislators with the aim of encouraging economically efficient strategies of litigation and settlement. Thus, while litigation and settlement models provide the sort of causal mechanism needed for a genuine functional account of the behavior of litigants, they unfortunately provide only a just-so story with respect to the other elements of the common law, including the core features of the law of torts.

Until now, we have simply granted the economic analyst's contention that tort law tends to produce an optimal reduction in accident costs. Our focus has been on the conditions under which such a tendency could figure in a functional explanation of tort law. It is not obvious, however, that our tort law produces anything like optimal deterrence. We can, no doubt, safely assume that on balance tort law reduces accident costs, as compared to a situation in which there is no legal recourse to recover for harm.[23] But lower costs than might exist in the absence of our tort law need hardly be optimal costs, nor even approach them. Economic analysis needs first an argument to show that tort law has developed over time in a way that approximates an efficient reduction in accident costs. Only then is there prima facie reason to look for a causal mechanism that would show why efficiency explains the shape of the legal institutions. In short, without both a *prima facie* demonstration of efficiency, and a plausible causal mechanism, it is hard to credit economic analysis with providing even a formally adequate functional explanation of tort law, let alone a convincing or persuasive one.

In contrast, the corrective justice account of tort law does not purport to provide a functional explanation in the sense we have been considering. Corrective justice invokes no opaque or hidden goal like efficiency. Indeed, the relationship between tort law and corrective justice is not even instrumental in any interesting sense; corrective justice itself may be a goal of the practice, but it is not a goal external to it and at which the practices of tort law are aimed. Rather, tort law expresses, embodies or articulates corrective justice. Tort law is a transparent institutional realization of principle, not an instrument in the pursuit of an external and hidden goal.[24]

Is this the end of the story? Perhaps not. We have been considering the explanatory claims of economic analysis; but in addition to explaining, economic analysis also seeks to recommend ways in which the law of torts might be improved. Perhaps this prescriptive aspect of the law and economics project can shed some light on its otherwise puzzling features.

On the economic analysis, the existence, endurance and shape of tort law are all to be understood *instrumentally* in terms of this economic goal. As with any instrument, we may evaluate tort law by its *effectiveness,* that is, how well or poorly it serves its function. Herein lies the great attraction of economic analysis for the reform-minded legal academic. It allows us not merely to understand and assess the law, but also to prescribe changes to our legal institutions. It gives us a purchase on every question we might ever ask about any rule of tort law – substantive, structural or procedural. All are measured by their economic efficiency, and endorsed or criticized depending on how well they serve that goal. Law review article after law review article is then published suggesting reforms – large and small, important and trivial.

Of course, it is no mean question what institutions would most effectively reduce accidents and their costs, or how, given our existing system of tort law, we might tinker with it in order optimally to serve that end. Such questions are not unreasonable. But claiming that the Anglo-American common law of torts should produce a certain outcome, or even that it tends to do so, is altogether different from claiming this outcome is the best or most plausible explanation of the law's existence and shape. This is not to say that a descriptive or explanatory account cannot have prescriptive implications; but if it is to succeed as an explanation, it must meet the adequacy conditions of an explanation – something that, as we have seen, the economic analysis appears inexplicably not to do. It is ironic that while the great majority of economic analysts of law claim to be explaining our existing institutions, their project may be in some deep way irreducibly evaluative or prescriptive.[25]

If economic analysis falls short of being a functional explanation in the familiar sense, might it be some other kind of theory altogether? The concept of a function plays a central role in certain forms of rational reconstructions that Dworkin labels, "constructive interpretations." In the Dworkinian picture, explanations of social practices and bodies of the law (or the whole of the law) are arrayed and assessed along two dimensions: fit and value. The interpretation must make sense of enough of the practice by showing how its component parts fit together (the fit requirement). However, many putative interpretations can satisfy this requirement. The best explanation is the one which not only fits the shape of the institutions or practice, but also reveals it in its best light, as the best version of the sort of thing it purports to be (the value component).

In offering an interpretation in this sense, one needs to posit a point, purpose or function of the institution or practice. The component parts must then be shown to hang together in a way that makes this function or point perspicuous. Thus, the function provides a lens through which the component aspects of the practice are seen to cohere and to be mutually supporting. At the same time, the posited purpose or function allows us to see the practice or institution as the best of its kind. All posited functions can be assessed both in terms of their capacity to shed light by unifying the practice, and in terms of their independent defensibility.[26]

Rather than conceiving of economic analysis as a functional explanation in the standard sense that characterized our earlier discussion, I suggest that we think of it in Dworkin's sense, as a constructive interpretation of tort law: what we might refer to as a functional explanation in the hermeneutic sense. In this way, positing the function of producing efficient accident cost avoidance reveals to us the way in which the disparate components of the structure and substance of tort law hang together in a way that is, at the same time, normatively attractive: in a way, in other words, that allows us to see tort law in its best light.

Thus, in the typical economic explanation, various parts of the law of torts – whether the rule of negligence, the definition of reasonableness, the but-for causation requirement, or the like – are each shown to further efficiency, and so efficiency is said to be the best interpretation of them, individually and collectively. No causal claim need be involved. Efficiency provides a matrix that holds the elements of the tort law together, and the coherence itself is grounds enough for the interpretation. If this matrix requires some procrustean modifications, they are justified by an attractive goal, because it is obviously preferable to have fewer accidents than to have more, and the fewest at the lowest possible cost.

The hermeneutic interpretation of the project may be the most charitable we can provide. After all, economic analysis has yet to provide the two essential components of a standard functional explanation: a demonstration that the outcome of tort law really is efficient cost reduction, and a causal mechanism that feeds back that outcome into an explanation of tort law's existence and shape. Moreover, while in the typical economic explanation of tort law the descriptive and prescriptive aims are combined in a way that would be indefensible for a

social-scientific functional account, this combination of descriptive and prescriptive elements is the very hallmark of an interpretive reconstruction.

Should economic analysis turn out to be an interpretive theory rather than a
traditional functionalist theory that would in itself be nothing to be embarrassed
about, though it might offend the positivistic social science scruples of some of
its proponents. That would be something to get over, not fret over. There would
be some things to fret over, though, and perhaps even to be embarrassed about.
Two of these are especially important. First, if economic analysis is an interpretive theory in the Dworkinian sense, then it is a particularly bad one on the
dimension of fit. Where an interpretation is supposed to help us see the way the
parts of an institution hang together, fit or cohere with one another – support
one another – economic analysis appears to do just the opposite with respect to
the structural features of tort law. It treats the victim and injurer as fundamentally unconnected to one another and the existence of the tort itself as merely
epistemically significant. The dimension of fit has, it appears, been sacrificed
altogether for the sake of the posited function, which now takes on the role of
cementing together the disjointed parts. The result is less an interpretation of
an actual institution than it is the imposition on it of a completely external goal –
like interpreting Christmas as a yearly boost for the retail industry.

Nor is the economic interpretation successful on the dimension of value,
where an argument is still required. Typically, economists of law shy away from
defending the normative attractiveness of efficiency. They have precious little
to say on the subject, and what they have said has not been particularly persuasive. But if the economic analysis of tort law (or of any body of law for that
matter) is to be an interpretation in the Dworkinian sense, then the argument for
efficiency as the best explanation of tort law requires an argument for the attractiveness of efficiency as a moral value, and indeed, an argument that efficiency is a more attractive moral value than the set of values embodied in corrective justice.[27]

I fear we may have raised deeper problems for economic analysis than those
with which we began. We have made some progress though. For in reinterpret-
ing the project as a form of normative reconstruction or interpretation, we have
freed the economist of the burden of providing the causal connection between
efficiency and the existence of tort law that is not likely available. For the interpretation to be a plausible one, however, the economist needs to provide a
better argument than he has so far to establish a "fit" between efficiency and the
structure and substance of tort law, and a much better defense of the moral value
of efficiency than has been offered to this point.

## III.

Instead of asking whether tort law is best understood on efficiency or justice
grounds, some economic analysts suggest that we ask the different question of

what best explains the general set of institutions and practices of risk regulation. Even if corrective justice provides the better explanation of tort law understood as a distinct and autonomous body of law, it fares worse than economic analysis as an account of our general practices of risk regulation. In fact, these analysts argue, tort law is not an autonomous body of law; it is just one of many parts of the law that have to do with regulating risk. Economic analysis provides the best explanation of tort law because tort law is an integral part of the institutional strategy of efficient risk regulation. Seeing tort law this way also allows us to uncover important connections between it and other parts of the whole.[28]

The strategy of meeting an objection by changing the subject is a familiar one. Even a sympathetic critic of economic analysis may be taken aback by the swiftness with which economic analysts are prepared to abandon their longtime poster child, the private law of tort. One needs, after all, a reason for changing the subject. The fact – if it is one – that thinking of tort law as part of a general approach to risk regulation fits better with economic analysis is, at best, a question-begging reason for shifting the subject matter of inquiry.

This is so even if there is a sense in which the current boundaries between various bodies of law are arbitrary. It is one thing to claim that the current divisions are neither fixed nor reflective of some natural ordering; it is another to claim that they are arbitrary. Even were the categories arbitrary in the sense of being "conventional" and neither "natural" nor "essential," that would not, by itself, be a reason for abandoning them. Still less would it be a reason for abandoning them in favor of the preferred economic set of categories. Only categories that are arbitrary in the sense of lacking adequate justification should be abandoned or ignored.

The claim that the boundaries between various bodies of law are arbitrary may, however, be a misleading way to put an interesting point.[29] There is no reason to suppose (in the absence of argument) that the categories of thought and morality expressed in various parts of the law instantiate conceptually or morally indispensable categories. For example, we should not be mislead into thinking that the distinction between "causing harm" and "failing to prevent harm," which is so fundamental to the law of torts, marks a independent moral difference.

In utilitarian moral theory, for example, the differences among causing harm, not preventing harm, and failing to benefit are not fundamental. Still a utilitarian can allow that some of these differences are reflected in different parts of the law for good utilitarian reasons.[30] Though the boundaries between categories of thought in law may not mark inherent moral differences, they may nonetheless be justifiable.

The question then becomes whether or not they are indeed justifiable – both morally and theoretically. We may wish to revise the categories if there are simpler or more elegant alternatives, or if they fail to hang together in a coherent way with other important concepts. Moreover, even if they conform to these

theoretical norms, we may find that the categories obscure important moral features of cases. In either instance, we may find that we have a reason to revise
or abandon the categories.

Still, we don't revise our boundaries between bodies of law just because we
can, or because doing so suits our prevailing theories. We cannot decide, as it
were, to drop the category of tort as uninteresting or unimportant just because
it would be more convenient for economic analysis to substitute the category
"practices of risk regulation" for it. Any such revision must be motivated by recalcitrant problems with the categories currently conceived – phenomena the
current architecture does not capture or which it illuminates for us only dimly.
Revisions can't be justified on the grounds that our favorite theory isn't working.

There are, moreover, criteria for revision – revision is a rational enterprise.
Typically, we make the smallest changes first. Only as a last resort do we jetti-
son the core of the distinctions, categories and beliefs with which we have
proceeded. Thus, we begin with the various distinctions between bodies of
law – torts, contract, criminal, and so on. We needn't show nor assume that these
distinctions are indispensable, or that they track some independent moral order.
We just have them and work with and within them. We do not inquire into their
justification unless we have reason to doubt their value or usefulness to us.[31]
Only when we have reason to worry about their theoretical or practical value
do we rethink them.

Are there reasons for revising our pretheoretic conception of tort law? Are
there reasons for revising the boundaries between tort and other bodies of law,
for substituting the law of risk regulation for the law of torts – for treating risk
regulation as more basic than tort law?

One possible reason might be that a concept of tort law that is bound by its
traditional categories fails to reflect the theoretical norm of consilience. To reflect this norm, a concept of tort law should provide insight into connections
among different bodies of the law. When we see tort law through the lens of
economic analysis, we can understand better the coherence in our general risk
regulatory practices. The better a theory of law is at unifying distinct areas, the
more attractive the theory is.

These considerations seem to provide an entirely different and better argument on behalf of the economic analysis of tort law. Even if economic analysis
does not have a good account of our pretheoretic conception of the bilateral
structure of tort law, considerations of consilience compel us to look beyond
tort law to other areas of the law, including parts of administrative law and regulatory law generally.

The price one has to pay in order to see these connections clearly is that one
has to revise one's pretheoretic understanding of the bilateral structure of tort
law. What once seemed necessary to our understanding of tort law must be
abandoned or rethought. We see a lot more in the law and in the way its com-

ponent parts are deeply connected to one another when we give up the view that in torts the victim and injurer are deeply connected in the way we might otherwise have thought they were.

This is the right kind of argument, but it is not yet a successful one for replacing the category of torts with that of risk regulation. There are many perspectives from which we might look at a body of law: the point of view of private parties concerned to plan their affairs; the point of view of those who have been mistreated by others; the point of view of lawyers, judges and perhaps that of reformers. The economic analysis of risk regulation seems to take the latter perspective only, and in so doing renders the other perspectives nearly unintelligible. For in asking us to revise our pretheoretic conception of tort law, it requires that we abandon the view that victims sue injurers because they have been wronged by them. We see lots of connections from the reformer's point of view, but at the cost of our inability, perhaps, to comprehend law from other points of view.

Thus, we do not yet have an argument for the economic analysis of tort law, just the outlines of what such an argument might look like. At the very least, we need a proponent of economic analysis to display in more detail the ways in which economic analysis illuminates the connections between torts and risk regulation. Still, the importance of the norm of consilience to theory construction authorizes an implicit challenge to the corrective justice account, one that we ought to take up. It would be odd if corrective justice explained tort law, yet failed to illuminate any other area of the law or of political morality. After all, the conceptual categories central both to tort law and to corrective justice – categories like responsibility, wrong, repair, and so on – are also important to our pretheoretical understanding of other parts of the law and of our political institutions more generally. The burden of the corrective justice theorist is thus not to show that corrective justice unifies tort law with regulatory practices in particular, but simply to show that the explanation of tort law in terms of corrective justice reveals the ways in which tort law hangs together with other legal and political practices.

## IV.

My view is that the best explanation of tort law will display its connections to our broader institutions of distributive and corrective justice in a way that illuminates and deepens our understanding of them all. Specifically, the institutions of tort law and distributive justice together articulate the requirements of fairness with respect to keeping track of the costs of life's misfortunes. There is a basic pretheoretical distinction between misfortunes owing to human agency and those that are attributable to no one's agency. The distinction between corrective and distributive justice reflects, among other things, this pretheoretical distinction between kinds of misfortunes.[32]

Corrective justice articulates the requirements of fairness with respect to the misfortunes we attribute to individual human agency; distributive justice articulates the demands of fairness with respect to other forms of misfortune. Many of the "problems" of tort law, corrective justice, and distributive justice are at bottom the same.[33]

Because the domain of distributive justice includes the class of misfortunes for which no one is responsible, whereas the domain of corrective justice is the class of misfortunes for which some human agency is responsible, it is natural to suggest that the difference in the requirements of fairness with respect to both is captured by the role the concept of personal responsibility plays in each.

Corrective justice says, in effect, that fairness in keeping track of the costs of life's misfortunes owing to individual human agency requires the imposition of a duty of repair for the compensable harms for which one is responsible: those owed, in an appropriate way, to one's responsible agency.[34] That is, I have a duty to repair your loss as a matter of corrective justice just because your loss is an outcome for which I am responsible.

In contrast, the scope of one's duties to come to the aid of others is not limited to alleviating the misfortunes for which one is responsible. Many duties of distributive justice require coming to the aid of others to alleviate misfortunes for which one is not causally or otherwise responsible. Corrective justice is a distinct kind of justice in precisely the sense that the duties imposed by it are grounded in the "responsibility for outcome" relationship.

Not every theorist of distributive justice holds that the claims of justice extend beyond the scope of the responsibility for outcomes relationship. The libertarian, for example, does not. According to the libertarian, the concept of responsibility for outcomes governs both distributive and corrective justice. Of course, there are at least as many formulations of libertarianism as there are libertarians. In its most familiar form, the animating concept is self-ownership. Responsibility for outcomes is explicated in terms of self-ownership in conjunction with causation and volition: roughly, X owns his body; X owns all those products (desirable or undesirable) that are the causal upshots of his voluntary doings – and nothing else. Volition and causation distinguish doings from mere happenings: actions from other events.

The concept of responsibility explicated in terms of ownership, volition and causation is general. It specifies the conditions that must be satisfied in order for it to be true that so-and-so is responsible for such-and-such (where "so-and-so" ranges over persons or other responsible agents and "such-and-such" ranges over states of affairs). Not only is the content of the principle of responsibility for outcomes specified independently of political or legal institutions and practices – this principle, for the libertarian, imposes constraints on political and legal institutions. In order to be just, institutions must conform to the demands of the principle of outcome responsibility. Legal institutions of responsibility, like tort law, must embody the principle of outcome responsibility.

For the libertarian, the institutions of property, tort liability and distributive justice – and perhaps more – are constrained by these conceptions of ownership and responsibility. The net effect is that the libertarian supports strict liability (as opposed to fault) in tort law and rejects redistribution of wealth as unjust. Under strict liability the injurer takes back what he rightfully owns, that is, the misfortunes that are the products of his agency. At the same time, redistribution violates the principle of agency by claiming that individuals own the misfortunes that have befallen others though they are not responsible for them in the relevant sense.

Though the libertarian is mistaken about both tort law and distributive justice, his position is not without interest. Three claims in particular warrant consideration: first, that there is a general concept of responsibility for outcomes that applies across contexts; second, that this concept of responsibility for outcomes imposes constraints on political or legal institutions; third, that the underlying problems and principles of distributive and corrective justice are the same.

It might be useful to compare the libertarian view with Stephen Perry's, in part because Perry is a leading critic of the libertarian theory of strict liability in tort law. Perry rejects the libertarian theory of distributive justice. For him the duties of distributive justice are not restricted to alleviating the misfortunes for which one is outcome-responsible.[35] Perry is best known, however, for his criticisms of the libertarian theory of strict liability in torts. As Perry notes, the libertarian reliance on ownership spelled out in terms of causation leads to indeterminacy. If X is liable strictly for the causal upshots of his voluntary actions, then in most cases, both the injurer and the victim own the victim's loss. This is because, in general, some voluntary actions of both parties are "but for" causes of the harm. A principle of strict causal liability leads not to strict injurer liability – as some, like Richard Epstein have thought – but to indeterminate liability. Perry is right about that.

Perry does not object to the view that outcome-responsibility should play a role in the proper account of tort law. His criticism is directed, rather, at the libertarian's conception of outcome-responsibility. Instead of analyzing it in terms of volition and causation, Perry analyzes it in terms of foreseeability and avoidability. Outcomes an agent can foresee and avoid are ones for which he is outcome-responsible. Perry maintains that, in order to be just, liability in torts must be grounded on this notion of outcome-responsibility.

Like the libertarian's conception, liability based on Perry's notion of outcome-responsibility is indeterminate. In most cases both the victim and the injurer will be outcome responsible in this sense. That is why Perry does not believe that strict liability follows from the concept of outcome-responsibility. Outcome-responsibility is, he believes, necessary but not sufficient for liability in torts. The criterion of outcome-responsibility determines the class of persons who can justly be held responsible for an outcome. For most injuries, both the victim and injurer will be members of the class: Both, after all, can typically foresee and avoid the danger. The loss must be imposed on one or the other on other grounds, and that, according to Perry, is where fault comes in. The party who is at fault bears the cost. The fault principle represents or expresses a criterion of "local distributive justice" applicable to the class selected by the criterion of outcome-responsibility.

Setting to one side the merits of Perry's overall position, I want to emphasize its similarities to the libertarian position. First, like the libertarian, Perry believes that there is a general set of conditions which, if satisfied, warrant the assertion that so-and-so is outcome-responsible for such-and-such state of affairs; that the content of these conditions is specifiable independent of the practices in which the concept of outcome-responsibility might figure; that, in other words, the conditions of outcome-responsibility apply across action contexts and are in that sense invariant; and, finally, that in order to be just, institutions in which liability is based on responsibility for outcomes must reflect this particular conception of it.

I reject these claims. Although I share with Perry and the libertarian the sense that the problems and principles of distributive justice and tort law are, in an abstract but important sense, the same, I reject the libertarian view that the bond that ties them together is some causal conception of responsibility for outcomes. More importantly, in contrast with both Perry and the libertarians, I deny that the justice of our tort institutions depends on a "moral" conception of responsibility for outcomes. There is a conception of responsibility for outcomes at the core of the concept of corrective justice and tort law – but this conception is not independent of tort institutions and practices, and its moral standing is of a piece with the moral standing of the institutions that embody it.

Whereas both Perry and the libertarian believe that in order to be just the imposition of liability in legal contexts must reflect the moral conception of outcome-responsibility, the view suggested here is that the concept of outcome-responsibility suitable to legal contexts must reflect the conditions under which the state's exercise of its authority is legitimate. These include constraints imposed by the fair terms of interaction which in turn reflect a fundamental conception of fairness as a kind of reciprocity. It is not obvious that our judgments of moral responsibility for outcomes, or of responsibility more generally, reflect or answer to a similar set of restrictions.

Put roughly, moral and political philosophy are independent in an important sense. The problem of political philosophy is not whether X is morally responsible for a loss, but whether the state would be justified in imposing liability on X for the adverse consequences of his conduct: for those untoward states of affairs for which he is outcome-responsible. Thus, the conditions under which the state is justified in imposing its coercive authority on someone are implicated in the political question (or legal one) in a way in which they are not in the moral one.

It is a further question whether, in order to be just, the politically relevant conception of responsibility should reflect or coincide with the moral conception. The answer to that question must depend on whether the conditions of legitimate political authority require such a relationship between the moral and legal conceptions of responsibility; and that is a question in political philosophy: Do the fair terms of interaction among persons require that responsibility for outcomes in legal contexts reflect the moral conception of outcome-responsibility? This, of course, is very different from the approach Perry and libertarians take, in which the moral conception of outcome-responsibility imposes constraints on the way we can think about political and legal institutions.

To clarify the differences between Perry and the libertarians on the one hand, and me on the other, I shall draw on a useful distinction of Thomas Scanlon's between *attribution* and *allocation* (Scanlon 1988). The attributive question is, who is responsible? The allocation question is, who should bear the costs? Suppose we begin with the latter question. One answer might be: the person who is responsible for the loss should bear it. This would be to say that the allocation question is to be answered in the light of the principle of attribution. More precisely, we might say that the costs of the accident should lie where they fall unless someone is responsible for having brought it about. If someone is responsible for having brought it about, that person must bear the loss. Any other way of allocating the loss would be unfair or unjust.

That the allocation question is to be resolved in terms of the attribution principle is what Perry shares with the libertarian. They differ, however, with respect to the conditions under which persons are outcome-responsible. And they also differ with respect to whether being outcome-responsible is sufficient to determine fully the answer to the allocation question. The libertarian believes being outcome-responsible is sufficient (at least for the *prima facie* case), whereas Perry does not. For him, liability requires both outcome-responsibility and fault.

In my view, the principle of allocation determines the appropriate principle of attribution – not the other way around. Once we determine what the allocative question is that a particular body of law seeks to answer, then we can determine which, if any, criteria of attribution (or responsibility) must be satisfied. The criteria of responsibility (attribution) suitable to create and enforce duties of repair in order to allocate costs that must fall on someone (injurer or victim) might well be different from those appropriate to the imposition of other duties (to apologize, or in other ways come to aid of others) (Coleman 1995).

Let me remind the reader where we are in the overall argument. In the first part of this essay, I argued that corrective justice explains the bilateral structure of tort law in a way that the economic analysis cannot. This led to the suggestion that perhaps, as a functional explanation, economic analysis should not be expected to account for the bilateral structure; but I argued in the second part of the essay that economic analysis fails to qualify as even a formally adequate functional explanation. I then considered the alternative of construing economic analysis as a kind of interpretive theory, one that employs the notion of a function in a less precise, formal or demanding way. Whereas this reconstruction more accurately captures what economic analysts actually appear to be doing, it proves ultimately unhelpful because the economic account fails on both the dimensions of fit and value.

I then introduced yet another reformulation of the economic argument by appealing to the theoretical norm of consilience. Perhaps explaining tort law in economic terms is illuminating because it reveals deep and important connections between tort law and other practices of risk regulation. One consequence of such an approach, however, is that it compels us to revise our pretheoretic conception of the importance of the bilateral structure of tort law. This may be a price worth paying, but the burden is on the proponent of economic analysis to show that it is. That would require that the supposed deep connections among the institutions of risk regulation be more fully developed. Meat must be put on the bones of the argument.

Nevertheless, the norm of consilience authorizes a challenge to the corrective justice explanation to demonstrate the ways in which corrective justice reveals connections to other legal practices. I took up this challenge by exploring some of the ways in which the corrective justice account of tort law reveals principled connections between it and the institutions of distributive justice. As it happens, a similar view is offered by libertarians, who see the connection between tort law and distributive justice in terms of a concept of outcome-responsibility. While I too defend the view that tort law and distributive justice are importantly connected, I deny that the principle of outcome-responsibility provides the link. The notion of responsibility that ties them together is, rather, one that can only be fully articulated by appeal to the practices of tort law itself.

This last claim, which is central to the view I endorse, may provoke the following objection: If the principle of outcome-responsibility suitable for corrective justice and tort law is not specifiable independently of tort law and corrective justice, just what is the relationship between tort law and the principle of outcome-responsibility? Isn't the relationship circular in a way that threatens the claim that corrective justice provides the best explanation of tort law? How can tort law be explained by corrective justice when the content of responsibility in corrective justice appears in part to depend on tort law? This is the problem to which I now turn.

## V.

Explanation requires a kind of conceptual distance between explanandum and explanans, in the same way that justification requires normative distance between that which is to be justified and that which purports to justify. Any other approach would seem to be question begging. It does not follow, however, that the content of the explanans and explanandum must be specified independently of one another. Independent formulations can, of course, suffice to create the necessary conceptual "distance"; they are not necessary, however. Let me explain.

Many, if not all, transparently attractive principles of political morality are, at the level at which their attractiveness is transparent, incapable of regulating the affairs among us. That is, they cannot give rise to particular rights, responsibilities and duties. In order to constitute regulative principles, rather than mere abstract ideals, their content must be made more concrete. They are made more concrete – their semantic content more fully specified – by social practices that articulate or embody them. Thus, we can understand social practices as ways of articulating principles of political morality. Social practices turn abstract ideals into regulative principles; they turn virtue into duty.

Take two principles that seem attractive enough on their face: "No one should be allowed to displace the costs of his activities onto others"; and "Each person should clean up his own mess." These are arguably expressions of fairness. It is not fair for one person to require others to clean up his mess or to displace, thereby, his costs on them. We might say that such a principle is itself an expression of the more basic requirement of fairness that no person be permitted to set the terms of cooperation between individuals unilaterally. What counts as a cost, a mess of the appropriate sort, displacement and cleaning up is filled out by practices that can be understood as embodiments, expressions or articulations of the more general principle of fairness. Only when these terms are specified are the principles capable of regulating affairs among individuals.

This is a semantic and not just an epistemic thesis. In other words, the practices we have do not merely reveal the content of the principles to which we are committed; the practices partially constitute that content. Nor is this the familiar view sometimes attributed to Aquinas that there are many ways of satisfying the demands of morality, all of which, from the point of view of morality, are equally good. On this Aquinean view, a moral principle's intension determines the extension of a set of justifiable practices, each member of the set equally well satisfying the principle. By contrast, on the view I am proposing, the intension of the principle itself is indeterminate and gets filled in differently depending on the practices of those who appeal to the principle. So its extension, the set of potentially justified realizations of the principle, is not determined by the principle independent of the practices. The extension might vary depending on the practices that constitute the actual realization of it.[36]

With respect to fairness, corrective justice and tort law, the idea is this: Fairness requires that no one be permitted to set the terms of cooperative interaction unilaterally. This invites the question, what are the requirements of fairness – how are we to understand its requirements – with respect to the activity of keeping track of (in the sense of allocating the costs of) some of life's misfortunes: namely, those owing to human agency.

Corrective justice and tort law articulate the requirements of fairness in the following way. The principle of corrective justice – that each of us has a duty to repair the wrongful losses for which we are responsible – specifies the content of fairness by articulating relationships among concepts central to the idea of fairness, concepts of loss, responsibility, and repair. Tort law in turn informs our concepts of responsibility, wrongful loss and repair.

Here's how I think it works. Some misfortunes owing to human action are the result of mischief whereas others are innocent. This difference matters to fairness. Again, some harms that are caused by mischievous conduct result from that aspect of the conduct that is mischievous, but some harm results from aspects of mischievous conduct that are without fault. It matters in other words whether the fault is responsible for the misfortune. Corrective justice informs fairness by telling us that when mischievous conduct is responsible for misfortune, the way to allocate misfortune's costs is by imposing a duty of repair.

Tort law further articulates the relevant conceptions of wrong, responsibility and the duty of repair. Tort law tells us that the concept of wrong relevant to fairness is objective: A person can act wrongly without having a wrong intention, and thus, plausibly, without being morally culpable for what he has done (this is the lesson of *Vaughan v. Menlove*). It also tells us that the duty of repair is to make good pecuniary but not necessarily nonpecuniary costs, that the default conception of repair is full compensation, and so on. Most importantly, it specifies the conditions of responsibility implicated by corrective justice.

There is no reason, then, to suppose that the criteria of responsibility in tort or corrective justice should match up with the general requirements of responsibility in criminal law or retributive justice, and so on. More generally, there is no reason why the criteria of responsibility in various areas of the law should coincide with any general moral notion of responsibility: whether responsibility for actions or responsibility for outcomes. There is no reason to think that a body of the law could not be just or fair otherwise. Rather than the institution's justice depending on its embodying an independently specified and independently defended criterion of responsibility for outcomes, the principle of responsibility in tort law helps make explicit the requirements of fairness within a very specific domain: the domain in which state power is brought to bear on individuals in order to allocate the costs of misfortunes resulting from individual agency. Thus I reject the position taken by Perry and the libertarians. There is no principle of outcome-responsibility that constrains tort law. Rather the conception of responsibility appropriate to tort law is partially given by its own institutions and practices, which in turn make explicit the requirements or content of fairness in this domain.

## VI.

If the conceptual distance between tort law and corrective justice depends on the kind of embodiment relation I have been describing, can this relation really explain the tort law? It may seem as though corrective justice is too "close" to tort law to explain it. Indeed, corrective justice may seem too indeterminate or, in any event, too inadequately specified to explain anything.

There are two distinct but related challenges here: The first asks what kind of an explanation is being offered; the second asks whether it succeeds as the kind of explanation it is. Turning to the first challenge: The embodiment relation purports to explain tort law by showing how its central concepts get their content. Their content is given, in part, by the practical inferences they warrant within the institution of tort law. Corrective justice describes the structure of those inferences in general terms; tort law as a set of practices embodies that general structure and gives it determinate shape. Corrective justice explains the concepts and the shape of the law not by determining them fully, but by showing how they hang together in the practical inferences that do give them determinate content.

This brings us to the second challenge: If the content of corrective justice is indeterminate prior to its practical realization or embodiment, then how can it really show the way the central concepts of the law hang together in warranting certain kinds of inferences and not others? What, to put the point more sharply, would count as a *wrong* inference, one that *didn't* connect the concepts of the law in the way corrective justice says they are connected? Unless corrective justice can exert some kind of "normative pressure" on the practices it explains, then anything goes; nothing that happens in our tort institutions could count as failing to embody corrective justice. That would make corrective justice worthless as an explanation.

The key to meeting this challenge is to see that while *part* of the content of corrective justice gets worked out in the embodiment relation I have described, tort law is not the *only* practice that helps to give content to corrective justice. Recall that corrective justice articulates part of the requirements of fairness with respect to the activity of keeping track of life's misfortunes owing to human agency. The concept of fairness is partly determined by tort law, but it is also determined in part by all of our other moral practices – legal, political, and private – in which fairness figures. The normative pressure fairness exerts in tort law is the pressure of every other practice in which fairness figures. This insures that not every practice of repair qualifies as an instance of or instantiation of corrective justice or fairness.

Fairness requires that no person be permitted to set the terms of cooperative interaction between individuals unilaterally. This assertion alone has a certain content independent of the law – content sufficient for us to say (with an argument) that a system of tort law cannot be fair if it employs a negligence standard understood along the lines of the famous Learned Hand Formula. According to the Learned Hand Formula, a person has a duty of care to another whenever the costs of the harm risked, discounted by the probability of its occurrence, is greater than the costs taking adequate precautions would impose on the risktaker. If precaution costs exceed the expected value of the harm, there is no duty to take precautions and the failure to do so would not be negligent or unreasonable.

The problem is that in the Learned Hand Formula, the degree of security to which the victim is entitled is entirely a function of the degree to which the potential injurer values his liberty. If precaution costs are foregone opportunities to engage in an activity the injurer values, then the measure of those costs is given by the value of the activity to him. The degree of security the victim is entitled to is fixed by the evaluations of the injurer in violation of the criterion of fairness, and, thus, corrective justice.[37] So even though tort law helps make the demands of fairness as expressed in the principle of corrective justice explicit, fairness and corrective justice provide criteria by which the practice of tort law can be assessed.

It should be noted, however, that while the norms of fairness and corrective justice are moral norms, the kind of normative pressure I have been describing is, in the first instance, tied to their theoretical justification rather than their moral justification. The Learned Hand Test is inappropriate to the practice of tort law because it runs afoul of the principle that best explains tort law – namely, the principle of corrective justice. If, in addition to being the best explanation of tort law, corrective justice turns out also to be a justified principle of morality, then the Learned Hand Test may be inappropriate in another way – it may be immoral.

## VII.

The idea of fairness that has been implicit in the discussion to this point is central to a range of political doctrines whose roots lie in the liberal tradition. In particular, I have relied on a notion of fairness as reciprocity among free and equal individuals. This notion of fairness is bound up with other ideals, such as freedom and equality; and all of these ideals are contested, as regards both their content and their relative priorities. It may lie somewhat beyond the scope of this essay to settle, once and for all, the most fundamental debates of modern political philosophy. I would like to conclude, however, by sketching what seems to me a particularly attractive view of what animates the best parts of the liberal tradition – including the ideal of fairness that is embodied, though imperfectly, in our institutions of corrective and distributive justice.

Libertarianism – to revisit our earlier discussion – could be characterized as that form of liberalism organized around the idea of outcome-responsibility, in which outcome-responsibility is itself to be analyzed in terms of morally prior notions such as self-ownership, agency, and a certain naturalist conception of causation. While I have rejected this conception of liberalism, I have not meant to dismiss the importance to liberalism of the concept of individual responsibility. I now want to suggest that a certain conception of individual responsibility is fundamental to the liberal ideal. This conception expresses the special relationship each of us bears to her own life, and does not bear to the lives of others.[38] We might express the liberal view of the individual's relationship to his own life in the proposition that each of us is responsible for how her life goes.

This could be understood as a kind of moral claim about the accountability of persons – about the fact that we can and sometimes do judge and evaluate individuals or their lives as good or bad, virtuous or vicious, successful or failed, and so on. However, the sense of responsibility I mean is not just accountability. Rather, it strikes me as a kind of conceptual claim at the core of the liberal ideal: that if we are to have a certain concept of the individual as an agent, as a being who acts and is not merely acted upon, then it must be true that the individual can have a certain kind of ultimate responsibility for how his life goes. That is to say, whatever the circumstances of his birth, his social status, nationality, religion, and so on, his authority over the course of his life is superior to these things; they have no ultimate claim on the way he chooses to lead his life.[39]

The idea of responsibility that I am describing is what makes possible a very strong sense in which I can say that my life is *mine:* I lead it, I have made it, it is my doing rather than something that has happened (and keeps happening) to me. This is an ideal of the person, and not a description of how all people necessarily are. Nonetheless, the ideal represents the realization of capacities that all normal persons have. Liberalism, I want to suggest, is the tradition that derives principles of political life from this ideal, and seeks to realize those principles in practice. Liberal political institutions are best understood as attempts to make it possible for individuals to be responsible for their lives, and to make that equally possible for all.

Any life, we might say, reflects a combination of two kinds of factors: What one does, and what merely happens to one. Ronald Dworkin usefully expresses the distinction between these factors as the difference between *choice* and *circumstance.* In order to realize the idea of responsibility implicated in the concept of a life lived rather than a life had, political institutions must be arranged so that individuals' lives reflect to a greater degree, or to the greatest possible degree, their choices rather than their circumstances of birth and the subsequent influences of fortune. The goal of making it equally possible for each to be responsible for the way her life goes is what grounds the centrality of freedom and equality in liberal doctrine: freedom inasmuch as it is necessary to enable a life to reflect individual choice; and equality inasmuch as no individual is entitled to a greater benefit of circumstance than any other.

This is, as I have said, my own view of what is most central as well as what is best in the liberal tradition. I cannot undertake here to defend it against rival views. But if one were to grant the attractiveness of the picture I am describing, the errors both of libertarianism and of a certain extreme egalitarianism would be apparent. By focusing on the idea of self-ownership as primary, the libertarian singles out one of the preconditions of responsibility, namely choice – but fails to equalize those circumstances that do not reflect choice; on the other hand, a crudely egalitarian liberalism that demands absolute equality of material standards tends to eliminate the element of choice in pursuit of equal circumstances.

If the aim is to give choice the preeminent role in human life, and to do so equally for all, then institutions should be arranged so that circumstances are equalized only insofar as they are not the effects of choice. This, I would maintain, is the concept of fairness that explains the distinction between redistributive and corrective institutions, and that is imperfectly embodied in them. It is the distinction between, on the one hand, those of life's misfortunes that are the result of someone's choices – and which are owed therefore to human agency – and on the other hand, those misfortunes that reflect the material conditions of choice. The principles of distributive justice govern the material conditions of choice, whereas the principle of corrective justice articulates the requirements of fairness with respect to the costs of misfortunes owing to human agency.[40] It does so by expressing the fact that fairness in keeping track of those misfortunes requires that the losses be imposed on the person (if any) whose wrongful conduct is responsible for them. Tort law further articulates the relevant conceptions of wrong, responsibility and the duty of repair. Tort law tells us that the concept of wrong relevant to fairness is objective: a person can act wrongly without having a wrong intention – and thus, plausibly, without being morally culpable for what he has done (this is the lesson of *Vaughan v. Menlove*). It also tells us that the duty of repair is to make good pecuniary but not necessarily non-pecuniary costs, that the default conception of repair is full compensation, and so on. Most importantly, tort law specifies the conditions of responsibility implicated by corrective justice. These requirements of fairness become clear to us in the circumstances that are delineated by our actual tort institutions; they could never be deduced from an abstract notion of fairness.

It would be in some ways neater, and might give the appearance of greater analytical power, to have a single principle of justice or efficiency from which one could derive a series of institutional forms and practices that would be defensible, perhaps even required by, the principle in question. But that would be to falsify the relationship between principles and the practices that articulate or realize them. The pragmatic method I have developed in this essay recognizes (for good reasons, but ones I have only been able to touch on here) that practices make the content of the principles determinate, while at the same time the principles themselves hang together as an articulation of a particular liberal ideal of the person and of the relationships among persons. The content of the most abstract and fundamental principles that form a coherent conception of liberalism is only fully determined by the relationship the principles bear to one another and to their practical embodiments. The pragmatic method implies that we can hope for no more than a revisable structure of independently intelligible and mutually coherent principles and practices. Justice requires that we accept no less.

## Notes

\* This essay is a shorter version of the first section of my Clarendon Lectures, which are published as *The Practice of Principle: In Defense of a Pragmatist Approach to Legal Theory* (Oxford University Press 2001). The emphasis of this essay is, however, somewhat different. An earlier and much rougher version of it was presented as part of the Clarendon Lectures at Oxford University. Several drafts were read by Arthur Ripstein, Benjamin Zipursky, Scott Shapiro, and Eric Cavallero. Ian Ayres, Stephen Perry, and Jody Kraus also read an earlier draft. All offered valuable criticisms and the paper has grown significantly as a result. I am, however, especially indebted to Eric Cavallero, who made several important editorial suggestions in addition to many valuable substantive suggestions and to Benjamin Zipursky, who, I believe, is on to something important and philosophically subtle in tort theory, and who has helped me see what I am up to in a way that had not fully occurred to me before.

[1] See Dworkin (1986); Perry (1998b).

[2] Scott Shapiro suggested this useful distinction.

[3] I defend the descriptive approach and criticize the Dworkinian alternative in Coleman (1998b).

[4] Elsewhere, I have explored the sense in which corrective justice expresses a requirement of justice – one that is independent of, but related to the demands of distributive justice. This is separate and distinct from the claim made here that the principle of corrective justice explains our tort law and practices. Corrective justice could be a morally attractive ideal, yet fail to explain tort law. Or corrective justice could explain tort law, yet not constitute an especially attractive moral ideal. In fact, corrective justice both explains tort law and is itself an attractive moral ideal, or so I have argued, see Coleman (1992a and 1998b).

[5] This line of argument is hinted at in Coleman (1995) and is further explicated in this essay.

[6] The case of New Zealand illustrates that the range of duties that fall under corrective justice is a contingent matter, and can vary between different legal systems. At one time, in New Zealand, there were no tort actions for accidentally caused harms – whether negligent or innocent – and the costs of such accidents were instead allocated through the general tax coffers. We could imagine a different society that not only had no tort system for enforcing private duties of repair in the case of accidents, but which had no tort system at all for enforcing any private duties of repair: suppose further that they had no practices of private repair at all. All misfortunes owing to human agency were held in common. What would we want to say about the status of the principle of corrective justice in such a society?

One thing we could say is that, in this fantasy world, those who wrongfully harm others still incur duties of repair; but that those duties of corrective justice are discharged collectively rather than privately. I have argued that it is more apt to say that if there are no practices of private repair for wrongfully inflicted loss (whether informal social practices or legal ones) then there are no duties of corrective justice.

This does not mean that individuals in such a society have no concept of corrective justice or that they do not understand the concept. They can know what it means to claim that when a person wrongfully injures another, the injurer has a duty to repair. They understand the concept of corrective justice, but their interpersonal lives are not regulated by it, and so they have no duties of corrective justice. This of course leaves open the question whether their moral and social lives are impoverished because they do not regulate their affairs by the principle of corrective justice

7   The sense of "owing to human agency" must remain vague for the moment. It will be seen below that tort law itself articulates and concretizes a distinctive sense of personal responsibility for actions. See Section V.

8   In fact, a no-fault or New Zealand plan might better serve the demands of efficiency and justice in allocating automobile accident costs than does the current tort system. This could be so even if the current tort system embodies the principle of corrective justice.

9   By a core of tort law I mean a set of features expressed at a certain level of generality that form part of our pretheoretic conception of the practice. The argument for including some features as part of the core and not others must be largely empirical: Most individuals familiar with tort law would include these features and not others. Which people? Tort scholars, judges, lawyers? I am not sure. I want to be open about my conception of the core of tort law. I could be wrong about what counts as the core of tort law, but offer it as a revisable working hypothesis.

Relatedly, two legal philosophers who share many of my views about the best explanation of tort law have taken issue with parts of my characterization of the core of tort law. Arthur Ripstein suggests that intentional torts are as much part of the core of tort law as anything. I do not deny this. I merely mean to include intentional torts within rules of fault liability. I have always understood that there were three ways of being at fault: Intentionally, recklessly and negligently. Ben Zipursky has suggested that the substantive core of tort law is best characterized in terms of a long list of different kinds of wrongs: That the basic category is the category of wrong which cuts across strict and fault liability.

The idea of wrong may be so basic to the entirety of the private law that it does not adequately distinguish the substance of tort law from the substantive core of any other body of law. Even if tort law is all about wrongs, we still tend to distinguish those which are addressed under a rule of strict liability from those addressed under a rule of fault liability.

10  It is possible, of course, that the best theory of tort law, tells us that the two principles of liability are inconsistent or represent conflicting ideals and, as a result, existing tort law needs to be reformed in a particular way, abandoning one principle of liability in favor of the other.

11  Even if it is controversial whether the elements of tort law I have identified constitute its core, it is *not* controversial that someone purporting to explain the fundamentals of tort law would miss something important were she to leave out these structural and substantive features. Any claim about the "core" of tort is bound to be controversial; tort scholars and others familiar with the law may plausibly disagree with one another regarding its essentials.

12  I use the term "economic analysis," "law and economics" and "economic analysis of law" interchangeably to refer to a range of theories that share a commitment to efficiency as a criterion of assessment. There are many other features of efficiency analysis including its commitment to marginalism. There are also many different conceptions of efficiency. For a discussion of these other features of economic analysis, see Coleman (1980).

13  For a full development of this line of argument, see Coleman (1988).

14  The familiar "rule-utilitarian" type strategy can be applied generally to all the features of

tort law I have called into question. But the strategy is not at all helpful, especially in this case.

15   Indeed, it is not obvious, as I will suggest below, that there is any significance left to be attached to the tortious action itself.

16   Moreover, the power in question is a power to seek out not the cheapest cost avoider, but rather the person the victim believes wrongfully harmed him. Nor is there any reason why the victim is in the best position to find the cheapest cost-avoider (he is, of course, in a relatively good position to locate his alleged injurer).

17   If search costs were low enough, it is hard to understand why we would even wait for a tort to occur. In economic analysis, the significance of the tort itself is only epistemic, and not justificatory. This is because the tort concerns something that has already occurred, whereas the point of practice is to secure some future-oriented goal. The fact that the injurer harmed the victim only matters if that fact gives us some reason for believing that either the injurer or the victim is in a good position to reduce accidents of this sort in the future. What happened between the injurer and the victim provides no reasons that justify liability or recovery, both of which are justified by their impact on future agents. When search costs are low enough, the epistemic value of the tort is lost. Without that, the tort has no significance at all.

18   That fact may, in conjunction with other generalizations, provide some reason for believing that the victim or injurer is in a relatively good position to reduce the costs of the accident in the future.

19   I do not repeat my defense of corrective justice as an explanation of tort law here or at this juncture. The bulk of my argument appears in Coleman (1992a). I also develop the argument in Coleman (1988). In this essay, I am more interested in getting at philosophically controversial features of my methodological position than in repeating the general substantive theory of tort law.

20   Perhaps some proponents of corrective justice have wanted to claim that the relationship between the victim and injurer reflected in its bilateral structure is necessary or essential to tort law and that the problem with economic analysis, therefore, is that it renders the relationship contingent. The problem with economic analysis, then, is that it renders a metaphysically essential component of tort law contingent. That is not my objection, however. I need make no metaphysical claim about the essence of tort law in order to argue that the normative significance of the relationship between victim and injurer is part of the best explanation of our tort institutions.

21   This is reminiscent of certain functional accounts in cultural anthropology. These accounts seek to establish that the reason for an institution or practice is not the one the natives believe, but is something completely different. I am indebted to Eric Cavallero for this point and for the general line of argument in these passages.

22   Some of the best critiques of functional explanations in the social sciences are developed in Elster (1985). Whatever the strengths of the economic analysis of the law may be, its proponents are not particularly reflective about the methodology of the social sciences.

23   Even that is not altogether obvious since many critics of tort law allege that its rules of strict products liability encourage overdeterrence.

24   To this point the situation appears to be as follows. Economic analysis offers a functional explanation of tort law. The problem is that the explanation it offers fails to meet the adequacy conditions of a functional explanation (the argument of this section); and, even if it did, it would not explain tort law since it blurs rather than illuminates and renders the ob-

vious mysterious (the argument of the first section). In contrast, corrective justice offers a non-instrumental, nonfunctionalist account in which tort law articulates corrective justice and in doing so exhibits the coherence of its component parts.

[25] In fact, their primary project seems rather to be prescriptive. In what follows, I suggest that the best interpretation of what economic analysts are up to merges the explanatory with the normative in a familiar way.

[26] Recall that in *Law's Empire,* after rejecting legal positivism as the victim of the deadly semantic sting, Dworkin reformulates it as an interpretive theory of law: what he calls "conventionalism." Dworkin criticizes conventionalism as a jurisprudence – the view that among other things posits that the point of law is to enforce and sustain a system of expectations – just because it fails fully to account for the scope of disagreement in law and because enforcing pre-existing expectations at the expense of doing justice or right between the parties is less attractive than are other normative "points, purposes or functions" of law. Thus it fails on both dimensions: fit and value.

[27] Of course, there are other options; for example, a reconstruction in which the alleged function plays no normative role at all. But that would be odd for a body of law that by all accounts is a normative practice of some sort. It would be odd to say that one had offered an explanation of a body of the law but for one minor feature of it, namely, that it was a normative practice. Perhaps it is time for economists of law to stop dismissing philosophy and start doing some of it, or at least using it to reflect on some of the basic methodological – if not substantive – issues at the core of their approach.

[28] I am not exactly sure what the argument for this claim is in part because I do not know what the content of risk regulation is taken to be, and what, therefore, we are to think of as our legal practices of risk regulation. I do not take up these issues here and simply bracket the question for now. My interest here is more methodological than substantive. I want to know why the fact that economic analysis might provide a better explanation (in the interpretive sense) than corrective justice of risk regulatory practices should count as a reason to think that it provides, therefore, a better explanation of tort law.

[29] No less respectable a figure than Ronald Dworkin claims that the boundaries between the various bodies of the law are not significant or fundamental. Even this may be a misleading way of making what may well be an important point.

[30] This is so even if the difference between causing harm and failing to prevent harm is a natural fallout from a normatively motivated feature of binary adjudication, or a presupposition of other kinds of private ordering. In neither case must the distinction be morally fundamental in general, no matter how fundamental it might be to tort law, indeed even to any morally defensible tort law.

[31] In the pragmatist tradition, this is often expressed as the "belief/doubt" principle. On this view, the Cartesian foundationalists have it all wrong. We do not suspend all belief pending some foundation of indubitability on which to ground it. Rather, we treat the set of beliefs that we happen to have as in no need of justification or foundation, indubitable or otherwise. Of course, our belief set is certain to contain some falsehoods, and we should be prepared to doubt and to revise any particular belief in the light of new experience or better theory.

[32] It is important to stress that this is not a theoretically precise distinction between kinds of misfortune. That, indeed, is one of the main points I hope to make in this essay. In order to articulate with precision the difference between the misfortunes that human agents are responsible for and the misfortunes that no one is responsible for, we need to appeal to the

whole conceptual and practical apparatus of the tort law. Once the tort law has clarified the class of misfortunes for which no individual is responsible, however, we confront the question of whether to hold those misfortunes in common as a society, or to let the losses lie where they fall. This of course is a question of distributive justice.

This much might suggest that corrective justice is prior to distributive justice, in that the former delimits the scope of the latter. Actually, the dependence goes in both directions. For example, if we decide as a matter of distributive justice to hold in common some class of misfortunes – for example, all of the costs of innocent or negligent accidents – we remove it from the area of misfortunes for which tort law allocates the costs. Distributive and corrective justice thus work together to sort out the costs of life's misfortunes.

33 Of course, distributive justice concerns the distribution of things other than misfortunes. Corrective and distributive justice overlap in their concerns and define one another's boundaries; but they do not coincide in their concerns.

34 This is an incomplete statement of the principle of corrective justice in part because it does not explicate the conditions of compensable loss. The point of this characterization is simply to draw attention to the centrality of human agency.

35 This, of course, is my view as well.

36 Nor is the view suggested here the familiar one that many moral principles are vague at their borders, and can only be made precise by practices. Again, the point is that many principles are indeterminate at their core.

37 As an aside, this fact about fairness and the Learned Hand Test is part of the reason that I have argued for the very different view that we should understand the fault requirement in tort law as setting out criteria of fairness with respect to the division of security and liberty interests between the parties. More importantly, the reader will recall that in fact *U.S. v. Carroll Towing* in which the Learned Hand Test was articulated is a comparative negligence case. The Learned Hand Test is not in that case an articulation of the duties injurers owe victims, but the responsibilities victims must take upon themselves. In that context, the context in which the test is created, there is no issue of interpersonal fairness. The problem with economic analysis is that it has interpreted the test in contexts in which the problems of interpersonal fairness arise.

38 This fact about the special relationship we bear to our lives is part of the reason why many liberals object to utilitarianism, claiming that the utilitarian is unable to take seriously – seriously enough, or seriously in the right way – the differences between persons.

39 Again, the relationship between this kind of responsibility and moral accountability is not my focus. I certainly do not mean to suggest that an individual is equally morally accountable for her actions, irrespective of hardship or privilege, or of the cultural and intellectual resources available to her. The basic elements of responsibility in the sense I am now using it may *be preconditions of moral judgment,* as Kant maintained (certainly if people did not have ultimate authority over how their lives go, then it would be hard to justify the desire to hold people to moral praise or blame for their lives or actions) but this kind of responsibility cannot be the whole story about moral accountability.

40 At the same time, both the boundaries between corrective and distributive justice, and the concept of what counts as a loss owing to human agency, are revisable notions: revisable in the light of the institutional and other practices that evolve as ways of expressing both.

# 6

# Corrective Justice in an Age of Mass Torts

ARTHUR RIPSTEIN AND BENJAMIN C. ZIPURSKY*

## I. Introduction

Corrective justice theory has been the subject of many, often inconsistent, attacks. Sometimes it is criticized on the ground that it provides no practical guidance as to how cutting edge issues of tort law ought to be resolved. Sometimes it is criticized for providing only normative guidance, and failing to accommodate what the tort law actually says. Sometimes it is criticized for both at once. And sometimes it is criticized for being simply off track – for missing what is central in law – the drive of money and deep pockets.

These objections are nicely exemplified in discussions of contemporary mass tort law. The question arises as to whether a plaintiff who suffered injuries from a defective product should ever be able to recover from a manufacturer of that type of product, even if the plaintiff cannot prove that the particular product or products that injured her were manufactured by the defendant. Corrective justice theory, it is sometimes complained, reveals only the rationale for the structures of the law we have, and does not tell us whether we should extend beyond that structure. Hence, corrective justice theory is patently correct that within the conceptual framework of the common law of torts, causation is required and liability would be denied in these cases. The question is whether the conceptual framework of corrective justice is one to which we must be limited. Corrective justice does not help with this.[1]

Or perhaps the argument is that corrective justice theory would clearly require a denial of liability in such cases, because causation is at the normative core of the concept of corrective justice, but tort law in various ways has now progressed to recognizing a right of action in the plaintiff under such circumstances, thus showing that corrective justice theory does not describe contemporary tort law.[2] And just the opposite has also been argued: that the tort law actually does not permit liability under these circumstances, save in the most exceptional cases, and yet corrective justice theory demands that it should, because there is wrongdoing that merits sanction and injury that merits rectification, and a nexus between the two that preserves proportionality central to the normative foundations of corrective justice.[3]

Finally, it is argued, corrective justice is irrelevant to the law in this area. What drives courts, as well as lawyers and commentators on each side of the issue, is the recognition that the manufacturer is the deep pocket. This is what permits the relaxation of causation rules; when causation rules are not relaxed, it is due to solicitousness for the manufacturer defendants.

In this article, we take the bull by the horns and use corrective justice theory[4] to do one of the things that legal theory is supposed to do: to frame a legal dilemma that needs to be probed more deeply in order to arrive at a more satisfactory resolution; to articulate the framework of goals and normative principles that animate the area of law in question; and to apply that framework to arrive at a conceptually and normatively satisfactory solution to the problem, one which coheres with the well-established precedent and principles of tort law, which reflects the principles of justice underlying the law, and which sits well with a pragmatic approach to the law.[5]

Two decisions adopting different versions of "market-share liability" provide focal points for our analysis. *Sindell v. Abbott Laboratories*[6] and *Hymowitz v. Eli Lilly Co.*[7] both involved large numbers of plaintiffs injured because their mothers had taken a drug, DES, which was marketed to prevent miscarriages. This product caused ovarian cancer in the adult daughters of some of the women who took it. The drug was produced by hundreds of manufacturers and marketed generically. Both that fact and the passage of time between the sale of the drug and the development of the cancer in adults a generation later made it impossible for plaintiffs to identify the particular manufacturers who had made the drug that injured them. In *Sindell,* the court held the manufacturers whom the plaintiffs were able to locate liable in proportion to their market share, but allowed any particular defendant to avoid liability to a particular plaintiff by showing that the drug it produced could not have caused that plaintiff's injury. In *Hymowitz,* by contrast, the court dispensed with the causation requirement, and held the defendant manufacturers liable in proportion to their national market share, and did not allow any defendant to avoid liability by showing that it had not injured some particular plaintiff.

*Sindell* and *Hymowitz* highlight two issues. First, should the requirement that defendant have caused plaintiff's injury be fundamental even in the mass tort context? Second, when, if ever, is it permissible to shift the burden of proof on the issue of causation to defendant? Although market-share liability is something of a rarity even in contemporary tort law, its permissibility and propriety continue to be a live question in many jurisdictions, and for many types of products.[8] More generally, the principles that market-share liability throws into question are felt in a wide range of mass tort and individual tort cases in which litigants and scholars propose a variety of ways to attenuate the requirement of causation.

Our answers are moderate. In a narrow range of cases, it is permissible for courts to shift the burden of proof on individualized causation, roughly as the California Supreme Court did in *Sindell.* However, it would be illegitimate to go beyond burden shifting and dispense with individualized causation altogether, as the New York Court of Appeals did in *Hymowitz,* and as numerous commentators have advocated. In defending these two claims, we shall provide philosophically detailed explanations in two areas. First, we shall explain why, as a substantive matter, causation is indeed a necessary precondition of liability from the point of view of corrective justice, and why it should be.[9] Second, we shall explain how equitable notions found throughout the law provide a principled ground for evidentiary burden shifting on individualized causation in certain mass tort cases. Although each of these philosophical tasks is undertaken with the ends of practical tort theory in mind, we believe that each bears its own fruit in legal philosophy more generally. In the course of developing a theory of evidentiary equity, we construct a more general account of the moral dimension of procedural law. It is a platitude that procedural and evidentiary rules are grounded in substantive policy choices. Our point is a rather different one. Corrective justice understands the relation between plaintiff and defendant as a particular kind of normative relation. If the tort system is understood as an implementation of corrective justice, its procedures must implement that relation in a world of uncertainty. The allocations of burdens and standards of proof in a regime of corrective justice is neither a civil analogue of the criminal law's presumption of innocence, nor a reflection of a general policy of leaving losses where they fall unless there is some compelling reasons to shift them. The rule that, in general, the plaintiff bears the burden of proving causation reflects the idea of doing justice in a world of uncertainty. So too does the rule adopted in *Sindell,* that as between an innocent party injured by one of the defendants she proved was a tortfeasor, and one of those defendants, the tortfeasor-defendant must bear the burden of proof on individualized causation.

In order to explain the allocation of burdens and standards of proof, then, we need to explain why causation is an element of tort liability at all. Section II develops a general analytical model of corrective justice. That model distinguishes between two senses in which one person may be said to have breached a duty to avoid injuring others. In one sense, whether the duty has been breached depends only on the actions of the defendant, without determining their effect on the plaintiff. Such duties might be called duties of non-injuriousness. But there is a second conception of duty – a conception of duties of non-injury – according to which the defendant has not breached a duty to avoid injuring another unless she has in fact injured that other. Some normative systems – criminal law and ordinary morality, for example – impose their distinctive forms of sanction for both types of breaches, albeit in different ways. Tort law, however, imposes the sanction of compensatory damages only where there has been a breach of relational duties of non-injury. If certain prominent contemporary accounts of tort law were correct, then the requirement of the breach of a relational duty of non-injury to trigger compensatory damages would be contingent, and *Hymowitz* would be defensible. We argue, from both an interpretive and a prescriptive point of view, that the breach of a relational duty of non-injury is essential to tort liability.

Section III offers an explanation of the normative principles underlying our tort system's focus on relational duties of non-injury as the basis of liability. Integrating and combining our prior work on the idea of recourse, and the idea of risk ownership, we provide a rational reconstruction of the nature of duty in tort law. This reconstruction yields a defence of the causation requirement.

In Section IV, we consider whether mass tort cases are different. A number of commentators have suggested that liability in proportion to risk-creation would provide a normatively superior system to the normal causation requirement, in cases in which product identification poses difficulties. We argue that such modifications would create more unfairness and arbitrariness than they would eliminate.

We offer our positive account of the mass tort cases in Section V. We show that the case that pioneered market-share liability, *Sindell,* keeps the central requirement of breach of a "duty of non-injury" in place. The key to *Sindell* is that a defendant is not entitled to the benefit of a presumption that its injurious conduct did not in fact injure plaintiffs, where the evidence demonstrates that each defendant's products did in fact injure a substantial range of the persons before the court, and where each plaintiff's case is only stymied by inability to mix and match concededly injured plaintiffs with defendants who have caused some share of the injuries. Rather than changing the role of causation, courts should be understood to be invoking their inherent powers to change the evidence required to make a *prima facie* case. We also explain how the *Sindell* court's resolution of other issues follows from this approach. We conclude this section by discussing the similarities and differences between *Sindell* and *Summers v. Tice.*[10] Like *Sindell, Summers* gives the illusion of altering the causation requirement while in fact merely altering its treatment of evidentiary issues.

## II. The Structure of Duty in Tort Law

### II.1 Three Dimensions of Duty

Theorists and courts often suggest that the law imposes obligations of repair on a defendant because that defendant has breached some legal duty. Our first question is: What kind of legal duty must the defendant have breached in order to trigger in her an obligation to repair the plaintiff's injury? It will be useful to begin by distinguishing among duties along three dimensions. Duties can be either *relational* or *non-relational,* depending upon the type of norm that imposes the duty (Zipursky 1998b, pp. 59–60). Relational norms prohibit a person from treating other persons in a certain manner. For example, a duty prohibiting persons from hitting one another is relational. It says to every person: as to each other person, you are not to hit him or her. By contrast, some duties are non-relational in that the conduct they prohibit or prescribe is not a way of treating or relating to another person. Thus, a duty prohibiting littering, or arson, or creation of a public nuisance, is a simple or non-relational duty.

Running perpendicular to the distinction between relational and simple (or non-relational) duties is a distinction between *duties of non-injuriousness* and *duties of non-injury*. If $X$ owes a duty of non-injury to $Y$, $X$ does not breach that duty unless $X$ has, in fact, injured $Y$. By contrast, duties of non-injuriousness prohibit persons from acting in certain potentially injurious ways. For example, a duty to take reasonable care is a duty of non-injuriousness. So too is a duty that one not market a defective product, or not utter fraudulent statements, and so on. Both duties of non-injury and duties of non-injuriousness may target a particular kind of injury – they may prohibit killing, for example, or conduct that tends to cause death – or they may target a broader range of conduct.

Finally, within the category of duties of non-injury, we can distinguish between *qualified* and *unqualified* duties. A qualified duty of non-injury is a duty not to injure someone by acting in a particular way: the duty not to batter another is a duty not to cause a harmful or offensive touching through intentional conduct. But it is also conceptually possible to have unqualified duties of non-injury – for example, a duty not to cause another to die.

## II.2 Duties in Tort Law and Compensatory Damages

The duty of repair – the duty to pay compensatory damages – is triggered by breach of a qualified relational duty of non-injury that runs to the plaintiff. Although one or more of these elements might be absent in grounding other tort remedies, such as punitive damages, nominal damages, and injunctions, all three are required for compensatory damages. Advocates of a relaxed causation requirement go awry in ways that can be stated in terms of qualified duties of non-injury: some take duties to be non-relational; some take note of the qualification and not the duties they qualify, concluding that they are duties of non-injuriousness, rather than non-injury. Some err on both points. Failure to focus on the nature of the relevant duties can make tort law seem arbitrary, hypocritical, or dogmatic. The tort law's approach can be shown to be none of these things by considering why it imposes qualified relational duties of non-injury.

RELATIONAL, RATHER THAN NON-RELATIONAL DUTIES. Many aspects of the law, particularly regulatory and criminal law, contain norms that are simple or non-relational. Not so for the tort law. It is about wrongs to others. It prohibits treating others in certain ways. In this respect, the norms of tort law are relational (Zipursky 1998b, pp. 60–3). Correspondingly, the duties that those norms impose are duties to treat others in certain ways, or to refrain from treating others in certain ways. For example, one may not defraud, defame, batter, maliciously prosecute, falsely imprison, or negligently injure another. These are all relational legal duties. Moreover, a plaintiff does not have a right of action against a defendant unless the duty breached was a duty to the plaintiff herself (Zipursky 1998b, pp. 15–39, 60–3).

DUTIES OF NON-INJURY, NOT DUTIES OF NON-INJURIOUSNESS. In general, a defendant does not owe plaintiff duty of repair unless she was the one who injured plaintiff, and unless her injuring of the plaintiff was the breach of a duty not to injure plaintiff. This requirement is embedded in the causation requirement in negligence law. Of course, in cases of proximate cause and concurrent causation, there is great debate as to what the causation element actually means and requires, but those are different issues than whether causation itself is a requirement. Some recent cases sidestep causation issues by redefining the category of injury that will permit recovery,[11] or by redefining the kind of relief sought.[12] All of these efforts tend to underscore, rather than to rebut, the centrality of causation in extant American tort law, as they indicate the need to shift to other categories, rather than abandoning causation itself.

QUALIFIED DUTIES OF NON-INJURY, NOT UNQUALIFIED DUTIES OF NON-INJURY. Finally, the duty of non-injury in torts is qualified, not unqualified. That is simply to say that causing a certain type of injury to another person is not sufficient for the imposition of a duty of repair. The defendant must have inflicted the injury by acting a certain way against the plaintiff. Thus, there is no trespass even if there has been an injury to land, unless the defendant intentionally used or possessed plaintiff's property. There is no fraud without an intentional or knowing misrepresentation. There is no negligent infliction of physical injury unless the defendant breached a duty of due care to the plaintiff, and caused the injury through that breach. And there is no liability for design defect, unless defendant's sold or marketed a dangerously defective product whose dangerous defect injured plaintiff.

The role of qualified duties of non-injury rather than of non-injuriousness is more apparent in areas in which liability is strict, such as the use of explosives or the transport of gasoline. Those who engage in ultrahazardous activities are liable for the injuries characteristic of those activities. The owner of a truck transporting gasoline is thus liable for the injuries caused by fire, regardless of the level of care exercised by the driver, or in maintaining the truck, but not for non-negligent road accidents that do not result in fire. If tort law enforced duties of non-injuriousness, strict liability would be puzzling, because the connection between liability and duty would be broken. Narrow areas of strict liability are unsurprising if tort law imposes qualified duties of non-injury. From the point of view of a qualified duty of non-injury, transporting gasoline is no less legitimate than are any number of risky activities that do not result in injuries. No duty is breached unless an injury results.

### II.3  A Potential Confusion

The fact that duties of non-injury are qualified has led many commentators to mistake the qualification for the duty, and so to suppose that the only normatively significant duty enforced by tort law is the qualification that the defendant's conduct have had a tendency to injure. The confusion is exacerbated by inherited terminology. "Duty" is one of the four official elements of the tort of negligence, and "breach" of that duty is another element. Because the remaining two elements of negligence are causation and injury, it may seem obvious that the duty involved in negligence law is independent of questions of causation and injury. While what is sometimes called the duty element of negligence concerns a duty of non-injuriousness, the tort of negligence itself imposes a duty of non-injury.

The potential for confusion runs deeper, however. The duty and breach elements play a critical role in the tort of negligence. A defendant's injuring of a plaintiff is actionable in negligence law only if defendant did so through a breach of a duty of due care owed to the plaintiff. The qualifier of the duty of non-injury, in negligence law, is *through breach of a duty of due care owed to the plaintiff.* So the qualifier is itself a duty of non-injuriousness. Hence, negligence law imposes liability on defendants who have, through breach of a duty of non-injuriousness owed to the plaintiff, injured the plaintiff. While the breach of a duty of non-injuriousness is pivotal in negligence law, it is not sufficient to ground liability.

When we look at how the primary norms of tort law function, the conceptual slide between these two kinds of duties is easy to understand. Tort law not only plays a role in assigning liabilities. It also serves to guide individual conduct. The apprehension of a primary norm of tort law consists, in part, in the recognition of a directive that one ought to conduct oneself in a particular way toward others. A variety of social, professional, institutional, and moral norms contribute to what we deem adequate care to others. These are plugged in as the qualifiers to the duty of non-injury in negligence law. In this manner, our conception of what we legally owe to others is harmonized with our broader normative conceptions of what we owe others, and we are, to a substantial extent, able to believe that the vulnerability to liability in negligence is limited to cases where we have failed to act toward others in the manner we are otherwise obliged to have done. Conversely, the rights and duties articulated under the law are concrete and public transformations of the moral relations that we recognize among one another. At the level of deliberation, and of moral appraisal of conduct, perhaps duties of non-injuriousness towards others play a relatively larger role. But although duties of non-injuriousness are incorporated into the tort of negligence, they are not enforced by the law. The legal rights we have against others, and the entitlement to act against another through the legal system to obtain compensation for an injury, turn on whether the other has breached a duty of non-injury.[13]

These points will be important when we turn to the DES cases, because our central claim is that *Sindell* cleaves to corrective justice precisely because it predicates liability on the breach of a duty of non-injury, rather than on the breach of a duty of non-injuriousness.

## III. In Defense of Causation

Each of these aspects of the duties of tort law has been contested by some movement or another within torts. There have been relatively few challenges to the interpretive claim that liability is in fact triggered by the defendant's breach of a duty of non-injury to plaintiff, not merely by a breach of a duty of non-injuriousness, by tortious conduct. To the extent that tort theorists have challenged the causation requirement, or the need for a duty of non-injury, they have done so principally from a prescriptive point of view, rather than the point of view of describing or interpreting actual American tort doctrine. It is to the prescriptive challenges that we now turn.

### III.1 The Moral Challenge to the Causation Requirement

Many scholars argue that a genuine understanding of what renders the tort system intelligible and justifiable will reveal that the causation requirement is not essential but contingent to our system.[14] When it ceases to serve the goals that it usually happens to serve well, its relaxation is consistent with what makes the tort system justifiable. To put it differently, they argue that our tort system *ought* to impose liability based on breach of duty of non-injuriousness, even absent a breach of the duty of non-injury to the plaintiff. This position challenges, from a prescriptive point of view, both the relationality requirement and the duty of non-injury requirement.

Christopher Schroeder offered a clear articulation of this line of argument (Schroeder 1990). Like others writing from the same perspective, Schroeder takes Kantian moral philosophy as his starting point. In Kant's moral thought, the only factor that is ultimately relevant to evaluating a person's moral worth is the quality of that person's will. As Kant puts it, a good will is the only thing that is good without qualification (Kant 1992). If we make the plausible supposition that institutions of liability should track what is morally most important, traditional tort law appears to face a serious difficulty. For, Schroeder suggests, there can be no morally defensible grounds for distinguishing between persons who are alike with respect to their moral worth. Yet traditional tort law's focus on duties of non-injury does exactly that. Suppose that both A and B tortiously market a certain defective product, and that C is injured by a product of this type. Both A and B are alike in violating their duties of non-injuriousness. As between A and B, it is merely fortuitous whether or not their product caused the injury. Justice permits, perhaps even requires, that A and B be sanctioned. C has an entitlement to compensation. Traditional tort law exacts compensation from whichever of A or B happens to have sold the particular product that injured C, and allows the other to escape liability altogether. As a result, Schroeder insists, it draws a morally arbitrary distinction, for it fails to treat relevantly like cases alike.

We will return to Schroeder's proposed alternative to traditional tort liability below. Our focus for now is on explaining why duties of non-injury are central to corrective justice.[15] To do so we offer two mutually supporting normative explanations of the requirement. The first of these draws attention to the role of the state when one person exacts compensation from another in tort; the second looks at the imposition of liability in terms of the fair allocation of a misfortune.

### III.2 Recourse

The argument that defendants who are alike in their fault should be treated alike grows out of a misconception about the role of the state in a tort action. The state does not appear as a party to a tort action in order to impose a sanction on a wrongdoer. Instead, the state empowers individuals to exact compensation for injuries. The plaintiff comes before the court seeking recourse from someone who injured her.[16] As a result, whether the defendant breached a duty of non-injury to plaintiff no longer appears arbitrary. It is not a sanction to fit the moral culpability of the act. It is a holding of liability to fit the rights invasion plaintiff has incurred.

The idea that the court provides civil recourse to the plaintiff contrasts in important ways with punishment. Punishment is widely thought to be appropriately keyed to only those features of an action that are fully within the wrongdoer's control.[17] To the extent that this is so, it is because punishment is the state's response to the wrongdoer's choice to do wrong, and so makes the choice to do wrong a central focus, and gives at most derivative status to consequences. By contrast, liability for an injury is properly keyed to the rights invasion experienced by plaintiff. If the plaintiff is seeking recourse for an injury, whether or not an injury results from defendant's acts is hardly an arbitrary feature.

When the state punishes, and even when it regulates, it is obligated to give notice of the conduct that will trigger such punishment or regulation, and the extent of the sanction that will be imposed. The state is under an obligation to treat like persons alike. As a result, decisions about who should bear some social costs ought to be public-minded. Fines or penalties, governmentally im-

posed, are typically set so as to be proportionate to conduct. All of these familiar features of punishment and regulation reflect fundamental norms governing
the relation between the state and an individual citizen.

Civil liability is different. Although decisions about liability are coercively
enforced by the state, in another sense they are fundamentally private matters
between the parties. One person comes before a court seeking recourse against
someone else in particular. Even if the state should treat all wrongdoers alike,
an injured person is only entitled to recourse against her injurer. Again, those
who are injured are entitled to sue for damages, but may decide not to. It is no
answer to a negligence action to point to other tortfeasors who escaped liability because those they injured declined to sue.

These familiar differences between punishment and civil liability reflect an
underlying difference: where the state appears as a party in cases of punishment
or regulation, and so is subject to appropriate limits governing that role, the role
of the state in a tort action is different. It is charged with upholding the rights
of citizens with respect to each other. Although it is permitted and enforced and
facilitated by the state, a right of action in tort is an action *by a plaintiff* against
a defendant. In affording plaintiffs such rights of action, the state is correspondingly rendering defendants vulnerable to plaintiffs. The question arises as
to what the appropriate conditions for the vulnerability are. The answer is that
the only ones who are empowered to act against the defendant through the state
are those whose rights have been violated by the defendant. More particularly,
the only plaintiffs who are allowed to use the state to force another person to
compensate them for an injury are those who were injured by that defendant.
Conversely, defendants are protected against actions by individuals seeking to
use the state to force them to compensate them for their injuries. The only persons to whom defendants are vulnerable are those to whom defendant breached
a duty.

### III.3  Risk Ownership and Injury

The structure of civil recourse explains why it is only relational, rather than simple duties whose breach triggers a right of action in the plaintiff against the defendant. Reflection on the relation between damages and injury lead to a complementary explanation of duties of non-injury. The idea of risk ownership
explains why compensatory damages are the appropriate remedy when a relational duty of non-injury is breached (Ripstein 1999).

The tort system can be thought of as a way of determining whose misfortune
a particular injury is. Neither tort law nor corrective justice takes an interest in
those who are injured by natural forces, such as hurricanes and hailstones.
Those who are so injured are simply unfortunate. Whether or not some general
scheme of social insurance ought to compensate them for their injuries, one
thing is clear: There is no other person *in particular* who should be singled out

to bear the cost instead. In the same way, if one person is injured through the agency of another, but that person was exercising appropriate care, the injurer will not be singled out to bear the burden. Instead, this misfortune too belongs to the person it befell.

Contrasting with these two cases in which losses are left where they fall is the case in which someone fails to exercise appropriate care towards another. In so doing, the careless one is creating a particular risk. If that risk ripens into an injury, it becomes attributable to the person who imposed it. Damages then serve to allocate the loss to a person who created the risk that ripened into the injury, insofar as it is possible to do so. In this sense, liability can be thought of on the model of ownership for a particular risk: If I create a risk, it is my risk, and if it ripens into an injury, the costs that it imposes are costs that others are entitled to force me to bear. The idea of ownership here is a thin one, familiar in the warning: "use at your own risk." The defendant is *not entitled* to be free of the costs associated with this injury. That is what we mean by saying that it is his loss to bear.

Although the idea that the risk properly belongs to the person who created it might seem to suggest that persons have a duty not to create risks, the situation is more complicated. The law takes an interest in where particular misfortunes lie against the background of a more general idea of social interaction, according to which, in the ordinary course of events, the results of voluntary interactions raise no questions of justice. Provided that people do not violate the rights of others, the fact that various holdings are the results of uncoerced social interaction and fair starting points is sufficient to address questions of their justice. (Of course, which terms are fair, and even more, which starting points, is controversial.) In order for interaction to justify its results, though, certain effects of interaction need to be undone. In particular, when people fail to treat each other appropriately, those who are injured can demand, as a matter of justice, that the costs of the injury be returned to those who properly bear them.

On this understanding, tort law does corrective justice by permitting those who have been wrongfully injured to demand that the costs of their injuries be borne by those who are responsible for them, and by enforcing these demands. It allows aggrieved parties to demand that those who are careless with the safety of others be treated as though they had been careless with their own safety. The liability that defendant is required to bear is not a punishment. It is simply the unfortunate outcome of a wrongful risk that was realized. Where another defendant takes a wrongful risk but that risk is not realized in plaintiff's injury, there is no basis for the plaintiff to demand that the defendant be forced to bear the plaintiff's loss, for there is no loss to bear. Those who are exposed to unrealized risks have no grounds for complaint, for their rights to security are intact. Those who have been wrongfully injured, by contrast, are entitled to proceed against their injurers, so as to return the loss to where it properly lies.

On the risk-ownership conception, then, duties of non-injury are imposed because only the breach of such a duty could give anyone grounds to demand, as a matter of justice, that the costs of that injury be returned to the person who properly bears it. *That injury* is one for which that defendant may be held liable because the injury is the realization of a wrongfully taken risk (to the plaintiff) by the defendant. A plaintiff who suffered an injury of a similar kind, which was not a realization of the risk created by the defendant in question cannot mount this argument. Even if the risk was a realization of someone's wrongfully created risk, if it was not the defendant's risk, it is not the defendant's loss, and liability should not be imposed.[18]

### III.4 Summary

A right in negligence law[19] is that the invasion of which provides an occasion for the state to permit one person to force another to bear liability for certain costs. Where the costs in question are the costs of bearing or correcting a particular kind of injury, the defendant's having undertaken action that inappropriately risked that injury is a reason for permitting the plaintiff to force defendant to bear that injury, at least if plaintiff herself did not inappropriately risk that injury too. When an inappropriately high risk of misfortune is realized, it is fair that if there is some description of the misfortune under which it was the realization of an inappropriately high risk, then the taker of the inappropriately high risk be forced to bear it. Liability is not primarily a punishment or deterrent, on this view, and its point is not to be retributive of or proportional to the wrongdoing. Compensatory damage awards are shifts of unfortunate losses to those who breached the duty not to create them. It is the inappropriate creation of the misfortune by the defendant that renders it permissible for the state to permit the plaintiff to shift the cost of that misfortune to the one who wrongfully created it.

Synthesizing these two points, a right of action is an entitlement to proceed against the defendant for damages to compensate an injury. The question is what sort of invasion of interest by plaintiff of defendant entitles plaintiff to this form of recourse against defendant. The answer is that plaintiff is entitled to return the cost of the injury on defendant if defendant has wrongfully inflicted its cost on him.

## IV. Are Mass Torts Different?

### IV.1 The Problem

We have offered two distinct but mutually supporting explanations of the existence of duties of non-injury in negligence law. As we said in the introduction, the rise of mass tort actions has been thought by many to bring about a substantial change in traditional tort doctrine, which one commentator has dubbed "the decline of cause."[20] Mass tort actions in which a large number of plaintiffs have been injured by defendants who can only be identified as members of a pool of risk imposers have led to what appear to be innovative judicial solutions, solutions which impose liability on negligent tortfeasors without requiring any proof of causation. Some commentators have taken these cases to vindicate economic analyses of tort law, either as ways of combining deterrence and compensation, or as ways of spreading losses appropriately. Others have taken them to reflect moral conceptions of responsibility that render causation irrelevant. Our own approach, which we will develop in the next section, shows why causation remains relevant to these cases, and interprets the judicial innovations at the level of evidentiary rules rather than substantive law. Before turning to our own solution, however, we pause here to consider some of the proposals that deem causation irrelevant to responsibility in these cases. The proposals we consider differ in a variety of ways. Our criticisms of them share a central theme: the basis of liability that each proposal suggests is overbroad, and, if followed through consistently, risks swallowing up all of tort law.

### IV.2  At-Fault Pools

One plausible way of accommodating the DES cases is to concede that they mark a departure from traditional corrective justice, but to see corrective justice as one among several ways of apportioning losses. This is essentially Jules Coleman's response in *Risks and Wrongs,* where he defends the *Hymowitz* approach to market-share liability. Coleman has no problem recognizing the possibility of a system of corrective justice based on who caused whose loss, but this is simply one option. Another option, seen in *Hymowitz,* would be to apportion liability among equally faulty parties according to their market share. Coleman's suggestion is that in certain situations it is appropriate to graft a narrow at-fault pool onto a more general regime of corrective justice (Coleman 1992a, p. 404).

Coleman's approach has many appealing features. Perhaps the most important of these is its focus on the significance of other institutions to duties of repair under corrective justice. Given that causation cannot be proved in certain cases, Coleman argues that there are compelling, but independent moral grounds for allocating accident costs. As Coleman puts it, the existence of other institutions for allocating costs is "neither an affront to corrective justice, nor irrelevant to it" (Coleman 1992a, p. 402). Instead, it is an institutional alternative, which, once in place, is relevant to questions of compensation. Absent an at-fault pool, corrective justice determines who must bear the costs of injuries. But once such a pool is in place, those in it remain responsible for the injuries they cause through their negligence, but no duty to repair flows from that responsibility. For Coleman, then, the court's solution in *Hymowitz* is a limited case of a general social insurance scheme. Like a generalized scheme, part of its rationale stems from a dysfunctional tort system. But rather than imposing the sort of across-the-board scheme advocated by some reformers,[21] displacing all of tort law, the *Hymowitz* court imposed a narrow scheme, tailored to those limited circumstances in which a corrective justice solution is infeasible on administrative grounds.

Coleman's parallel with a generalized system of social insurance is appealing. Our criticisms of Coleman's position are not meant to be incompatible with any sort of social insurance scheme. Our concern is that the proposal of a local at-fault pool added to the rest of tort law represents an unstable compromise between two very different ways of managing injuries and two very different approaches to the regulation of behaviour.

In tort law, the defendants are selected by the plaintiff, and each of their identities as risk-imposers, their fault levels and their relation to the case are picked and proved by the plaintiff. There is no notice as to the extent of damages to which a defendant may be subject. Consequential damages are broad, typically including pain and suffering, a wide variety of losses other than medical expenses, various pecuniary losses, and sometimes punitive damages. Determinations of defendant's liability and of its scope are made by a handful of laypersons under the circumstances of a ripened, individualized injury, or set of injuries. Limitations periods are tied to discovery of actual injury, rather than the occurrence of the tortfeasor's conduct. Degree of liability turns on the happenstance of who was in fact injured, how great their injuries were, and who decides to bring suit.

All of these observations about the American system for resolving tort disputes are commonly heard. And it might seem odd that we are using them as criticisms of an at-fault pool, which at least seems to avoid arbitrariness and unfairness in one dimension – distinctions among equally negligent actors. But that is our very point. The aspects of procedural law that we have described may trouble some observers of the tort system. But they would be strikingly egregious if they were the conditions under which the state imposed a fine or a penalty. An at-fault pool does exactly that, for in such a pool, the breach of the non-relational duty of risk generation is the trigger of the imposition of a penalty, whereas under rules of traditional causation, the breach of a duty of non-injury to plaintiff is the trigger of liability.

The conception of procedural fairness that is applicable when plaintiff is redressing a violation of her right and the conception of fairness applicable when the state is imposing a fine are quite different. The meagre notice, predictability, objectivity, and even-handedness that we note in the tort system are inexcusable when the state is in the business of administering penalties and fines.

But we believe that a substantial portion of these aspects of American procedural law are not simply artifacts of a deviant system, but rather systemic and
appropriate aspects of a system designed to permit private individuals to redress
what they believe to be rights invasions inflicted on them by others. The differences between individual recourse and state administration make adminis-
tratively mandated contributions to an at-fault pool inappropriate as an after-
the-fact response to injury. To graft an at-fault pool onto the tort law, as the
*Hymowitz* court did, is highly problematic for all of these reasons.[22]

Second, if Coleman's approach is procedurally unfair to defendants, it is also
arguably unfair in its treatment of those who are left within the traditional tort
system. Coleman is right to suggest that the existence of an at-fault pool is normatively relevant to the corrective justice duties of those who carelessly injure
others. But it is also relevant to the rights of those who are injured. Consider
the case of those people who are injured by negligent persons who can, in principle, be identified, but cannot in fact be identified. Where those who are injured by members of a local at-fault pool can recover from the members of the
pool as a group, those who are injured by negligent persons who are not in such
a group can only recover from their injurers. This is a point with considerable
practical import, since it makes a wrongfully injured plaintiff's ability to recover depend on such irrelevant features of his injurer as the structural features
of the industry to which the injurer belongs. Whether or not a plaintiff injured
by a negligent defendant who disappeared into the crowd would be left to deal
with his injuries would depend on whether the injurer was a member of a class
for whom an at-fault pool had been constructed. Again, a manufacturer whose
only business is as the sole producer of a defective product might well be bank-
rupted by litigation. Because such a manufacturer would not be a member of a
Coleman-type at-fault pool, those injured by it would be able to recoup, at most,
a fraction of the costs of their injuries. By contrast, if a number of manufacturers produce the same defective product, but it represents a fraction of each company's sales, they will fit into an at-fault pool, and those injured by their products will probably recover fully. The arbitrariness of this contrast is significant,
because whether or not a particular plaintiff recovers depends on business decisions having nothing to do with negligence.

We have offered two objections to Coleman's approach. The first focussed
on the role of courts and legislatures in imposing burdens, the second on the potentially arbitrary distinction that approach draws between those who do and do
not face the burden of proving causation. Both of these concerns about Coleman's approach reflect the respects in which it imposes distinct normative
schemes on cases which are normatively indistinguishable (albeit evidentially
distinguishable). We do not mean to deny Coleman's claim that both normative
approaches are legitimate. Our concern is that deploying them together is troubling. Both of the competing normative principles are capable in principle of

broader application. Combining them in the way that Coleman recommends undermines the legitimating role of each.

### IV.3  One Big At-Fault Pool?

There appears to be a clear path out of at least one of the difficulties we have identified for Coleman's approach, namely to replace the tort system with an administrative scheme that would join all negligent persons together into an at-fault pool. Then the ability of any particular plaintiff to recover will no longer depend on structural features of the industry to which his injurer belongs. Christopher Schroeder has advocated just such a system.[23] As we noted earlier, Schroeder's approach is animated by unease about the role of chance in tort liability. In place of this morally arbitrary outcome, Schroeder advocates a different interpretation of corrective justice. For Schroeder, cases like *Sindell* and *Hymowitz* are paradigmatic rather than exceptional, because they treat defendants alike based on the injuriousness of their conduct. As a result, they are coherent regimes of individual responsibility, for they evaluate agents in light of things that they can be expected to control, notably the degree of care they exercise with respect to the security of others. By eliminating luck, those cases tie responsibility exclusively to agency. By tying liability to both responsibility and compensation, such an approach preserves what is most valuable in traditional tort law, while ridding it of its arbitrary elements. Thus, in an important sense, the DES cases mark an opportunity for the law to "work itself pure," by isolating its animating principles, and discarding arbitrary relics of its procedural past. On Schroeder's account, corrective justice requires three things: agency-based responsibility, compensation of wrongfully injured plaintiffs, and internal financing, so that the sum total of compensation is exacted from defendants in proportion to their wrongdoing. Hence, we arrive at a general scheme of at-fault pools. The causation requirement is dropped, as both unfair and irrelevant to the purposes of sanctioning carelessness and compensating its victims.

Schroeder's proposal is also arguably free of worries about judicial activism, since its obvious home is as a legislative solution. Once in place, such a scheme does not require the sort of findings of fact about individualised causation in which courts specialize. Instead, it is an administrative system, which serves to ensure that those who expose others to risks bear the full costs of careless behaviour.

Despite its focus on removing the supposedly arbitrary features of tort law's causation requirement, Schroeder's approach may lead to new arbitrary distinctions. In this, Schroeder's approach illustrates a general pattern. Attempts to remove seemingly arbitrary distinctions from accident law often lead to the drawing of other distinctions, which are themselves objectionable because arbitrary. For example, Schroeder's proposal gets its impetus from a desire to treat negligent defendants alike apart from any question of the harm that ensues as a result of their carelessness. He thus seeks to treat the wrongs to which corrective justice responds as *non-relational,* that is, wrongs to the world in general, or perhaps society, rather than to the particular injured plaintiffs. Thus he rejects Cardozo's dictum that "negligence in the air . . . will not do."[24] Now there is nothing troubling in itself with defining wrongs non-relationally. Much regulatory legislation does so, and does so appropriately. But once they are so defined, it is difficult to understand their relation to the other features of corrective justice that Schroeder deems essential. For example, Schroeder's requirement of internal financing – the requirement that the costs of compensation be borne by those who create risks – is unmotivated, once wrongs are defined non-relationally. Perhaps there are administrative reasons for keeping various budgets separate, parallel to the reasons some have suggested for treating Social Security as a self-funding program, both safe against other government shortfalls, and unable to appeal to general revenues if it faces a shortfall. The point is that once duties are defined non-relationally, there are no reasons of justice to focus on internal financing.

The fact that various parts of Schroeder's view are not internally related does not in itself mean that the account draws arbitrary distinctions. But once the requirements of relational duties and causation are dropped, the rationale for treating all morally similar defendants alike leads to arbitrary distinctions among those who are injured. Those who are injured without negligence, whether as a result of natural catastrophes or just plain bad luck, are left to bear their own injuries, no matter how severe, while those who are injured as a result of negligence receive compensation from the at-fault fund. Looked at from the perspective of those who are injured, this difference reflects the utterly arbitrary effects of fortune, and reflects it in a way that will surely strike them as terribly unfair.[25]

This may seem like an odd complaint for the defender of corrective justice to lay at Schroeder's feet. Corrective justice only compensates those injured through wrongdoing; why should Schroeder's scheme do otherwise? The answer is that corrective justice explains this focus in terms of relational duties of non-injury. Those who injure others must bear the costs of so doing; *this* defendant must pay damages to *this* plaintiff *because he wronged her.* Schroeder's scheme cannot give this sort of answer, because it imposes non-relational duties of non-injuriousness. What happens as a result of the violation of those duties is irrelevant to the moral assessment of those who breach them. Chance and causation only matter to those who are injured. Yet if the putatively morally arbitrary factor of causation gives a claim to compensation to some but not others, those who do not receive compensation are right to complain. Creating a risk gives rise to a negative moral evaluation on Schroeder's approach. Once a risk has been created, it is a free-floating, and ultimately arbitrary factor that is no different from the other arbitrary risks thrown up by both nature and non-negligent conduct. A consistent application of that approach would treat accident victims alike, for all are alike in having faced misfortune not of their choosing. Consistently applied, Schroeder's approach leads to a scheme of general social insurance covering all accidental losses.[26]

## V. Market-Share Liability, Evidence, and Corrective Justice: Understanding *Sindell*

### *V.1 Introduction*

We have argued above that, under actual American tort law, a plaintiff is not permitted to recover compensation for an injury from a defendant unless the defendant has breached a relational duty of non-injury to that plaintiff – i.e., unless the defendant has caused an injury to that plaintiff. We have argued, moreover, that this requirement is not a contingent feature of the tort system, but is essential to its normative structure. And we have provided an explanation of why that should be so, and why certain kinds of attempts to predicate recovery of compensatory damages on mere breaches of a duty of non-injuriousness would be unjustifiable within the structure of the tort law.

On first blush, the requirement of a duty of non-injury appears to produce harsh and impractical results. Recall that in *Sindell* and *Hymowitz*, each of the plaintiffs could prove that defendants had manufactured products of the type that injured her, and that one of the defendants probably caused her injury, but could not identify which one, largely due to the fact that decades had passed between the litigation and the mothers' ingestion of the product, and the fact that defendants' products were, to a great degree, fungible. Hence, through no fault of their own, seriously injured plaintiffs were unable to recover against anyone, and defendants who had been proven to have caused some tortious injuries were to go free of liability.

In what follows, we argue that certain forms of market-share liability are indeed consistent with the view we are offering of the normative foundations of tort law, and are indeed consistent with the contention that liability in tort is based on breaches of duties of non-injury. Our positive account relies largely upon certain ideas in the normative theory of procedure and evidence.

We also limit our analysis to the argumentative strategy on which the *Sindell* plaintiffs in fact prevailed, according to which individual defendants had wrongfully injured individual plaintiffs. Many of the best-known mass tort litigations, such as DES, asbestos,[27] agent orange,[28] and tobacco,[29] have in fact involved a broader range of legal theories. Complaints in these cases have typically asserted that defendants conspired, or engaged in concert of action, and also that they individually caused the injuries by negligent or fraudulent conduct, or by marketing to plaintiff a defective product. And plaintiffs have typically asserted that these torts were committed to them personally, but sometimes also asserted the tortiousness of the defendants toward the group of persons to which the plaintiff belongs.[30]

The intuitive justice of *Sindell* requires no novel strategies of these sorts. None of the mass tort cases litigations has in fact been resolved or justified by courts in this aggregating manner. Instead, they have been treated by the courts as cases in which particular defendants have injured particular plaintiffs. It is to that account that we now turn.

## V.2  The Argument of Sindell

Our basic account is simple. The requirement that defendant breached a duty of non-injury to plaintiff is not a self-executing requirement. A court cannot reach a conclusion on whether defendant did or did not breach such a duty except relative to certain evidentiary standards. The normal evidentiary standard in cases where a negligently manufactured product is alleged to have injured a plaintiff is that the plaintiff must provide specific evidence linking the defendant's particular product to her particular injury. Otherwise the court will deem defendant not to have breached a duty of non-injury to plaintiff. If that *evidentiary* requirement is conjoined with the *substantive requirement* that defendant have breached a duty of non-injury to plaintiff, then the plaintiff in *Sindell* should lose. On its own, though, the substantive requirement of a breach of a duty of non-injury does not itself yield such a conclusion. The *Sindell* court declined to dismiss plaintiff's case, notwithstanding acceptance of this requirement, *precisely because it rejected the ordinary evidentiary standard*. And, we shall argue, the *Sindell* court was right to keep plaintiff's case alive precisely because it was right to reject the ordinary evidentiary standard.

## V.3  The Normative Basis of Burdens of Proof

Ordinarily, in order to prove that the defendant breached a duty of non-injury, the plaintiff must first identify the defendants. One of the striking features of *Sindell* is that plaintiffs had no real difficulty in proving that each of the defendants had breached duties of non-injury to plaintiffs. The combination of the scale on which DES was marketed and the hazards attendant on its use were enough to prove more probably than not that *each* defendant had injured some plaintiffs through its negligence. In this sense, the problem in *Sindell* is not exactly about causation. In an ordinary causation injury, two closely related questions arise (at least implicitly): (i) Did defendant breach a duty of non-injury, or merely a duty of non-injuriousness, i.e., did the conduct result in injury, or was this merely tortuous conduct that did not come to fruition as injury? (ii) Was the plaintiff's injury a result of the defendant's negligence? In *Sindell*, these two issues had already been resolved; the fact that each defendant had breached a duty of non-injury was beyond serious dispute, as was the fact that plaintiff's injuries were the result of the negligence of defendants. The real issue of *Sindell* concerns the burdens and standards of proof of identification. The source of the problem faced by the plaintiffs is the ordinary burden of proof; to understand the solution, we must examine why it is ordinarily set the way that it is, and how the distinctive circumstances of *Sindell* make it acceptable to shift it.[31]

To a significant extent, decisions about which evidentiary principles to accept rest on views of accuracy and reliability as to the substantive law. To take an extreme example, using a roulette wheel as the means of determining whether defendant injured plaintiff is unfair, because it is not sufficiently reliable as a way of producing just results in particular cases. At the same time, reliability is not the only factor that is relevant. The requirement that a criminal be proved guilty beyond a reasonable doubt rests also on a normative conception of the legitimate occasions of punishment, which insists that punishment of the innocent is far worse than failure to punish the guilty.

In the civil law, burdens and standards of proof also reflect views about the legitimate exercise of the court's power.[32] They also reflect the requirement that a court do justice to the parties before it. It is important to be clear that setting the *standard* of proof does not determine where the *burden* of proof should lie. The burden of proof is normally placed on the plaintiff. This does not reflect a general philosophical reluctance to engage in state action. Nor is it motivated by the costs of litigation, or the equivalent in tort law of the criminal law's presumption of innocence. The idea of recourse explains why the plaintiff faces the burden of proof (although it does not determine the magnitude of that burden). The plaintiff appeals to a court for recourse against a defendant who has wronged him. Because the plaintiff is demanding that the court do something, the burden ordinarily lies with him of convincing the court that he is entitled to a remedy.[33]

Outside of the paradigmatic case of a single plaintiff proceeding against a single defendant, though, the general normative rationale for both burdens and standards of proof may make different burdens and standards appropriate. If we understand the requirement that the plaintiff show more probably than not the defendant has negligently caused his injury on the model of the criminal law's presumption of innocence, any change in the burdens and standards of proof will look like an injustice to the defendant. But the requirements appropriate to a showing of guilt, prerequisite to the state punishing a person do not carry over to the occasions on which one person may act against another.

### V.4 *Shifting the Burden in* Sindell

With this apparatus in place, we are now in a position to explain why the *Sindell* court's decision to assign liability to the defendants in proportion to their market share within the court's jurisdiction abandoned neither corrective justice principles nor the idea that tort law imposes only duties of non-injury.

The *Sindell* court reasoned that the normal rule should be altered because "as between an innocent plaintiff and negligent defendants, the latter should bear the cost of the injury" (*Sindell* at 936). This language is far broader than the court intended. Taken at face value, it is broad enough to warrant a shift of the presumption on causation in *any* case in which negligence has been established. The California Supreme Court intended no such thing. The plaintiffs in *Sindell* were not only able to offer proof that defendants had been negligent; they also offered proof that a large number of plaintiffs had been injured and that each of the defendants was likely to have caused a share of these injuries. In short, the plaintiffs in *Sindell* offered proof not only that each defendant had breached a duty of non-injuriousness, but also that each had breached relational duties of non-injury and that plaintiffs in the pool were injured by those breaches. The situation thus differs markedly from more typical cases in which causation is in dispute. In such cases, the plaintiff must show that defendant's negligence was the cause of plaintiff's injury in order to show that defendant has breached a legal duty at all. If causation cannot be proved in such cases the defendant is entitled to be free of liability as a matter of right.

The large scale of DES manufacture changes the situation. The scale on which DES was manufactured makes it possible for plaintiffs to establish more probably than not that each defendant had completed torts against many of the plaintiffs. Had the numbers been much smaller, the fact that DES was negligently produced would not have been sufficient to establish that any duties of non-injury were breached. Given the evidence that each of the defendants had completed a tort, the only remaining question concerns the identity of the plaintiff against whom they have committed it. If the burden of proving identification was left with the plaintiffs, each of the defendants would have a ready answer in each case. Each defendant would be able to claim of each plaintiff that *some other* defendant had injured *that* plaintiff, and that any injuries caused by the defendant in question had been inflicted on *some other* plaintiff. That is just the result the court was unwilling to allow. The defendant's "ready answer" in each case implicitly concedes responsibility for injuries to some other plaintiff. To allow it would be to allow each defendant to assert serially both that it was not responsible for her injuries (when confronted by her) and that it was responsible for them (when confronted by others). Such a merry-go-round of defences would have allowed each defendant to show, as to each plaintiff, that its negligence had not caused her any injury, even while conceding that it had caused a significant number of injuries of precisely that type to some, unidentifiable members of the pool of plaintiffs. The court chose to prevent the defendants from doing so.

The point is not that the plaintiffs in *Sindell* faced difficulties of proof as a result of the wrongdoing of the defendants.[34] The difficulties of proof arose only because the defendants had engaged in generic marketing of their product, a practice which ordinarily provides considerable benefits to consumers and is not wrongful in itself. Instead, the court's concern was with the ability of the defendants to concede and deny their liability to each plaintiff. Defendants were effectively estopped from making this move, given that they were seeking an identification defence that would have prevailed even where defendants conceded that they were not entitled to be free of liability as a matter of right. At most they could claim that they were entitled to the usual burdens and standards of proof. But that claim rings hollow. Any procedure is at best an imperfect way of realizing corrective justice in a world of uncertainty. As a result, procedural rules may work an injustice in a particular case. If they do, the party who would stand to benefit from that injustice cannot complain that he is being wronged if a court acts to prevent it. For neither party to a lawsuit has the right to procedures that favour him; at most each party has a right to procedures that are not unfair.

The California Supreme Court's readiness to change the rule of evidence in *Sindell* was an exercise of the general power of courts to shape their procedures and evidentiary rules in a manner that is conducive to doing justice. The general idea underlying such powers – familiar from such doctrines as unclean hands, estoppel, and laches – is that a court protects its own integrity by protecting rights in a particular case against the untoward effects of procedures that are normally acceptable. Related principles can be found throughout the law of evidence. A party who has destroyed evidence on a particular issue is not permitted to benefit from the evidentiary uncertainty due to the destroyed evidence. The government, having procured evidence by unconstitutional means, may not use it to establish its case. A party's misconduct or sloppiness in discovery may give rise to a presumption for the benefit of its adversary. The successful maintenance of a particular substantive position in one litigation may estop that party from contesting that position in later litigation. In all of these cases, the court uses facts about a party's prior conduct to alter the usual evidentiary framework for arriving at its substantive determinations of the facts.

Within American law, classic expression of this kind of equitable evidentiary principle is provided by no less hard-headed a judge than Learned Hand. In *Navigazione Libera Triestina Societa Anonima v. Newtown Creek Towing Co.*,[35] a defendant who was proved to have caused certain damages to a ship argued that it should not be responsible for the cost of docking the ship for repair because the repair of the damages it caused were not the only repairs needed, and the other repairs would also have necessitated docking the ship. Judge Hand rejected this argument. He began by noting a category of cases of joint tortfeasors in which, because of the impossibility of proof, the normal presumption in favor of the defendant would lead to all tortfeasors escaping liability, and an innocent party bearing the loss itself – "an absurd result." He then noted that this absurdity is avoided by shifting the "impossible" burden of proof in such cases to the defendant (*Navigazione* at 697). By way of explaining why this shift was equitably appropriate, Hand reasoned that the "tortfeasor cannot be allowed to escape through the meshes of a logical net. He is a wrongdoer;

let him unravel the casuistries resulting from his wrong" (*Navigazione* at 697, citations omitted).

The judicial power to fashion procedures so as to do justice – in some (non-technical) sense an "equitable" power – is especially important in cases in which the wrong to be avoided is the result of one party seeking to use procedures to frustrate another's legitimate claim. That is just what is going on in *Sindell*. Each of the defendants breached relational duties of non-injury. Moreover, in light of the group of plaintiffs and defendants before the court, the plaintiffs' evidence tended to show, for each of the defendants, that it had breached a relational duty of non-injury to several (hundreds or thousands) of the plaintiffs. Each of the defendants was arguing, in effect, that despite this proof, the plaintiffs' failure to match each defendant with the particular plaintiffs whose injuries it caused should prevent all plaintiffs from recovering from any defendant. The court rightly refused to permit such arguments to defeat plaintiffs' case.

Like Learned Hand, the California Supreme Court sought to prevent an "absurd" result. It gave defendants the (nearly) "impossible" burden on product identification, permitting them to "unravel" the casuistries of product identification and thereby rebut the presumption of market-share liability, if they were able to do so. Having blocked the defendants from using the difficulties of identification to prevent plaintiffs from making their case, the court took the further step of shifting the burden of disproof to them. In the cases in which it is appropriate to shift the burden, the burden of proof only shifts after the plaintiff has proved that the defendant has completed a legal wrong. Moreover, the wrong in question must be the one that is at issue in the tort action in question. Thus, this procedural solution to *Sindell* does not run the risk of swallowing up the entire law. If mere negligence were enough to shift the burden of proving causation, tort law would make the breach of duties of non-injuriousness the condition of liability, and the retention of the causation requirement in other cases would be puzzling. But because the wrong that dirties the hands of a defendant must be a completed tort, the procedural solution does not wreak havoc with the rest of tort law.

Duties of non-injury are therefore not only not alien to the burden-shifting in *Sindell,* but essential to it. It is only because the defendants have been proved to have breached duties of non-injury that a modified presumption is available to plaintiffs.

### V.5 Market-Share Liability

Duties of non-injury are essential in a second way to *Sindell;* they explain the apportionment of liability by market share, which is the innovation for which the case is best known. We have argued thus far that *Sindell* permits plaintiffs a presumption against defendant whom they have proved negligently marketed a product that could have injured them and did in fact injure some persons. Defendants argued that this result was unfair because it left each defendant potentially liable for the injuries of all plaintiffs. Even if, *arguendo,* some of the injuries suffered by members of the plaintiff pool were realizations of risks created by our product, they argued, we surely cannot be held responsible for all of the realized risks, for we had only a fraction of the market. In short, we cannot be responsible for more harm than we did.

Market-share liability can be seen as a response to this complaint. The California Supreme Court crafted a rule that would ensure that defendants could not be held liable for greater than their market share. Its reason for doing so was not, as some commentators have suggested, to tie liability to *risk creation,* but to tie it to *injury causation.* Indeed, the court concludes its opinion by explicitly stating this as the response to defendants' arguments over the need for responsibility as a predicate for liability:

> Defendants urge that it would be both unfair and contrary to public policy to hold them liable for plaintiff's injuries in the absence of proof that one of them supplied the drug responsible for the damage. Most of their arguments, however, are based on the assumption that one manufacturer would be held responsible for the products of another or for those of all manufacturers if plaintiff ultimately prevails. But under the rule we adopt, each manufacturer's liability for an injury would be approximately equivalent to *the damages caused by the DES it manufactured. (Sindell* at 938, emphasis added)

Market-share liability can be understood as ensuring that defendants' liabilities are (at least roughly) limited by the harm they did. Under *Sindell,* the tort system will do corrective justice by requiring defendants to bear roughly the costs they have wrongfully imposed, and by unburdening plaintiffs of roughly the costs of injuries of which they were entitled to be free. That the match is rough in both directions need not concern us; *any* implementation of corrective justice will depend on imperfect judgments about causation, and on imperfect estimations of the extent of injuries. In this *Sindell* is no different from any other case. Its only novelty is in the evidence it was willing to accept in making a *prima facie* matching of plaintiffs to defendants.

Even if each defendant is not entitled to a presumption as to all injuries and liability, it does not follow that each defendant is not entitled to a presumption for *some* range of liability. In particular, defendant *is* entitled to be presumed free of liability for any beyond the injury it has been proved (without identification) to have caused. In short, the presumption should go only as far as the defendant's market share – precisely the rule in *Sindell.*

### V.6 Doctrinal Controversies over Market-Share Liability

In the twenty years since *Sindell* was decided, numerous issues have arisen concerning the contours and conditions of market-share liability. The analysis above sheds light on how some of these issues should be resolved: (A) whether the presumption that the defendant is liable to each plaintiff is rebuttable or irrebuttable; (B) whether the relevant market share is national market share, or the market share in a more narrowly defined region, such as a state; (C) whether the fungibility of products is a precondition of the imposition of liability; (D) whether joint liability is appropriate.

**A. REBUTTABLE OR IRREBUTTABLE PRESUMPTION.** In *Hymowitz,* the New York Court of Appeals held that the presumption that a manufacturers' liability should be at the level of its market share is an *irrebuttable* presumption, even as to plaintiffs for whom defendants proffer proof that it was not their product that injured the plaintiff. Several scholars have reached similar conclusions.[36] The California Supreme Court held in *Sindell,* however, that the presumption was *rebuttable,* and the overwhelming majority of courts adopting some form of market-share liability have agreed (Twerski 1989). Our account shows why California is right and New York wrong. Plaintiffs are permitted to recover from defendants on a market share theory, notwithstanding the tort law's requirement of a breach of the duty of non-injury to the plaintiff, only because there is insufficient evidence in either direction on whether defendant in fact breached a duty of non-injury to plaintiff. But if defendant can actually provide specific evidence showing that its product could not have been linked or was not in fact linked to plaintiff's injury, then the imposition of liability violates the rule that a plaintiff may not recover against a defendant who did not breach a relational duty of non-injury to her, and forces defendant to bear a loss of which he is entitled to be free.

**B. STATE V. NATIONAL MARKET SHARE.** It is one thing to say that a defendant's liability should be limited by its market share, and quite another to say what "market share" actually means. The place, time, and nature of this market are often hotly contested. Most notably, courts are often forced to decide whether they ought to use defendants' national market share of the product in question at the relevant point in time,[37] or defendants' market share within the geographical region in which the plaintiffs (or the users whose use injured plaintiff – in DES cases, their mothers) resided – typically a state market share. The California Supreme Court did not define market share in *Sindell,* and other courts have divided on the issue.

Our account of the rationale for market-share liability favors state over national market share. More particularly, it is essential that each plaintiff who recovers mount a case that defendant's product *could* have injured plaintiff, and that there be a genuinely open question as to whether defendant's product did injure it. It is only within this evidentiary uncertainty that market-share liability plays a role. A manufacturer with no market in the jurisdiction in which plaintiff was injured should not be subject to such liability.

This is not just to reiterate our point about rebuttability. The point is broader than this. Suppose that a defendant's national market share is greater than its market share in the state in which the court is sitting, and in which the plaintiffs reside. Then this percentage of each plaintiff's injuries, multiplied by the plaintiffs litigating against it, will produce a total liability that is likely to exceed the injury the defendant in fact imposed *on the plaintiffs before the court.* Recall that defendant is able to limit its liability to its market share precisely because liability beyond its market share will in effect force defendant to be liable for the costs of injuries that it is entitled to be free of. Hence, a condition of the permissibility of market-share liability is violated if the court selects a market in which some defendant has a share greater than in the market in which the plaintiffs reside. This inevitably will mean that state market share should be selected over national market share.[38]

C. FUNGIBLE PRODUCTS. DES and certain other pharmaceutical products (such as, perhaps, blood-clotting factor) present natural opportunities for the imposition of market-share liability because the products of different manufacturers are fungible. Intuitively, fungibility is relevant to market-share liability for two reasons. First, it is the fungibility that often creates the problem of tortfeasor identification. Second, where there is fungibility because products are identically designed, and the cause of action is predicated on a negligent or defective design, warranty, or failure to warn, identical products are equally likely to produce injuries. The question arises, however, as to whether the fungibility of the products manufactured by alleged tortfeasors is a necessary condition for the imposition of market-share liability.

Our account shows that fungibility is a precondition for the legitimacy of market-share liability. The reason is not that blameless-plaintiff/tortfeasor-identification problems could not arise without fungibility. They clearly could and have. Fungibility is relevant because fungible products from different manufacturers are equally likely to produce injuries. More exactly, the court has before it a pool of plaintiffs who have proved that the members of a certain industry, through producing a certain product, have caused a certain number of injuries. In fact, the court envisions that each plaintiff's injury was caused by some particular defendant. Product identification problems prevent the matching of the defendant with the plaintiff. If the products were in fact fungible, then, assuming the demographics of product use among the plaintiff pool roughly matched the market share in the relevant jurisdiction, market share will reflect roughly the injury-imposition of each defendant.[39]

D. JOINT LIABILITY. Eight years after *Sindell,* the California Supreme Court was forced to decide whether or not market-share liability was a form of joint liability. From a practical point of view, the issue was whether plaintiffs who were unable to collect a certain portion of their damages from insolvent defendants could proceed against other defendants beyond their market share (presumably leaving those other defendants with a right of contribution against its insolvent co-defendant). In *Brown v. Superior Court*,[40] that court rejected joint liability, holding that each manufacturer's liability was limited to its market share. Many jurisdictions follow *Brown*[41] but some do not, reasoning that it is better for the negligent manufacturer to bear the cost of the injury than the innocent plaintiff, in the event that one of the manufacturers is insolvent.[42]

Joint liability in market-share cases is unwarranted, for it undermines the rationale for imposing market-share liability at all. To permit liability to be imposed on a defendant beyond its market share is, in effect, to permit liability without a breach of the duty of non-injury. This is unacceptable from a normative point of view for the reasons we set out above. The temptation to impose a form of joint liability is the product of two errors. One is the supposition that market-share liability is a form of group liability, in other words, that the defendants are liable as a unit. Aggregative liability is sometimes possible, and is seen in conspiracy and concert-of-action cases, but it requires a substantive legal and factual theory of joint tortious conduct.[43] Although, as we have stated, we regard it as an important question worthy of further attention whether such a case could be made out, this case was not made out in *Brown* or *Sindell*, and therefore the theory of liability it licenses cannot be used. The second error is a more subtle one. It involves the misuse of an equitable idea, that the negligent tortfeasor should bear the loss rather than the innocent plaintiff. To be sure, this vaguely captures an important way of thinking in the law, and an idea that played a role in *Sindell*. It should be evident, however, that unless this principle is used within a carefully defined context, it could swamp a great deal of the law, because it would eliminate the requirement that defendant breach a duty of non-injury to the plaintiff.

The key to our account of *Sindell* was that it is narrow. It applies only to a negligent tortfeasor who has breached a duty of non-injury; it affects only the selection of evidentiary burden; it applies only to product identification problem in aggregative litigation; and it is applicable only to the extent that those against whom it is used cannot a claim a right to be free of costs that it seeks to impose. It is only because the place of this principle is so narrow that it was properly used within the law. To apply the same principle outside of its proper place is to miss all that is distinctive about *Sindell*.

### V.7  Summers v. Tice

Our account of liability shifting requires a completed wrong. The temptation to see *Sindell* as overwhelming the rest of tort law rests in part on a failure to distinguish between duties of non-injury and duties of non-injuriousness. But it also rests, at least in part, on the fact that *Sindell* is a California case, and that plaintiffs argued to the court that they should win on the strength of the legal theory in the famous California case of *Summers v. Tice*.[44] In *Summers,* three men were hunting quail. The plaintiff, Summers, flushed a quail, and the two defendants, Tice and Simonson, negligently fired their shotguns in his direction. A pellet lodged in Summers's eye (and another lodged in his lip). The two defendants were using identical guns and shot, so there was no way for Summers to establish which one had injured him. The plaintiff thus not only failed to identify his injurer, but also failed to prove that either defendant had breached a duty of non-injury at all. Nonetheless, the court shifted the burden of proof of causation to the defendants. Since neither could disprove his role in the injury, they were held jointly and severally liable, with the provision that should either one be able to carry the burden of proof that it was not he himself who injured the plaintiff, he could escape liability altogether.

It is important to our analysis that the *Sindell* court did not follow *Summers.* It explicitly rejected it,[45] and imposed a form of liability, namely market-share liability, quite different from that in *Summers* (which it referred to as "alternative liability"). But it did shift the burden of proof of causation in cases of tortfeasor uncertainty, and its readiness to do so was motivated in part by *Summers.* So it is not surprising that scholars have seen *Sindell* as an extension of *Summers.*[46] This leaves us, however, with the prickly question of why it was all right for the court in *Summers* to shift the burden of proof on causation absent a showing of a breach of a duty of non-injury, even though this is not generally permissible, and is not permissible under *Sindell.*

The burden shifted in *Summers* for a reason that was not present in *Sindell.* The plaintiff in *Summers* had evidence as to each defendant that he negligently caused his injury. The problem in *Summers* was that each defendant was able to argue, by pointing to the other, that the chance that he caused the injury was at most 50 percent. Thus, as between plaintiff and each defendant, plaintiff was able to claim a 50 percent likelihood that defendant did it and defendant was able to claim a 50 percent likelihood that he did not. Yet only one of the defendants had completed a tort against the plaintiff. Although the other had been negligent, he had not breached a duty of non-injury. Unfortunately, neither the plaintiff nor either of the defendants knew which was which.

Normally, of course, defendants win on the cusp. But this result is not dictated by the structure of tort law, as we have analyzed it. That structure requires that if the court determines that defendant did not breach a duty of non-injury to plaintiff, then defendant should not be liable, but it does not say what standard ought to be used for this determination; that is a matter of evidentiary rules. However, even if one decides to permit defendants to prove that they did not injure the plaintiff by using probabilistic evidence, and even if one decides that showing that the probability is greater than 50 percent that defendant did not cause plaintiff's injury is grounds for a court determination that defendant did not injure plaintiff, that leaves open the question of what to do *at* 50 percent. It is the combination of leaving the burden with the plaintiff and the more-probably-than-not standard that creates the problem in *Summers.*

The solution is to limit the reach of the tie-breaking rule to cases in which it is guaranteed to lead to a misfortune being left with the wrong person. Ordinarily, a variety of considerations line up in favor of setting a tie-breaking rule in favor of the defendant. The fact that the plaintiff appears before the court seeking recourse is one such reason. Another is the concerns the court might have about discouraging frivolous litigation. But if there are normally good reasons for setting the tie-breaking rule to favor the defendant, any such reasons are reasons of process and policy rather than right. In the case of a particular tie, it is at least permissible for the court to look at a variety of other factors.

Courts have, in fact, considered a wide range of instrumentalist and non-instrumentalist considerations, including evidentiary matters, such as access to proof, concerns about the likelihood that a scheme of rights will be sufficiently respected and enforced, public goals, such as regulation, prevention, and compensation; equitable concerns about the fairness of the treatment of the parties in resolution of these cases.[47] Not all of these factors carry equal weight in *Summers.* One of them is particularly salient: the equitable concern that leaving the burden with the plaintiff in this case is *guaranteed* to leave the loss with the innocent plaintiff, and to relieve the negligent tortfeasor of liability. On the cusp, a court normally has no choice but to take a 50 percent chance of making a mistake. In *Summers,* though, the ordinary rule would have guaranteed a mistake; the changed rule still enables the plaintiff to proceed against the defendant who did not in fact cause his injury, but the chance of this error is only 50 percent, which is ordinarily deemed acceptable. Although ordinary procedures ordinarily approximate justice, employing them in this case would ensure injustice. Where the plaintiff has established that one of the defendants caused the injury, the defendants cannot claim that, as a matter of justice, they are entitled to the benefits of the tie-breaking rule. Still, to shift the burden is not to leave the defendants without a defence. If either defendant can show more probably than not that they did not cause the injury, he thereby shows that the loss does not properly lie with him, and so escapes liability. Now it is true that the entire problem in *Summers v. Tice* arises because neither defendant has the information at his disposal to absolve himself in this way. But placing the burden of proving causation on the defendants is a response to the uncertainty faced by the court. The fact that the defendants in the instant case will lack the means of proof does not render the assignment of the burden to them unfair.

The *Summers* court also mentions a variety of other considerations. The defendants had better access to proof than the plaintiff; the defendants' rights would be respected by permitting each not only to prove its own nonliability by a preponderance, but to argue that the other's conduct caused the injury; the goal of compensating the injured and deterring injurious behavior would be furthered. The more instrumental of these considerations are not out of place in deciding what to do about the tie-breaking rule. Instrumental arguments are not introduced to determine liability; they are at most relevant to the wisdom of shifting the tie-breaking rule. In cases of a tie, the court must resign itself to the fact that it is as likely as not that the wrong person will end up bearing a loss. The court lacks the information necessary to decide between the parties on grounds of justice. In such a case it may be *permissible* to consider other factors. Given the certainty that the loss will lie with the wrong person if the burden is not shifted, though, it is not clear that consideration of such factors is necessary to reach the result.

### V.8  Sindell *Revisited*

The above account provides a narrow solution to *Summers* – "narrow" because it will not generalize to other cases. It does this while recognizing the diversity of reasons the *Summers* court took into account. A precondition to the consideration of these reasons of policy and fairness is the decision of whether shifting the burden of proof is consistent with defendant's right to be free of liability where it has not breached a duty of non-injury. The *Summers* court was able to decide that this burden-shifting was consistent with defendants' rights because the case concerns what to do where the fact-finder put the probability of the defendant's having breached a duty of non-injury to plaintiff at exactly 50 percent. The court's analysis would therefore not extend to a hypothetical case of shots by three negligent hunters, each of whom could show the chance was 66.67 percent that he did not injure the plaintiff. By extension, it would also not apply in a case like *Sindell*, in which each of the defendants was less than 50 percent likely to have caused any particular injury. This is exactly what the California Supreme Court decided in *Sindell*, declining to apply the "alternative" liability theory of *Summers*.

Both *Summers* and *Sindell* are cases about the permissibility of shifting the burden of proof on tortfeasor identification. Despite this similarity, neither is a helpful guide to the other. The reason for shifting in *Summers* is that the probabilities are balanced; the result is a rebuttable presumption of full liability in *Summers*. The reason for the shifting in *Sindell* is the defendants' having breached duties of non-injury to the plaintiffs; the result is a rebuttable presumption that the defendant injured each plaintiff, but only to such a degree that, cumulatively, defendant will bear liability no greater than the breach of duties of non-injury it is proved to have committed. The *Sindell* option is unavailable in *Summers*, because defendant was not proved to have breached any duty of non-injury. Conversely, the *Summers* option is unavailable in *Sindell* because the probability of each defendant having injured a particular plaintiff is less than 50 percent.

In other ways, though, the reasoning of *Sindell* resembles the reasoning of

*Summers.* In both cases, in light of the court's decision on the *permissibility* of burden-shifting, the question arose as to whether such burden-shifting was actually a good idea, and ought to be done. The Court in *Summers* noted a wide range of reasons for altering the ordinary evidentiary rules: reasons of evidence availability, adequately protecting defendants' rights, furthering the goals of loss-spreading and plaintiff compensation, and recognizing the unfairness of letting wrongdoers go free while innocent parties must bear losses not rightfully theirs. All of these considerations are found in *Sindell* as well, and provide some of the more salient language of the court's discussion: "The most persuasive reason for finding plaintiff states a cause of action is that advanced in *Summers:* as between an innocent plaintiff and negligent defendants, the latter should bear the cost of the injury. . . . From a broader policy standpoint, defendants are better able to bear the cost of injury resulting from the manufacture of a defective product."[48] As we have explained, these reasons of policy and principle, difficult, important, and interesting as they may be, are not reasons advanced for the contention that *there is a cause of action absent breach of a duty of non-injury.* Nor are they reasons for the contention that burden-shifting does not impermissibly offend against defendants' rights. They are reasons used to decide whether, if it is permissible to shift the burden for some share of liability, under some conditions, the burden ought to be so shifted. Unsurprisingly, the court decides that it should.

*Sindell* thus does not disturb the interpretation of tort law we have offered. To the contrary, our account provides a framework for understanding the exception that the California Supreme Court fashioned in *Sindell.* If causation (or breach of duty of non-injury) were not essential, then *Sindell* would be about substantive rules of liability, not about evidentiary presumptions. More importantly, the difficult problems of mass torts and product identification presented by DES and other torts like it, do not necessarily call for an abandonment of the conceptual framework of tort law. What they call for – and what the California Supreme Court gave them – is a sensitive and pragmatic approach in the elaboration and modification of the procedures through which this normative structure is applied.

## VI. Conclusion

Both instrumentalists and moralists are often puzzled by the central role that our tort law gives to causation. Addressing largely the moralists, we have provided a two-fold explanation of this aspect of tort law. In the first instance, tort law provides an avenue of recourse to those who have been wronged against those who have wronged them, not a means of punishment for those who have acted badly. It is therefore essential that defendant have wronged plaintiff if plaintiff is to recover from her; it is essential that defendant have breached a duty to plaintiff not to injure her. Moreover, when the tort law permits a plaintiff to exact compensation from defendant for an injury, it does so only because it treats that injury as the realization of a risk for which defendant is responsible. If it was not defendant who caused plaintiff's injury, then the injury is not a realization of the risk defendant created, and defendant cannot fairly be held responsible for it. The causation requirement reflects the fact that the rights protected by the tort law are rights against being injured, and the duties it imposes are duties not to injure others. Although these rights and duties are both qualified – it is only injury imposed *through some* injurious kind of conduct that permits the imposition of liability – it is not the potentially injurious conduct but the actual injury that creates a violation of legal right.

Tort law undoubtedly serves many functions in the American legal system, and it is understandable that we should want it to serve those functions more effectively and fairly. With this in mind, many tort scholars have favored the abandonment or at least the relaxation of the causation requirement. The supposed deterrent and compensatory functions of the tort law seem ill-served by a causation rule in a wide variety of cases. These shortcomings, they claim, are most notable in mass tort cases where causation appears to be a stumbling block because of poor information on product identification. Moreover, as we have detailed above, even some of those scholars committed to thinking about tort law from a moral point of view have urged that a fairer treatment of both victims and injurers would be facilitated by attenuating the causation requirement.

Our analysis suggests that these critics have understated both the weaknesses and the strengths of tort law. They have said too little about its weaknesses by focusing on the arbitrariness of a compensation system that permits those injured by torts to go uncompensated when their injurers cannot be identified, and a regulatory system that sanctions those who behave in a socially harmful manner only when their victim can identify them. These are the problems that an attenuation of the causation requirement in tort law will supposedly solve. But to solve these problems is not enough; we are left with the problem of explaining why only those serious injuries caused by torts are compensated. Once we abandon the idea that compensation is provided in tort because it is part of a recognition of the tortfeasor's *responsibility* for the plaintiff's injury (which we must, if we are to abandon causation), there is no reason to limit compensation to tortiously caused injuries or accidents. Similarly, if we are willing to hold defendants liable to those they have not injured, we must ask why it is fair or effective to use private litigation, with awards based on the happenstance of various injuries, to determine the sanctions paid by defendants. Once we are in the business of evaluating the tort law's capacity to realize these goals, we must recognize that it is not contingently but essentially incomplete and arbitrary relative to these goals. In short, all of the considerations put forward as reasons for attenuating the causation requirement in tort law are more plausibly viewed as reasons for supplementing the legal system with public compensatory and deterrent systems, for tort law without causation will be both ineffective and arbitrary to the core.

On the other hand, critics of the causation requirement have also underestimated its strengths, for they have suggested that the causation requirement is a symptom of the impractical and antiquated nature of the tort law, its inability to come to terms with contemporary problems. *Sindell* shows just the reverse. Faced with thousands of persons seeking to hold numerous manufacturers responsible for injuries caused by modern pharmaceuticals placed on a sophisticated market and delayed for decades, the court used the common law of torts and evidence to craft a solution that would work. It recognized that the framework of duties and rights that gives the law meaning at a substantive level does not in and of itself yield answers to disputes brought before a court; procedural and evidentiary rules are also required. The selection of those rules involves normative choices of its own. Although the evidentiary rules must be crafted so as to respect the substantive rules of law, this precondition still leaves room for procedures that realistically engage the situation that classes of litigants find themselves in, and the equitable posture of the parties before the court. When this was done, the California Supreme Court showed that it was able to maintain the causation requirement, respect a defendant's right to be free of liability for injuries she is not responsible for, and yet simultaneously recognize the rights of those injured to hold responsible those who tortiously injured them.

Of course, we have focused here only on the issue of causation and product identification in mass torts. But in so doing, we hope to have illustrated a larger point. Corrective justice theory can illuminate the concepts of right and responsibility embedded in tort law. The reason for doing so is not to neglect the practical effects of tort law, or to close it off from change. On the contrary, it is only when we understand how the concepts of tort law are structured that we can evaluate its capacity to serve our favored goals, and we can decide how, in a changing world, these concepts are to be given content.

## Notes

* We are grateful to the participants in the UNC Law and Philosophy Workshop on Tort Theory, September 1997, and especially to our commentator, Bruce Chapman. We have also received important help from Dan Capra, Greg Keating, Jill Fisch, John Goldberg, Michael Martin, Dan Richman, Tony Sebok, and Martin Stone, and valuable research assistance from Gita Cale, Philip Pfeffer, and Maria Rivera.
[1] See, e.g., Robert L. Rabin (1996) (reviewing Weinrib (1995)). Rabin argues that Weinrib's corrective justice theory has nothing to offer in resolving new questions about damage apportionment in torts.
[2] See, e.g., Alan Strudler (1992). Jody Kraus's use of the lottery paradox in his critique of Strudler is illuminating. See Jody S. Kraus (1997).
[3] See, e.g., Schroeder (1990).
[4] There is potential for confusion over our use of the phrase "corrective justice." Used in a broad sense, it refers to a range of theories that emphasize the concepts of rights, duties, and fairness in explaining tort law, and embraces works as diverse as, e.g., Jules L. Coleman (1992a); Ernest J. Weinrib (1995); Arthur Ripstein (1999); Richard A. Epstein (1973); George P. Fletcher (1972); Stephen R. Perry (1992b); and Benjamin C. Zipursky (1998b).

But "corrective justice theory" is sometimes used in a narrower sense to refer to a particular hybrid of Aristotelian and "duty-of-repair" theories exemplified by Weinrib's *The Idea of Private Law*. In this essay, we mean corrective justice theory in the broader sense.

5   Cf. Zipursky (2000) (providing philosophical foundations for a pragmatic, rather than formalistic version of corrective justice).

6   *Sindell v. Abbott Laboratories*, 607 P. 2d 294 (Cal. 1980).

7   *Hymowitz v. Eli Lilly Co.*, 539 N.E. 2d 1069 (N.Y. 1989).

8   Compare, e.g., *Smith v. Cutter Biological Serv's., Inc.*, 830 P.2d 717 (Haw. 1991) (applying market-share liability to manufacturers of blood product that caused AIDS in hemophiliacs); *Kennedy v. Baxter Healthcare Corp.*, 50 Cal. Rptr. 2d 736 (Cal. Ct. App. 1996) (declining to apply market-share liability to manufacturers of latex gloves). See also *Hamilton v. Accu-tek*, 62 F. Supp. 2d 802 (E.D.N.Y. 1999) (Weinstein, J.), *on appeal* (applying modified form of market-share liability to negligence claim against handgun manufacturers on the basis of lack of precautions taken in wholesale distribution conduct).

9   There is a large literature on causation in torts. See, e.g., Coleman (1992a, pp.270–84); Weinrib, (1995 pp. 153–67); Epstein (1973); Wright (1987, 1988); Rizzo (1987).

10  199 P.2d 1 (Cal. 1948) (shifting burden of proof to two defendant hunters to disprove causation, where injured plaintiff cannot prove which one injured him).

11  See, e.g., *Falcon v. Memorial Hospital*, 462 N.W.2d 44 (Mich. 1990) (loss of 37.5% chance of surviving embolism is an actionable injury under Michigan medical malpractice law). For an illuminating discussion of similar cases, see Stephen R. Perry (1995).

12  *Metro-North Commuter R.R. Co. v. Buckley*, 117 S. Ct. 2114 (1997) (considering, but rejecting actionability of emotional injury occasioned by heightened risk of asbestos-related disease caused by negligent exposure to asbestos).

13  For a more complete elaboration and defense of these points, see Goldberg and Zipursky (1998); Zipursky (1998a).

14  Schroeder (1990); Coleman (1992a, chapter 19); Rosenberg (1984); Berger (1997).

15  Including Kant's own legal theory, and his more general account of moral imputability. On the former, see Kant (1991); on the latter see his "On a Supposed Right to Lie from Benevolent Motives," appended to Kant (1992).

16  This idea is developed in greater detail in Zipursky (1998b, pp. 82–7) and Zipursky, "Civil Recourse and Corrective Justice" at p. 62–89 (manuscript on file with author).

17  Actual legal practice is somewhat more complicated: attempted crimes are punished less severely than completed ones, and many crimes receive the same punishment whether committed recklessly or intentionally. For one attempt to explain these departures from an emphasis on control, see Ripstein (1999, chapter 7).

18  These points are developed in more detail in Ripstein (1999) and Coleman and Ripstein (1995). There are, of course, many areas of tort law that involve imposition of liability for compensation of injuries, but do not involve activity that is normally described as wrongful risk creation. The most obvious example is an intentional tort, such as a battery. Injury through wrongful risk creation is our focus here not because risk is necessarily a paradigm for all of torts, but because it is, in some ways, the hardest case to explain. Hence the plaintiff's broken nose, inflicted through an intentional battery, is an injury the defendant is responsible for because the defendant breached a duty not to injure others through intentionally battering them. That the injury was intentionally inflicted, rather than being inflicting through wrongful risk imposition, makes the case easier, not harder.

19  The statement also applies to product liability law regarding design defects.

[20] Thomson (1987a); Thomson (1987b); and Thomson, "Remarks on Causation and Liability," in Thomson (1986).

[21] For example, Schroeder's argument discussed below, and the New Zealand system defended by Waldron (1995).

[22] We leave to another occasion the question of whether there were special circumstances in *Hymowitz* – e.g., the presence of New York statute of limitations legislation specifically designed for DES daughters – that had an impact on the justifiability of the court's decision.

[23] Schroeder (1990). In more recent work, Schroeder has modified his position somewhat. See Schroeder (1995).

[24] *Palsgraf v. Long Island Rail Road,* 162 N.E. 99 (N.Y. 1928).

[25] See the discussion of this point in Atiyah (1997)

[26] Indeed, Schroeder appears to have moved in this direction in Schroeder (1995).

[27] *In re Related Asbestos Cases,* 534 F. Supp. 1152 (N.D. Ca. 1982).

[28] *In re "Agent Orange" Product Liability Litigation,* 818 F.2d 145 (2d Cir. 1987).

[29] *Castano v. American Tobacco Co.,* 84 F.3d 734 (5th Cir. 1996).

[30] For a sensitive discussion of the range of different issues and problems presented in mass tort cases, see Abraham (1987). Beyond the subtleties of substantive law theories and evidentiary rules that we address here, there are obviously numerous procedural and choice of law issues that loom large in mass tort law, that we do not purport to address here. See generally Mullenix (1996).

[31] The possibility of a genuine evidence-based rationale is prematurely abandoned in Robinson (1982).

[32] For an important recognition of the respects in which evidentiary issues in identification cases implicate broader questions about the proper exercise of power within the legal system, see Nesson (1985).

[33] We do not mean to deny that placing the burden in this way has benefits a court might welcome, such as reducing opportunistic litigation. Our claim is only that a concern with recourse also animates it.

[34] But see note 48.

[35] 98 F.2d 694 (2d Cir. 1938).

[36] See Twerski (1989); Rheingold, (1989, n. 25); Epstein (1985b).

[37] See *Ashley v. Abbott Laboratories,* 789 F.Supp. 552 (E.D.N.Y. 1992); see generally Bunting (1994) (arguing that a national market-share approach represents a laudable attempt to reconcile the disparate and conflicting pronouncements of the Supreme Court on the issue of personal jurisdiction).

[38] Perhaps a narrower geographic distribution would be even better; if different defendants had different shares of the market in different areas of a state, tying their liability to those regions would come closer to tying their liability to the extent of their completed legal wrongs. See *Martin v. Abbott Laboratories,* 102 Wash. 2d 581, 689 P. 2d 368 (1984); see also *Conley v. Boyle Drug Co.,* 477 So. 2d 600 (Fla. Dist. Ct. App. 1985).

[39] See *In Re New York State Silicone Breast Implant Litigation,* 166 Misc. 2d 85, 631 N.Y.S. 2d 491 (Sup. Ct., N.Y. Co. 1995); see also *Goldman v. Johns-Manville Sales Corp.,* 33 Ohio St. 3d 40, 514 N.E. 2d 691, 700 (1987) (holding that asbestos litigation does not lend itself to market-share liability because asbestos is not a fungible product). See also, *Kennedy v. Baxter Healthcare Corp.,* 50 Cal. Rptr. 2d 736 (Cal. Ct. App. 1996) (market-share liability inapplicable, in part, because latex gloves are not fungible); *Edwards v.*

*A. L. Lease & Co.,* 54 Cal. Rptr. 2d 259 (Cal. Ct. App. 1996) (no market-share liability for nonfungible products under California law).

40  751 P.2d 470 (Cal. 1988).

41  See *Rogers v. Miles Laboratories, Inc.,* 116 Wash. 2d 195, 802 P. 2d 1346 (1991); see also *Shackil v. Lederle Laboratories,* 530 A. 2d 1287, 1303–4 (N.J. Super. Ct. App. Div. 1987); *Hymowitz v. Eli Lilly & Co.,* 639 N.E. 2d 1069, 1078; see generally Schwartz and Mahshigian (1988).

42  See *Abel v. Eli Lilly & Co.,* 418 Mich. 311, 343 N.W. 2d 164 (1984) (exceptional decision expressly allowing joint and several liability).

43  See *Nicolet Inc. v. Nutt,* 525 A.2d 146 (Del. Sup. Ct. 1987) (holding that defendant may be jointly and severally liable for damages caused by the acts of coconspirators if such acts were committed in furtherance of the scheme).

44  199 P.2d 1 (Cal. 1948).

45  607 P.2d at 931

46  The court also quoted a student comment from the *Fordham Law Review* that drew a parallel between *Summers* and the DES cases. *Sindell* at 937, quoting Comment (1978).

47  The United States Supreme Court has decided on several occasions that a burden may be shifted to the defendant when the probabilities are in "equipoise." The first, and analytically crucial step is the recognition that the presumption "would affect only [a] narrow class of cases in which the evidence on either side was equally balanced." *Cooper v. Oklahoma,* 116 S. Ct. 1373, 1381 (1996) (citing *Medina v. California,* 505 U.S. 1244 (1992)). In *Cooper,* the court struck down a Kentucky evidentiary rule requiring defendants in criminal trials to prove their incompetence by clear and convincing evidence. It was forced to reconcile this decision with *Medina,* which permitted states to place the burden of proving incompetence to the criminal defendant. The fact that *Medina* concerned only those cases in equipoise was critical to the court's distinction.

48  *Sindell,* 607 P.2d at 936. The quoted passage omits the following "Here, as in *Summers,* plaintiff is not at fault in failing to provide evidence of causation, and although the absence of such evidence is not attributable to the defendants either, their conduct in marketing a drug the effects of which are delayed for many years played a significant role in creating the unavailability of proof." In this passage, the court is speaking out of both sides of its mouth. On the one hand, it recognizes that "the absence of [causation] evidence is not attributable to defendants," on the other hand, it insinuates the defendants' culpability *for the lack of causation evidence* by stating that "their conduct . . . played a significant role in creating the unavailability of proof." Ultimately, the court does not make a persuasive case that defendants bear any responsibility or culpability for the lack of evidence. Although they are surely responsible for producing the drug that ended up injuring people many years later, this is in no recognizable sense an evidentiary wrongdoing. It is curious that the court strains to equivocate on this point. Our account suggests that the court recognized it was engaged in equity-based burden shifting, and recognized a more familiar and well-established version of such burden shifting where there was evidentiary wrongdoing or responsibility for evidentiary gaps. As we have explained, *Sindell* cannot and does not depend on such an allegation.

# 7

# Economics, Moral Philosophy, and the Positive Analysis of Tort Law

MARK GEISTFELD

The positive analysis of tort law is descriptive in the sense that it ascribes a purpose to tort liability, such as one based on corrective justice or wealth maximization, and then interprets tort law in those terms. An interpretation that adequately describes tort practice is thought to support the claim that the tort system serves the purpose upon which the interpretation is based, even if participants in the system do not consciously pursue that purpose.

This analytical approach is partially motivated by the role that precedent plays in the justification of legal decisions. If positive analysis shows that most of tort law maximizes wealth, for example, then one may have substantial precedent for justifying the wealth-maximizing outcome in the case at hand. Similarly, a greater ability to discern commonality in prior cases makes one more capable of predicting the outcome of future cases, insofar as "like" cases are supposed to be treated alike.

By enhancing the ability of the tort system to handle cases in a uniform and consistent manner, positive analysis promotes or protects the values of equality and reliance. Positive analysis has only limited normative value, however. Even if positive analysis shows that most of tort practice can be adequately described as serving some purpose, a purpose that is not morally justified probably does not provide a good reason for deciding the present case (Alexander 1989). Any purpose ascribed to tort law must be normatively justified, so the positive analysis of tort law cannot substitute for normative theory.

Not surprisingly, there has been much debate about the appropriate purpose of tort liability, with the most attention being paid to the competing claims that either corrective justice or wealth maximization provides the appropriate rationale for tort liability. Unfortunately, there is no consensus on the proper objective of tort liability, explaining why so much attention has been paid to the positive analysis of tort law. Those who believe that tort law should maximize wealth have often appealed to the theory's descriptive power as proof that "the logic of the law is really economics.[1] To rebut this claim, philosophers have argued that moral principles, typically based on corrective justice, provide a better description of tort practice.[2] This critique has two aspects. First, it shows how much of tort law implements moral principles. Second, it argues that the economic interpretation provides a poor explanation of important tort practices.

As Sections I and II below show, these objections to the positive economic analysis of tort law are answerable. This analysis does not show that wealth maximization provides a better description of tort law or a more defensible basis for tort liability. Instead, by showing that the economic and moral interpretations can each provide persuasive descriptions of tort practice, the analysis suggests that the two interpretations must share substantial similarities. Section III accordingly seeks to understand why the two interpretations are able to provide such good descriptions of tort practice. Despite their fundamental differences, each justifies an important subset of tort rules, albeit for different reasons. These rules therefore can be justified on the basis of an overlapping consensus. Of course, the overlapping consensus does not encompass all tort rules. Most notably, the conventional economic rationale for tort liability always requires deterrence, whereas the corrective justice rationale does not. But any form of tort liability is likely to have some deterrence impact, making it difficult to determine whether the justification for any given rule depends on deterrence or some other moral reason. Hence it is unsurprising that the economic and moral interpretations each yield persuasive descriptions of tort practice.

For various reasons, then, there are considerable obstacles faced by those who want to rely on positive analysis to resolve the issue of whether the tort system pursues an economic or moral objective. Positive analysis, however, has another, underappreciated role, one that connects economic analysis to moral reasoning rather than providing grounds for choosing between the economic and moral interpretations of tort law. As Section IV shows, economic analysis necessarily depends on moral argumentation regarding the way in which social welfare depends on individual welfare, an issue implicating the requirements or restrictions that inhere in the principles of equality and justice. Different versions of equality or justice yield different specifications of social welfare. Consequently, even though the conventional economic interpretation of tort law defines the social objective as one of maximizing utility or wealth, that definition is not required by modern welfare economics. The few restrictions that welfare economics places on the definition of social welfare are likely to be satisfied by any moral theory of tort law that operates within a domain defined by the injurious consequences of human behavior, a domain that includes most moral theories of tort law, including those based on corrective justice. The choice among the various moral theories depends on moral argumentation, rather than economic analysis, concerning the appropriate justification for tort liability. The economic analysis of tort law, in turn, is merely a form of positive analysis seeking to determine whether any given tort rule is likely to affect individual welfare in the normatively justified manner. Positive analysis therefore does not provide grounds for choosing between economic and moral interpretations of tort law; it is the ground that unites them.

## I. Positive Analysis of the Structure of Tort

Moral philosophers have provided convincing moral reasons that justify the tort system's reliance on case-by-case adjudication involving an injured plaintiff and a defendant who causally contributed to the injury. By definition, corrective justice seeks to restore an antecedent equality between two parties that was lost in an interaction between them. Consequently, "[t]he defendant's injuring of the plaintiff and the plaintiff's recovery of damages from the defendant are mutually connected, so that the procedure is the precisely appropriate response to what the defendant has done to the plaintiff."[3]

The conventional economic interpretation of this tort practice, by contrast, argues that it minimizes accident costs – the sum of injury and prevention costs – and therefore maximizes utility and wealth. Moral philosophers claim that this argument is lacking in important respects, leading them to conclude that positive analysis favors the moral over the economic interpretation.[4] In evaluating this claim, I will not dispute the moral justifications for the practice. Rather, I will show why the conventional economic interpretation can be refined so that it too can persuasively explain the structure of tort adjudication.

### A. Case-by-Case Adjudication

Moral philosophers have argued that the tort system is an unlikely institutional choice for minimizing accident costs, implying that its immanent purpose is unlikely to be based on economic considerations.[5] The premise of this argument has merit, particularly in light of economic analyses showing that case-by-case adjudication is not likely to generate the liability rules or the number of suits that minimize costs (Hadfield 1992; Shavell 1997). Hence I will grant the claim that the tort system is an imperfect regulatory institution for minimizing accident costs. I will also assume that the tort system is a perfect institution for implementing corrective justice. My argument is that this difference in institutional capabilities does not undermine the proposition that the tort system currently tries to minimize accident costs. The argument is based on an historical understanding of the origin and evolution of the tort system, an understanding derived from the work of legal historians who do not believe that the purpose of the tort system is based on utility or wealth maximization.

The argument is as follows. The tort system was initially designed in the twelfth and thirteenth centuries to implement corrective justice for cases in which the defendant criminally injured the plaintiff. The institution of case-by-case adjudication involving injurers and victims matured over the centuries and was highly developed when the industrial revolution occurred in the United States during the nineteenth century. As that century progressed, the common law changed in two fundamental ways that could have allowed judges to reorient the tort system so that it served an economic rather than corrective justice purpose. The writ system, in which formal procedural requirements often obscured considerations of the substantive law, was abolished, allowing judges for the first time to squarely face various substantive issues of tort law. In addition, the jurisprudence of the time rejected natural-law justifications for the common law in favor of instrumentalist justifications. The confluence of these two developments plausibly suggests that the structure of case-by-case adjudication, with its corrective justice origins, evolved during the nineteenth century into a system for regulating the increased number of accidental injuries characteristic of an industrialized society. As time passed, the tort system became even more entrenched, so that today it continues to serve as one of the primary social institutions for reducing accident costs, even though other modes of regulation might serve that economic goal more effectively.

1. Corrective justice origins of the tort system. In the early English common-law system, tort law – that is, civil actions for damages not based upon contract – grew out of the criminal law. The reasons for the initial connection between tort and criminal law are succinctly set forth by the English legal historian J. H. Baker:

In early societies there is no concept of the 'state.' Both compensation and retribution for wrongdoing are exacted at the instance of the wronged individual and his kin. Either there will be a feud between one family member and another until satisfaction is wrought, or the potential feud will be averted by customary arbitration processes designed to secure the payment of 'emendation' for the wrong. The purpose of emendation payments was overtly retributive, yet it was also compensatory: in modern language, it was both a fine and damages at the same time. In so far as feuds and their settlement were governed by rules about compensation, there was a law of wrongs. But there was no division of wrongs into crimes and torts. And the main purpose of introducing fixed law into the matter was to protect the wrongdoer against excessive private vengeance, rather than to punish him or deter others. (Baker 1990, p. 571)

One obvious method of protecting a wrongdoer against "excessive private vengeance" is to force him to compensate the victim of the crime, because doing so reduces the victim's need to make things even by exacting revenge. Such payment also penalizes the wrongdoer for the criminal conduct, and gives the victim added reason for initiating the suit or supplying proof of the crime to the authorities. For these and other reasons, the "king's courts . . . were approaching the field of tort through the field of crime."[6]

Tort actions were quasi-criminal until the late seventeenth century.[7] For approximately five centuries, then, tort liability exclusively addressed situations in which the defendant wrongfully (criminally) injured the plaintiff and was required to compensate the plaintiff for that wrong. These situations are paradigmatic examples of corrective justice. Hence there is little doubt that the tort system first developed as an institution for implementing corrective justice, explaining why the structure of tort adjudication fully reflects a corrective justice rationale.

2. The U.S. tort system in the eighteenth and nineteenth centuries. Shortly after the American Revolution, most states decided to retain the English common law, despite anti-British sentiments.[8] The reason was simple. According to the jurisprudence of the time, common-law doctrines were derived from principles of natural law. Due to the universal nature of these principles, legal decision makers thought that common-law doctrines for the most part were equally applicable in England and the United States.[9]

In the ensuing decades, legal decision makers rejected natural-law justifications in favor of more pragmatic, instrumentalist justifications. Whether this shift occurred before or after the Civil War is a point of some contention, but it is clear that judicial decision-making became increasingly pragmatic and policy oriented as the nineteenth century progressed.[10]

The tort system could not wholly reject its corrective justice origins in favor of an overtly instrumentalist approach, as any change in judicial decision-making is constrained by the requirements of *stare decisis* – the need to maintain consistency and uniformity of the law over time. But the constraints of *stare decisis* were considerably weakened during the nineteenth century. One by one, the states abolished the writ system, which used pleading requirements in a manner that often masked difficult issues of substantive law. Although this procedural reform was not supposed to affect the substantive law, eliminating the practice meant that some substantive issues of great importance, such as the choice between negligence and strict liability, were for the first time presented in their most general form to the courts.

The abolition of the writ system accordingly created an opportunity for tort law to evolve into something new. This opportunity occurred at a time when judges were increasingly embracing a pragmatic jurisprudence that conceptualized law as an evolutionary process rather than as a body of rules eternally fixed by principles of natural justice. The question, then, is how judges might have responded to this evolutionary opportunity. One way to assess how the jurisprudence of tort law might have changed in this period is to look at the criminal law. The historical connection between criminal and tort law suggests that changes in the jurisprudence of criminal law probably were reflected in tort law, particularly since most nineteenth-century lawyers handled both criminal and civil matters (Friedman 1985, p. 572).

"According to the new penology, the proper goal of criminal law was deterrence of crime and rehabilitation of the criminal" (Friedman 1985, p. 281, note 14). Relatedly, criminal laws in the nineteenth century were often used to regulate business conduct.[11] But "[t]he multiplication of economic crimes did not mean, necessarily, that people looked on sharp business behavior with more and more a sense of moral outrage. [Rather], the states, and the federal government, invoked criminal law more and more in one of its historic functions – as a low level, low-paid administrative aid" (Freedman 1985, p. 584).

It made sense for state governments to use the court system as an "administrative aid" because other types of state regulatory institutions were not well developed at the time. "Two pillars of the modern state were missing: a strong tax base and a trained civil service. Without these two, and perhaps without a firmer grip on economic information, the state could not hope to master and control behavior in the market" (Freedman 1985, p. 185). Due to the lack of regulatory alternatives, the court system was probably the most effective regulatory mechanism available to the states during this period.[12]

Given that the criminal law was used for such instrumental, regulatory purposes, it would be extraordinary if tort law were not used for similar purposes. Moreover, the need to use tort law as a method of regulating business practices became more pronounced as the century progressed, because increased industrialization and use of technology, particularly the railroad, substantially increased the number of personal injuries.[13] A pressing social need to regulate business conduct in light of an increasing number of accidental injuries; the increased use of the criminal law to regulate business conduct; and a jurisprudence that sanctioned the use of the common law to pursue pragmatic ends – all undoubtedly influenced the judicial approach to tort law, making it quite likely that judges in this era fashioned tort rules to minimize the accident costs of industrial enterprise.

The changes in tort law during the period were profound. Many legal historians attribute the development of the modern tort system to the industrial revolution.[14] The attribution becomes particularly plausible in light of the fact that no treatises were published on the law of torts, in either England or the United States, before 1850 (Friedman 1985, p. 299). The numerous changes that occurred in the nineteenth century in turn strongly suggest that the tort system evolved from a system of corrective justice to a regulatory institution concerned about reducing accident costs, a conclusion supported by Gary Schwartz's study of tort law in this period:

Two [themes that recurred in the case law] were a judicial concern for the risks created by modern enterprise and a judicial willingness to deploy liability rules so as to control those risks. Another set of themes included a judicial solicitude for the victims of enterprise-occasioned accidents and a judicial willingness to resolve uncertainties in the law liberally in favor of those victims' opportunities to secure recoveries. (Schwartz 1988 p. 665)

Although Schwartz argues that his study does not support the thesis that nineteenth-century tort law was based on an economic rationale, the themes he finds are broadly consistent with the minimization of accident costs.[15] Similarly, although Morton Horwitz claims the historical record shows that courts in this period altered tort doctrine for the instrumental purpose of subsidizing business development (Horwitz 1977), his findings can also be construed as being broadly consistent with the requirements of wealth maximization (Hovenkamp 1983; Williams 1978).

The crucial issue is not whether the historical record shows that the nineteenth-century tort system minimized accident costs. That result would be surprising, for as will become apparent below, there are numerous reasons why the tort system is unlikely to maximize wealth. Rather, the more interesting conclusion is that the historical record shows that the tort system in the nineteenth century began pursuing the instrumentalist objectives of compensation and deterrence in a manner consistent with the minimization of accident costs.

3. Continued reliance on the tort system despite its high cost. Even though the tort system was the best available institution for regulating accidents in the nineteenth century, the rise of the administrative state in the twentieth century means that other forms of regulation are now feasible. Whether the tort system continues to be the best institution for minimizing accident costs is highly debatable.[16] For purposes of argument, suppose another form of regulation is more effective at reducing accident costs than the tort system. This supposition is thought to undermine the proposition that the immanent purpose of the tort system is based on economic considerations. After all, if society truly wanted to minimize accident costs, wouldn't it eliminate the tort system in favor of a regulatory institution more capable of achieving that goal? The continued existence of the tort system in light of less costly regulatory alternatives therefore could imply that the immanent purpose of tort liability is not based on an economic rationale.

Despite the logic of this argument, the availability of more effective regulatory institutions does not undermine the economic justification for the tort system. Understanding why requires some understanding of institutional choice.[17] Once society has invested in an institution, whether change is cost-effective depends on how the costs of change compare with its benefits. Consider a road that for historical reasons is quite curvy. Over time, development occurs along the road. Today, all else being equal, a straight road would be a less costly transportation route. But all else is not equal. The advantages of a straight road can only be obtained at the costs of displacing existing development along the curvy road. These costs could outweigh the benefits of the straighter road. Consequently, although a straight road reduces transportation costs, it is not necessarily cost-effective for society to replace the curvy road with a straight one.

These same considerations apply to regulatory institutions. Even if there were a regulatory institution that could reduce accident costs more effectively than the tort system, replacing the tort system would create various displacement costs. Not only would those who work in the current system have to change jobs, but the new institution would have its own start-up costs. Errors would be made, and there would be other costs of transition until there were sufficient learning for the new institution to function properly. The displacement and transition costs in the aggregate may exceed any benefits that would occur if the tort system were replaced by the other regulatory institution. Thus, it can make sense for society to continue its reliance on the tort system to reduce accident costs, even if a different form of regulation would be more effective at reducing accident costs.

Moreover, even if it would be cost-effective to change regulatory institutions, that change must be legislatively implemented. The various costs that individuals or groups would incur due to the displacement of the tort system give them a substantial incentive for forming interests groups to defeat such legislation. Interest groups could block any cost-effective change for a variety of reasons, many of which are reflected in the current political struggle over tort reform.[18] Hence the existence or possibility of more cost-effective regulatory institutions says nothing about the immanent purpose of the tort system.

## B. The Role of Injurers and Victims, and the Significance of Causality

Despite the good reasons for concluding that tort law has evolved into a form of economic regulation, the viability of the economic interpretation depends on whether courts have adopted tort doctrines that minimize accident costs. Perhaps the most pressing question in this respect is why an economically oriented tort system would rely on case-by-case adjudication involving injurers and their victims? An evolutionary tort system could have retained case-by-case adjudication in an effort to minimize accident costs, while eliminating the common-law requirement that the plaintiff must have suffered an injury caused by the defendant's tortious conduct. Explaining the role of injurers and victims, and the requirement of causation that connects the two parties, is particularly important for those committed to an economic interpretation of tort law, because moral philosophers have made strong arguments that these tort practices are inadequately explained by the economic interpretation of tort law.

According to the conventional economic explanation, giving victims full compensation for their injuries gives them the necessary financial incentive to sue their injurers. Imposing such liability on injurers in turn gives risk-creating actors an incentive to reduce risk in a cost-effective manner. The requirement of causation, according to this account, is not analytically necessary: "If the purpose of tort law is to promote economic efficiency, a defendant's conduct will be deemed the cause of an injury when making him liable for the consequences of the injury will promote an efficient allocation of resources to safety and care" (Landes and Posner 1987, p. 229).

Although this explanation is logically coherent, moral philosophers claim it is an implausible justification for these important tort practices. This critique has obvious merit. Any party, not only the victim, could be enticed to sue in-

jurers in exchange for sufficient tort compensation. Moreover, risk-creating actors would take the cost-minimizing amount of care if they were exposed to liability whenever they failed to take such care, whether or not their failure to do
so caused injury. The tort practice of limiting the class of defendants to those
who created a tortious risk that caused injury to the plaintiff accordingly needs
further economic justification. Such justification is readily available.

Consider the role of the injurer. Typically, the common-law requirement of
misfeasance limits the class of potential defendants to those who created or contributed to a risk that caused the plaintiff's injury, even though other parties
could have prevented the injury. Whether this requirement is cost-effective depends on whether accident costs would be further reduced by a more expansive
duty requiring an individual who did not create a risk to take actions to help another who is subjected to that peril. Although such a duty to rescue would reduce the number of accidents, it would significantly increase precaution costs.
Whether the duty minimizes accident cost – the sum of injury and prevention
costs – accordingly depends on how various empirical issues are resolved.[19]
Absent the empirical evidence that would resolve these difficult issues, there is
no reason for concluding that the common-law requirement of misfeasance is
not cost-effective.

Now consider the role played by the victim, including the requirement of causation. As Ernest Weinrib has pointed out, "[c]ausation becomes pertinent only
when we focus on the plaintiff's receipt from the defendant of an amount of
money representing the harm suffered" (Weinrib 1987, p. 414). This observation is consistent with an economic justification for the causation requirement.

To see why the economic interpretation of causation focuses on the harm
suffered by the plaintiff, consider how damages would be calculated if the plaintiff suffered no harm. In theory, if the defendant were forced to pay the average
amount of damages defined by reference to the parties exposed to the risk, then
risk-creating actors would have the correct incentive for reducing risk.[20] This
approach would obviate the need for having a victim initiate the tort suit, as anyone could establish average damages. However, if these damages were set too
low, there would be an insufficient safety incentive, whereas if the damages
were set too high, risk-creating actors could take too much care (Shavell 1987,
p. 131). Such erroneous damages calculations would be common. The correct
estimation of the average damages award requires information about the range
and frequency of damages that could be suffered by the group of potential victims, information that typically will not be available to a court. Estimates of the
average damages award based on incomplete information are likely to be erroneous. The resultant error costs can be avoided, and the correct safety incentive
maintained, if courts instead undertake the more limited factual inquiry concerning the actual harm suffered by an individual victim, and then make the defendant liable for those damages. The savings in information and error costs
provide an economic justification for basing the damages award on the full
amount of damages suffered by a particular victim.[21] The economic rationale

for fully compensatory damages, in turn, justifies the requirement of causation, because "[c]ausation becomes pertinent only when we focus on the plaintiff's receipt from the defendant of an amount of money representing the harm suffered."

The requirement of causation reduces error costs in another way. To determine the optimal level of care, courts need data pertaining to the range and frequency of damages that could be suffered by those exposed to the risk, the same data needed to derive good estimates of average damages. The difficulty that courts face in estimating average damages therefore implies that they often will be unable to set the standard of care at the optimal level. The possibility of court error in setting the standard of care, and the resultant uncertainty, tends to give risk-creating actors an incentive to exercise more than the cost-effective amount of care. These error costs, however, are reduced by the cause-in-fact requirement: when courts perfectly enforce this requirement, total accident costs are lower than when courts underenforce the requirement (Marks 1994, p. 287).

These considerations also explain why the tort claim must be pursued by the victim rather than a third party. The need to determine the actual damages suffered by the victim of the tortious conduct leaves little reason for expecting that a third party would be more capable of proving those damages, particularly pain and suffering. And even if a third party were as capable as the victim in this respect, the monetary compensation ordinarily will be more valuable to the victim, who has suffered a loss, than to the third party. Interpreting the role of the victim-plaintiff in this manner not only is consistent with economic considerations, it also is consistent with historical understandings.[22]

Suits between injurers and their victims therefore make a great deal of economic sense. According to this account, this tort practice is a cost-effective way of giving risk-creating actors the appropriate incentives for minimizing accident costs. To be sure, this analysis provides further reasons for concluding that the tort system is an imperfect institution for minimizing accident costs. But as argued earlier, such imperfections do not undermine the economic interpretation of tort law. Rather, the crucial point is that tort practice pertaining to injurers, victims, and the causal relation between the two, appears to rely on the most cost-effective approach that courts could feasibly implement. The economic interpretation of tort liability accordingly provides a satisfactory account of these important practices, leaving no persuasive reason why positive analysis favors the moral rather than the economic interpretation of this aspect of tort law.

## II. Positive Analysis of Substantive Tort Law

Negligence is probably the most significant form of tort liability. Moral philosophers have argued that important negligence doctrines are more readily explained in moral rather than economic terms. As before, I will accept the claim that these practices can be morally justified and argue that they also have a persuasive economic justification.

## A. Objective Versus Subjective Valuation of Individual Interests

Risky behavior promotes the actor's individual interests while threatening the interests of third parties. Whether someone should forego such behavior in order to reduce risk therefore requires a valuation of the relevant interests. Under current tort law, individual interests are evaluated objectively rather than in terms of the individual's own subjective valuation.[23]

An objective valuation of interests can be morally justified on the ground that it treats both parties to the lawsuit equally, whereas a subjective standard would let the injurer set the terms of the relationship unilaterally, violating the principle of equality according to some moral theories.[24] An economic justification for this doctrine, by contrast, would seem to be more problematic. An objective, uniform valuation of interests does not account for individual differences, so it cannot yield tort rules that are cost-effective for each person.

Despite this problem, the conventional economic interpretation of tort law finds this tort practice to be economically justified. A negligence standard defined in terms of the subjective valuations of the plaintiff and defendant would require interpersonal comparisons of utility. Economists have long eschewed this type of analysis due, in part, to the difficulty of observing and verifying subjective valuations.[25] And even if such valuation were feasible, it would be more expensive to administer than the objective standard. Consequently, the savings in administrative costs are likely to outweigh any benefit that would stem from the use of a subjective standard, implying that the objective standard is probably cost-effective (Landes and Posner 1987, pp. 121–31; Shavell 1987, p. 76).

Whether this tort practice is better described by the economic or moral interpretation is hard to determine, particularly since each relies on rationales that have long been recognized by courts and commentators.[26] Moral philosophers nevertheless reject the economic interpretation on the ground that it makes the tort system's reliance on objective valuations contingent on informational problems, whereas an objective valuation of interests is desirable as a matter of moral principle. This argument is unpersuasive, however. Economic arguments are necessarily fact dependent, making any economic justification contingent in that sense. Moreover, the economic justification of the objective standard is not necessarily contingent on informational problems, as there is no compelling reason for assuming that a tort system committed to the reduction of accident costs would rely on subjective valuations if it were possible to do so.

Economic analysis typically takes tastes or preferences as given or exogenous to the analysis, seeking instead to determine the consequences that flow from individuals' self-interested attempts to satisfy their (given) preferences.[27] Yet, economists, influenced by sociology, psychology, and other disciplines, have recognized that economic behavior can affect the formation of preferences, so that standard economic analysis yields incorrect conclusions in some instances unless it properly accounts for the possibility of endogenous preferences.[28] Importantly, there seems to be an emerging view, held by economists and noneconomists alike, that social and legal norms are important determinants of individual preferences.[29] The norms expressed by tort rules therefore may shape individual preferences in a manner not sufficiently captured by the conventional economic analysis of tort law, suggesting that an objective valuation of individual interests may be desirable due to the way in which such valuation influences individual preferences for creating risk.[30]

Suppose the tort system were to rely on subjective valuations. If an individual could avoid negligence liability merely because she derived great pleasure from an activity that exposed others to unreasonable risk, then the norm expressed by this tort practice tells people that it is permissible to injure others as long as you derive a significant benefit, of any type, from the risky activity. One message sent by such a norm is that it is socially acceptable for individuals to feel good about imposing risks on others. Insofar as this norm enhances a preference that individuals have for engaging in risky behavior, the tort system would be increasing the amount of risk in society. Compare this outcome to the one produced by an objective standard. If an individual faces negligence liability even though she greatly benefited from the risky activity, then the norm expressed by the tort rule tells people that certain motivations for such behavior are not acceptable. One message sent by such a norm is that it is *not* socially acceptable for individuals to feel good about imposing risks on others. Insofar as such a norm diminishes any preference or desire that individuals have for engaging in such behavior, an objective valuation of interests will reduce risk relative to the level that obtains in a system that subjectively values interests.[31]

A subjective standard also allows for various kinds of undesirable strategic behavior. It would give risk-creating actors an incentive to be uninformed or otherwise poorly positioned to reduce risks, for these diminished capabilities would often relieve actors of the duty to take the precautions required of those who are better informed or positioned to reduce risks. A subjective standard also makes it more difficult for potential victims to determine how much precaution they should take to protect themselves from being injured by others. The resultant uncertainty could cause risk-averse potential victims to exercise too much care. An objective standard, by contrast, eliminates this problem: the amount of care required by the negligence standard cannot be manipulated by potential injurers, and potential victims can take cost-minimizing precautions by assuming that others are conforming to the objective standard.[32] Interestingly, these problems of strategic behavior are reflected in the moral argument rejecting the subjective standard on the ground that it would be undesirable if injurers could unilaterally set the terms of the relationship.

Hence the objective valuation of interests has at least two persuasive economic rationales. First, as conventionally stated, the approach avoids the intractable administrative difficulties that would arise if the system were to rely

on subjective valuations. In addition, objective valuations are more likely to reduce risk and the total cost of safety precautions. The norm expressed by a tort
rule represents a social expression of appropriate behavior, making it likely that
the subjective valuation of interests would increase risk over the levels attained
by an objective valuation of interests. A tort rule wholly dependent on individual characteristics can also be manipulated by self-interested behavior, making
it likely that some of the burden of risk reduction would be inefficiently shifted
from potential injurers to potential victims. For these reasons, a tort system that
seeks to minimize accident costs probably would rely on an objective valuation
of interests, even if subjective valuations were feasible. The positive analysis of
tort law therefore fails to yield any persuasive reason why the objective valuation of interests favors the economic or moral conceptions of tort law.[33]

## B. Weighting Individual Interests

Tort liability protects the interest that potential victims have in being free of injury, while at the same time it burdens the economic or liberty interests of potential injurers by requiring them to take safety precautions or pay damages.
Because more (or less) tort liability promotes or protects the interests of one
group while burdening the other, there is a moral issue regarding the appropriate reconciliation of these conflicting interests. Differing positions on this issue underlie much of the disagreement about the fairness of cost-minimizing
tort rules.

One group of moral theories gives equal weight to the interests of injurers
and victims. This form of equality is the essential characteristic of utilitarianism, so these moral theories can be called utilitarian.[34] The utilitarian weighting of interests justifies cost-effective tort rules. Accident costs are minimized
by a tort rule requiring safety precautions up to the point at which the additional
or marginal cost of the precaution (borne by potential injurers) equals the marginal benefit of risk reduction (received by potential victims). To reject a cost-
minimizing rule in favor of an alternative liability rule would burden one set of
interests by more than the protection provided to the other set of interests. Giving equal weight to the interests of the respective parties accordingly requires
the adoption of cost-minimizing liability rules.

Other moral theories, by contrast, give greater weight to safety considerations than to economic concerns, reasoning that the interest potential victims
have in their physical security is more important than the burdens imposed on
potential injurers (Keating 1996, pp. 349–60; Weinrib 1995, pp. 147–52;
Wright 1995, pp. 249–75). The principle that "safety matters more than
money" would seem to justify safety precautions greater than the cost-minimizing amount. Although a tort rule that required such precautions would impose economic or liberty burdens on potential injurers that exceed the safety

benefit conferred on potential victims, the added weight given to safety interests can justify the liability rule.

Whether tort rules minimize accident costs would seem to depend on whether tort practice gives safety interests equal or greater weight than economic interests. The principle that safety matters more than money is firmly established in the context of intentional torts.[35] This principle is also reflected in the disproportionate standard for negligence liability, which gives proportionately greater weight to safety interests as the risk in question increases. Under this standard, potential injurers have a duty to take safety precautions that do not cost disproportionately more than the safety benefit created by the precaution. The standard apparently has been adopted by the English and Commonwealth courts (Gilles 1994; Keating 1996, pp. 349–60), and some scholars argue that courts in the United States also rely on it (Wright 1995, pp. 260–1). Others, including legal economists, argue that courts in the United States use a cost–benefit standard for negligence (the Learned Hand Formula) that gives equal weight to safety and liberty interests (Posner 1972).

It is unclear how the tort system actually weights individual interests in negligence actions. Although the *Restatement (Second) of Torts* explicitly adopts the Learned Hand cost–benefit test, the vast majority of jurisdictions in the United States rely on jury instructions that define negligence in terms of how a reasonably prudent person would act under the circumstances (Gilles 1994). The few jurisdictions that require more specific guidelines use jury instructions general enough to be consistent with both the cost–benefit and disproportionate standard. The generality of the jury instructions on negligence enables one to argue for or against the positive claim that juries use the cost–benefit negligence standard.[36]

Although it is difficult to determine what the tort system is actually doing in this regard, the conventional economic interpretation is unpersuasive, for it seems implausible that an economically oriented tort system would rely upon a generalized jury instruction that gives jurors the opportunity to apply something other than the Learned Hand cost–benefit test. That conclusion, however, is based on the erroneous assumption that it would always be economically desirable for juries to apply the Hand Formula. The stronger economic argument is that a generalized jury instruction is likely to be more cost-effective across a range of cases.

The Hand Formula compares the cost of a safety precaution with a benefit defined solely in terms of the expected cost of the injuries that would be avoided if the precaution were taken. This negligence standard does not fully account for risk aversion – the cost individuals incur when exposed to risk that is additional to the expected cost of injury. Most people are risk averse.[37] Consequently, safety precautions typically have two benefits: reduction in the expected cost of injury, and reduction in the cost of risk aversion. Because the Hand Formula adequately accounts for only one of these benefits, it may require less safety than would be cost-effective.

To be sure, law-and-economics scholars have claimed that there is no need for the Hand Formula to account for the costs of risk aversion (Landes and Posner 1987, p. 57). This claim is only partially true, however. Insofar as risk-averse individuals are fully insured, they will behave as if they are risk neutral when choosing safety precautions.[38] In these cases, the Hand Formula will minimize accident costs. But tort plaintiffs are not fully insured against all tortiously caused injuries. They do not receive compensation for legal expenses, which typically consume about one-third of their total compensation,[39] nor can they purchase insurance coverage for such expenses. Tort plaintiffs also do not receive compensation for every type of nonmonetary injury caused by tortfeasors, nor can they fully insure themselves against such injuries. Most jurisdictions, for example, do not allow damages for the victim's lost enjoyment of life in wrongful death actions (Tabbacchi 1991). And even if such damages were available, the tort award would not always represent the kind of "full compensation" that is required to eliminate considerations of risk aversion.[40] For a broad range of tort cases, then, potential tort victims are not fully insured, implying that the economic analysis of negligence must account for the cost of risk aversion.

Unlike the Learned Hand cost–benefit negligence standard, the disproportionate negligence standard can fully account for risk aversion. As potential victims are exposed to increasingly higher risks, they can incur a higher cost of risk aversion in addition to the cost of injury threatened by the risk. Consequently, if safety interests are defined solely in terms of the expected cost of injury, to account for risk aversion these interests should be given proportionately greater weight as the risk increases. The disproportionate negligence standard operates in this manner, which is why it can be more cost-effective than the Hand cost–benefit negligence standard. By this same reasoning, the Hand Formula for negligence tends to be more cost-effective when the tortious risk threatens monetary damages for which insurance is available, because individuals are significantly less likely to be risk averse with respect to such losses.

The cost-minimizing negligence standard accordingly depends on the type of case, suggesting that a uniform negligence standard applicable to all cases could be less effective than the current tort practice of instructing jurors that negligence depends upon how a reasonably prudent person would act under the circumstances. Jurors are likely to feel that safety matters more than money when the risk threatens nonmonetary injuries such as death. If so, they are likely to apply the disproportionate negligence standard, which can be the more cost-effective rule for these cases. For cases in which the risk threatens only monetary injury such as property damage, jurors are more likely to equate safety with money. If so, they are likely to apply the cost–benefit negligence standard, which tends to be the better rule for cases of this type. Hence there is no compelling reason for concluding that this tort practice favors the economic or moral interpretation of tort law.

### III. Implications of the Positive Analysis of Tort Law

Of the many lessons that could be drawn from the positive analysis of tort law, one seems clear: the important tort doctrines can be adequately interpreted in economic or moral terms. That the two interpretations can explain so much of tort law suggests that they can each justify substantially similar tort practices. Despite this rather obvious point, few tort scholars have shown interest in exploring whether an overlapping consensus might be sufficient to justify important tort practices.[41] For this reason, it is worth trying to identify the common ground shared by the economic and moral interpretations of tort law. Identifying the overlapping consensus also helps to identify the differences between the interpretations. The nature of these differences explains why positive analysis is unlikely to favor one interpretation over the other.

The structural aspects of the two interpretations can be developed by analyzing how tort liability implicates the individual interests in liberty and security that "have always, historically speaking, been of central concern to tort law."[42] By focusing on these interests, it becomes clear why the economic and moral interpretations of tort law each justify substantially similar tort practices.

First, consider the relevant interests of potential victims. The fact of injury grounds all of tort liability, making it necessary to conceptualize how a victim can be injured. Some injuries, such as those involving fungible property, would be eliminated for the victim if she were given enough money to repair the damage or purchase an identical good. Absent the receipt of this money, these injuries burden the economic, liberty interests of victims. Other injuries, such as physical injury, cannot be fully cured by the receipt of money. One who suffers such injury is changed by it; monetary compensation will help the victim, but money will not fully restore what has been damaged. These injuries therefore do not burden the economic, liberty interest of individuals, but instead burden their interest in maintaining physical integrity – the security interest.[43]

The requirement of equality also mandates consideration of the interests of those who must bear the burdens of tort liability – potential injurers. The burdens of tort liability involve the expenditure of money (for liability judgments and safety devices) or effort. Tort rules accordingly only implicate the liberty interests of risk-creating actors, whereas they implicate the liberty and security interests of potential victims. Promoting or protecting the interests of one group necessarily burdens the interests of the other. These competing interests must be mediated by the principle of equality.

Consider a form of tort liability that does not reduce risk. Absent risk reduction, tort liability merely involves wealth transfers between injurers and victims, thereby implicating only the liberty interests of the two parties. The liberty interests of one party must necessarily be burdened. If the liberty interests of the two parties are to be treated equally pursuant to the relevant moral theory, then the party who is least burdened by the loss must bear it. A tort rule that satisfies this requirement also minimizes the cost of injury compensation and therefore maximizes wealth. (The cost of precaution is not relevant because this form of liability does not affect risk.) In these cases, then, both the economic and moral rationales justify the same tort practice.

Moral theories, however, do not require that liberty interests always be given equal weight. Most notably, for some theories the liberty interests of potential injurers are not given the same weight or respect as the liberty interests of potential victims absent a sufficiently good reason for the risky behavior. What type of reasons justify risky behavior is determined by an objective valuation of interests. This class of cases therefore implicates the question of whether the tort system should use objective or subjective valuations of interests. As previously discussed in Section II.A, both the economic and moral rationales for tort liability justify the objective valuation of interests. The two rationales do not necessarily justify the same objective valuations, but there is a substantial overlap between the two.

The final set of cases involve situations in which tort liability reduces risk, thereby protecting the interest that potential victims have in their physical security. The justification for tort liability no longer depends upon a comparison of the liberty interests of potential injurers and victims, as occurs in settings of no risk reduction, but instead depends upon how the liberty interests of potential injurers compare with the liberty and security interests of potential victims. Adding the security interests of potential victims to the mix makes it easier to justify any given burden imposed on the liberty interests of potential injurers. The more that tort law deters, the more easily it can be justified.

How much risk reduction any given form of tort liability must achieve to make it justifiable depends on how liberty and security interests are weighted. As previously discussed in Section II.B, both the economic and moral rationales for tort liability countenance an approach that gives security interests greater weight than liberty interests. Indeed, the similarity of the two approaches for resolving this critical issue helps to explain why such a weighting of interests finds justification in the utilitarian moral theory of John Stuart Mill and the nonutilitarian moral theories of Immanuel Kant and John Rawls.[44] To be sure, the economic and moral rationales for tort liability might diverge over the appropriate degree to which safety interests should outweigh economic interests, but this difference, if it exists, ought not to obscure the more important point that risk reduction makes it easier to justify tort liability under either rationale, creating a substantial similarity that helps to explain why each can offer descriptively powerful explanations of tort practice.

Deterrence considerations also largely explain why the economic and moral interpretations can each yield good descriptions of important tort practices, despite the structural differences of the two approaches. According to the economic interpretation, a tort rule can minimize accident costs only if it reduces risk. (This is because of the relatively high cost of providing injury compensation through the tort system as compared to other currently available modes of compensation, such as first-party insurance.) In theory, most forms of tort liability are likely to reduce risk, giving proponents of the economic interpretation the necessary deterrence rationale for the tort practice in question. Consequently, even if proponents of a moral interpretation can also give persuasive reasons for the tort practice that is not dependent on risk reduction, it is difficult to determine whether the justification for the practice depends on deterrence or some other moral reason.

## IV. Positive Analysis: The Link Between Economics and Moral Philosophy

Although tort law can be adequately described in terms of utility or wealth maximization, neither of those objectives adequately describe the economic analysis of tort law. Economic analysis does not justify or depend upon any particular objective of tort law, including utility or wealth maximization. Rather, the economic analysis of tort law can only help determine the forms of tort liability most likely to further the appropriate purposes of the tort system. Those purposes cannot be derived by economic analysis, but instead depend on moral justification. Hence the economic analysis of tort law is nothing more than a positive analysis that complements, rather than competes with, the appropriate moral theory of tort law.

The limited, positive role of economic analysis stems from the focus of welfare economics on the maximization of social welfare. Welfare economics requires some relationship between social welfare and individual well-being, but the way in which social welfare depends on individual welfare is not prescribed by economic analysis. Social welfare could consist of the aggregation of individual utilities, for example, with each individual receiving equal weight. Social welfare defined in this manner finds moral justification in utilitarianism. Alternatively, social welfare could be defined exclusively in terms of the well-being of the individuals who are worst off in society. Such a social-welfare function finds moral justification in the work of John Rawls (1971). Numerous other social-welfare functions are possible. Which of them ought to be used depends on moral argumentation regarding the merits of proposed formulation. That choice cannot be made by economic analysis. Instead, economic analysis can only determine whether any given social practice is likely to maximize the social-welfare function otherwise justified by moral argumentation.

Economic analysis obviously requires a social-welfare function that is capable of being maximized. These requirements are few in number. As Paul Samuelson, one of the founders of modern welfare economics, describes them:

[W]e take as a starting point . . . a function of all the economic magnitudes of a system which is supposed to characterize some ethical belief. . . . We only require that the belief be such as to admit of an unequivocal answer as to whether one configuration of the economic system is 'better' or 'worse' than any other or 'indifferent,' and that these relationships are transitive; i.e., A is better than B, B better than C, implies A better than C, etc. . . . Utilizing one out of an infinity of possible indicators or cardinal indices, we may write this function in the form

$$W = W(z1, z2, \ldots )$$

where the z's represent all possible variables, many of them non-economic in character.[45]

In addition to the requirements of completeness and transitivity, economists often impose an additional condition that the social-welfare function must depend non-negatively on individual utilities, which means that social welfare is increased by any action that makes at least one person better off and no one worse off (the Pareto principle). Such a social-welfare function is called "individualistic" or "welfarist" because it makes all questions of social ordering entirely dependent on individual-utility orderings (Sen 1982a).

The few essential requirements for a social-welfare function are likely to be satisfied by any plausible moral theory of tort law that limits tort liability to behavior resulting in injury. As described earlier, such a moral theory determines the weights to be given to the liberty and security interests of potential injurers and victims in any given context. This moral theory accordingly specifies the "ethical belief" that the social-welfare function should reflect that weighting of individual interests for the entire range of injurious conduct (the requirement of completeness). As long as the theory is also logically consistent (transitive), it can be translated into a social-welfare function.

Consider a moral theory that justifies tort liability for a given form of injurious conduct on the ground that the liberty interests of potential injurers who engage in such behavior deserve less weight or respect than the liberty and security interests of potential victims. In effect, this moral theory defines a social-welfare function that gives zero weight to the individual benefit derived from conduct that is morally inadequate or blameworthy and causes injury to another. According to this definition of social welfare, morally objectionable risky behavior has no social benefit, but creates a social cost captured by the decreased welfare of the individual who suffers injury. Morally objectionable conduct that causes injury necessarily reduces social welfare, then, so tort liability that deterred such conduct, e.g., would increase social welfare.

In this case, economic analysis is appropriately limited to determining the form of liability rule that would deter such morally objectionable conduct at minimal cost.[46] Economic analysis cannot answer the question of whether such conduct *should* be deterred, because modern welfare economics provides no grounds for rejecting this definition of social welfare. Presumably, the social-welfare function (that is, the underlying moral theory) is capable of yielding a consistent answer to the question of whether one configuration of the economic system (no tort liability of a particular type) is better or worse than another configuration (tort liability of that type). As long as this definition of social welfare enables one to make complete and transitive welfare judgments over alternative social states, it satisfies the essential requirements of welfare economics.

To be sure, this non-utilitarian social-welfare function does not conform to the conventional economic interpretation of tort law, nor does it conform to the social-welfare function typically used by economists.[47] In particular, a nonutilitarian social-welfare function might not satisfy the Pareto principle, because that principle cannot accommodate the moral concern for protecting individual rights.[48] The Pareto principle asks only who prefers what, and disregards entirely the reasons for each preference. For nonutilitarian moral theories, these reasons typically matter, as in the foregoing example involving tort liability for "morally objectionable" conduct. Not surprisingly, then, there is a conflict between rights-based nonutilitarian concerns and the Pareto principle: "Non-utility considerations cannot be immovable objects if utility considerations, even in a rather limited context (as in the Pareto principle), are made into an irresistible force" ( Sen 1987, pp. 382, 388). But even if the Pareto principle is violated by a nonutilitarian moral theory of tort law, the economist *qua* economist has no reason for rejecting that moral theory. The Pareto principle requires that social welfare be defined solely in terms of individual welfare. Welfare economics, by contrast, only requires that social welfare be somewhat dependent on individual welfare, explaining why economic analysis does not require adherence to the Pareto principle.

The requirement that social welfare be somewhat dependent on individual welfare is likely to be satisfied by any plausible moral theory of tort law. The domain of tort law is defined by the injurious consequences of human behavior. Those consequences obviously affect individual welfare, so any moral theory of tort law, including noninstrumental justifications, must pay at least some attention to the impact of tort liability on individual welfare. The social-welfare function implicitly defined by a moral interpretation of tort law therefore depends at least somewhat on individual welfare, providing the necessary connection between the moral philosophy of tort law and modern welfare economics.

## Conclusion

Moral philosophers have offered cogent criticisms of the positive economic analysis of tort law. Those who believe that the tort system minimizes accident costs can counter this criticism. The economic and moral interpretations each provide good explanations of important tort practices. This conclusion suggests that the two theories complement each other in ways that have not been adequately appreciated. The overlapping consensus, for example, might be sufficient to justify various tort practices. As I have argued elsewhere, the current rule of strict liability for abnormally dangerous activities can be justified in this way (Geistfeld 1998).

A focus on the positive analysis of tort law reveals a different connection between economic analysis and moral philosophy, however. Economic analysis is incomplete. The purpose of a social practice – that is, the specification of the social-welfare function – is largely outside the domain of economics. Consequently, the economic analysis of tort law cannot provide a moral justification for tort law; it can only determine whether a tort rule furthers the morally justified purpose of tort law.[49] Hence economic analysis is a form of positive analysis that can only complement, rather than displace, moral theories of tort law.

Indeed, a moral theory concerned about how tort liability affects liberty and security interests must rely on the economic analysis of tort law. To understand how tort liability affects the economic liberty interests of injurers and victims, one must know about the cost of different types of compensation and insurance systems. To understand how tort liability can protect security interests, one must have a theory of how individuals respond to the incentives created by tort liability. The economic analysis of tort law addresses both sets of issues. The failure to incorporate the economic understanding of these issues into moral theories of tort law is likely to yield liability rules that do not promote or protect liberty and security interests in the morally justified manner. Economic and moral reasoning therefore complement one another as long as the underlying moral philosophy of tort law centers on the question of how to protect some individuals without overly infringing on the liberty of others.

### Notes

[1] Posner (1975, p. 764). The claim that tort law maximizes wealth is developed most extensively in Landes and Posner (1987). Usually I will refer to the conventional economic approach as one that seeks to maximize wealth, even though law-and-economics scholars do not all share the notion that wealth maximization is the appropriate goal of tort law. A more defensible approach seeks to maximize social welfare rather than to maximize wealth. Despite this important analytical difference, the two approaches have tended to be similar in practice. This is because economically oriented torts scholars have defined social welfare in terms that are essentially utilitarian, so that social welfare is usually maximized by tort rules that minimize the sum of prevention costs and injury costs. See, e.g., Shavell (1987). See also infra note 34 (explaining that utilitarianism is characterized by the equal weighting of different individual interests). A tort rule that minimizes the sum of prevention costs and injury costs also maximizes wealth, so the two approaches justify the same rules.

2  For persuasive arguments of this type, see Coleman (1992a); Keating (1996); Weinrib (1995); Wright (1995).

3  Weinrib (1989c, p. 511). See also Coleman (1992a, pp. 374–85).

4  Many moral philosophers find this to be the most persuasive critique of the economic account. See, e.g., Perry (1996).

5  For example, Stephen Perry argues that the economic understanding of tort law is problematic because one could imagine a less costly system in which "victims had to bear their own losses and injurers were required to pay to the state, rather than to the victim, fines equal to the harm done or taxes equal to expected loss" (Perry 1996, p. 67). Such a system would require some form of administrative regulation to compute and collect the appropriate taxes, and thus does not depend upon case-by-case adjudication in the tort system.

6  Pollock and Maitland (1898, p. 530). See also Milsom (1981, p. 285): "[A]ll wrongs are criminal, presumably because there is offence to the community as well as to the victim so that penal consequences may follow. But of course penal consequences did not exclude redress for the victim; and if he himself brought the charges home to the wrongdoer, then he might recover goods taken or other compensation, and the wrongdoer would still be punished."; Keeton (1984, p. 8): "Originally the two remedies [criminal and tort] were administered by the same court, and in the same action. Tort damages were at first awarded to the injured individual as an incident to a criminal prosecution."

7  See Keeton (1984, p. 8 note 9): "as late as 1694 the defendant to a writ of trespass was still theoretically liable to a criminal fine and imprisonment."

8  See Horwitz (1977, p. 4): "Between 1776 and 1784, eleven of the thirteen original states adopted, directly or indirectly, some provisions for the reception of the common law as well as of limited classes of British statutes."

9  See Horwitz (1977, pp. 4–9); Feldman (1997, pp. 1394–1404).

10  See Feldman (1997, pp 1404–9, note 12) explaining the views of leading legal historians on the issue of when jurisprudence became pragmatically oriented and arguing that the period was characterized by a mixture of natural law and pragmatic reasoning, with the latter gaining ascendancy as the century progressed.

11  Friedman (1985, p. 584): "In every state, every extension of governmental power, every new form of regulation, brought in a new batch of criminal law. . . . The full discussion of these statutes belongs more to the story of government regulation of business than to criminal justice."

12  Regulation by the states, rather than the federal government, also made sense. "Most government intervention, and government regulation, was carried on, in 1800 or 1830, by the states, not the federal government." Friedman (1985, p. 177). Indeed, "[i]n 1900, nobody expected much out of a national government. It ran the Army, the post office, supervised railroads – all this was important, of course, but the bulk of the governing process was lodged in the states" Friedman (1985, p. 658).

13  "In preindustrial society, there are few personal injuries, except as a result of assault and battery. Modern tools and machines, however, have a marvelous capacity to cripple and maim their servants. From about 1840 on, one specific machine, the railroad locomotive, generated, on its own steam (so to speak), more tort law than any other in the 19th century" Friedman (1985, p. 300).

14  See Friedman (1985, p. 300): "Tort law was new law in the 19th century." Horwitz (1977) found that American tort law had been "transformed" by 1860; see also White (1980, pp.

3–19), who argued that the "modern negligence principle" was "an intellectual response" to the increased number of accidents in the nineteenth century. Schwartz (1981, pp. 1727) rejected the view that tort law was "new law" in the nineteenth century, claiming instead that the new nineteenth-century liability standards developed from precedent in an evolutionary way.

[15] See Schwartz (1988, p. 643 note 8). In the nineteenth century, first-party insurance schemes for victims were not available, making the compensation afforded by the tort system the only available form of insurance for many accident victims. Hence increased tort liability tended to minimize accident costs by reducing the number of accidents while providing a cost-effective form of compensation. The judicial concern for regulating risks and providing injury compensation therefore was directly connected to the minimization of accident costs.

Note that an emphasis on compensation is, for the most part, no longer consistent with the minimization of accident costs. Today, the widespread availability of first-party insurance mechanisms makes tort liability a relatively expensive form of compensation. For this reason, the economic rationale for tort liability currently depends on deterrence.

[16] For a flavor of this debate, see Croley and Hanson (1993).

[17] The argument in this section is based on Roe (1996).

[18] For an introduction to the way in which interest groups affect lawmaking, see Farber and Frickey (1991). For a discussion of tort reform and the role played by interest groups, see Geistfeld (1994) and Komesar (1990).

[19] It would be cost-effective to impose tort liability on one who fails to take an "easy" rescue that would have saved another. See Hasen (1995). However, it would be very difficult, if not impossible, to limit such a duty in a principled way. See Epstein (1973, pp. 198–200). There is no good reason, for example, why an "easy" rescue does not encompass the case in which a wealthy individual could spend a few dollars to save another. The economic properties of such a duty therefore depend upon how it would affect individual incentives to accumulate wealth and the other costs it would impose on individuals by infringing upon their personal liberty. Once "rescue becomes more expensive, and certainly when rescue becomes more dangerous, efficiency arguments vary" (Hasen 1995, p. 146).

[20] More precisely, an optimal damages award must be an unbiased estimator of the damages that could be suffered by the parties exposed to the risk. Average damages satisfy this criterion if injurers cannot choose their victims, and if victims cannot affect the chance they will be harmed. The discussion in text is applicable to any unbiased estimator other than damages awards based on the victim's actual harm.

[21] Basing damages on actual injury rather than risk exposure can be justified with this same argument.

[22] See Milsom (1981, p. 285): "Early law-suits revolved around proof; and the essence of the victim's role in such proceedings lay not in their initiation, as has been supposed, but in his making of proof"; see also supra pp., describing the compensatory nature of tort damages in the early common-law system.

[23] See *Restatement (Second) of Torts* §283 cmt. e (1965) stating that the interests advanced by an injurer's conduct do not depend upon the actor's subjective evaluation, but rather on "the value which the law attaches to [them]"; id. §291 stating that a party "is not excused because he is peculiarly inconsiderate of others . . . nor is he negligent if his moral or social conscience is so sensitive that he regards as improper conduct what a reasonable man would regard as proper."

[24] See, for example Coleman and Ripstein (1995, pp. 112–13).

[25] Welfare economics once relied on interpersonally comparable and cardinal utility measures. Serious doubts were subsequently raised about the scientific possibility of verifying such welfare comparisons, and whether an economist *qua* economist was qualified to judge aggregate welfare improvement or detriment. See Robbins (1935). In light of these concerns, modern welfare economics attempts to avoid interpersonal utility comparisons.

[26] See, e.g., Holmes (1963, pp. 108–9) recognizing both justifications for the objective standard. *Restatement (Second) of Torts* §283B (1965) justifies the objective standard in part due to the difficulties of "drawing any satisfactory line[s] between . . . variations in temperament [and] intellect."

[27] For clear statements regarding the way in which modern economic analysis proceeds by assuming that preferences are exogenous or fixed, see Friedman (1962); Becker and Stigler (1977).

[28] For a collection of articles dealing with the interplay between economic analysis and preference formation, see Casson (1997).

[29] Much of this literature is surveyed and cited in McAdams (1997). For a sampling of the legal scholars who have claimed that legal rules shape preferences, see Gordon (1984, p. 109): "[T]he power exerted by a legal regime consists less in the force it can bring to bear against violators of its rules than in its capacity to persuade people that the world described in its images and categories is the only attainable world in which a sane person would want to live."); Radin (1996, p. 173): "Legal institutions can express culture, or they can help shape it. Where legal institutions help shape culture, they do so in part by instantiating and reinforcing particular conceptions of the nature of persons and their good." Sunstein (1990, pp. 64–7) argues that most preferences are endogenous to legal rules and norms. For notable examples of economists who have embraced this approach, see Becker (1996) and Sen (1976).

[30] A similar point has been made by scholars regarding the way in which criminal laws can enforce morals, see, e.g., Devlin (1965), or change norms, see, e.g., Simpson (1987), arguing that the laws of the English King Ethelbert were an attempt to displace the social norm that one had to avenge the death of a family member – the "feud" – with the idea "that it was not wrong to take money instead of blood."

[31] If an objective valuation changes preferences, it yields outcomes that can be compared to the outcomes produced by a system relying on subjective valuations only if one is willing to compare the utility levels of the same individual with different sets of preferences. In effect, such a comparison involves an interpersonal comparison of utility (different preferences correspond to different selves of an individual), a practice greatly disfavored by modern welfare economics. Because the two systems cannot be directly compared, it seems more appropriate to compare them in terms of risk levels and total precaution costs for those risk levels.

[32] Compare Landes and Posner (1987, p. 88): "The negligence-contributory negligence approach, defined in marginal Hand Formula terms, yields optimal results so long as the law applies the Hand Formula to each party on the assumption that the other party is exercising due care." The Hand Formula for negligence is discussed in the ensuing section in text.

[33] The issue of whether the tort system should use an objective or subjective standard also arises with respect to an individual's ability to take care. For these issues, the tort system relies on subjective and objective considerations in a manner consistent with the minimization of accident costs. See Schwartz (1989).

[34] "The Utilitarian doctrine is that each man ought to consider the happiness of any other as theoretically of equal importance with his own, and only of less importance practically, in so far as he is better able to realize the latter" (Sidgwick 1907, p. 252). All moral theories of this type can be called "utilitarian," even if they are meant to be nonutilitarian, because they "are based directly on the utilitarian conception of equality, according to which treating people as equals simply means counting each person's interests equally while maximizing the total satisfaction of interests" Wright (1995, p. 253).

[35] See Keeton (1984, p. 132): "the law has always placed a higher value on human safety than upon mere rights in property." There are good reasons for doubting that a principle applicable to intentional harms necessarily applies to accidental harms. Owen (1993, esp. pp. 469–71) argues that tort law's recognition of this ethic "is rooted generally in the context of truly intentional takings." See also Keating (1997).

[36] Compare Gilles (1994, pp. 1027–39): arguing that the reasonable person standard can serve as a heuristic that implements the cost–benefit negligence standard, with Wells (1990): arguing that the jury is expected to reach a case-specific consensus across "a cross section of normative viewpoints."

[37] Risk aversion occurs whenever individuals experience declining marginal utility of wealth, which seems to be a common phenomenon. The assumption that most individuals are risk averse is supported by the fact that individuals commonly purchase insurance, because this expenditure is one that only risk-averse individuals would make.

[38] See Becker and Ehrlich (1972). The logic of this result is straightforward. Full insurance equalizes utility across all potential states of the world, eliminating the element of risk from the individual's decision-making calculus.

[39] See Kakalik and Pace (1986, pp. 68–9 and table 2) describing study showing that for average tort lawsuit in 1985, approximately 30% to 31% of total compensation paid to plaintiffs was used to pay plaintiffs' legal fees and expenses.

[40] According to the economic account, a fully compensatory tort award equalizes the victim's utility across the injured and noninjured states of the world. In a wrongful death action, a victim without a bequest motive receives no utility from the tort award, so there is no tort award in such a suit that can satisfy this definition of full compensation.

[41] Compare Rawls (1993) arguing that a political conception of justice can accommodate a plurality of incompatible doctrines by focusing on the overlapping consensus of reasonable, comprehensive doctrines.

[42] Perry (1996, p. 57). See also Keeton (1984, pp. 16–17), observing that "weighing the interests [of security and liberty] is by no means peculiar to the law of torts, but it has been carried to its greatest lengths and has received its most general conscious recognition in this field."

[43] Thus, for example, economic analysis treats one type of injuries as involving nothing other than a reduction in wealth or income for a given utility function, whereas nonmonetary injuries change the individual's utility function.

[44] For Mill, "an extraordinarily important and impressive kind of utility" attaches to physical security, because "security no human being can possibly do without" (Mill 1861, p. 50). According to Weinrib, "[U]nder Kantian right bodily integrity is an innate right and thus prior to the acquired rights of property" (Weinrib 1995, p. 202 note 73). Similarly, Keating writes that although "[t]he liberties at stake in accidental risk impositions are not part of the equal basic liberties of Rawls's first principle of justice . . . liberties protected

by accident law have an analogous priority over our interests in acquiring wealth and income" (Keating 1997, p. 1313).

45  Samuelson (1947). A similar formulation of the social-welfare function was derived by Bergson (1930). Social-welfare functions that satisfy these conditions are called Bergson-Samuelson social welfare functions, and provide the most commonly used approach for welfare economics. See, e.g., Tresch (1981).

46  Minimizing the costs of deterrence protects the liberty and security interests of potential victims in the least burdensome manner for potential injurers. Hence such a rule would maximize social welfare as defined above. Note that the maximization of social welfare does not always depend on deterrence. The social-welfare function could be defined so that in the context of the tortious conduct in question, the liberty interests of potential injurers receive less weight than the liberty interests of potential victims. In this case, wealth transfers between an injurer and victim would increase social welfare.

47  Modern welfare economics typically relies on a social-welfare function based only on the welfare levels of individuals, typically disregarding the identity of the individuals and the sources of their utility. See, e.g., Mas-Colell (1995, pp. 825–38) describing variations of the Bergson-Samuelson social-welfare function defined solely in terms of individual utilities with distributional weights attached only to the total amount of each individual's utility. This approach, however, is merely one of mathematical convenience. See, e.g., Mueller (1989, pp. 373–4). Indeed, Paul Samuelson expressly recognized that the social-welfare function could depend upon the source of individual utilities: "one of the $z$'s [in the social-welfare function] may be the amount of tea consumed by John Jones, or the amount of labor which he provides" (Samuelson 1947, p. 222). This is because the distributional weights given to the individual utilities need only satisfy the general requirements for a properly specified social-welfare function. See Tresch (1981, p. 26). As long as these requirements are satisfied by the distributional weights attached to the various sources of individual utility, social welfare can be defined in a manner that disaggregates the sources of individual utility; moreover, any approach to welfare economics that does not rely on such disaggregation is likely to be based on utilitarianism or the Rawls-inspired leximin principle. See Sen (1982a).

48  See Sen (1970).

49  In discussing the "fashionable [stance] for the modern economist to insist that ethical value judgments have no place in scientific analysis," Paul Samuelson observed that "It is a legitimate exercise of economic analysis to examine the consequences of various value judgments, whether or not they are shared by the theorist. . . . That part [of welfare economics] which *does* involve inter-personal comparisons of utility also has real content and interest for the scientific analyst, even though the scientist does not consider it any part of his task to deduce or verify (except on the anthropological level) the value judgments whose implications he grinds out" (Samuelson 1947, pp. 219–20).

# 8

# Pluralism in Tort and Accident Law
## Toward a Reasonable Accommodation[1]

### BRUCE CHAPMAN

## I. Introduction

When we make choices, even such everyday choices as how to spend an evening
(or what restaurant to choose beforehand, or what mode of transport to use in
getting there), we are typically confronted with a plurality of different criteria
informing the choice. In choosing, for example, between spending the evening
at the movies or at a philosophy lecture, we might have to consider whether on
this particular evening we wish to be pleasurably entertained or intellectually
challenged. There might also be good reason for considering cost, convenience
of parking, and the amount of time involved. Moreover, these various criteria
seem to flow from quite different and independent sorts of values. It seems hard
to believe that the purely hedonic pleasure involved in watching some action
film is really an aspect of a larger philosophical understanding, or that the understanding offered by the philosophy lecture, although pleasurable, is the same
kind of pleasure as that offered by the movie. Indeed, it seems likely that the
last three considerations mentioned (cost, convenience, time), which are of a
more practical nature, will be as much informed by how we might otherwise
spend our time and money, that is, by the broad range of very different forms
of experience that could be enjoyed beyond the two options mentioned here,
and thus that they implicate an even more diverse array of criteria and values
than pleasure and understanding.

Plurality, then, is the rule rather than the exception when we make choices.
Yet we do make these choices, often without all that much difficulty and, after-
wards, they can even seem reasonable to us, something we might justify. Moreover, we do so even though the different choice criteria typically order the available options in different ways so that no one option dominates (or, according to
each and every criterion, is better than) all the others. The action film might provide more pleasure, for example, but less understanding than the philosophy lecture. Thus, our judgments of what is best (or what we have most reason to do[2])
"all things considered" seem to imply that we have methods for resolving con-

flicts between the different criteria informing our choices. That is, we operate, daily it seems, with some method of integrating plural choice criteria.

Is there any real puzzle in this? There might be, at least on some views of what is entailed by value or criterial pluralism. On these views, pluralism *of* choice criteria seems to imply incomparability *between* criteria, and this incomparability implies in turn that any choice in the face of criterial conflict cannot be justified or even involve sound judgement (Chang 1998). How could it? If diverse criteria cannot be compared, then there is no sense in which an option recommended by one of the criteria could be thought to be better than a different option recommended by another. On this sort of view, pluralism implies that the different criteria are genuinely independent of, or external to, one another, and that a truncation in the satisfaction of any one in the name of another is, from the viewpoint of that one, normatively arbitrary.

In *The Idea of Private Law,* Ernest Weinrib (1995) would appear to have in mind just these sorts of concerns about the pluralism he sees in many contemporary understandings of the normative structure of tort law. According to Weinrib, the standard view in contemporary tort scholarship is "functionalist," that is, one which understands all of private law, including tort law, by way of externally specified purposes. Moreover, these externally specified purposes, Weinrib says, are independently justified:

[T]he favored goals of the functionalists are independent not only of private law but also of one another. For example, compensation and deterrence, the two standard goals ascribed to tort law, have no intrinsic connection: nothing about compensation as such justifies its limitation to those who are victims of deterrable harms, just as nothing about deterrence as such justifies its limitation to acts that produce compensable injury. Understood from the viewpoint of mutually independent goals, private law is a congeries of unharmonized and competing purposes. (Weinrib 1995, p. 5)

This apparent lack of harmony in the different goals which are commonly announced for tort law has been noticed by others as well. Michael Trebilcock, for example, has pointed to the indeterminacy that plagues any attempt to confine one's concern for compensation, to be achieved efficiently through some least cost insurer, to those parties most immediately (privately) connected to the loss-generating interaction. On compensation or insurance grounds, Trebilcock remarks, it may simply be better to "cast privity, proximate cause constraints, and the like aside and expand the search to a broader net of parties" (Trebilock 1988, p. 243). However, as Trebilcock has himself argued elsewhere (Trebilock 1987), it is this broader net of possibilities that explains much of what some have called "the insurance crisis" in tort law. The incoherence of conjoining the plurality of deterrence and compensation criteria within a single instance of adjudication (which Trebilcock refers to as a "dilemma," a term itself suggestive of unordered plurality) has simply made tort liability so indeterminate as to be unpredictable and, therefore, uninsurable.

However, in Weinrib's view, it is particularly problematic for the law to manifest such a cacophony of unordered purposes, since the law holds itself out as an "exhibition of intelligence," a self-consciously rational enterprise which constantly aspires, by way of publicly articulated and objectively comprehensible reasons, "to avoid contradiction, to smooth out inconsistencies, and to realize a self-adjusting harmony of principles, rules, and standards" (Weinrib 1995, pp. 12, 14). Weinrib argues that a pluralism of mutually independent ends entails a kind of incoherence and that law, if it is to satisfy its own ambitions for itself, must, somehow, be single-minded in a way that pluralism denies.

Of course, some will object that this argument for single-mindedness, or monism, goes through too easily. Different values or choice criteria might in some direct sense be independent of one another, but nevertheless be indirectly related and, therefore, systematizable under some more comprehensive justificatory purpose. Such systematization, after all, is what the utilitarian has always promised to deliver (Sidgwick 1907). Of course, this suggests that the pluralism with which we began is more apparent than real, for now the many criteria so systematized, while not immediately related to one another, are construed as mere aspects of some overarching super-value, such as utility or welfare, which provides a common measure, or commensurability, for them all.[3]

However, Weinrib explicitly considers this possibility for justifying tort law by reference to the independent goals of deterrence and compensation and, just as explicitly, rejects it as implausible. He writes, "Can one seriously believe that deterrence and compensation are optimally combined when the incidence and amount of deterrence are set by the fortuity of the plaintiff's injury, and when the occurrence of compensation for the injured is determined by the need to deter potential injuries? That would be a coincidence of Panglossian proportion" (Weinrib 1995, p. 41). In this repudiation of the possibility of attending sensibly, within tort law, to the two goals of compensation and deterrence, it may sound as if Weinrib is simply reiterating his earlier point that there is something normatively arbitrary in limiting one goal by another. However, his point here is really quite different. Here he entertains at least the logical possibility that the two goals might be ordered with respect to one another; indeed, they might even be "optimally combined." But he disputes that this optimal tradeoff is likely to be achieved at just those moments where tort law makes it possible. After all, tort law combines the moment of deterrence against the defendant with the moment of compensation to the plaintiff. Alternative institutions for dealing with compensation and deterrence, specifically those outside the private law of tort, would not face this constraint.

Thus, for Weinrib the possibility of offering a justified framework for decision-making within tort law in the name of compensation and deterrence is bleak. Either these goals are commensurable under, say, the overarching aspect of welfare, or they are not. If they are not, then they represent an irreducible pluralism any accommodation of which is normatively arbitrary. On the other hand, if they are commensurable the optimal combination of the two according to their common measure of performance is not likely to be found at any of the available points made possible by private law adjudication.

It is a familiar idea that rational judgement or choice must be based on reason, and that the only route to a reasoned choice is either through a single normative value that can order the alternatives or, what appears to be the same thing, through the commensurability of the different criteria or values informing the choice under some sort of super value. As already suggested, this is the stuff of utilitarianism in almost all its guises. However, it is a little surprising to see that Weinrib buys so heavily into this framework, given his strong rejection of welfaristic instrumentalism, at least as a way of understanding tort law. Of course, Weinrib can claim that there is nothing in this monistic framework that requires him to be a commensurist, and certainly nothing to require that his single normative value be welfarist.

However, conjoining monism with the rejection of welfare as a possible organizing value is troubling in itself, as more than a few commentators on Weinrib have pointed out. Martin Stone, for example, has offered these remarks about Weinrib's welfare-deficient formalism:

> [I]f formalism thus requires that the law have no purposes related to the conditions of well being, it seems bound to foster the sort of anxiety concerning the law's 'why' that motivates functionalism. . . . *Vis à vis* the formalist, the functionalist has a good point: If the perpetuation of the law in social institutions is something we can rationally endorse, we ought to be able to see the law as advancing our well being, as making our life better rather than worse. (Stone 1996)[4]

Stone concedes that if welfare or well-being is framed as the tort law functionalist would have it, that is, as constituting a free-standing value that is prior to, and independent of, tort law, then Weinrib's argument that tort law cannot sensibly be about achieving some such welfare optimum probably succeeds. Such a conception of welfare is inherently nonrelational and, therefore, necessarily foreign to the demands of private law adjudication. But Stone asks us to consider the possibility that the normative significance of welfare might be framed relationally, and even uses Weinrib's own example of "love" to motivate that thought. Weinrib uses love to illustrate the idea that some of the most normatively significant phenomena in our lives are best understood only in their own terms, that is, not as instrumental to the achievement of some independently conceived external good (Weinrib 1995, pp. 5–6). But Stone invokes love to exemplify the thought that some of the most important components of our well-being or welfare are inherently relational in their nature. If the problem with the functionalist's use of welfare is that it aspires to achieve an inherently nonrelational optimum by way of the essentially relational structure of private law, then the difficulty might not be the same for a relational conception of welfare. Thus, in Weinrib's analysis the real problem might not be with welfare as such, but rather with the particular nonrelational version that he considers.

The thought that there might be a relational conception of welfare deals with one possible difficulty with Weinrib's understanding of tort law, namely, that it so rules out any conscious concern for well-being that we might well wonder whether we should be normatively interested in tort law at all. But there is still the problem with which we began. Pluralism, I have suggested, is the rule rather than the exception in decision-making, and for good reason. Plural considerations are plural because they are different in their nature and not because they simply differ in the amounts they offer of some common nature (Stocker 1990, p. 177). It is for this reason that the assumption of commensurability does a kind of conceptual violence to the underlying values, converting genuinely qualitative differences into quantitative ones. Moreover, it is this same recalcitrant irreducibility of plural considerations which, understandably, motivates Weinrib to think that a mere noncommensurable aggregation of them in decision-making, and more particularly in tort law, will only provide for an accidental unity, the stuff of incoherence. But the pervasiveness of pluralism, combined with the fact that our choices nevertheless seem rationalizable, at least in many cases, belies that anxiety. What is needed, therefore, is not so much a relational conception of welfare that still, single-mindedly, imposes commensurability and the denial of pluralism onto tort law, but, instead, an essentially relational framework that allows a sensible role to be given to welfare even as it admits other values which might be noncommensurable with it.

In this essay, I shall provide the beginnings of such an account. Or, more accurately, I shall provide the structure for such an account and provide illustrations of how the most relevant pluralisms are accommodated both within tort law in particular and across accident law more generally. What I propose is an ordering of genuinely plural values according to a conceptually sequenced argument.[5] Such a conceptual ordering should provide, even in the face of an incommensurable pluralism, for Weinrib's conception of law as an "exhibition of intelligence." The result is a kind of path dependent choice, of course, but because the path is conceptually ordered it is not, for like reason, the sort of *arbitrary* path dependence which is the usual concern of decision theorists. Finally, the notion of a conceptually sequenced argument, where each protagonist offers arguments in direct reply to what is put at issue by the other, provides the essentially relational structure for the accommodation of competing values which is so prized by the private law of tort.

## II. The Logic of Multicriterial Decision-making

### A. *Impossibilities and Limited Possibilities*

Value conflicts within a person, which provides an occasion for individual deliberation and choice, are in many respects similar to value conflicts between or among persons, the focus of social choice. Moreover, this similarity has not gone unnoticed. Kenneth Arrow, the originator of social choice theory (Arrow 1963) has (along with Hervé Raynaud) borrowed from his own social choice framework and provided a systematic account of multi-criterial decision-making for an analysis of the problem of policy choice faced by a single professional decision-maker (Arrow and Raynaud 1986). In this section, we will also borrow some of the technique developed within social choice theory to provide a framework for analyzing the problem of multi-criterial decision-making.

It was Arrow's original contribution to show that certain seemingly weak conditions for the rational integration of disparate orderings of various alternatives for choice are not compatible. Arrow's original problem was one of social choice for which the different orderings provided were simply the preference orderings provided by the different individuals in a given society. But, as alluded to above, the structure of this problem is formally equivalent to the problem involved in the rational integration of orderings provided by different criteria. Thus, Arrow's proof that it is logically impossible to combine certain seemingly reasonable conditions for the integration of these criteria into some "best, all-things-considered" choice is troubling in a much more general way.

Could it be that Arrow's impossibility result provides support for Weinrib's claim that there is no coherent way to combine genuinely plural considerations short of assuming their commensurability, something that sounds a lot like assuming away pluralism altogether? Are the only possibilities the ones identified by Weinrib, namely, an irrational or incoherent pluralism, a single-minded or coherent monism, or a commensurability of plural considerations of a sort that only allows them the freedom to range quantitatively and subverts their genuine qualitative differences? These would indeed appear to be the lessons offered by social choice theory to multi-criterial decision-making.

Consider first the possibility of pluralism without commensurability. This was the problem originally considered by Arrow under the aspect of noninterpersonally comparable individual preference orderings. In the multi-criterial setting, the impossibility reduces to the claim that any integration function satisfying certain other reasonable conditions (still to be discussed) must be (in Arrow's terms) "dictatorial," that is to say, monistic, or responsive only to the recommendations of *one* of the many criteria informing the choice.[6] Of course, since Arrow was originally interested in minimally democratic forms of social decision-making, a dictatorial result, where some one individual's preference ordering was everywhere decisive for social choice, was unacceptable; hence the "impossibility" in his result. Weinrib, on the other hand, seems prepared to accept the monistic analogue to this result for deliberative multi-criterial decision-making.

Furthermore, Weinrib's idea that plural considerations might be logically commensurable and optimally combined under a more comprehensive justificatory purpose (while inappropriate in his view as a measure of what is likely to be achieved within tort law) also receives some support from certain results in social choice theory. If one assumes that commensurability means that the different criteria can be compared with one another on a *cardinal* scale, then the *only* method for rationally integrating the criteria, and which otherwise satisfies Arrow-like conditions for a reasonable integration, is utilitarian, that is, one which orders the alternatives according to the sum total of the quantity which makes the criteria commensurable (Sen 1982a, pp. 233–8; Deschamps and Gevers 1978; Roberts 1980). On the other hand, if one assumes that intercriterial commensurability is *ordinal* and not cardinal, that is, that one can make sense of the *level* at which some criterion is satisfied in comparison to another, but not of the relative *gains* and *losses* in choosing between criteria, then only a small adjustment in the Arrow framework (introducing the idea that at *some* point the multi-criterial decision-maker must reasonably be moved, if possible, to achieve higher levels of satisfaction of that criterion which is otherwise least satisfied) means that the only method for rationally integrating the criteria is one analogous to Rawls' maximin or "difference" principle. This principle, in the multi-criterial setting, would have us choose so that we maximize the level of satisfaction of that criterion which of all the different criteria is least satisfied.[7]

That the only alternatives for a rational integration of criteria, assuming inter-criterial commensurability, are either versions of utilitarianism or of the Rawlsian maximin principle provides for a stark choice indeed. It seems that, despite assuming commensurability between plural considerations in the way suggested by Weinrib's analysis, we are still plagued with the same kind of single-mindedness which, without assuming commensurability, drives him, for example, to require a (dictatorial) monism for a coherent account of tort law. One might have hoped that commensurability would have allowed for more than this, and in particular that it might have permitted some attention to be given to overall gains and losses in criteria (the stuff of utilitarianism and cardinal commensurability) *as well as* some attention to the more egalitarian concern for how deeply some given criterion is denied (the stuff of maximin and ordinal commensurability). Yet the framework provided by Arrow, and seemingly assumed by Weinrib as well, for the rational integration of different criteria seems not to allow for this more pluralistic mode of integration. It is as if we can admit pluralism in our criteria, but not be pluralistic in our rational accommodation of those criteria. Perhaps the time has come to examine this framework more closely.

### B. Independence Conditions and Problematic Profiles

In her thorough investigation of the relevance of the Arrow framework for the problem of multi-criterial decision-making, Susan Hurley has been critical of some of the seemingly reasonable conditions which are imposed on the rational integration of criteria by that framework (Hurley 1989, pp. 225–70). It is worthwhile considering these objections even as we introduce the reader to the Arrow conditions for the first time. Sometimes, a considered objection can provide an excellent lens through which to see the real significance of some normative concept against which an objection has been made.

Hurley accepts that multi-criterial decision-making, if it is to be genuinely pluralistic, should be "nondictatorial" (or nonmonistic) in Arrow's sense, arguing that it is a quite different matter from monism to introduce, say, cardinal commensurability of different criteria under the aspect of a single comprehensive theory. "We must distinguish," Hurley says, "the domination of a particular theory about values over others on theoretical grounds from the dictatorial status of a particular value, which may be asserted by a theory about values" (Hurley 1989, p. 233).[8] Good theory, she suggests, ought to be dictatorial even if the values that are the subject matter of that theory are not. Thus, she accepts Arrow's nondictatorship condition.

She also accepts the Pareto condition, which in the multi-criterial context amounts to a condition of dominance: If *all* the criteria rank some alternative $x$ as better or more choiceworthy than some other alternative $y$, then a reasonable integration of these criteria should rank $x$ as better or more choiceworthy than $y$. Concerns about the acceptability of the Pareto principle within conventional social choice theory, such as those captured by Amartya Sen in his theorem about "the impossibility of a Paretian liberal" (Sen 1982b, p. 285), involve (as Sen himself recognized) the purely welfarist content of the Pareto principle in that context, and are not relevant, Hurley says, to the analogous (dominance) principle in multi-criterial decision-making (Hurley 1989, p. 232).

What Hurley finds more problematic than the nondictatorship and Pareto conditions are the conditions of "universal domain" and "independence of irrelevant alternatives," conditions that she is forced to consider together because of the special way they interact in Arrow's proof of the impossibility result. The independence of irrelevant alternatives condition requires that the choice between any pair of alternatives depend only on the criterial rankings of those alternatives, and not on criterial rankings of other alternatives (and, in particular, how these might vary). Although this might seem a reasonable enough requirement at first glance, it turns out, as we shall see, that this condition imposes a very powerful form of choice consistency on multi-criterial decision-making.

The condition of universal domain requires that the rational integration of criterial orderings apply not only to such orderings as they actually are, but to all such orderings that are logically possible. The idea is to preclude closing off any possible combination of criteria orderings *ab initio*, something that would cut against the openness of the rational integration exercise to the broadest possible range of difficulties. Surely, one does not want to be able to merely conjure up such a very convenient and limited domain of criterial orderings that all problems of integrating a more difficult domain are effectively assumed away.

Whereas this openness even to the most remote logical possibility might seem commendable, and not all that threatening given our choice criteria as they actually are, the effect of combining this with the condition of independence of irrelevant alternatives is that remote logical difficulties are immediately converted into general impossibilities, *including* the impossibility of dealing reasonably with the rational integration of our criterial orderings as they actually are! This is why the Arrow theorem is properly described as a *general impossibility* theorem. The independence of irrelevant alternatives condition effectively turns a "not generally possible" result for some particular counterfactual profile of criterial orderings (available only as a logical matter, perhaps, because of universal domain) into a "generally not possible" result for all possible criterial orderings, including the much more limited profile of criterial orderings that exists as a matter of fact.

Hurley convincingly objects to these interprofile effects of the independence of irrelevant alternatives condition. She suggests that we might be interested in what our various criteria say about different counter*factuals,* as, for example, when we appeal to certain hypothetical cases to isolate and better understand what our criteria or values really require. However, it does not seem that we should be likewise interested in counter*criterials* and, in particular, whether there is any consistency between, on the one hand, our all-things-considered judgments as these are informed by the profile of criteria as they actually are and, on the other hand, our judgments as they might be in some different and only remotely possible world with a quite different profile of criterial orderings. Yet this sort of interprofile consistency is what the independence of irrelevant alternatives condition imposes (Hurley 1989, pp. 234–41).[9]

At this point the reader might well wonder if the Arrow impossibility result is so troubling after all. It seems to provide for a very strong exclusion against the general possibility of rational multi-criterial decision-making only because it imposes such a strongly counterintuitive interprofile consistency condition. Whatever the merits of such a condition in the interpersonal social choice context that originally concerned Arrow, Hurley seems right to question the attractiveness of this condition in multi-criterial choice. And if the conditions imposed by Arrow seem less compelling, then so too is his impossibility result that had seemed to force us to choose uncomfortably between a dictatorial monism and an incoherent pluralism.

However, as Hurley recognizes herself, this would be an overly hasty conclusion. If a certain profile of criterial orderings can be shown to actually exist for some choice problems, then there is a risk of incoherence even without reference to the sort of consistency across logically possible profiles that is contemplated by the condition of independence of irrelevant alternatives. In other words, there are *intra*profile versions of Arrow-like impossibility results, and in the context of accident law, and tort law more specifically, these results continue to suggest a substantive difficulty that needs to be addressed.

Intraprofile impossibility results come in two basic forms, neutral and non-neutral. Since this distinction is of some relevance for the different institutional strategies that are used for dealing with pluralism, it is important to understand the difference. Neutral intraprofile impossibility results assume a neutrality condition as one of their underlying (logically incompatible) conditions. Neutrality requires that for any alternatives $w$, $x$, $y$, and $z$, if all criteria rank $w$ and $z$ in the same way they rank $x$ and $y$ (that is, if whenever $w$ ranks above $z$ for any criterion, so does $x$ rank above $y$, and vice versa), then $w$ and $z$ must be ranked in the same way, all things considered, as $x$ and $y$. Thus, unlike the condition of independence of irrelevant alternatives, which requires a kind of interprofile consistency in the ranking of a given pair of (relevant) alternatives, neutrality requires consistency for a given profile of orderings (or intraprofile consistency) if the different orderings rank different pairs of alternatives in the same way. Nonneutral intraprofile impossibility results, by contrast, do not rely on neutrality as one of their underlying conditions.

Neutral intraprofile impossibility can be exemplified by simple majority voting. Majority voting, of course, is something which we more usually think of as applicable to individuals, but, as Arrow and others have suggested, it can sensibly be applied to multi-criterial decision-making as well. In this context the method simply selects that choice in any pair of alternatives that is ranked higher, or preferred, by a majority of the criteria informing the choice. The difficulty, or impossibility (given the other defining conditions for the method of majority decision[10]), is that for a certain profile of criterial orderings, there is no way for the majority to choose anything but a minority preferred alternative. This is the familiar paradox of majority voting and is illustrated below for the three criteria $C_1$, $C_2$, and $C_3$ in their respective rankings (in order of preference from top to bottom) of the three alternatives $x$, $y$, and $z$.

| $C_1$ | $C_2$ | $C_3$ |
|-------|-------|-------|
| $x$ | $y$ | $z$ |
| $y$ | $z$ | $x$ |
| $z$ | $x$ | $y$ |

It is easy to see that a majority of these criteria prefer $x$ to $y$, $y$ to $z$, and $z$ to $x$. Thus, it is not possible for a majority of the criteria to choose any of the three alternatives without there being another alternative, available for choice, which a majority of the criteria prefers to that choice.

It is easy to prove that if a majority voting paradox is to occur, then the particular configuration or matrix of preferences over three alternatives which is exemplified here for alternatives $x$, $y$, and $z$, and which is often referred to as a Latin square, must occur somewhere in the given profile of criterial orderings.[11] Moreover, close examination of the proof shows the essential role which is played by neutrality in generating this particular intraprofile impossibility result. Since this particular configuration of criterial preferences is necessary for the impossibility, it becomes very interesting to ask whether there is any reason in specific contexts for choice to expect this pattern of orderings to occur for the relevant criteria. As we shall see in Section III.A, there is every reason to expect this pattern for the sorts of criteria relevant to accident law in general and, arguably, for tort law in particular.

However, before dealing with the specifics of accident law, more needs to be said about the overall structure of intraprofile impossibility. For, as already suggested, there are also nonneutral intraprofile impossibility results. Nonneutrality permits, in a way that neutrality does not, that if a given pair of alternatives $w$ and $z$ are ranked in the same way by all criterial orderings as some other pair of alternatives $x$ and $y$, nevertheless, the "all-things-considered" ranking of $w$ and $z$ need not be the same as for $x$ and $y$. Thus, non-neutrality allows for the possibility of some criteria being "jurisdictionally decisive" for some alternatives, but not others, even though the different criteria might rank the different alternatives within the different jurisdictions in identical ways.

Nonneutrality is an important feature for some strategic approaches to multi-criterial decision-making. If different criteria can be separated into different domains where they reign supreme, perhaps because the criteria are in some sense a good match for the alternatives considered there, then it might seem that some of the conflict between criteria, so characteristic of pluralism, can be avoided. Indeed, it is arguable that this might be how Weinrib would approach the problem of pluralism within accident law. One of the alternative strategies that he identifies for dealing with plural considerations, beyond postulating some comprehensive justificatory purpose which provides for their commensurability and calls for their optimal combination, is to "translate each goal into the legal ordering appropriate to its particular requirements. We would then have one set of institutions that dealt with deterrence and another that dealt with compensation" (Weinrib 1995, pp. 41–2). Where the first of these strategies, involving commensurability, implies neutrality, the second, which provides for the separate consideration of different criteria in jurisdictions in which each rules supreme, implies nonneutrality.

There are at least two difficulties with this nonneutral strategy for dealing with pluralism. One is that it is unclear that it forms a genuine alternative to commensurability. In Section III.A I shall show that any attempt, for example, to concentrate exclusively on the goal of compensation within, say, some no-fault scheme inevitably confronts the demands of the deterrence goal if the costs of compensation are to be sufficiently contained to be fundable. And within tort law itself I shall suggest (in Section IV) that the purity of corrective justice, even for Weinrib, must give way at some point (within a conceptually sequenced argument) to some considerations of efficiency.

The second difficulty with the nonneutral strategy of using separate spheres or jurisdictions for different criteria is the one captured by Amartya Sen's intraprofile theorem on "the impossibility of the Paretian liberal." Sen meant to capture a tension between a concern for rights and even the minimal concern for welfare that is implied by the Pareto principle (viz., that a social choice rule should never choose an alternative that all individuals consider inferior to another that is available), but the structure of his result implies a more general difficulty. Suppose one criterion $C_1$ is given supreme jurisdiction over alternatives $w$ and $x$ and another criterion $C_2$ is given supreme jurisdiction over alternatives $y$ and $z$. Now suppose that $C_1$ orders the four alternatives (from left to right) as $z\ w\ x\ y$, and that $C_2$ orders them $x\ y\ z\ w$. Then, since $C_1$ is supreme over $w$ and $x$, and $C_2$ is supreme over $y$ and $z$, it is arguable that neither $x$ nor $z$ should be chosen since the jurisdictionally relevant criterion judges each of those alternatives to be inferior to another that is available in its proper domain. But that only leaves alternatives $w$ and $y$ available for choice. However, both of these are inferior to other alternatives that could have been chosen according to *all* the relevant criteria (i.e., they are Pareto inferior or dominated alternatives), something that makes the choice of either of them seem particularly perverse all things considered. Thus, it is not possible to choose any of the alternatives $w$, $x$, $y$, or $z$ without violating either one of the identified criteria or the Pareto principle.

Or so the arguments typically go. However, notice that although this sort of nonneutral intraprofile impossibility result does not assume the condition of independence of irrelevant alternatives (there not being any interprofile consistency to worry about), nevertheless, there is still a strong sort of "independence effect" in allowing a criterion *absolute* jurisdictional supremacy over some alternatives, that is, supremacy regardless of how that criterion ranks other (irrelevant) alternatives and, more specifically, how that criterion ranks those other alternatives in comparison to how some different criterion happens to rank them. This is, after all, how the jurisdictional separation strategy deals with the fact of noncommensurable pluralism; comparison between different criteria over the same alternatives is not required. But this sort of "independence," as the intraprofile impossibility results suggest, has its own difficulties, at least in the face of certain profiles of criterial orderings. To avoid them, it seems, we may need to drop the independence and make the criterial dominion over some alternatives more sensitive to some sort of *inter*-criterial comparability.

In the course of this essay, I shall be sketching one possible form that such inter-criterial comparability could take without reducing to full commensurability, and illustrating it with examples from accident law generally (Section III) and tort law more specifically (Section IV). However, before turning to the details of that analysis, it is useful to consider one other general kind of decision rule that sometimes informs multi-criterial decision-making. This rule is interesting because it introduces the idea of a conceptually sensitive ordering for different choices and shows how this form of ordering can differ fundamentally from the more conventional choice-theoretic notions of ordering, based on value maximization, that are usually required by decision theory. This decision rule also usefully exemplifies a special version of non-independent multi-criterial choice.

## C. Two Different Forms of Multi-Criterial Ordering

It is sometimes claimed that if one faces a choice between two goods, and even if one chooses the greater good, it is nevertheless rational to feel some regret for the foregone lesser good (Hurka 1996; Williams 1973). It is also claimed, although this appears to be more controversial, that it is *only* rational to feel this regret if the two goods are in some sense generically different from each other, that is, if one has a pluralistic theory of goods.[12] Whether this is the only way to have rational regret is not something we need to settle here. However, if pluralism provides for one of the ways, then it is interesting to consider the role that regret might play in multi-criterial decision-making. It may be that regret is more than a symptom of unruly pluralism; it could be that rational regret, or rational choice in the face of regret, can provide a way for ordering pluralism. In this section I shall suggest that it does, and that it does so in a way quite different from that provided by conventional decision theory.

Suppose that it is rational to feel regret for the failure to satisfy a given criterion in a difficult choice situation in which the various criteria are in conflict with one another. Moreover, suppose that it is rational to feel this regret for each criterion in proportion to the loss one experiences in that criterion in not having chosen other than one did. This clearly suggests that regret depends on cardinality and that is what I assume here. However, unlike in utilitarianism, we do not aggregate regret across different criteria. Regret, I suggest, is something we feel for each criterion considered singly.[13]

For example, in the following choice A between alternatives $x$ and $y$, we have three criteria informing the choice, $C_1$, $C_2$, and $C_3$, and cardinal payoffs for each criterion in each choice. We can also construct a corresponding regret matrix, here represented by the numbers appearing in parentheses after each of the cardinal entries; in terms of the payoff matrix, this regret number represents the cardinal difference between a particular row item and the maximum number in the column in which that row item appears.

Choice A:

|               | $C_1$   | $C_2$  | $C_3$    |
| ------------- | ------- | ------ | -------- |
| alternative $x$ | 12 (0)  | 7 (0)  | 3 (9)    |
| alternative $y$ | 5 (7)   | 4 (3)  | 12 (0)   |

Now suppose the decision rule (borrowed from decision theory, but criticized there (Luce and Raffia 1957) is to choose so as to minimize the maximum possible (criterial) regret, or "minimax regret." After all, regret is something one will experience in each choice, and surely it is best to minimize the maximum possible regret that one might feel. By inspection this means that one should choose $y$ over $x$ since the maximum regret experienced with that choice is 7 as opposed to 9.

Likewise, for the following pairs of choices, B:$(y, z)$ and C:$(z, x)$, one should choose $z$ and $x$, respectively.

*Choice B:*

|  | $C_1$ | $C_2$ | $C_3$ |
|---|---|---|---|
| alternative $y$ | 5 (0) | 4 (8) | 12 (0) |
| alternative $z$ | 2 (3) | 12 (0) | 6 (6) |

*Choice C:*

|  | $C_1$ | $C_2$ | $C_3$ |
|---|---|---|---|
| alternative $z$ | 2 (10) | 12 (0) | 6 (0) |
| alternative $x$ | 12 (0) | 7 (5) | 3 (3) |

However, now some will surely say that there is a problem here.[14] Should not a rule for rational decision-making generate a transitive ordering of the alternatives for choice? Transitivity requires that if some alternative $y$ is chosen over another alternative $x$, and alternative $z$ is likewise chosen over alternative $y$, then alternative $z$ should be chosen over alternative $x$. Yet that is precisely what the minimax regret rule does not do (compare Choice C).

There is another way to see the apparent irrationality of minimax regret. Suppose that the choice is to be exercised over all three alternatives at once as in Choice D.[15]

*Choice D:*

|  | $C_1$ | $C_2$ | $C_3$ |
|---|---|---|---|
| alternative $x$ | 12 (0) | 7 (5) | 3 (9) |
| alternative $y$ | 5 (7) | 4 (8) | 12 (0) |
| alternative $z$ | 2 (10) | 12 (0) | 6 (6) |

Then, minimax regret recommends choosing alternative $y$ since the maximum possible regret with that choice (regret of 8) is less than with alternative $x$ (regret of 9) or alternative $z$ (regret of 10). But, the argument will go, surely it is odd to choose $y$ over $z$ from the set of three alternatives $(x, y, z)$ in choice D, but $z$ over $y$ in choice B when there are only the two alternatives $(y, z)$. Why should adding the third alternative $x$ to the set of opportunities make a difference to the choice between $y$ and $z$? One might have thought that the latter choice would have been independent of any such influence. Indeed, economists typically insist on just this sort of independence in their revealed preference axioms.[16]

Yet this last way of putting the point suggests that we have returned to an earlier set of difficulties discussed in Section II.B. There we saw that insistence on certain notions of independence was highly problematic for multi-criterial choice. Perhaps it is also problematic to insist on the analogous notion of independence here. However, while the notion of an intransitive ordering may be problematic for the idea of value maximization or "preference, all things considered," and likewise problematic for revealed preference theory, why should an ordering based on regret be transitive or consistent in that way? After all, the various choices from the varying sets of alternatives considered above are perfectly *comprehensible,* or rationally ordered, under the quite different concept of regret. (There simply *is* more regret to be avoided in choosing alternative $y$ rather than alternative $z$ when alternative $x$ is available than when it is not.) Perhaps such a concept provides an ordering for multi-criterial choice that is structurally different from that provided by, and assumed so uniformly as rational in, the concept of value maximization or an all-things-considered preference ordering.

It should not be surprising, really, that some forms of conceptually ordered multi-criterial choice might be structurally different from the sort of ordering provided by the idea of an all-things-considered preference. After all, as the economist's revealed preference axioms suggest, choice informed by preference should, for any pair of alternatives, be independent of how those alternatives are combined, or partitioned, with other alternatives. This is what looked odd, initially, about choice based on minimax regret. But different partitions of the alternatives, in making different alternatives available for choice, define what is "at issue" for choice in quite different ways. Thus, on a second look, it should not be surprising that under the aspect of different issues or concepts, different because differently available alternatives have defined the choice problem in a new way, choices between even the same pair of alternatives might not be the same. We should expect, therefore, under a conceptually *sensitive* theory of decision-making, that choices will be systematically issue- or partition-dependent in a way that preference theory denies is rational.[17]

We should also expect, therefore, that some conceptually ordered choice will be path-dependent. After all, path dependence is simply partition dependence with a temporal dimension; some partitions of the set of overall alternatives are considered before others, with the final choice being the one that survives the sequence as a non-rejected alternative. But path dependence has a bad name in preference theory. Arrow, for example, first imposed his condition of transitivity on the all-things-considered social preference relation because he felt that, without it, social choice would be arbitrarily dependent on the order, or path, in which the different alternatives were considered (Arrow 1963, p. 120). (The majority voting paradox, considered above, illustrates the problem; whichever alternative of the three not considered first in a pairwise majority vote of the criteria will end up being chosen by a majority of the criteria, at least if previously rejected alternatives are not reconsidered.) But if the different partitions of the alternatives, or the paths of choice, are conceptually ordered, as in the structured presentation of issues within a sequenced and concept-sensitive argument, then there is less reason to think that the final choice is *arbitrary* in the way that originally concerned Arrow. A sequence of choice, or partitioning of alternatives, ordered by concepts is one which is permeated with thought, the very opposite of arbitrary or non-rational choice.

In the next section of the paper I shall begin to illustrate what I mean by a conceptually sequenced argument in the context of accident law. Moreover, I shall suggest that it provides a rational way to accommodate plural criteria which is different both from the strategy of assuming single valued commensurability and from the strategy of assigning supreme jurisdictional authority to single-minded criteria within special domains, strategies which we have already seen are problematic for genuinely plural or multi-criterial choice. However, to motivate the relevance of that sort of exercise in the context of accident law, we need first to leave our more abstract discussions of the problematic structures of multi-criterial choice behind, and to show that there is a content for these sorts of problems in the particular normative criteria that animate accident law.

## III. Intraprofile Impossibilities in Accident Law

In our discussion of the general difficulties encountered in multi-criterial choice, we saw that, short of assuming the full commensurability of different criteria (in either its cardinal or ordinal forms), there were two sorts of problem to be encountered. The first of these was the interprofile impossibility that was first unearthed by Arrow. However, it seemed that this powerful result may depend too much upon assuming a strong interprofile consistency condition, namely, the independence of irrelevant alternatives, a condition which, in the context of multi-criterial choice, it may not make much sense to assume.

However, it was also pointed out that the second sort of difficulty, characterized by intraprofile impossibility results, and which can show up in either neutral or nonneutral forms, did not depend on this strong condition, although it did depend upon certain problematic profiles of criterial orderings existing as a matter of fact. This might suggest that if these particular profiles did not really exist, or at least did not typically exist in some contexts, then intraprofile impossibility might not be much of a problem for multi-criterial choice in those contexts. However, in this section, I shall argue that in the context of accident law, this is likely to be an empty dream. The very concerns for deterrence, compensation, and general welfare, which Weinrib has rightly identified as the ones current in contemporary theorizing about accident law, are the very criteria that one should expect to generate the sort of neutral intraprofile impossibility that we earlier saw exemplified in the majority voting paradox. When all of these relevant criteria are all at once allowed access to all the salient alternatives for choice, including tort law, in the way that neutrality permits, either incoherence or arbitrary path dependence would appear to be the result.

This may suggest that a nonneutral strategy for dealing with plural criteria might fare better in dealing with the problematic criterial profile that exists as a matter of fact for accident law. This, for example, is the strategy chosen by Weinrib himself when he chooses to comprehend tort law purely from the point of view of corrective justice, leaving the concern for deterrence, compensation and welfare to be satisfied by other institutions. However, over the course of this paper, I shall argue, first, that this strategy also falls prey to the perils of intraprofile impossibility (Section III.B) and, second, that there is evidence that tort law has itself recognized this fact, Weinrib's claims notwithstanding (Section IV). The form that tort law takes to accommodate these plural considerations, I shall suggest, is the one that admits them according to a non-arbitrary, conceptually sequenced, issue- or path-dependent argument.

## A. Neutral Intraprofile Impossibility in Accident Law: The Case of Majority Voting

To outline a neutral strategy for dealing with the plural criteria that inform accident law, we obviously need to have some sense of what the alternatives for choice are and, more particularly for the purposes of this paper, how these alternatives relate to tort law. In an earlier article, in which we discussed in some detail the options relevant to automobile accidents, Michael Trebilcock and I identified four alternatives that are typically debated as possible substitutes for a pure tort regime (Chapman and Trebilcock 1992). Three of these were a pure no-fault compensation scheme (where tort law had no role at all), an add-on no-fault scheme (where tort law is left intact and merely supplemented by some no-fault system), and a threshold no-fault scheme (where tort law is displaced by no-fault up to some threshold, but still operates thereafter as the exclusive remedy for recovery against accident loss). (We also considered a fourth scheme, elective no-fault, which was different from the others in focusing less on the character of the scheme designed to replace pure tort and more on the possibility of providing for individual rather than legislative choice of the substitute scheme; this possibility we ignore here.[18])

In the earlier article, we argued that these three alternatives naturally organized themselves into two categories, namely, according to whether they were designed to supplement or to replace (in whole or in part) the law of tort (Chapman and Trebilcock 1992, p. 809). We shall have reason to return briefly to this two-fold categorization later in this section, but for the moment I wish to emphasize a slightly different, although related, point. We argued in our earlier article that those who focus on the viewpoint of the plaintiff, and who, accordingly, emphasize the compensation criterion in accident law, would be inclined to rank the add-on no-fault scheme, as provided for by a strategy of supplementation to tort law, as their most preferred of the options. Next to that they would prefer one of the various replacement no-fault schemes (with the threshold scheme possibly ranked ahead of pure no-fault), ranking tort law, with its traditional emphasis on the defendant's fault as a necessary prerequisite for the plaintiff to recover for loss, as least preferred. The deterrence criterion, on the other hand, more focused on fault and the costs which tort law can selectively bring to bear on the defendant, would rank tort law as most preferred, would be prepared to contemplate an add-on scheme that did not replace tort law at all as second, and rank the replacement alternatives in their various forms as last, with threshold no-fault likely being preferred to pure no-fault since tort law is still to some extent preserved there. Finally, we identified a criterion which would be advanced by those whose concerns might be more about general social welfare than about the plight of either plaintiffs or defendants in particular, and who would be most concerned about the costs of administering and funding any scheme for allocating accident losses. This criterion, we suggested, would rank the replacement no-fault alternatives as most preferred (likely in the order of the extent of replacement, with pure no-fault ahead of threshold no-fault), tort law as second, and the add-on scheme, with all its costs of duplication, as last.[19]

Thus, our arguments effectively generated the following three orderings (from top to bottom) by the three relevant criteria of the four alternatives, including tort law:

| *Compensation* | *Deterrence* | *Admin./Funding Costs* |
|---|---|---|
| add-on no-fault | tort | pure no-fault |
| threshold no-fault | add-on no-fault | threshold no-fault |
| pure no-fault | threshold no-fault | tort |
| tort | pure no-fault | add-on no-fault |

It will be apparent that, given these criterial orderings, a majority of the criteria cannot identify any one of the four alternatives as majority preferred without another one of the four alternatives also being majority preferred to that choice. A majority of the criteria prefers the add-on scheme to the threshold scheme, the threshold scheme to the pure scheme, and the pure scheme to tort law. Yet tort law is majority preferred to the add-on scheme. If any attempt is made to avoid the paradox by using criterial majorities to eliminate alternatives in sequence, then which alternative survives as the final choice, not rejected by any majority of the criteria, will be entirely dependent on the order in which the alternatives were presented for consideration, that is, it will be path dependent.

We argued in section II that for a majority voting paradox like this to occur, it is necessary (although not sufficient) that a particular matrix of orderings, referred to as a Latin square, over some possible triple of alternatives must be present somewhere within the given profile of criterial orderings. (In the above profile of criterial orderings, the Latin square is present, for example, with respect to the add-on no-fault alternative, the threshold no-fault alternative, and tort law.) Conversely, for the paradox to be avoided it is sufficient that this particular matrix be absent. This makes it interesting to examine the Latin square matrix in some greater detail. What, precisely, is the sort of pluralistic diversity it identifies as problematic for majoritarian decision-making? Or, equivalently, what kind of consensus or coordination does it suggest is required across plural considerations if the sorts of majoritarian difficulties highlighted here are to be avoided?

What the Latin square captures is the idea that for the three alternatives in the square there is no unanimous agreement across all the relevant criteria that any one of alternatives is either "not best" of the three, or "not worst" of the three, or "not between" the other two. That is, the three rankings together show that, for *each* of the three alternatives, at least one of the criteria ranks that alternative as worst, another that that same alternative is best, and a third that that same alternative is between the other two. Thus, because this particular pattern of criterial rankings is necessary for the majoritarian voting paradox to occur, one way of avoiding the paradox is by insisting on a very particular kind of unanimous agreement across the criteria, namely, that they all agree that there is at least one alternative in every triple which is "not best," or "not worst," or "not between" the two others. In the social choice literature this special form of unanimity requirement is called *value restriction* (Sen 1970, pp. 166–86).

Now, as many social choice theorists have pointed out, there is reason to believe that in some choice situations such consensus or value restriction will arise spontaneously across certain criteria. For example, if there is a single dimension along which all the different criteria measure the worth of all the alternatives for choice and, further, if there is some consensus across the criteria that one of the alternatives in every set of three has some intermediate amount of that decisive dimension, then that intermediate alternative will be a "not worst" alternative for every one of the criteria (Mueller 1989, p. 69). That is, every criterion will rank this intermediate alternative as either best, in that the alternative has *neither* too much nor too little of the decisive dimension, or in between the other two alternatives, in that it has *either* too much *or* too little as compared to some other alternative which is more extreme on this decisive dimension. No criterion, however, will rank this alternative as worst of the three, since that would imply that the intermediate alternative has *both* too much *and* too little of the one dimension that is allegedly decisive for that criterion, something which is obviously self-contradictory.

The problem with this "not worst" route to satisfying value restriction is that it is very restrictive indeed and, therefore, unlikely to arise spontaneously across criterial rankings in many choice situations. Not only must all criteria agree that there is a single decisive dimension for the evaluation of all three alternatives in any given set of three, they must also agree that the facts show that some particular alternative is unambiguously of intermediate value on that dimension.

Social choice theorists have now shown that these are very demanding require-ments, and that as soon as one introduces more than one evaluative dimension into a choice situation, it is extremely unlikely that the "not worst" form of value restriction will be satisfied in fact.[20]

Indeed, the above example of the majority voting paradox can be used to il-lustrate the difficulty in an interesting and suggestive way. Suppose, for exam-ple, that it could be said that the only really decisive issue in accident law was the extent to which the tort law regime was *replaced* by some other policy al-ternative. This general view of the matter might arise if everyone agreed that tort law was effective in meeting some relevant goal (e.g., deterrence), but var-ied in their willingness to pay its high costs in achieving that goal. Some might want most to replace tort law completely (e.g., a compensation proponent who, while admitting deterrence was relevant, was not much interested in it), others not at all (the full blown deterrence proponent), and still others might prefer most a partial replacement, all of this depending on their point of optimal trade-off between the benefits and costs of achieving tort's agreed upon goal. But no one would rank the partial replacement alternative, or the threshold regime, as worst in their ranking. And, in such a situation where replacement of tort law is the only issue up for consideration, no one would even get to consider a pol-icy option that introduced some new issue for consideration. So the add-on no-fault regime, which provides for having both tort law and a no-fault option for all accidents, that is, introduces for consideration a new issue, namely whether we should *add to* rather than merely replace tort law, would not arise as one of the alternatives for choice.

In fact, in the above table of criterial orderings one can see that there is no majority voting cycle in the absence of the add-on no-fault alternative, that is, if the choice criteria are permitted to range only over those (single issue) alter-natives that involve varying degrees of replacement of tort law (viz., tort law with no replacement, the threshold regime with partial replacement, and pure no-fault with full replacement). This is because there is unanimous agreement across all criteria that, in all the possible sets of three alternatives, the thresh-old regime (or partial replacement alternative) is an intermediate alternative on the decisive replacement dimension and, therefore, is "not worst." It is only when we allow other dimensions of evaluation to become importantly decisive in this choice situation, such as the extent to which the victim is compensated, so that the compensation criterion is motivated and permitted to propose an add-on regime rather than one of the replacement no-fault alternatives as the best of all possible worlds, that we undermine this "not worst" form of value restric-tion. But this is exactly what we should expect if there is no longer just a sin-gle decisive dimension along which all the choice criteria are to evaluate all of the alternatives for choice. With the addition of the add-on scheme, we now have two such dimensions, one which values the *replacement* of tort law to varying degrees, and another which values *supplementing* tort law with a compensation scheme. In the face of this new plurality of issues, we should not be surprised, therefore, that one of the forms of consensus sufficient for avoiding the majority voting paradox, namely, the "not worst" form of value restriction, has been lost.

However, this example is also usefully suggestive of how we might *impose* a form of value restriction on pluralistic criteria by way of appropriate institutional design, and even if the criterial orderings do not satisfy the requirement spontaneously or as a matter of brute fact. Recall that before the possibility of an add-on regime was introduced, the above criterial orderings did not show the Latin square pattern which is necessary for the majority voting paradox to occur. This, we argued, was the consequence of placing only the replacement alternatives before the criteria for their consideration, a single and decisive dimension for the evaluation of all the alternatives other than the add-on regime, and one, therefore, that could provide a basis for satisfying the "not worst" form of value restriction. This suggests that it would be useful for avoiding the majority voting paradox if the criteria could somehow be precluded, *at least initially*, from considering those alternatives which introduce these new dimensions of choice into the choice problem.[21] Then the different criteria would come to bear on the alternatives *as if* their shared profile of orderings exhibited the sort of unanimity that value restriction required even if as a matter of fact it did not.

We can think of this imposed form of value restriction, at least initially, as having the following sequenced structure. First, for any possible triple of alternatives, the idea is to have the criteria compare, and choose between one of the three alternatives considered on its own and the other two alternatives considered as a packaged pair. Then, if the packaged pair is chosen, the criteria can go on to consider and choose, which of these previously packaged alternatives in particular is to be the final choice. Such a choice sequence would not permit the singled out alternative ever to be compared with any one of the packaged alternatives. Rather, the packaged alternatives are never compared as such with the singled out alternative and are only compared with each other if the package is chosen in the first round of the choice sequence. If the packaging is done so that one decisive dimension for choice is at issue in the first round when the singled out alternative is compared with the package, and another dimension for choice is at issue in the second round if and when choice is exercised over the alternatives in the package, then the effect of packaging is to force the voters to confront a sequence of choices which considers alternatives on only one decisive choice dimension at a time, thereby avoiding the majority voting paradox.[22]

The above example of criterial orderings for accident law alternatives can be used to illustrate the choice sequence in a less abstract way. Suppose, before the different criteria were permitted to consider individually all the replacement no-fault alternatives which we described above (including the tort law alternative as a limiting case, or zero point, on that replacement continuum; more on this below), that we insisted that they first resolve the conceptually prior issue as to what overall "form" the no-fault alternative should take. No-fault could be considered either as a replacement for, or as a supplement to, tort law. Such a prior choice would have the effect of singling out the add-on no-fault alternative to be compared with a replacement package comprised of the other alternatives. But the choice sequence would not permit any of the packaged replacement alternatives to be compared individually with the add-on alternative. In this way the *extent* of tort law's replacement is kept apart as an issue, or as a decisive dimension for choice, from the question that asks first whether the replacing or the supplementing of tort law with no-fault is more appropriate as an overall strategy. Thus, the choice sequence avoids the majority voting paradox, first, by separating out the different dimensions for the evaluation of the various policy options into different rounds of choice and, second, by keeping these different dimensions apart from each other by precluding any pairwise comparison of previously rejected alternatives with those individual alternatives which are within the packages being considered in subsequent rounds.

That this particular form, or structure, of choice sequence is enough to avoid the majority voting paradox is easily shown. For while we may have motivated our argument for the adoption of choice sequences which proceed one dimension at a time by way of a discussion of how the "not worst" form of value restriction is undermined by multi-dimensional choice, the real gain in adopting a choice sequence of this form lies in the fact that it effectively imposes the "not between" form of value restriction on all criterial orderings. Given this as one of the forms of value restriction, of course, a majority voting paradox cannot occur.

If the first round of the choice sequence concerns the issue of whether no-fault should, on the one hand, replace or, on the other hand, supplement tort law, then, as already suggested, the effective choice over this set of alternatives is between the add-on regime and the other alternatives packaged together as variations on replacement. Now, since neither the compensation criterion nor the administrative/funding cost criterion puts the add-on no-fault alternative *between* the other two alternatives in their respective orderings, it is easy to see how each criterion would vote in such a first round of choice. The compensation criterion would favour supplementing tort with no-fault and, therefore, would unambiguously vote for the add-on regime. The administrative cost/funding criterion, on the other hand, would equally unambiguously favour replacing tort law to some (even zero) extent over supplementing it with no-fault and, therefore, would vote for the replacement package.

But what about the deterrence criterion? Because it does put the add-on no-fault alternative *between* the two replacement alternatives, first round voting is less easy to predict for it. If it chooses replacement (or, as it might better be put, if it chooses to put the extent of replacement on the agenda for choice in the second round), it may help to preserve tort law, or its most preferred option, but it runs the risk of also bringing about its least preferred options, namely, the threshold and pure no-fault schemes. This presents the deterrence criterion with a dilemma to be sure, but that is the consequence of the choice sequence imposing "not between" value restriction on criteria with respect to the add-on no-fault alternative. Thus, the dilemma is not one the deterrence criterion would face if its ordering satisfied this form of "not between" value restriction as a matter of fact. But since the ordering does not satisfy it, the effect of the choice sequence being organized in this way is that this form of value restriction is imposed upon this criterion *as if* it really did. In this sense, therefore, the structure of the choice sequence captures the demands of "not between" value restriction as one of the methods for avoiding the majority voting cycle.

At this point in the argument one might be prepared to accept the idea that the general concept of value restriction, and the concept of "not between" value restriction in particular, might help to provide the appropriate form or structure of a choice sequence or process which will avoid the majority voting paradox. However, one might still object, since different versions of "not between" value restriction can be imposed depending on which of the different alternatives is singled out in the choice sequence, and since the final policy outcome that results from the sequence depends crucially on which particular version is imposed, that we are still mired in the same problem of social choice that prompted our search for an appropriate choice sequence in the first place. Have we not simply substituted a new form of criterial conflict, one now focused on the particulars of a choice sequence, for the original one that focused on the choice of final alternatives?

However, this objection overstates the degree of freedom one really has in packaging the options for choice into a sensible sequence of choice. Some choice sequences (or paths), or choice packages (or partitions of the alternatives), simply make more sense than others, at least in a given context where real alternatives are standing in for the merely lettered abstractions, $x, y,$ and $z$. Consider again the above criterial orderings. We have already suggested that a plausible choice sequence might be one that considered first whether the reform of tort law should take on a replacement or supplementary aspect. This choice sequence, which had the consequence of singling out the add-on alternative and packaging the others as replacement alternatives, was particularly burdensome for the deterrence criterion, which put the add-on no-fault alternative between the other replacement alternatives in its ordering. Might not a proponent of the deterrence criterion propose some other packaging of the alternatives which would capture the essence of a different choice sequence, and which would confront some other criterion with the burden of meeting the demands of "not between" value restriction? Suppose, for example, that a deterrence proponent suggested that we single out the tort law alternative instead. She might argue that the conceptually prior issue for choice, and the one that should be settled first in the choice sequence, is whether *any* change in favour of one of the no-fault alternatives, be it supplemental or replacement in form, should be made. Only if we have decided to make some change, she might argue, should we then go on to consider the secondary issue as to whether the change should be supplemental or replacement in form.

As suggested, this choice sequence singles out the tort law alternative for special consideration in the first round. No longer is it merely to be considered as one of the replacement alternatives to be decided upon after the decision is made (if it is) to choose the replacement over the supplemental form of no-fault. And surely that is right. There is certainly something odd in characterizing the tort law alternative as one of the replacement alternatives; zero replacement is not really a degree of replacement at all. Moreover, this is not an abstract mathematical point about the nature of zero; at that level the point may well be ambiguous, or even wrong. Rather, the point being made operates at a more substantial level than that, and surely that is the level appropriate to the topic under discussion. It suggests that we would all recognize something opportunistic in any attempt by a proponent of some criterion to exploit the purely mathematical idea that zero replacement was a degree of replacement. We would see that for what it really was, that is, as an attempt to rig the choice sequence or agenda to effect a final choice that was to the particular advantage of one criterion, not to seek what is reasonable in the accommodation of plural criteria. It is for this reason that the argument advanced by the proponent of the deterrence criterion to single out the tort law alternative in the way described is particularly compelling. It responds to any attempt to characterize the choice of tort law alternative as involving some degree of replacement of tort law (where replacement occurs in a very limited way indeed) in exactly the way it should, with skepticism.

So now we have three rounds of choice in our choice sequence, with each round addressing a different issue. The first round emphasizes the issue of *change,* and singles out the tort law alternative against a package of all the possible no-fault reforms. Then, if change is chosen, the issue becomes what *form* the change to no-fault should take; in particular should no-fault be thought of as replacing or supplementing tort law? This second round of choice, therefore, would single out the add-on alternative against a package of possible replacement alternatives, that is, threshold or pure no-fault, in the manner we have already described. Should replacement be the form of change which is chosen in the second round, then the third and final round of choice would be over the *extent* of replacement, or a choice over these last two alternatives. I suggest that this sequence of choice from change to the form of change and, lastly, to the final specification of the extent of change in that form, is non-arbitrary in a way that the path dependent choices which originally concerned Kenneth Arrow are not. Indeed, if I could avoid the theoretical baggage that so often accompanies the term, I might even describe the decision to use this choice sequence, which moves so logically from the general and prior issue of change to the final spec-ification of the extent of change in one particular form, as "natural."[23]

However, it might be objected that what is natural about the choice sequence I have proposed is more in its partitioning of the overall choice problem into different issues for choice than it is in any particular sequence in which those issues are addressed. In particular, it might be thought that it is just as natural to suggest that the details of no-fault reform should be completely specified be-fore any prior commitment to such a change or reform is even made. Thus, on this argument, the first round of the choice sequence would consider the extent of replacement issue and determine first which of the replacement alternatives should be chosen. Having decided that matter the choice sequence would then compare the add-on no-fault regime with the replacement alternative already chosen as best so as to resolve the issue as to the proper form that no-fault should take. Finally, having resolved all the details as to the form and extent of reform, the choice sequence would then compare the most preferred no-fault reform al-ternative with the tort law alternative to resolve the issue as to whether there should be any such change at all. This alternative choice sequence considers the same issues (or partitions) that my proposed sequence of choice does, only it does so in a reverse order that moves, apparently, from the particular to the gen-eral rather than the general to the particular.

However, there is more than just a reversal in the order in which the differ-ent issues are considered which distinguishes the two choice sequences. Where my proposed choice sequence, moving from the general issue of change to a fi-nal specification of its details, confronts the criteria with the burden of meeting the requirements of "not between" value restriction at various points in the choice sequence because some of the alternatives are presented in packages, the alternative choice sequence that works from the particular to the general never confronts the criteria with anything other than *unpackaged* and *particular* (un-categorized) choices, for example, the choice between the best replacement al-ternative and the add-on regime, or the choice between either of those two and tort law. But this means that in the alternative choice sequence there is only the appearance of an institutional commitment to a particular series of issues as im-portant since there is no corresponding requirement, without the burden of "not between" value restriction also being imposed, that the criteria themselves be ordered around, or supportive of, these issues as the most salient. Thus, even though it *appears* to attend to the same issues as our proposed choice sequence which moves from the general to the particular, the alternative choice sequence, which moves from the particular to the general, exhibits only a formal com-mitment to those issues for choice, and one which is devoid of the real substance that is provided by a corresponding judgment as to the appropriate value re-strictions which should be required of the criterial orderings that are to inform pluralistic choice. I prefer our proposed choice sequence to the alternative choice sequence because it preserves a coherence that should exist between the *conceptual* (partition dependent) ordering of issues and the *value* restrictions which are imposed on criteria. As promised, the latter is ordered by the former.

### B. Nonneutral Intraprofile Impossibility in Accident Law: The Strategy of Criterial Separation

In the previous subsection, I examined the possibility of combining the different criteria that inform accident law in a neutral way, that is, in a way that allows all the criteria equal and simultaneous access to all the alternatives for choice. However, we discovered that the multi-criterial profile of orderings of relevant alternatives, which is so problematic for integrating these criteria under majority rule, was likely to be the rule rather than the exception in this accident law context. To avoid the problematic profile, or at least to discipline its arbitrary effects on multi-criterial choice, I proposed that choice be conceptually sequenced in a way that was coherent with the spirit of requiring value restriction as an ordering to be imposed across criterial pluralism.

However, it might be thought that these problematic forms of pluralism could be handled in a quite different way altogether. Specifically, the idea would be to separate the application of different criteria into domains where each criterion would reign supreme (that is, unanswerable to other criteria), perhaps because the dominant criterion is somehow a good match for the alternatives considered there. In doing this, the argument might go, conflicts between different criteria, the stuff of incoherence, can simply be avoided. Indeed, as suggested above, this would appear to be the strategy supported by Weinrib for accommodating the otherwise competing concerns about defendant deterrence and plaintiff compensation. Corrective justice, he would suggest, should be the special province of tort law.

In this subsection I shall more closely look into this non-neutral strategy for dealing with pluralism within accident law. I shall argue that the criterial purist within any one sphere will have great difficulty maintaining the integrity of that sphere against influences from other criteria. Sometimes my arguments will only appeal to the sort of pluralist who admits the worth of competing criteria but thinks that they are best or most coherently satisfied within separate jurisdictional domains. To this sort of pluralist we shall only suggest that some greater mixing of criteria within domains is more likely to satisfy each and every criterion that she has admitted is worthy of pursuit. But there will be pluralists, perhaps, who will hang on somewhat more single-mindedly to the separate pursuit of plural criteria, arguing that any kind of mixing of criteria across domains must either be incoherent or (as in the case of mixing according to quantitative commensurability) do conceptual violence to the genuine qualitative differences which exist between plural criteria. To these sorts of pluralists I offer a two-pronged reply. First (in the remainder of Section III.B), I argue that there is often incoherence in *not* admitting some consideration of alternative criteria; failure to do so undermines the satisfaction of the single-minded pluralist's own primary value. Second (in Section IV), I argue that there *is* a way to admit the consideration of multiple criteria without assuming their (full) commensurability. That way is to admit them (and their only partial commensurability) in the order required by a conceptually sequenced argument. I argue, further, that this is precisely the way competing criteria are coherently accommodated within tort law even now, and I provide some examples to illustrate the point.

**I. CORRECTIVE JUSTICE AND COMPENSATION.** I begin with Weinrib's claim that the single organizing principle for tort law is corrective justice and his idea that, if there is a concern for compensation that needs to be addressed, then the proper and only coherent way to do so is outside tort law within an institution specifically designed for compensatory requirements. Call this outside institution the social compensation scheme, or SCS.

Now imagine that there has been an accident the facts of which would normally bring it within the purview of tort law and the concerns of corrective justice: Able has negligently injured Baker. But suppose too that the SCS has some concerns here. In particular, the SCS wants to insure that Baker is compensated for her injury regardless of fault. So the SCS pays Baker compensation.

What is the corrective justice adjudicator to do when Baker now appears at the doors of the tort system with the intention of suing Able for his wrongdoing? There appear to be three options. First, the corrective justice adjudicator can deny access to Baker on the grounds that she has already received compensation elsewhere. But this is (reciprocally) to deny tort law its proper access to the very sort of wrongful interaction which is relevant to corrective justice. That seems to hold both tort law and corrective justice hostage to what is decided under the compensation criterion in the SCS, hardly the stuff of criterial separation.

Second, the corrective justice adjudicator can choose to ignore, at least initially, what has happened in the SCS and allow Baker to bring her suit in tort. But at some point in the action, and in particular when it has come time to consider the determination of what damages are appropriate, the court will have to consider the argument that Able will advance, namely, that Baker, while wrongfully injured as a result of Able's negligence, is none the worse off for that injury, having already been completely compensated. If the principle governing the award of damages in tort law is *restitutio in integrum,* or to restore the plaintiff to the position that he or she would have been in had the tort not occurred, *but no more,* then it is unclear that Able should have to pay Baker any damages at all. Yet that too leaves the wrongful interaction between Able and Baker somehow unaddressed, a denial of corrective justice. The dilemma is a familiar one: where the plaintiff has access to some sort of collateral benefits scheme, then the remedy in tort law can choose either to ignore that fact, and allow the plaintiff to recover damages in excess of her loss (or double recovery), or to take account of the loss but leave some of the relational wrong, appropriate to tort law and corrective justice, and visited upon the plaintiff by the defendant, unattended. Each one of these choices manages to do some violence to tort law and the requirements of corrective justice.

There is, of course, a third option. The corrective justice adjudicator in tort law could deny Baker her right to recover for losses already compensated by the SCS, but allow the SCS a right of subrogation to sue in her name. This is, of course, exactly how the law of tort does handle the problem of collateral benefits (although there are complications to be addressed below) and it seems to allow for the neat accommodation of all the considerations relevant to corrective justice. Now the plaintiff Baker is not permitted to have double recovery, yet the defendant Able is forced to address the relational wrong that he visited upon Baker and for which it is important that corrective justice have some sort of application.

However, the problem of criterial integrity, originally foisted upon tort law, has simply shifted now to the SCS. For now it appears that the SCS, whose only job is to provide for compensation, is implicated by the requirements of corrective justice. The solution to this point is to have the SCS provide for a right of subrogation in the tort system in the name of wrongfully injured plaintiffs. But suppose the SCS wants nothing to do with tort law or corrective justice, and wants only to devote itself to the compensation criterion. Can it do so without shifting its difficulties back to the corrective justice adjudicator? It seems that it can. For suppose the SCS simply made it part of its legislative package that neither plaintiffs like Baker nor the SCS itself (in subrogation) would have a right to sue in tort law for wrongfully imposed injuries. For then it is not as if the corrective justice adjudicator is ever confronted, *qua* adjudicator, with a plaintiff willing to sue and with respect to whom the adjudicator denies corrective justice where it is properly applicable. Such a plaintiff simply never knocks at the door of tort law, this right having been legislated away. But it cannot be that there is something inapposite for adjudication in a plaintiff not coming to tort law despite having a claim. For that is something tort law contemplates every day, when plaintiffs choose, for any number of different reasons, not to sue in tort.

**II. THE DETERRENCE OBJECTION.** So it appears that we have now arrived at some sort of equilibrium between the concerns of corrective justice, singlemindedly pursued through tort, and the concerns for compensation, just as singlemindedly pursued through the SCS. But the argument cannot safely stop here. For despite the fact that we have avoided, at least as an adjudicative matter, denying any plaintiffs who are wrongfully injured by defendants their day in court, and despite the fact that we have provided for their effective compensation by the SCS without at the same time allowing them double recovery, we have, nonetheless, left some wrongdoing by some defendants unattended as a legislative matter.

It is clear that this residual problem is of some interest to proponents of the deterrence criterion. To the extent that wrongdoers are not held accountable for their wrongdoing they are less likely to be deterred from causing wrongful injury. But the pluralist can simply say that this is why the non-neutral strategy of criterial separation needs to have an institution devoted to deterrence considerations, where the conduct of the wrongdoer is addressed in a way appropriate to that criterion. However, some pluralists can say this more easily than others. For the sort of pluralist who admits the relevance of deterrence as a value, abstracted from any particular institution, there should be a willingness to at least consider the possibly that *both* deterrence *and* compensation might be better achieved by mixing their joint consideration into single institutions. This would be to use a multi-criterial version of Sen's theorem on the Pareto-impossible liberal against this sort of pluralist. It seems particularly perverse, the argument might go, to so insist on institutional purity that every one of the criteria that the pluralist admits is worthy of attention is less satisfied than it otherwise could be under a mixing strategy. Nor would this argument, based as it is on the Pareto principle, commit the pluralist to any kind of commensurability.

I do not choose here to demonstrate that the criterial separation strategy for dealing with pluralism necessarily performs worse in some Pareto sense than a strategy of criterial mixing across institutions.[24] It seems as likely as not that the mixing strategy will have mixed results as compared to the criterial separation strategy, meaning that neither strategy will Pareto dominate the other with respect to all relevant criteria. But I leave that issue here. Instead, I choose to address the other sort of pluralist who, much more single-mindedly, only seems to attach significance, for example, to the satisfaction of the deterrence and compensation criteria within, respectively, properly constituted compensation and deterrence institutions. Such a pluralist, it seems, will not be much moved by any suggestion that there is some greater deterrence to be achieved when a compensation institution compromises on the deterrence-limiting effects of full (or flat priced[25]) plaintiff compensation, or that there is some compensation-enhancing impact in having a deterrence institution consider the effects of plaintiff compensation on deterrence (e.g., through private rather than public regulatory enforcement). The different criteria are simply *defined* for such a pluralist such that extra deterrence within a compensation institution, and/or extra compensation within a deterrence institution, are without the value they have in institutions properly (and single-mindedly) devoted to their particular satisfaction.

To see if this is really a logically possible position for a pluralist, consider first the compensation criterion as satisfied, purely, in a compensation institution. Suppose that it is proposed that there be full recovery for all accident or personal injury losses. Surely, such a compensation proponent, even one moved only by the satisfaction of the compensation criterion in its own proper domain, has to be concerned that, without any attention to the incidence of accidents, there is every reason to think that such a proposal will be unfundable. Moreover, the reason that the scheme will be unfundable is precisely that the person who is fully compensated for injury does not, given that compensation, much care about the incidence of injury. Now the deterrence theorist, of course, has a special sort of concern about this indifference to injury, as would a responsibility theorist, but the compensation theorist too has to be concerned, even in her own terms, if the implication is that some other injuries will of necessity go uncompensated. On the other hand, if it is assumed that the compensation scheme provides, as most do, only for partial recovery, then almost by definition of limited recovery as limited compensation, the compensation theorist has to be concerned about the incidence of accidents. The greater the number of accidents, the greater the incidence of less than complete compensation.

Again, however, it will be said by this sort of pluralist that the way to deal with a higher incidence of injury is not by limiting recovery within the compensation scheme, but rather by attending to the incidence of injury directly within institutions specifically (and purely) designed for the purpose. So, for example, one might attend to the deterrence of injury or the incapacitation of injurers by having appropriate criminal or regulatory institutions in place. But what would this mean? Would it mean that a speeding driver who has an accident and negligently causes injury both to himself and another would be allowed, with one hand, to recover for his own injuries regardless of fault from the SCS, but, with the other, be obliged to pay back a deterrence focused fine to the regulatory institution? This would mean that the injurer is still the worse off for the accident. Would full compensation regardless of fault now mean that the injurer is to recover for the costs of the fine as well? Then what has happened to the effect of the fine on deterrence? Or perhaps the regulatory institution should focus less on deterrence and monetary fines and more on the strategy of incapacitation as, say, in the use of jail terms or the revocation of one's licence to drive. But these strategies too have their implications for full compensation. Even if one is prepared to ignore, somehow regardless of fault, the loss experienced by the injurer, the fact remains that the injurer will have dependents for whom the regulatory sanction, visited upon the injurer to avoid incidence of injury, represents a real loss as a result of the accident. Is the SCS, committed to full compensation regardless of fault, not also committed to compensating for these losses? It is easy to see that, in only a few steps, the pluralist who demands that institutions remain pure to their dominant and defining criterion are confronted with the possibility that their single-minded pluralism is self-defeating.

It will be argued in reply that no sensible compensation theorist has ever intended that full compensation must extend to compensation for the sanctions meted out in the name, say, of deterrence. While these latter sorts of losses are, admittedly, losses that would not have occurred "but for the injury causing accident," the argument will be that they are, nevertheless, not within the category of losses which it is the intention of the compensation scheme to cover. And, of course, that seems right. The issue is again what sorts of collateral impacts, while *historically* connected to the accident as its cause-in-fact consequences, are *normatively* the sorts of losses that are relevant to a victim's recovery. The argument here is that a scheme focused only on pure compensation for the fact of loss on the one hand, and pure deterrence or incapacitation on the other, without ever attending to any issues of coordination between the two, seems doomed to be self-defeating at one of the two extremes.

III. PROBLEMS FOR THE PURITY OF CORRECTIVE JUSTICE AND TORT LAW. In the argument to this point, I have shown that there is a kind of reciprocal implication between corrective justice and compensation (Section III.B.i), and between compensation and deterrence (Section III.B.ii). I have also shown, moreover, that this requires the sort of coordinating response across institutions that would be difficult under any strict adherence to a criterial separation strategy. In the next section, I shall show that tort law provides a kind of coordinating response to multi-criterial choice that makes sense of the private law nature of tort law adjudication in particular, as well as the aspirations to rationality which are characteristic of law more generally. The mode of response, I shall suggest, is a conceptually sequenced argument, the one we have already suggested falls out of an analysis of difficulties unearthed by the theory of social choice.

However, before turning to this more positive description of tort law, it is worthwhile saying a few words about why a tort law animated by corrective justice, as much as any scheme focused on compensation, cannot be indifferent to the incidence of accidents. This will allow us to complete the round, having in this section related to each other, in pairwise combination, all three sorts of concerns originally identified by Weinrib, namely, compensation, deterrence, and corrective justice.

In tort law, the typical remedy takes the form of a payment by the defendant to the plaintiff of a sum of money sufficient to restore the plaintiff (so far as it is possible to do this with money) to the position she was in prior to the defendant's wrongful conduct. According to corrective justice, this remedy is designed to accomplish two things at once, namely, to annul the defendant's wrong and to vindicate the plaintiff's right. Weinrib's argument is that the vindication of the plaintiff's right only requires a remedy moving *from the tortfeasor,* and the tortfeasor need only make his payment *to the plaintiff* (that is, only requires a private law remedy), if the victim's loss and the tortfeasor's gain are somehow seen as correlative. Loss and gain are correlative if one person's gain implies another person's loss and vice versa, and it is Weinrib's point that it is only possible to see the losses and gains of tort law as correlative in this way if one measures them, and their normative significance, under the aspect of corrective justice, where the equality, from which gain and loss is measured, is the formal equality of persons, an equality which abstracts from the particularity which distinguishes persons. Moreover, says Weinrib, it is precisely this need for a correlative gain and loss which must preclude both deterrence and compensation from providing the required normative measure of gain and loss for tort law, since what is a wrongful gain from the point of view of deterrence will not (except by accident) also be a wrongful loss from a quite independently conceived compensatory point of view.

Weinrib's invocation of the notion of an abstract "normative" gain and loss to preserve the possibility of correlativity between gains and losses that would otherwise obviously differ in their particularity has not gone uncriticized. Stephen Perry, for example, has argued that such a normative abstraction from particularity and, more specifically, from welfare renders Weinrib's theory incapable of accommodating tort law's concern for welfare at the very point in the action when damages are to be paid as reparation of the wrong, for some the defining moment in a tort action (Perry 1992b).[26] Perry suggests that if the norms of tort law operate in abstraction from all particularity and welfare, it should be enough for tort law to address the mere indignity of the wrongful interaction by having the defendant offer a public apology to the plaintiff (Perry 1993, p. 36). The need to pay actual monetary compensation, therefore, is not explained.

However, an apology would not redress the denial of liberty or right as it is manifested in actual harm, something which *is* normatively significant in a transactional wrong. It is simply a mistake to think, because Weinrib claims that the right is *prior* to the good and, therefore, that the good of welfare has no *independent* normative significance, that it has no normative significance at all. Rather, welfare does have normative significance, but only under the aspect of the plaintiff's right or the defendant's correlative wrong. Actual injury or harm does not count as such, but it does count as the completion of the very risk which, if unreasonable, made the defendant's conduct wrongful in the first place. Just as it would be incoherent within a single account of transactional wrongdoing to "piggyback" some particular harm on the back of a quite unrelated notion of wrongful risk (the sort of thing that was seen in *Polemis*[27] and corrected in *Wagon Mound*[28]), so it would be incomplete to attend to risk without attending in any way to what it is a risk *of.*[29]

Nevertheless, the fact that the plaintiff's welfare loss only has the normative significance it has under the aspect of the defendant's wrongdoing does pose a different sort of difficulty for Weinrib at the point of reparation. Some welfare losses, in particular nonpecuniary losses such as past pain and suffering, are losses for which the payment of money can make no difference. Thus, there is no possibility, whatever the money might do for the plaintiff more generally, that the payment of money damages can do any real work within the space of welfare identified as normatively significant by the defendant's wrongdoing. This means, for a significant number of cases at least, that the compensation achieved for wrongful losses within tort law, and which should receive reparation according to corrective justice, will only be partial compensation. To do more is to step outside the space of welfare made salient by the category of right.[30]

However, if compensation according to the demands of corrective justice can only be partial (at least in cases involving nonpecuniary loss), then a corrective justice theorist like Weinrib has to be concerned about the *incidence* of wrongdoing in addition to its correction. This is, of course, precisely what the deterrence (and incapacitation) theorist would emphasize. After all, the greater the incidence of wrongdoing, the greater the incidence of uncompensated wrongful losses and the more there is a deficiency in the correction of correlative wrongful gain and loss. In other words, not only does the normativity of wrongdoing implicate the normativity of reparation, as argued above in response to Perry, but also, given the possibility of non-pecuniary loss, the limited reach of the normativity of reparation implicates a normative concern for the incidence of wrong.[31] It would seem, therefore, that just as the compensation theorist could not purge the system of compensation completely of deterrence-like concerns under a strategy of criterial separation, so the corrective justice theorist cannot, even in his own terms, hold onto the purity of corrective justice within tort law.

This completes our account of the mutual pairwise implication of deterrence, compensation, and corrective justice. Such mutual pairwise implication, we have tried to suggest, makes a nonsense of the non-neutral strategy of criterial separation for dealing with pluralism. Some other strategy, therefore, is called for. Moreover, what is needed is a strategy which, unlike the strategy of commensurability with its emphasis on merely quantitative variation, allows for this mutual implication between criteria without eliding their qualitative differences. In the next section of the paper I argue that such a strategy is available by way of the sequenced consideration of plural criteria under the aspect of a conceptually ordered argument, and illustrate the workings of this strategy with examples from the law of tort.

## IV. The Sequenced Consideration of Plural Criteria in Tort Law

### A. *Conceptual Orderings and Relational Welfare: The Relevance of Excuses*

In his survey of the inadequacies of contemporary understandings of tort law, Weinrib (1995, pp. 53–5) considers George Fletcher's innovative account based on the imposition of non-reciprocal risk (Fletcher 1972). Weinrib rightly characterizes Fletcher's theory as non-instrumental and, therefore, to be contrasted with those theories that construe tort law "as a medium for accident insurance or as a mechanism for maximizing social utility" (Weinrib 1995, p. 53). But his concern about Fletcher's theory of tort law is similar to that which he has about deterrence; Fletcher, he says, "postulates a justificatory consideration that applies to the defendant independent of the plaintiff." In particular, Weinrib argues, "[h]is approach to excuses severs the defendant's moral position from the plaintiff's entitlement, and thus precludes conceiving of the plaintiff-defendant relationship as an intrinsic unity" (Weinrib 1995, p. 55).

While I hold no torch here for Fletcher's account of tort law in general, in this section of the paper I do want to argue that Weinrib overstates his case against excuses.[32] Excuses, I shall suggest, provide us with an example of how there can be, within tort law, a conceptually ordered concern for welfare that is appropriately relational in form so that it does make sense of the equal (and exclusive) standing of the plaintiff and defendant in a private law action. Moreover, it does so in a way that, as Weinrib suggests with his characterization of the theory as non-instrumental, makes sense of the separate and distinct (i.e., plural) qualities of rights and welfare.[33]

The problem with excuses, according to Weinrib, is that they provide for a too one-sided concern for the defendant: "What matters is the relationship between the defendant's act and the defendant's excusing conditions of compulsion or ignorance" (Weinrib 1995, p. 54). For Weinrib the question that naturally arises in a bilateral private law action, which gives equal standing to *both* the plaintiff and the defendant, is why moral considerations that are relevant only to the defendant as actor should affect the legal position of the plaintiff as victim. However, this question ignores the conceptual ordering that is implied by the invocation of an excuse. As Weinrib admits, excuses presuppose wrongdoing and necessarily occupy a second stage in a multistaged argument. But this presupposition of wrong must mean that the plaintiff has already had standing in the action; she has gone first and proven her prima facie case against the defendant. What could be more essentially bilateral than that? The idea of an excuse (and all that goes with it in what the defendant says, what considerations he appeals to, and so on) has no independent standing in the action; it can only go forward into the overall calculus of legal decision-making if the plaintiff has already (and *independently*) gone first.

However, for Weinrib, this analytic truth about excuses only serves to aggravate the problem. For now the excuse operates to exculpate the defendant on the basis of defendant-specific considerations *despite* the fact that the plaintiff has already shown that she has an entitlement to recover (Weinrib 1995). But this begs the question as to whether there really is an entitlement "all things considered," that is, whether the entitlement should be recognized in the plaintiff against the defendant without considering the defendant's excuse. Nor does it seem quite right to characterize the content of the excuse as invoking considerations "relevant only to the actor" and not relevant to the plaintiff. In Fletcher's account of excuses, for example, the organizing idea for excuses is *com*passion, that is, that any reasonable person similarly situated would have acted as the defendant did. Presumably, this includes the plaintiff.[34] Thus, the argument for allowing the relevance of excuses reduces to the idea that the plaintiff cannot admit the truth of this claim and yet still make a claim for damages against the defendant without asserting a kind of inequality or priority over him.

Weinrib would likely object at this point that the "kind of inequality" that is in play in the argument from compassion is a kind very different from, and one which is inappropriate to, the equality of abstractly free agents. These, after all, are the sorts of beings that have the capacity for freedom precisely because they can rise above their particular circumstances and *not* succumb, however reasonably, to them. Any other concern for welfare, even the sort of reasonable concern for welfare that is exercised in compassion, is welfare uninformed by the aspect of right (and correlative wrongdoing) which properly grounds, and otherwise makes sense of, the private law tort action.

But this objection also begs the question. The reason Weinrib is driven to the equality of abstract freedom is that he is looking for an account of tort law, and of normative gain and loss, that makes sense of the equal and exclusive standing of the plaintiff and the defendant in the private law action. Other normative accounts of gain and loss in tort law do not provide for this equal and exclusive standing. But an action that allows the plaintiff to go first against the defendant with her prima facie case, because that particular defendant has wrongfully caused her injury, and then, once the plaintiff has put the matter at issue, allows the defendant to invoke compassion against that particular plaintiff under a standard of reasonableness equally applicable to each, is as particularly relational, exclusive, and equal as the sort of private law action envisaged by Weinrib's theory of tort law.

It is true, of course, that the second stage of the action brings in a relational notion of welfare that is not entirely ordered by the criterion of equal abstract freedom. In fact, the concern for relational welfare that is evidenced by compassion seems to cut back against (or defease[35]) the notion of abstract freedom, even as it awaits the (nonlexical) priority of that notion to put compassion at issue. But that is a difficulty only for the single-minded monist. For the pluralist, the fact that a sequenced argument of the sort exemplified by the notion of excuses might provide for the rational (conceptually ordered) and, therefore, coherent accommodation of multiple independent criteria is hardly a problem at all. Indeed, it is exactly what one should expect from results in the literature on social choice.

## B. *Tort Law, Corrective Justice, and Reasonable Deterrence*

Having introduced the idea, through an analysis of the notion of excuse, that a conceptually sequenced argument might allow welfare to play a role in tort law, even as it also concedes a defeasible priority to abstractly equal freedom, the time has come to see if a like-minded concern for welfaristic deterrence can also be coherently admitted into the tort action. In this section I shall suggest that it can and, indeed, already has been admitted in just this way, not only into the law, but also into Weinrib's own account of the law.

To make the point, I focus on Weinrib's analysis of some leading common law cases involving reasonable care (Weinrib 1995, pp. 147–52). The standard of reasonable care is breached in tort law when the defendant undertakes an action that imposes an unreasonable risk on the plaintiff. According to Weinrib, there have been two systematic attempts to unpack the different elements of unreasonable risk. In the American version, exemplified most explicitly by the Hand Formula from *United States v. Carroll Towing Co.,*[36] the idea is to compare the risk of loss to the plaintiff with the defendant's burden of precautions. A reasonable person undertakes precautions up to the point where the costs of the precautions cease to be less than the expected loss to the plaintiff. By contrast, the English and Commonwealth approach, exemplified by the case *Bolton v. Stone,*[37] Weinrib says "disregards the cost of precautions" (Weinrib 1995, p. 148).

Weinrib argues that the English and Commonwealth approach is less problematic for corrective justice because risk is a relational concept in a way that the defendant's burden of precautions is not (Weinrib 1995, p. 148).[38] Again, the point is that the defendant's burden of precautions is a burden peculiar to him and the natural question to ask is why this burden should matter to the plaintiff's entitlement to be free from the effects of unreasonable risk. As Lord Reid observes of the defendant cricket club in *Bolton,* "If cricket cannot be played on a ground without creating a substantial risk, then it should not be played there at all" (*Bolton,* at 867). Thus, on the Commonwealth analysis as provided so far, the plaintiff's entitlement to be free of such risk would appear to be absolute.

But Weinrib recognizes that it is an exaggeration to say that the Commonwealth cases "disregard" the burden of precautions. As he observes, the Commonwealth courts proceed with their analysis of unreasonable risk "in several stages" (*ibid.*). The first stage asks whether the risk was reasonably foreseeable, which is to ask whether the risk was "real" or "so fantastic or far fetched" that a reasonable person would not have paid much attention to it. Then, having passed over this undemanding threshold, the court is to ask what a reasonable person does in the face of a real risk. Real risks fall into two categories, "substantial" (which does not mean large) and "small." For substantial risks, it is true that the burden of precautions is irrelevant; the defendant can be liable in a Commonwealth court even for cost-justified, or efficient, action. But for small (insubstantial) risks, which normally would not attract liability, there is a third stage of analysis in which the burden of precautions does become relevant. In particular there can be liability even for small risks if it would not involve "considerable expense to eliminate the risk."[39] Thus, where the burden of precautions can never work to contract the scope of liability at a second stage deter-

mination that the risk is substantial (and even if the burden is large), it can work
to enlarge the scope of liability at a third stage for small risks if the burden of
precautions is small.[40]

Weinrib rightly points out that this third stage attention to the burden of precautions is a long way from the Hand Formula, which would admit the burden
of precautions into consideration at every stage and for all risks. But that is only
to say that the concern for the efficient avoidance of accidents that is evidenced
here, viz., in the fact that reasonable persons, when they can, undertake cheap
precautions to avoid small risks, is admitted in a way that avoids *full* commensurability of rights under the aspect of welfare, something that would make nonsense of a genuinely plural (i.e., independently significant) consideration of
welfare *and* rights. But Weinrib fails to recognize adequately that the Commonwealth cases that he chooses to discuss as the leading cases dealing with
the notion of reasonable care are cases that admit plural considerations. The
very welfare concerns that would never be in play if, as he suggested initially,
precaution costs were really "disregarded," *are* given consideration.

Moreover, the sequenced consideration of welfare under the aspect of an efficient avoidance of small risks is conceptually ordered. The conceptual ordering borrows from the priority of the right to the good, requiring in the first stage
of the analysis that the plaintiff's rights against risk of physical loss be respected
even if the defendant's burden of precautions is large. No social calculus, priv-
ileging only one side of a wrongful interaction, will exculpate the defendant
from wrongdoing.[41] Reasonable persons do not impose their own special problems on others. On the other hand, a genuinely plural concern for an independent notion of welfare (i.e., one not completely under the aspect of right) does
put in an appearance under the standard of reasonable care; reasonable persons,
if they can do so cheaply, restrain themselves from injuring others even if the
risks are otherwise small enough not to be their concern. This limited concern
for welfare can, it seems, defease the priority of right even as it recognizes it at
the first stage; it can inculpate even if it cannot exculpate a wrongdoer. Welfare,
under a conceptual ordering, has a direction as well as a weight. Again, this is
exactly what we should expect under a path dependent integration of plural criteria into a coherent social choice.

## C. Tort Law, Corrective Justice, and Reasonable Compensation

Our final illustration of issue-dependent sequenced argument as a method for
dealing with plural considerations within tort law will deal with the problem of
collateral benefits. It will be recalled from Section III.B.i that this problem
arises for the criterial separation strategy when the plaintiff has access both to
tort law and to some sort of compensation scheme for reparation of her injury.
Tort law can choose to take the collateral compensation into account, in which
case the plaintiff would be denied recovery and an instance of correlative

wrongful gain and loss, otherwise relevant to corrective justice, would not be annulled. Or tort law can choose to be sovereign in its proper domain and ignore the plaintiff's collateral compensation, in which case the plaintiff's recovery in tort seems to put her in a position that is *better* than she would have been in had the tort not occurred, a violation of the *restitutio in integrum* principle. It is not surprising that the courts have seemed to vacillate incoherently between these choices, not always able to articulate a reasoned equilibrium.

In our earlier discussion, we identified a further difficulty for the criterial separation strategy in this context. While a right of subrogation in tort law for the collateral compensation scheme might provide for some sort of equilibrium between compensation and corrective justice, other concerns for the loss of deterrence values might generate the need for sanctions within the deterrence system, wherever that may be. But these sanctions too might call for compensation within the compensation scheme, at least if that scheme was fault-insensitive in the way usually suggested. After all, these sanction-based losses are no less a consequence of the tort than the original injury. They are a form of collateral loss.

We suggested, however, that most compensation theorists would deny that their favored compensation scheme would provide for compensation against these sorts of collateral losses. Such losses, they might say, are simply too remote from the original accident and from the intent of their scheme. But this means that these compensation theorists must have a way of categorizing losses that, admittedly, would not have occurred "but for" the accident (and so are caused by it) into those worthy of compensation and those not so worthy. In this section we suggest that the manner in which tort law handles the analogous remoteness problem of collateral benefits, under a sequenced argument, provides a useful way through the maze. By illustrating the tort law solution, of course, I will also have shown how tort law coherently accommodates our pluralist concerns for both the rights of corrective justice and the welfarism of reasonable compensation.[42]

The common law approach to collateral benefits can be seen most clearly in a leading House of Lords case *Parry v. Cleaver.*[43] In this case, a police constable was injured while directing traffic and was unable to return to work. For over a year after the accident the plaintiff remained with the police force and continued to receive his full salary. After being discharged from the force, the plaintiff, in addition to receiving wages from other employment, also received a police force disability pension to run for the rest of his life. Eligibility for this disability pension was contingent on an individual having put in ten years of pensionable service and on the injury having been sustained while on duty. It was also agreed that both the plaintiff and the police authority had made (at least notional) contributions to the disability pension fund.

The law lords were agreed that the full wages which the plaintiff received after the accident but before discharge from the force should be deducted from any damages received from the defendant for lost wages. Similarly, there was agreement that the wages received from the plaintiff's civilian employment subsequent to discharge should be deducted. Finally, the law lords also were agreed that, for the time period after the date on which the plaintiff would normally have retired from the force, the money received from the disability pension should be deducted from any damages claimed for the loss of the full pension which he would normally have received had he retired at that date. However, the law lords were divided (3 to 2) on whether the disability pension should be deducted from damages claimed for lost wages over the period between the plaintiff's discharge from the police force and the time of normal retirement. Five different opinions were delivered, with the majority supporting nondeductibility.

The different treatment of the disability pension benefit with respect to its deductibility against the claim for lost wages before normal retirement and the claim for lost pension benefits after normal retirement is puzzling. Some courts emphasize that deductibility differences are to be explained by whether the plaintiff has either paid for them or otherwise earned them through providing some service.[44] But here the disability pension benefit received after the time of normal retirement was no less "paid for" than the same benefit received before that time; yet there was deductibility of the collateral benefit for the former period but not the latter.

Lord Reid explicitly addresses this different treatment of the disability pension in the two time periods, and his reasons for doing so suggest that there is more to the issue of deductibility than whether the plaintiff has paid for the collateral benefit in question. Indeed, they reveal a judge attempting to wrestle with plural considerations:

The answer is that in the earlier period [before retirement] we are not comparing like with like. He lost wages, but he gained something different in kind, a pension. But with regard to the period after retirement we are comparing like with like. Both the ill-health pension and the full retirement pension are the products of the same insurance scheme; his loss in the later period is caused by his having been deprived of the opportunity to continue in insurance so as to swell the ultimate product of that insurance from an ill-health to a retirement pension. There is no question as regards that period of a loss of one kind and a gain of a different kind. (*Parry v. Cleaver,* at 564)

Thus, for Lord Reid it is not sufficient that the plaintiff paid for the benefit if its deductibility against damages is to be avoided; it must also be the case that the benefit falls within the same category as, or is of "like kind" with, the damages against which it is to be offset.

However, why should this be? While Lord Reid does not give any explicit reason, Lord Wilberforce's majority judgment in *Parry* offers us a clue. Lord Wilberforce quotes the following passage from the judgment of Windeyer J. in *Paff v. Speed:*

It is, in my view, a mistake to think that there is some general rule governing the admissibility of evidence of pensions of all sorts in all cases of personal injury. Damages for personal injury are compensatory. The first consideration is what is the nature of the loss or damage which the plaintiff says he has suffered. A defendant can always call evidence that contradicts the case the plaintiff seeks to establish. If, as here, a plaintiff claims that he has been deprived of a pension that was one of the advantages of the particular service in which he was, the defendant can prove that, in fact, he has a pension. If a plaintiff claims that he has incurred expenses for medical treatment or for an artificial limb, the defendant can show that these things were provided for without charge. But a claim that because of physical injuries the plaintiff's capacity to earn money has been destroyed is not met simply by showing that he has received money or other assistance from a charity, a former employer, a friend or the State.[45]

According to Windeyer J. and Lord Wilberforce, therefore, it is the plaintiff's own prior claim for damages that determines the category within which the defendant must work in arguing, in reply to that claim, for the deductibility from damages of certain benefits already paid to the plaintiff. Thus, a plaintiff's damages claim for a lost pension that he would otherwise have received from his former employer *is* met by the defendant showing that the plaintiff is receiving an alternative pension that the plaintiff would not have received but for the accident. On the other hand, a plaintiff's claim for damages for lost earnings arising out of an inability to work at his former job, while they are met by the defendant pointing out that the plaintiff has earnings from alternative employment, are *not* met by the defendant showing that the plaintiff is receiving money from another source, be it charity, the state, or even a disability pension provided by that same employer. The latter payments to the plaintiff, while obviously beneficial to him and quite possibly contingent on the occurrence of the accident, are simply irrelevant to the specific claim for damages for lost earnings that he is making against the defendant.

Why irrelevant? Why should the plaintiff, by choosing certain categories of damages, be able to restrict the defendant's ability to introduce set-offs between categories? Why not some more global and less category-specific accounting of how *in toto* the accident has made the plaintiff worse off? The arguments provided in this paper provide an answer. Tort law's method for selecting out those categories of collateral benefit that are properly "in play," or deductible against any claim for loss, is structured as a path-dependent choice. The plaintiff, in making out her prima facie claim to damages of a certain kind, puts certain categories of loss at issue, *and not others*.[46] Within the category at issue, the defendant can argue that the plaintiff has enjoyed offsetting benefits. This is another example of the sequenced consideration of competing considerations, where this time the sequence admits, first, a concern for right and corrective justice in giving the plaintiff standing to make her claim for some particular wrongful loss and, second, the concern for compensation, where the defendant, under the aspect of the plaintiff's claim, can point to collateral benefits the plaintiff has already received. The alternative method, which in a less category-specific and sequenced manner, asks only (and all at once) whether the plaintiff is any the worse off for the accident all things considered, allows welfare to obliterate the priority of right in the typical way that full commensurability does. On the other hand, as we have seen, the failure to attend at all to the fact of collateral benefits, as in the strategy of criterial separation, is in danger of doing its own sort of conceptual violence to the demands of corrective justice. The method of sequenced argument, I suggest here, is tort law's way of steering between these difficulties, and of accommodating plural criteria, including the compensation criterion, even as it recognizes the priority of right.

## V. Conclusion

In my introduction to this essay, I referred sympathetically to Weinrib's characterization of private law in general, and tort law more specifically, as an "exhibition of intelligence." To grasp private law is to come to terms with it, not merely as a set of decisions authoritatively imposed upon litigants, but as an engagement of thought where, says Weinrib, "the process of justification is at least as important as the result of individual adjudications" (Weinrib 1995, p. 12), and where "a conceptual structure finds expression in the arguments of those who take the task of legal thinking upon themselves" (Weinrib 1995, p. 14). For Weinrib such a conceptual structure has to be coherent in a very special way; the concepts that form the elements of the structure have somehow to be ordered "as parts of a whole in which each part conditions, and is *simultaneously* conditioned by, the other parts" (Weinrib 1995, p. 87, emphasis added). Morever, "being reciprocally connected in terms of the unity in which they all partake, the parts are themselves not individually self-sufficient" (Weinrib 1995, p. 87).

In this essay I have also tried to take seriously the idea that the private law is an engagement of thought or an exhibition of intelligence. But I have tried to do so in a way that allows, more than Weinrib does, for the self-sufficiency, or independent significance, of genuinely plural criteria. The concern for law as an engagement of thought is evidenced, first, by the fact that I find the foundations for my particular path-dependent method for accommodating pluralism within the logically rigorous analyses provided by the theory of social choice and, second, by the fact that I interpret this path-dependence as a conceptually sequenced argument developed between two litigants. The respect I attach to the independent significance of plural criteria, and in particular to the significance of both rights and welfare as criteria properly relevant to tort law, is shown by the way I give rights and corrective justice their priority in this argument, even as I allow the more welfarist concerns for efficient deterrence and reasonable compensation to defease this priority at some subsequent stage of the argument. The danger of such defeasibility being arbitrary or ad hoc is avoided precisely because it is *conceptually* ordered. Moreover, because the plural values are accommodated *in sequence* rather than under a simultaneous mutual conditioning of parts, as Weinrib seems to require, the sort of contradiction that we might otherwise observe within flat legal thinking is avoided. Thus, a conceptual ordering, which allows for the defeasible priority of genuinely plural criteria, seems to provide both for a formal structure of *coherent* pluralism, in a way that Weinrib denied was possible, and for a normatively *attractive* content for that structure in the combined consideration of rights *and* welfare. Indeed, this combination is sufficiently attractive, I think, to compel our continued allegiance to tort law as one of the more reasonable methods for dealing with the costs of wrongful interactions between persons.

### Notes

[1] I am particularly grateful to Mark Grady, Gerald Postema, Michael Trebikock, and Ernest Weinrib, as well as to the various participants at the McGill Legal Theory Workshop, the Georgetown Law and Economics Workshop, and the UNC Workshop in Law and Philosophy, where this paper was first presented, for helpful discussions on ealrier drafts. Financial assistance from the Connaught Fund of the Univeristy of Toronto is also gratefully acknowledged.

[2] Whether "best" and "most reason to do" track the same recommendations for action is one of the questions to be addressed in this essay.

[3] Although see Sen (1981) for an interesting account of different sorts of pluralism even within a utilitarian framework. Also, it is important not to confuse the quite general claim that there might be (*contra* Weinrib) a rational way to integrate plural criteria with the more specific claim that the only way to do so is under the aspect of some larger over-arching value. The former admits the existence of pluralism and argues that there is a coherent way to accommodate it; the latter essentially denies the pluralism from the beginning. On the relevance of this distinction for social choice theory and the Arrow framework which I use in this essay, see the discussion in Hurley (1989, p. 233). In this essay the method of conceptually ordered multi-criterial decision-making is proposed as an example of the former.

[4] Also, see Trebilcock (1989a, p. 480): "Criticisms of autonomy theories of tort law stress the barrenness of non-instrumental rationales for tort law that ignore the relevance of the goals of both accident reduction and accident compensation, which are the only two concerns that are likely to matter to most members of the community contemplating the likely impact of an accident on their lives. To claim that tort law is inherently incapable of serving these objectives, which must be advanced through other policy instruments, is to avoid joining the debate over whether tort law is, in that event, worth preserving."

[5] I have already suggested elsewhere that this idea of a "conceptually sequenced argument" might provide a way of handling the problem of incommensurability which is quite different from the methods conventionally proposed by rational choice theorists. See Chapman (1998a).

[6] Arrow and Raynaud provide the proof for this result in the context of multi-criterial choice. See Arrow and Raynaud (1986, pp. 20–1).

[7] See Sen (1982a, p. 235); d'Aspremont and Gevers (1977); Hammond (1976); Strasnick (1976a, 1976b). Strictly speaking, the principle proved in this literature is "leximin" rather

than maximin. In other words, one maximizes the satisfaction of that criterion which is least satisfied, but if there is a tie in this respect between two or more possible choices, one goes on to consider the second least satisfied criterion, and so on.

[8] This is the distinction between, on the one hand, the general idea of a rational integration of plural criteria and, on the other hand, the idea that it might be possible to provide an integration of the apparently plural criteria as mere aspects of a single larger overarching value, something which effectively denies the pluralism altogether.

[9] Hurley is careful to consider a counterfactual version of the independence of irrelevant alternatives condition, but finds that it violates the most basic requirement that normative concepts supervene on non-normative information of some kind. In particular, if there is to be a difference or change in a given criterial ordering, then this must be because something in the factual alternative has changed. While a given criterion can rank factually different alternatives identically, it cannot rank factually identical alternatives differently. Yet this is what the counterfactual version of the independence of irrelevant alternatives condition would seek to do.

[10] For the axiomatization of the method of simple majority voting as a social choice rule, see May (1952).

[11] For an easy exposition of the proof in the context of strict preferences (i.e., without the possibility of indifference), see Sugden (1981, pp. 156–9). Sugden uses the term Latin square; the square can be seen in the symmetry of each alternative appearing just once in each column and each row of the matrix.

[12] See, e.g., Stocker (1990). Hurka (1996) discusses and disputes Stocker's views, as well as the views of others like Wiggins and Nussbaum, who believe that rational regret evidences pluralism.

[13] However, I do suppose, for the purposes of this example, that regret is cardinally comparable across different criteria. Thus, choices based on regret (what I will call "minimax regret" choices) are not invariant with respect to linear (or affine) transformations of the numbers used for any one (as opposed to all) of the criteria. On the relationship between informational significance and choice invariance, see Sen (1986 and 1982a). The comparability of criterion-dependent regret is to be distinguished from assuming the comparability of the criteria themselves.

[14] As, indeed, some decision theorists do; see the discussion of Chernoff's objection in Luce and Raffia (1957).

[15] It is worth noting that the criterial orderings in this example are the ones that would also support the familiar majority voting paradox. Alternative $x$ is preferred by a majority of the criteria to alternative $y$, $y$ is so preferred to $z$, and $z$ to $x$.

[16] See, e.g., Arrow (1959) and Sen (1971). For criticism of these conditions as consistency requirements for common law decision-making, together with exemplification of the argument from tort law, see Chapman (1994). For argument that certain values or choice criteria, which are categorical (but not absolute) in their application to certain partitions of alternatives (and not others), will demonstrate precisely the sort of choice "inconsistency" that is exemplified here by the regret matrix, see Chapman (1998a, pp. 1496–1507).

[17] Regret and preference are both concepts, of course. So the point is not that regret provides a conceptual ordering and preference does not. Rather, it is that regret provides a partition-dependent ordering in a way that preference does not because regret is a *different* concept. Thus, there is concept *insensitivity* in the rational choice theorist's typical assumption that all rational choice should be partition independent choice. For further argument to this ef-

fect, see Chapman (1994, pp. 58–64); and Chapman (1998a, pp. 1496–1507). Also see Chapman (1998b), for an argument that certain systematic difficulties encountered in preference-oriented rational choice might be avoided if concept sensitivity is introduced into the space of alternatives.

18  The elective no-fault scheme has been much promoted by its originator, Professor Jeffrey O'Connell of the University of Virginia; see, e.g., O'Connell and Joost (1986). For criticism of the elective scheme, suggesting that it gives rise to a problem of adverse selection, see Carr (1989).

19  I supply only the barest of suggestions here for these particular rankings of these options by these criteria. For the arguments in greater detail, and for their support within the empirical work on accident law, see Chapman and Trebilcock (1992, pp. 812–29).

20  See, e.g., Kramer (1973) and McKelvey (1976). For good discussion, see Mueller (1989, pp. 79–82).

21  This is comparable to the method of achieving a structurally induced equilibrium in legislative choice by imposing the requirement that legislative voting be restricted to one issue at a time. See the discussion in Mueller (1989, pp. 89–91); and Strom (1990, pp. 98–106). For further discussion of these matters as they relate to common law decision-making, see Chapman (1998b, pp. 303–18).

22  Of course, in one sense the majority voting paradox is not so much "avoided" as "obscured." It is present in the given criterial orderings as these are expressed over the alternatives directly, but the packaging of the alternatives restricts the issues for choice (and, therefore, the comparability of the alternatives) and so does not allow the paradox to manifest itself.

23  For interesting and, I think, related discussion of how the model of "specification" provides for a way to deliberate over incommensurable ends, see Richardson (1990 and 1997).

24  For examples of the mixing strategy in the context of compensation schemes, where deterrence concerns are explicitly addressed, see Trebilcock (1989).

25  See Trebilock (1989). Pricing the plaintiff's insurance according to the plaintiff's propensity for accidents (i.e., non-flat pricing) would compromise on compensation, but enhance deterrence.

26  Others have made related arguments, including Stone (1996, pp. 265–9); and Brudner (1995, pp.196–200), although Brudner claims that the criticism of Weinrib is only "partially correct" (at 323). Weinrib attempts to answer Perry's version of the argument in Weinrib (1993, pp. 20–3), an answer that is largely echoed in Chapman (1995b).

27  *In Re Polemis,* [1921] 3 K.B. 560 (C.A.).

28  *The Wagon Mound, No. 1,* [1961] A.C. 388 (P.C.).

29  Compare Weinrib (1995, p.160): "Risk is not intelligible in abstraction from a set of perils and a set of persons imperiled." The need to attend to the completion of risk and wrongdoing in actual injury is also important for understanding why the law punishes criminal attempts differently from completed crimes; see Chapman (1988b).

30  For this argument in more detail, see Chapman (1995b).

31  Although the argument presented here depends upon the inevitability of partial compensation, it can be argued by way of the paradoxes of "derived obligation" and "contrary-to-duty imperatives" that the (secondary) duties of reparation, highlighted by corrective justice, must implicate (primary) duties to avoid wrongdoing even if full compensation is paid. Otherwise, one will end up, under the logic of "ought," positively prescribing wrong rather than prohibiting it. For discussion, see Richardson (1997, pp. 80–2); and Richard-

son (1990, pp. 298–300). Richardson's discussion of these paradoxes is interesting because it highlights the fact that different and seemingly conflicting decision criteria can apply to a choice problem within an ordered sequence of specification, something which allows for the revision (or qualification) of one criterion (e.g., the primary duty not to wrong) in the light of another which must (conceptually) come after it (e.g., the secondary duty to repair or mitigate harm). The terminology of primary and secondary duties is Jules Coleman's; see Coleman (1992b).

[32] For excellent criticism of Fletcher's theory of nonreciprocal risk, see Coleman (1975).

[33] For a similarly structured account of the role of excuses in the criminal law, but one which denies a like space for them in tort law, see Chapman (1988a).

[34] Throughout his discussion of Fletcher, Weinrib attempts to put the plaintiff out of reach of the general sense of compassion which the excuse is meant to invoke. He asks, for example: "Why should the probability that *most* [emphasis added] people in the defendant's position would have committed the same wrong lead to the cancellation of a particular plaintiff's right? . . . Even if the excusing condition moves *us* to compassion, on what grounds does our compassion operate at the *plaintiff's* expense?" (Weirib 1995, p. 54). But once the plaintiff is included within the scope of reasonable compassion, then holding the plaintiff to that standard of reasonableness seems less unfair and inappropriate.

[35] The legal theorist whose name is most closely associated with the concept of defeasibility is H. L. A. Hart; see Hart (1952, pp. 145–66). For discussion of the significance of Hart's analysis, see Baker (1977). The fundamental difference between a preference ordering (either continuous or lexical) and a defeasible ordering is discussed in Chapman (1998a, 1998b).

[36] 159 F. 2d 169, at 173 (2d Cir., 1947).

[37] [1951] App. Cas. 850 (H.L.).

[38] As Weinrib observes elsewhere (1995, p. 160), this characterization of risk was shared by Justice Cardozo; see his opinion in *Palsgraf v. Long Island Railroad,* 162 N.E. 99, 100 (N.Y.C.A., 1928):"The risk reasonably to be perceived defines the duty to be obeyed and risk imports relation."

[39] *Overseas Tankship (U.K.) Ltd. v. The Miller Steamship Co. Pty. Ltd. (Wagon Mound No.2),* [1967] 1 App. Cas. 617, 641 (P.C.).

[40] This way of characterizing the effect of the burden of precautions on the scope of liability, viz., as expanding it but not contracting it, can be found in Brudner (1995, p. 191).

[41] In this respect, the exculpatory effect of an excuse at the second stage of an action, where the excuse, by way of compassion, reaches both parties equally, is to be contrasted with the one-sided invocation of a burden of high precaution costs.

[42] The following analysis of the collateral benefits problem is developed in more detail in Chapman (1995a).

[43] [1969] 1 All E.R. 555 (H.L.).

[44] See, e.g., *Cunningham v. Wheeler,* [1994] 1 S.C.R. 359, 558–560 (S.C.C.). It is hard to rationalize nondeductibility this way, however, since the other well-established situation giving rise to nondeductibility is where the plaintiff has received a charitable payment from some third party to compensate for the loss, precisely the opposite of a situation in which the plaintiff has paid for the collateral benefit.

[45] *Paff v. Speed,* (1961) 105 C.L.R. 549, 567.

[46] The fact that the plaintiff only puts some categories of loss at issue in her claim is usually thought to disadvantage her under the notion of remoteness. But, as argued here in the text,

it can also limit what the defendant can say in reply to that claim, and not just for the case of collateral benefits. Consider, for example, this old chestnut: because the defendant has negligently collided with the plaintiff's car, the plaintiff fails to sail on time with the *Titanic,* an accident that has the effect, therefore, of saving the plaintiff's life. Had the plaintiff sailed with the ship, it is almost certain that she would have drowned. Why not set this benefit off against any damages which the plaintiff suffers in the car accident? After all, it does not seem that the accident has made the plaintiff worse off, *all things considered.* But the accident has caused the plaintiff a loss (i.e., a damaged car, personal injury), and for this there is little doubt that she will recover in tort, whatever the more global calculus of costs and benefits might suggest. And the reason for this is remoteness. What might have happened to the plaintiff on the *Titanic* had the accident not occurred, or even what did happen there to others, is simply too remote from the accident linking the plaintiff with the defendant. More specifically, it is no part of what makes the defendant's negligent behaviour wrong that the plaintiff might, even with reasonable foreseeability, fail to be at some dock in sufficient time to sail with her ship. Rather, what makes negligent driving wrong is that it might result in foreseeable injury to the plaintiff's person or property, consequences which in turn might make it impossible for the plaintiff to work and, therefore, earn wages or a pension for retirement. Thus, the plaintiff can properly bring these last mentioned categories of injury into account in her claim for damages in a way that the defendant cannot properly bring into account the offsetting benefits to the plaintiff of her having missed the ship's sailing. The former losses from the accident lie within the ambit of the defendant's wrongdoing, or are proximate to it, in a way that the latter benefits of the accident are not. In this way, therefore, the issue of remoteness not only limits the *plaintiff* to the sort of damages which she can claim are proximately consequential to the defendant's wrongdoing, but it also restricts the range of benefits which the *defendant* can properly identify as an offset to the plaintiff's damages. The example of the *Titanic* is a variation on one found in Weinrib (1989a). For developments of this example into further variations, all in order to show that corrective justice need not provide for compensation for nonpecuniary loss, see Chapman (1995b).

# References

Abraham, Kenneth S. (1987) "Individual Action and Collective Responsibility: The Dilemma of Mass Tort Reform." *Virginia Law Review* 73: 845–890.

Ackerman, Bruce. (1977) *Private Property and the Constitution*. New Haven, CT: Yale University Press.

Ackrill, J. L. (1980) "Aristotle on Action." In *Essays on Aristotle's Ethics*. Berkeley, CA: University of California Press.

Alexander, Larry. (1989) "Constrained by Precedent." *Southern California Law Review* 63: 1–64.

(1990) "Reconsidering the Relationship among Voluntary Acts, Strict Liability, and Negligence in Criminal Law." *Social Philosophy and Policy* 7: 84–104.

Aquinas, Thomas. (1975) *Summa Theologiciae*. Translated by T. Gilby. London: Oxford University Press.

Aristotle. (1959) *Rhetoric*. Edited by W. D. Ross. Oxford: Oxford University Press.

(1985) *Nicomachean Ethics*. Translated by Terrence Irwin. Indianapolis: Hackett Publishing.

Arrow, Kenneth. (1959) "Rational Choice Functions and Orderings." *Economica* 26: 121–127.

(1963) *Social Choice and Individual Values*. 2nd edition, New Haven, CT: Yale University Press.

Arrow, Kenneth, and Hervé Raynaud. (1986) *Social Choice and Multicriterion Decision-making*. Cambridge, MA: MIT Press.

Atiyah, Patrick. (1997) *The Damages Lottery*. Oxford: Hart Publishing.

Baker, G. P. (1977) "Defeasibility and Meaning." In *Law, Morality and Society*. Edited by P. M. S. Hacker and J. Raz. Oxford: Clarendon Press.

Baker, J. H. (1990) *An Introduction to English Legal History*. 3rd edition, London: Butterworths.

Balkin, J. M. (1986) "The Crystalline Structure of Legal Thought." *Rutgers Law Review* 39: 1–110.

Barry, Brian. (1989) *Theories of Justice*. Berkeley, CA: University of California Press.

Becker, Gary. (1996) *Accounting for Tastes*. Cambridge, MA: Harvard University Press.

Becker, Gary, and Isaac Ehrlich. (1972) "Market Insurance, Self-Insurance, and Self-Protection." *Journal of Political Economy* 80: 623–648.

Becker, Gary, and George Stigler. (1977) "De Gustibus Non Est Disputandum." *American Economic Review* 67: 76–90.

Bender, Leslie. (1988) "A Lawyer's Primer on Feminist Theory and Tort." *Journal of Legal Education* 38: 3–38.

Benson, Peter. (1989) "Abstract Right and the Possibility of a Nondistributive Conception of Contract: Hegel and Contemporary Contract Theory." *Cardozo Law Review* 10: 1077–1198.

   (1992) "The Basis of Corrective Justice and Its Relation to Distributive Justice." *Iowa Law Review* 77: 515–624.

Berger, Margaret. (1997) "Eliminating General Causation: Notes Towards a New Theory of Justice and Toxic Torts." *Columbia Law Review* 97: 2117–2152.

Bergson, Abram. (1930) "A Reformulation of Certain Aspects of Welfare Economics." *Quarterly Journal of Economics* 52: 310–344.

Blair, Douglas H., George Bordes, Jenny S. Kelly, et al. (1976) "Impossibility Theorems without Collective Rationality." *Journal of Economic Theory* 13: 361–379.

Bohlen, Francis H. (1926) "The Rule in Rylands v. Fletcher." In *Studies in the Law of Torts.* Indianapolis, IN: Bobbs Merrill Co.

Brudner, Alan. (1995) *The Unity of the Common Law: Studies in Hegelian Jurisprudence.* Berkeley, CA: University of California Press.

Bunting, Julia Christine. (1994) "Ashley v. Abbott Laboratories: Reconfiguring the Personal Jurisdiction Analysis in Mass Tort Litigation." *Vanderbilt Law Review* 47: 189–233.

Calabresi, Guido. (1970) *The Costs of Accidents.* New Haven, CT: Yale University Press.

   (1975) "Concerning Cause and the Law of Torts." *University of Chicago Law Review* 43: 69–108.

   (1985) *Ideals, Beliefs, Attitudes and the Law: Private Perspectives on a Public Law Problem.* Syracuse, NY: Syracuse University Press.

Calabresi, Guido, and Jon T. Hirschoff. (1972) "Toward a Test for Strict Liability in Torts." *Yale Law Journal* 81: 1055–1085.

Carr, Jack L. (1989) "Giving Motorists a Choice Between Fault and No-Fault Insurance: An Economic Critique." *San Diego Law Review* 26: 1087–1094.

Casson, Mark. (1997) Editor, *Culture, Social Norms and Economics.* Northampton, MA: Edward Elgar.

Cavell, Stanley. (1989) *This New Yet Unapproachable America: Lectures After Emerson After Wittgenstein.* Albuquerque, NM: Living Batch Press.

Chang, Ruth. (1998) "Comparison and the Justification of Choice." *University of Pennsylvania Law Review* 146: 1569–1598.

Chapman, Bruce. (1988a) "A Theory of Criminal Law Excuses." *Canadian Journal of Law and Jurisprudence* 1: 75–86.

   (1988b) "Agency and Contingency: The Case of Criminal Attempts." *University of Toronto Law Journal* 38: 355–377.

   "The Rational and the Reasonable: Social Choice Theory and Adjudication." *University of Chicago Law Review* 61: 41–122.

   (1995a) "Developments in Tort Law: The 1993–4 Term," *The Supreme Court Law Review* 6: 487–544.

   (1995b) "Wrongdoing, Welfare and Damages: Recovery for Non-Pecuniary Loss in Corrective Justice." In *Philosophical Foundations of Tort Law.* Edited by David Owen. Oxford: Clarendon Press.

(1998a) "Law, Incommensurability and Conceptually Sequenced Argument." *University of Pennsylvania Law Review* 146: 1487–1528.

(1998b) "More Easily Done Than Said: Rules, Reasons and Rational Social Choice." *Oxford Journal of Legal Studies* 18: 293–330.

Chapman, Bruce and Michael Trebilcock. (1992) "Making Hard Social Choices: Lessons From the Automobile Accident Compensation Debate." *Rutgers Law Review* 44: 797–870.

Coase, Ronald. (1960) "The Problem of Social Cost." *The Journal of Law and Economics* 3: 1–44.

Coleman, Jules L. (1974) "On the Moral Argument for the Fault System." *Journal of Philosophy* 71: 473–490.

(1975) "Justice and Reciprocity in Tort Theory." *Western Ontario Law Review* 14: 105–118.

(1980) "Efficiency, Utility, and Wealth Maximization." *Hofstra Law Review* 8: 509–551.

(1982) "Corrective Justice and Wrongful Gain." *Journal of Legal Studies* 11: 421–440.

(1988) "The Economic Structure of Tort Law." *Yale Law Journal* 97: 1233–1253.

(1992a) *Risks and Wrongs*. Cambridge: Cambridge University Press.

(1992b) "Tort Law and the Demands of Justice." *Indiana Law Journal* 67: 349–379.

(1995) "The Practice of Corrective Justice." *Arizona Law Review* 37: 15–31.

(1998a) "Incorporationism, Conventionality and the Practical Difference Thesis." *Legal Theory* 4: 381–425.

(1998b) "Second Thoughts and Other First Impressions." In *Analyzing Law: New Essays in Legal Theory*. Edited by Brian Bix. Oxford: Clarendon Press.

Coleman, Jules, and Arthur Ripstein. (1995) "Mischief and Misfortune." *McGill Law Journal* 41: 91–130.

Cooter, Robert D. (1996) "Decentralized Law for a Complex Economy: The Structural Approach to Adjudicating the New Law Merchant." *University of Pennsylvania Law Review* 144: 1643–1696.

Cooter, Robert D., and Thomas Ulen. (1988) *Law and Economics*. Glenview, IL: Scott, Foresman.

Craswell, Richard. (1991) "Passing On the Cost of Legal Rules." *Stanford Law Review* 43: 361–398.

Croley, Steven P., and Jon D. Hanson. (1993) "Rescuing the Revolution: The Revived Case for Enterprise Liability." *Michigan Law Review* 91: 683–797.

D'Aspremont, Claude, and Louis Gevers. (1977) "Equity and the Informational Basis of Collective Choice." *Review of Economic Studies* 44: 199–209.

Dennett, Daniel C. (1985) *Elbow Room: The Varieties of Free Will Worth Wanting*. Cambridge, MA: MIT Press.

Deschamps, Robert, and Louis Gevers. (1978) "Leximin and Utilitarian Rules: A Joint Characterization." *Journal of Economic Theory* 17: 143–163.

Devlin, Patrick. (1965) *The Enforcement of Morals*. New York: Oxford University Press.

Duff, R. A. (1990) *Intention, Agency and Criminal Liability*. Oxford: Basil Blackwell.

Dworkin, Ronald. (1978) *Taking Rights Seriously*. Cambridge, MA: Harvard University Press.

(1980) "Is Wealth a Value?" *Journal of Legal Studies* 9: 191–226.

(1986) *Law's Empire*. Cambridge, MA: Harvard University Press.

Ehrenzweig, A. (1953) "A Psychoanalysis of Negligence." *Northwestern University Law Review* 47: 855–872.

Elster, Jon. (1985) *Making Sense of Marx.* Cambridge: Cambridge University Press.

Epstein, Richard A. (1973) "A Theory of Strict Liability." *Journal of Legal Studies* 2: 151–204.

(1985a) *Takings: Private Property and the Power of Eminent Domain.* Cambridge, MA: Harvard University Press.

(1985b) "Two Fallacies in the Law of Joint Torts." *Georgetown Law Journal* 73: 1377–1388.

Farber, Daniel A., and Philip P. Frickey. (1991) *Law and Public Choice.* Chicago, IL: University of Chicago Press.

Feinberg, Joel. (1970) *Doing and Deserving.* Princeton, NJ: Princeton University Press.

Feldman, Stephen M. (1997) "From Premodern to Modern American Jurisprudence: The Onset of Positivism." *Vanderbilt Law Review* 50: 1387–1448.

Finkelstein, Claire. (1992) "Tort Law as a Comparative Institution: Reply to Perry." *Harvard Journal of Law and Public Policy* 15: 939–963.

Fletcher, George. (1972) "Fairness and Utility in Tort Theory." *Harvard Law Review* 85: 537–573.

(1993) "Corrective Justice for Moderns." *Harvard Law Review* 106: 1658–1678.

Frank, Jerome. (1963) *Law and the Modern Mind.* 2nd edition, Gloucester, MA: Peter Smith.

Franklin, Marc A. (1967) "Replacing the Negligence Lottery: Compensation and Selective Reimbursement." *Virginia Law Review* 53: 774–814.

Fried, Charles. (1970) *An Anatomy of Values: Problems of Personal and Social Choice.* Cambridge, MA: Harvard University Press.

Friedman, Lawrence M. (1985) *A History of American Law.* 2nd edition, New York: Simon and Schuster.

Friedman, Milton. (1962) *Price Theory.* Chicago, IL: Aldine Publishing Co.

Geistfeld, Mark. (1994) "The Political Economy of Noncontractual Proposals for Products Liability Reform." *Texas Law Review* 72: 803–847.

(1995) "Placing a Price on Pain and Suffering: A Method for Helping Juries Determine Tort Damages for Nonmonetary Injuries." *California Law Review* 83: 773–852.

(1998) "Should Enterprise Liability Replace the Rule of Strict Liability for Abnormally Dangerous Activities?" *UCLA Law Review* 45: 611–672.

Gibbard, Alan. (1991) "Constructing Justice." *Philosophy & Public Affairs* 20: 264–279.

Gilles, Stephen. (1994) "The Invisible Hand Formula." *Virginia Law Review* 80: 1015–1054.

Glionna, John M. (1992) "Trestle-Jumping Fad Puts Youths in Path of Danger." *Los Angeles Times,* Aug. 10, 1992.

Goldberg, John C. P., and Benjamin C. Zipursky. (1998) "The Moral of *Macpherson.*" *University of Pennsylvania Law Review* 146: 1733–1848.

Gordon, Robert W. (1984) "Critical Legal Histories." *Stanford Law Review* 36: 57–125.

Grady, Mark F. (1989) "Untaken Precautions." *Journal of Legal Studies* 18: 139–156.

Hadfield, Gillian. (1982) "Bias in the Evolution of Legal Rules." *Georgetown Law Journal* 80: 583–616.

Hammond, Peter J. (1976) "Equity, Arrow's Conditions and Rawls' Difference Principle." *Econometrica* 44 (1976): 793–804.

Hart, H. L. A. (1952) "The Ascription of Responsibility and Rights." In *Essays in Logic and Language.* Edited by Anthony Flew. Oxford: Oxford University Press.

(1961) *The Concept of Law.* Oxford: Clarendon Press.

(1968) *Punishment and Responsibility: Essays in the Philosophy of Law.* New York: Oxford University Press.

Hart, H. L. A., and Tony Honoré. (1985) *Causation in The Law.* 2nd edition, New York: Clarendon Press.

Hasen, Richard L. (1995) "The Efficient Duty to Rescue." *International Review of Law and Economics* 15: 143–152.

Hegel, G. W. F. (1991) *Elements of The Philosophy of Right.* Edited by Allen W. Wood. Translated by H. B. Nisbett. Cambridge: Cambridge University Press.

Holmes, Oliver Wendell. (1870) Review of T. E. Holland's *Essays upon the Form of the Law* (1870). *American Law Review,* vol. 5, pp. 114–115.

(1920) "The Path of Law," In *Collected Legal Papers.* New York: Harcourt, Brace and Co.

(1963) *The Common Law.* Cambridge, MA: Harvard University Press.

Honoré, Tony. (1964) "Can and Can't." *Mind* 73: 463–479.

(1988) "Responsibility and Luck." *Law Quarterly Review* 104: 530–553.

Horwitz, Morton J. (1977) *The Transformation of American Law, 1780–1860.* Cambridge, MA: Harvard University Press.

Hovekamp, Herbert. (1983) "The Economics of Legal History." *Minnesota Law Review* 67: 645–697.

Hurd, Heidi. (1994) "What in the World is Wrong?" *Journal of Contemporary Legal Issues* 5: 157–216.

(1996) "The Deontology of Negligence." *Boston University Law Review* 76: 249–272.

Hurka, Thomas. (1996) "Monism, Pluralism and Rational Regret." *Ethics* 106: 555–575.

Hurley, Susan. (1989) *Natural Reasons.* New York: Oxford University Press.

Ison, Terence G. (1967) *The Forensic Lottery.* London: Staples Press.

James, Fleming Jr. (1948) "Accident Liability Reconsidered." *Yale Law Journal* 58: 549–570.

Johnson, Conrad D. (1976) "On Deciding and Setting Precedent for the Reasonable Man." *Archiv fuer Rechts- und Sozialphilosophie* 161: 161–187.

Kakalik, James S., and Nicholas M. Pace. (1986) *Costs and Compensation Pain in Tort Litigation.* Santa Monica, CA: Rand Institute for Civil Justice.

Kamm, Francis M. (1996) *Morality, Mortality, Volume II: Rights, Duties and Status.* New York: Oxford University Press.

Kant, Immanuel. (1991) *Metaphysics of Morals.* Translated by Mary Gregor. Cambridge: Cambridge University Press.

(1992) *Grounding for the Metaphysics of Morals.* Translated by James Ellington. Indianapolis, IN: Hackett Publishing.

Kaplow, Louis, and Steven Shavell. (1994) "Why the Legal System is Less Efficient then the Income Tax System in Redistributing Income." *Journal of Legal Studies* 23: 667–681.

Keating, Gregory C. (1993) "Fidelity to Pre-Existing Law and the Legitimacy of Legal Decision." *Notre Dame Law Review* 69: 1–55.

(1996) "Reasonableness and Rationality in Negligence Theory." *Stanford Law Review* 48: 311–384.

(1997) "The Idea of Fairness in the Law of Enterprise Liability." *Michigan Law Review* 95: 1266–1380.

Keeton, Robert E. (1963) *Legal Cause in the Law of Torts.* Columbus, OH: Ohio State University Press.

Keeton, Robert, Lewis D. Sargentich, Gregory C. Keating. (1998) *Cases and Materials on Tort and Accident Law.* St. Paul, MN: West Publishing.

Keeton, W. Page. (1984) *Prosser and Keeton on the Law of Torts.* 5th edition, St. Paul: West Publishing.

Kelsen, Hans. (1957) "Aristotle's Doctrine of Justice." In *What is Justice?* Berkeley, CA: University of California Press.

Komesar, Neil K. (1990) "Injuries and Institutions: Tort Reform, Tort Theory, and Beyond." *New York University Law Review* 65: 23–77.

Kramer, Gerald H. (1973) "On a Class of Equilibrium Conditions for Majority Rule." *Econometrica* 41: 285–297.

Kraus, Jody S. (1997) "A Non-Solution to a Non-Problem: A Comment on Alan Strudler's 'Mass Torts and Moral Principles.'" *Law and Philosophy* 16: 91–100.

Lacey, Nicola. (1988) *State Punishment: Political Principles and Community Values.* London: Routledge.

Landes, William M., and Richard A. Posner. (1987) *The Economic Structure of Tort Law.* Cambridge, MA: Harvard University Press.

Locke, John. (1980) *The Second Treatise of Government.* Indianapolis, IN: Hackett Publishing.

Luce, R. Duncan, and Howard Raiffa. (1957) *Games and Decisions.* New York: Wiley.

Marks, Stephen. (1994) "Discontinuities, Causation and Grady's Uncertainty Theorem." *Journal of Legal Studies* 23: 287–301.

Mas-Collel, Andreu. (1995) *Microeconomic Theory.* New York: Oxford University Press.

May, Kenneth O. (1952) "A Set of Independent, Necessary and Sufficient Conditions for Simple Majority Decision." *Econometrica* 20: 680–684.

McAdams, Richard H. (1997) "The Origin, Development and Regulation of Legal Norms." *Michigan Law Review* 96: 338–433.

McDowell, John. (1998) *Mind, Value and Reality.* Cambridge, MA: Harvard University Press.

McKelvey, Richard O. (1976) "Intransitivities in Multi-Dimensional Voting Models and Some Implications for Agenda Control." *Journal of Economic Theory* 12: 472–482.

Mehr, Robert I., Emerson Cammack, and Terry Rose. (1985) *The Principles of Insurance.* 8th edition, Homewood, IL: R.D. Irwin.

Michelman, Frank. (1967) "Property, Utility and Fairness: Comments on the Ethical Foundations of 'Just Compensation' Law." *Harvard Law Review* 80: 1165–1259.

Mill, John Stuart. (1861) *Utilitarianism.* Edited by Samuel Gorowitz. Indianapolis, IN: Bobbs Merrill Co. (1971).

Milsom, S. F. C. (1981) *Historical Foundations of the Common Law.* 2nd edition, Boston, MA: Butterworths.

Moore, Michael S. (1990) "Choice, Character and Excuse." *Social Philosophy & Policy* 7: 29–58.

(1993) "Foreseeing Harm Opaquely." In *Action and Value in Criminal Law.* Edited by J. Gardener, J. Horder, and S. Shute. Oxford: Clarendon Press.

(1994) "The Independent Moral Significance of Wrongdoing." *Journal of Contemporary Legal Issues* 327: 237–281.

(1999) "Causation and Responsibility." *Social Philosophy & Policy* 16: 1–51.

Morris, Clarence. (1952) "Duty, Negligence and Causation." *University of Pennsylvania Law Review* 101: 189–222.

Mueller, Dennis C. (1989) *Public Choice II.* Cambridge: Cambridge University Press.

Mullenix, Linda S. (1996) *Mass Tort Litigation: Cases and Materials*. St. Paul: West Publishing.

Nagel, Thomas. (1979) "Moral Luck." In *Mortal Questions*. Cambridge: Cambridge University Press.

Nesson, Charles. (1985) "The Evidence or the Event? On Judicial Proof and the Acceptability of Verdicts." *Harvard Law Review* 98:1357–1392.

Nozick, Robert. (1974) *Anarchy, State and Utopia*. New York: Basic Books.

O'Connell, Jeffrey, and Robert H. Joost. (1986) "Giving Motorists a Choice Between Fault and No-Fault Insurance." *Virginia Law Review* 72: 61–90.

Owen, David G. (1993) "The Moral Foundations of Products Liability Law." *Notre Dame Law Review* 68: 427–506.

(1995) Editor. *Philosophical Foundations of Tort Law*. Oxford: Clarendon Press.

Perry, Stephen. (1988) "The Impossibility of a General Strict Liability." *Canadian Journal of Law and Jurisprudence* 1: 147–171.

(1992a) "The Mixed Conception of Corrective Justice." *Harvard Journal of Law and Public Policy* 15: 917–937.

(1992b) "The Moral Foundations of Tort Law." *Iowa Law Review* 77: 449–514.

(1993) "Loss, Agency, and Responsibility for Outcomes: Three Conceptions of Corrective Justice." In *Tort Theory*. Edited by K. Cooper-Stephenson and E. Gibson. North York, Ontario: Captus Press.

(1995) "Risk, Harm, and Responsibility." In *Philosophical Foundations of Tort Law*. Edited by David Owen. Oxford: Clarendon Press.

(1996) "Tort Law." In *A Companion to Philosophy of Law and Legal Theory*. Edited by Dennis Patterson. Oxford: Blackwell Publishers.

(1997) "Libertarianism, Entitlement, and Responsibility." *Philosophy & Public Affairs* 26: 351–396.

(1998a) "The Distributive Turn: Mischief, Misfortune, and Tort Law." In *Analyzing Law: New Essays in Legal Theory*. Edited by Brian Bix. Oxford: Clarendon Press.

(1998b) "Hart's Methodological Positivism." *Legal Theory* 4: 427–467.

(2000) "On The Relationship between Corrective and Distributive Justice." In *Oxford Essays in Jurisprudence*. Edited by J. Horder. Oxford: Clarendon Press.

(unpublished) "Risk and the Meaning of Negligence."

Plott, Charles R. (1973) "Path Dependence, Rationality and Social Choice." *Econometrica* 42: 1075–1091.

Pollack, Frederick, and Frederick Maitland. (1898) *The History of English Law Before the Time of Edward I*. 2nd edition, Cambridge: Cambridge University Press (1968).

Posner, Richard A. (1970) "Book Review." *University of Chicago Law Review* 37: 636-648.

(1972) "A Theory of Negligence." *Journal of Legal Studies* 1: 29–96.

(1975) "The Economic Approach to Law." *Texas Law Review* 53: 757–782.

(1977) *Economic Analysis of Law*. 2nd edition, Boston, MA: Little, Brown and Co.

(1981) "The Concept of Corrective Justice in Recent Theories of Tort Law." *Journal of Legal Studies* 10: 187–206.

(1990) *The Problems of Jurisprudence*. Cambridge, MA: Harvard University Press.

(1992) "Legal Reasoning from the Top Down and From the Bottom Up: The Question of Unenumerated Rights." *University of Chicago Law Review* 59: 433–450.

Priest, George L., and Benjamin Klein. (1984) "The Selection of Disputes for Litigation." *Journal of Legal Studies* 13: 1–55.

Prosser, William L. (1941) *Handbook of the Law of Torts*. St Paul, MN: West Publishing Co.

(1953) "Palsgraf Revisited." *Michigan Law Review* 52: 1–32.

Quinn, Warren. (1993) "Actions, Intentions, and Consequences: the Doctrine of Doing and Allowing." In *Morality and Action*. Cambridge: Cambridge University Press.

Rabin, Robert L. (1996) "Law for Law's Sake." *Yale Law Journal* 105: 2261–2283.

Radin, Margaret Jane. (1996) *Contested Commodities*. Cambridge, MA: Harvard University Press.

Rawls, John. (1971) *A Theory of Justice*. Cambridge, MA: Harvard University Press.

(1993) *Political Liberalism*. New York: Columbia University Press.

Rhees, Rush. (1970) "Some Developments in Wittgenstein's View of Ethics." In *Discussions of Wittgenstein*. London: Routledge & Kegan Paul.

Rheingold, Paul D. (1989) "The Hymowitz Decision – Practical Aspects of New York DES Litigation." *Brooklyn Law Review* 55: 883–897.

Richardson, Henry S. (1990) "Specifying Norms as a Way to Resolve Concrete Ethical Problems." *Philosophy & Public Affairs* 19: 279–310.

(1997) *Practical Reasoning About Final Ends*. Cambridge: Cambridge University Press.

Ripstein, Arthur. (1994) "Equality, Luck and Responsibility." *Philosophy & Public Affairs* 23: 3–23.

(1999) *Equality, Responsibility, and the Law*. Cambridge: Cambridge University Press.

Rizzo, Mario J. (1987) *Symposium on Causation in the Law of Torts*. *Chicago-Kent Law Review* 63:397–680.

Robbins, Lionel. (1935) *An Essay on the Nature and Significance of Economic Science*. 2nd edition, London: Macmillan.

Roberts, Kevin W. S. (1980) "Interpersonal Comparability and Social Choice Theory." *Review of Economic Studies* 47: 421–439.

Robinson, Glen O. (1982) "Multiple Causation in Tort Law: Reflections on the DES Cases." *Virginia Law Review* 68: 713–770.

Roe, Mark J. (1996) "Chaos and Evolution in Law and Economics." *Harvard Law Review* 109: 641–712.

Rosenberg, David. (1984) "The Causal Connection in Mass Exposure Cases: a 'Public Law' Vision of the Tort System." *Harvard Law Review* 97: 849–929.

(1995) *The Hidden Holmes: His Theory of Torts in History*. Cambridge, MA: Harvard University Press.

Samuelson, Paul A. (1947) *Foundations of Economic Analysis*. Cambridge, MA: Harvard University Press.

Scanlon, Thomas M. Jr. (1975) "Preference and Urgency." *Journal of Philosophy* 72: 655–669.

(1982) "Contractualism and Utilitarianism." In *Utilitarianism and Beyond*. Edited by Amartya Sen and B. A. O. Williams. Cambridge: Cambridge University Press.

(1988) "The Significance of Choice." In *The Tanner Lectures on Human Values*. Edited by S. M. McMurrin. Salt Lake City, UT: University of Utah Press.

(1991) "The Moral Basis of Interpersonal Comparisons." In *Interpersonal Comparisons of Well-Being*. Edited by Jon Elster and John E. Roemer. Cambridge: Cambridge University Press.

Schelling, Thomas C. (1980) *The Strategy of Conflict*. Cambridge, MA: Harvard University Press.

Schroeder, Christopher H. (1990) "Corrective Justice, Liability for Risks, and Tort Law." *UCLA Law Review* 38: 143–162.

(1995) "Causation, Compensation, and Moral Responsibility." In *Philosophical Foundations of Tort Law*. Edited by David Owen. Oxford: Clarendon Press.

Schwartz, Gary T. (1981) "Tort Law and the Economy in Nineteenth Century America: A Reinterpretation." *Yale Law Journal* 90: 1717–1775.

(1988) "The Character of Early American Tort Law." *UCLA Law Review* 36: 641–718.

Schwartz, Victor E., and Liberty Mahshigian. (1988) "Failure to Identify the Defendant in Tort Law: Towards a Legislative Solution." *California Law Review* 73: 941–975.

Schwartz, Warren F. (1989) "Objective and Subjective Standards of Negligence: Defining the Reasonable Person to Induce Optimal Care and Optimal Populations of Injurers and Victims." *Georgetown Law Journal* 78: 241–279.

Seavey, Waren. (1939) "Mr. Justice Cardozo and the Law of Torts." *Columbia Law Review* 39: 20–55.

Sen, Amartya. (1970) *Collective Choice and Social Welfare*. London: Oliver and Boyd.

(1971) "Choice Functions and Revealed Preference." *Review of Economic Studies* 38: 307–317.

(1976) "Liberty, Unanimity and Rights." *Economica* 43: 217–245.

(1981) "Plural Utility." *Proceeding from the Aristotelian Society* 81: 193–215.

(1982a) "On Weights and Measures: Informational Constraints in Social Welfare Analysis." In *Choice, Welfare and Measurement*. Cambridge, MA: MIT Press.

(1982b) "The Impossibility of the Paretian Liberal." In *Choice , Welfare and Measurement*. Cambridge MA: MIT Press.

(1986) "Information and Invariance in Normative Choice." In *Social Choice and Public Decision-making*. Edited by Walter P. Heller, Ross M. Starr, and David A. Starrett. Cambridge: Cambridge University Press.

(1987) "Social Choice." In *The New Palgrave Dictionary of Economics*. Edited by John Eatwell, Murray Millgate, and Peter Newman. New York: Macmillan Reference.

Shavell, Steven. (1987) *Economic Analysis of Accident Law*. Cambridge, MA: Harvard University Press.

(1997) "The Fundamental Divergence Between the Private and Social Motive to Use the Legal System." *Journal of Legal Studies* 26: 575–612.

Shulman, Harry. (1928) "The Standard of Care Required of Children." *Yale Law Journal* 37: 618–625.

Shute, Stephen, John Gardner, and Jeremy Horder. (1993) Editors, *Action and Value in Criminal Law*. Oxford: Clarendon Press.

Sidgwick, Henry. (1907) *The Methods of Ethics*. 7th edition, reprinted Indianapolis, IN: Hackett Publishing (1981).

Simester, A. P. (1996) "Agency." *Law and Philosophy* 15: 159–181.

Simons, Kenneth W. (1996) "Deontology, Negligence, Tort, and Crime." *Boston University Law Review* 76: 273–299.

Simpson, A. W. Brian. (1987) "The Laws of Ethelbert." In *Legal Theory and Legal History: Essays on the Common Law*. London: Hambledon Press.

Stocker, Michael. (1990) *Plural and Conflicting Values*. Oxford: Clarendon Press.

Stone, Martin. (1996) "On the Idea of Private Law." *Canadian Journal of Law and Jurisprudence* 9: 235–277.

Strasnick, Steven. (1976a) "Social Choice Theory and the Derivation of Rawls' Difference Principle." *Journal of Philosophy* 73: 85–99.

(1976b) "The Problem of Social Choice: Arrow to Rawls." *Philosophy & Public Affairs* 5: 241–273.

Strom, Gerald Steven. (1990) *The Logic of Lawmaking.* Baltimore, MD: Johns Hopkins University Press.

Strudler, Alan. (1992) "Mass Torts and Moral Principles." *Law and Philosophy* 11: 297–330.

Sugarman, Steven. (1985) "Doing Away with Tort Law." *California Law Review* 73: 555–664.

Sugden, Robert. (1981) *The Political Economy of Public Choice.* Oxford: Martin Robertson.

Sunstein, Cass R. (1990) *After the Rights Revolution.* Cambridge, MA: Harvard University Press.

Sverdlik, Steven. (1993) "Pure Negligence." *American Philosophical Quarterly* 30: 137–147.

Tabbacchi, Tina M. (1991) "Note: Hedonic Damages: A New Trend in Compensation?" *Ohio State Law Journal* 512: 331–349.

Thomson, Judith Jarvis. (1986) *Rights, Restitution and Risk: Essays in Moral Theory.* Cambridge, MA: Harvard University Press.

(1987a) "Causality and Rights: Some Preliminaries." *Chicago-Kent Law Review* 63: 471–496.

(1987b) "The Decline of Cause." *Georgetown Law Review* 76: 137–150.

Trebilcock, Michael. (1987) "The Social Insurance-Deterrence Dilemma of Modern North American Tort Law: A Canadian Perspective on the Liability Insurance Crisis." *San Diego Law Review* 24: 929–1002.

(1988) "The Role of Insurance Considerations in the Choice of Efficient Liability Rules." *Journal of Law Economics and Organization* 4: 243–265.

(1989a) "The Future of Tort Law: Mapping the Contours of the Debate." *Canadian Business Law Journal* 15: 471–488.

(1989b) "Incentive Issues in the Design of 'No-Fault' Compensation Systems." *University of Toronto Law Journal* 39: 19–54.

Tresch, Richard. (1981) *Public Finance: A Normative Theory.* Georgetown, Ontario: Irwin-Dorsey.

Twerski, Aaron D. (1989) "Symposium: The Problem of Indeterminate Defendants: Marketshare and Non-Marketshare Liability." *Brooklyn Law Review* 55: 869–882.

Waldron, Jeremy. (1995) "Moments of Carelessness and Massive Loss." In *Philosophical Foundations of Tort Law.* Edited by David Owen. Oxford: Clarendon Press.

Walker, Margaret Urban. (1992) "Moral Luck and The Virtues of Impure Agency." *Metaphilosophy* 22: 14–27.

Weinrib, Ernest J. (1983) "Toward a Moral Theory of Negligence Law." *Law and Philosophy* 37: 37–62.

(1987) "Causation and Wrongdoing." *Chicago-Kent Law Review* 63: 407–450.

(1989a) "Right and Advantage in Private Law." *Cardozo Law Review* 10: 1283–1310.

(1989b) "The Special Morality of Tort Law." *McGill Law Journal* 34: 403–413.

(1989c) "Understanding Tort Law." *Valparaiso Law Review* 23: 485–526.

(1993) "Formalism and its Canadian Critics." In *Tort Theory.* Edited by K. Cooper-Stephenson and E. Gibson. North York, Ontario: Captus Press.

(1994) "The Gains and Losses of Corrective Justice." *Duke Law Journal* 44: 277–297.

(1995) *The Idea of Private Law.* Cambridge, MA: Harvard University Press.

Wells, Catherine Pierce. (1990) "Tort Law as Corrective Justice: A Pragmatic Justification for Jury Adjudication." *Michigan Law Review* 88: 2348–2413.

White, G. Edward. (1980) *Tort Law in America: An Intellectual History.* New York: Oxford University Press.

Williams, Bernard. (1973) *Problems of the Self.* Cambridge: Cambridge University Press.

(1981) "Moral Luck." In *Moral Luck: Philosophical Papers 1973–1980.* Cambridge: Cambridge University Press.

Williams, Stephen. (1978) "Transforming American Law: Doubtful Economics Makes Doubtful History." *UCLA Law Review* 25: 1187–1218.

Winch, Peter. (1972) "Ethical Reward and Punishment." In *Ethics and Action.* London: Routledge and Kegan Paul.

Wittgenstein, Ludwig. (1958) *Philosophical Investigations.* Translated by G. E. M. Anscombe. Oxford: Blackwell.

Wright, Richard W. (1987) "The Efficiency Theory of Causation and Responsibility: Unscientific Formalism and False Semantics." *Chicago-Kent Law Review* 63:553–578.

(1988) "Causation, Responsibility, Risk, Probability, Naked Statistics, and Proof: Pruning the Bramble Bush by Clarifying the Concepts." *Iowa Law Review* 73: 1001–1077.

(1995) "The Standard of Care in Negligence Law." In *Philosophical Foundations of Tort Law.* Edited by David Owen. Oxford: Clarendon Press.

Zipursky, Benjamin C. (1998a) "Legal Malpractice and the Structure of Negligence Law." *Fordham Law Review* 67: 649–690

(1998b) "Rights, Wrongs, and Recourse in the Law of Torts." *Vanderbilt Law Review* 51: 1–102.

(2000) "Pragmatic Conceptualism." *Legal Theory* 6: 457–485.

# Index

Printed in the United States
200288BV00004B/193-195/A